ROLLING STONES ON AIR

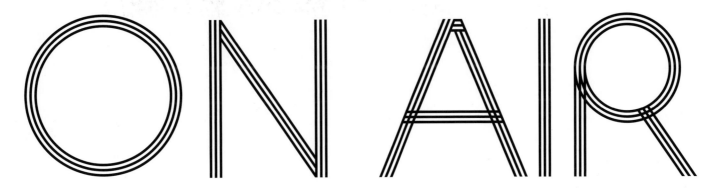

IN THE SIXTIES

TV AND RADIO HISTORY AS IT HAPPENED

Richard Havers

Virgin BOOKS

1963
1964
1965
1966

1967
1968
1969

CONTENTS

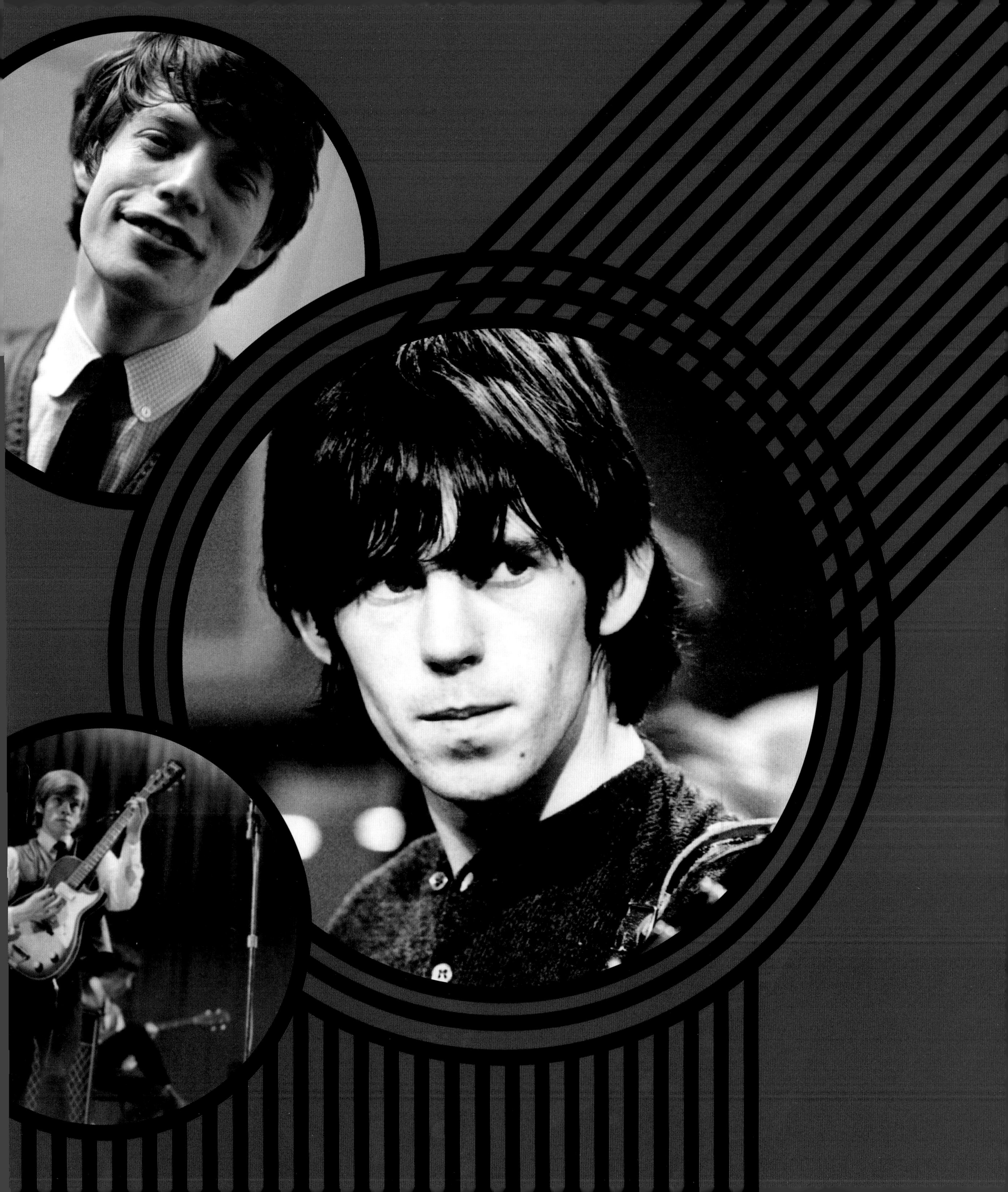

THIS AIN'T NO ROCK 'N' ROLL OUTFIT

The Rolling Stones were war babies. They were all born or grew up during the Second World War.

Keith Richards is the youngest of the original band members, born in December 1943, on the day that the Mills Brothers were at the top of the American charts; they were the first African-American artists to have the honour following the launch of the first official *Billboard* chart in January 1940. The UK would have to wait for almost thirteen years until the *New Musical Express* published the first 'singles' chart.

Mick Jagger is five months older than Keith, having been born in July, on the day that the Allies captured Palermo in Sicily, the island from which the families of Frank Sinatra, Dean Martin and Frankie Laine originated.

Of the original members, Brian Jones was the middle ranking in terms of age, having been born in February 1942, a point in the war when things were going badly for the Allies in the Far East following the fall of Singapore to the Japanese. Charlie Watts was born in June 1941 at University College Hospital London, as the Luftwaffe Blitz on the UK's capital was coming to an end. Bill Wyman was born in October 1936 and he is the only one of the original band members who has significant recollections of the war.

The first television broadcasts in Britain began shortly before World War Two, but hardly anyone had a TV and they were stopped immediately when war broke out in September 1939. Television went back on air in 1947, but even by 1951 there were only two transmitters (one in London, the other in Birmingham), which meant that fewer than 10 per cent of British homes had a TV set. In the *BBC Year Book of 1946* the corporation had this to say about the future of television: 'As for

Previous page: The Stones on Edith Grove, 1963

Opposite: The first official photoshoot, beside the River Thames in London, 4 May 1963

programmes, there is no limit to what viewers can hope to see. Judging from previous experience, the most popular items will probably be television 'outside broadcasts' of sporting events – Cup Finals, the Derby, big boxing matches, tennis, cricket, seen whilst they are actually taking place – and from theatres, with of course big public events such as the opening of Parliament and the Lord Mayor's Show. These outside shows will always appeal particularly to the new viewer. The old hand may in time come to earmark his evenings primarily for full-length television plays, which were the other great attraction in pre-war days. And then of course there will be variety, cabaret, ballet, fashion shows, demonstrations of everything from cooking to carpentry, talks, discussions, and quiz programmes, art shows, personality interviews, visits to the Zoo, street interviews with ordinary Londoners, jazz sessions, recitals, and films.'

Interestingly, there's no mention of news, which given the modern obsession with twenty-four-hour rolling news is surprising. Perhaps less surprising is the omission of music, apart from jazz: the BBC – like most broadcasters in the late 1940s and 1950s – saw radio as the place for popular music. It was not until the second half of the 1950s, and for some time afterwards, that if pop did appear on British screens it was on variety shows, shoe-horned between comedy sketches or performing animals, and it was usually performed by artists that no self-respecting teenager gave a hoot about.

In 1950s America, just as in Britain, teenagers, packed off to bed at an unreasonably early hour, went beneath the bed covers to listen to crackling medium-wave radio broadcasts – there seemed to be more static than music. In the USA, this was the heyday of powerful AM radio stations, where men with strange names like Wolfman Jack broadcast to teenage America. Meanwhile, in Britain and Europe, teens listened to Radio Luxembourg, at least they did in the evening, because during the day everyone was stuck with the BBC who seemed to think that pop music was, at best, harming the moral fibre of the nation's youth. In early 1960s America, FM radio was becoming more widely available, but initially it was used only to simulcast AM broadcasts and orchestral concerts – all too soon, however, it would help power a revolution.

'The one that really turned me on, like an explosion one night, listening to Radio Luxembourg on my little radio when I was supposed to be in bed asleep, was "Heartbreak Hotel".'

Keith Richards

RUDOLF
RASMUSSEN
SPORT

'The first person I really admired was Little Richard. I wasn't particularly fond of Elvis or Bill Haley. They were very good, but for some reason they didn't appeal to me. I was more into Jerry Lee Lewis, Chuck Berry and a bit later Buddy Holly.'

Mick Jagger

While America had thousands of radio stations, the only place where pop music could be heard in the UK throughout most of the two decades after the war ended was the BBC's Light Programme, and even then it was restricted by the number of records that could be played for fear of putting musicians out of work. Wartime had brought about a rise in the number of music programmes that were broadcast, often featuring singers and live bands of the 'big band' type – all of whom helped define middle of the road.

The Stones, like many people of a certain age, would cringe at *Sing Something Simple*, which first broadcast in 1959 and featured half an hour of the blandest songs that broadcast, for much of its forty-two years, immediately before *Pick of the Pops*, the weekly chart countdown and essential listening for every music-loving teenager.

In the second half of the 1950s, the young future Stones, like just about every British teenager, listened to whatever music they could on the BBC and occasionally managed to see something of the exciting sound of rock and roll that had crossed the Atlantic on new TV shows, which were only partially aimed at young people.

Bill Haley's 'Rock Around The Clock' was recorded in New York City in April 1954, but it only topped the US charts in the summer of 1955 after it featured in the film *Blackboard Jungle*. To the casual observer it is *the* record that signifies the birth of rock and roll. Haley's anthem to sexual gymnastics was totally misunderstood by the nice people at the BBC as they played it and helped it to the top of the charts in the UK in January 1956.

Then along came Elvis who had his first UK hit in June 1956. The following year, Chuck Berry had his first minor success in Britain with 'School Day', although he had his first American hit in late summer 1955. Nearly a year separated Little Richard's first US hit and British hit, and Fats Domino's 'Ain't It A Shame' took almost eighteen months to cross the Atlantic. Jerry Lee Lewis's 'Whole Lot A Shakin' Goin' On' took just three months, hitting the UK charts in September 1957. Rock and roll had well and truly arrived.

Up until 1955, the BBC, with its single channel, was the only television available for viewing in Britain – then along came ITV. That made a grand total of two channels, but at least it meant a choice. It was not until 1964 that finally BBC 2 began broadcasting ... and of course it was only in black and white, added to which everything shut down at 11 p.m. or thereabouts.

In 1957, *Six-Five Special* broadcast for the first time in February on the BBC. It is a revelation, although only relative to what else was on. It featured artists such as Lonnie Donegan, Cleo Laine, Wee Willie Harris, Marty Wilde, Petula Clark and Tommy Steele.

Around the same time, ITV came up with *Cool for Cats*, a fifteen-minute show that featured a similar cast of British performers. Things did perk up in 1958 when Jack Good, the producer of *Six-Five Special*, defected to ITV to create *Oh Boy!* Among the resident performers were Cuddly Dudley, who sang on twenty-one shows, Cliff Richard (twenty shows), the Drifters or the Shadows as they later became known (seventeen shows), and Marty Wilde (seventeen shows). Guests included Billy Fury, Tony Sheridan, Shirley Bassey and Lonnie Donegan, along with some occasional American visitors including Conway Twitty, Brenda Lee and most importantly Eddie Cochran.

Left: Elvis Presley
Below: Little Richard

'His violent hip-swinging was revolting, hardly the kind of performance any parent could wish their children to see. He was wearing so much eyeliner he looked like Jayne Mansfield. If we are expected to believe that Cliff was acting naturally, then consideration for medical treatment may be advisable.'

The *New Musical Express* on Cliff Richard's first appearance on *Oh Boy!*

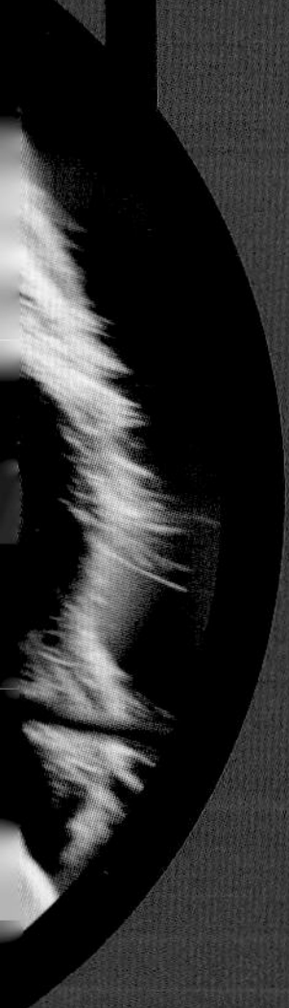

In 1959, Mick became the first Rolling Stone to appear on television, but in a very different guise than we have become used to. Mick's father, Basil, or Joe as he was always known, was a lecturer in physical education as well as working for the British Sports Council, and a pioneer of the British basketball movement. Joe got involved in producing an ATV programme called *Seeing Sport* that aired from 1957 until 1965. On the 14 September 1959 edition of the show, 16-year-old Mick is seen rock climbing near Tunbridge Wells in Kent. He and his brother Chris featured in several other episodes in the series.

Mick, Keith, Charlie, Bill and Brian obviously watched television, but it was inevitably to the radio that they turned to hear the kind of music that they found inspiring. Jazz in Britain was in a funny old place at the time. Men like Chris Barber were bringing in American blues performers to play in jazz clubs, although some audience members got rather irritated by the fact that Muddy Waters insisted on playing his guitar through an amplifier: all very irregular.

Jazz Club on the BBC offered the chance to hear some blues, albeit sporadically. By 1962 it was occasionally presented by George Melly, who was infatuated with Bessie Smith. As often as not, though, those appearing were bands such as Mickey Ashman's Ragtime Jazz Band or Humphrey Lyttelton and his Band or Ken Colyer's Jazzmen, but at least they all had one foot in the blues.

'I practised at home to jazz records all the time. The only rock and roll I ever listened to was after the Stones turned me on to it.'

Charlie Watts

Opposite left: Jimmy Reed
Opposite right: Chuck Berry

In the spring of 1962, Mick, Keith, Brian and Charlie all spent time at the Ealing Club, a regular spot for blues lovers in west London that had been started by Alexis Korner and Cyril Davies. On one of their first visits to the Ealing Club, Mick and Keith saw Brian playing Elmore James-style slide guitar. Later Mick sang with Alexis and Cyril's Blues Incorporated, and Charlie sometimes sat in on drums with the band. Over time all manner of future stars played with Blues Incorporated, including Jack Bruce and Ginger Baker (later to form Cream with Eric Clapton), Graham Bond, Long John Baldry, Art Wood (Ronnie Wood's brother) and Paul Jones who went on to front Manfred Mann.

By the summer of 1962, Blues Incorporated had a regular Thursday-night gig at the Marquee Club in London's Oxford Street. In the first week of July they were offered the chance to appear on the BBC's *Jazz Club*, which didn't go down well with the Marquee's owner, Harold Pendleton, who issued a blunt ultimatum: 'If you leave this Thursday to do the broadcast, I will not guarantee your gig the Thursday after.'

Korner had a plan. He asked his friends and acolytes, Mick Jagger, Ian Stewart, Keith Richards and Brian Jones, to deputize for him at the Marquee. Having secured the gig, Mick's first ever utterance in the press was carried by *Jazz News*: 'I hope they don't think we're a rock 'n' roll outfit.' According to Mick, 'In those days there was a lot of music snobbery. People wanted their music in genre-specific boxes. When we played the Marquee Club in July 1962 this was principally a jazz club and so even the blues were a bit of a stretch for them; they wanted us to remain within our genre.'

Before they could play their Marquee gig there was the small matter of what they should call themselves. They came up with Rollin' Stones, named for a Muddy Waters song that was included on his first British album release.

Jazz News previewed the gig, saying: 'Mick Jagger, R&B vocalist, is taking an R&B group into the Marquee tomorrow night, while Blues Incorporated do their *Jazz Club* gig. Called the Rollin' Stones. The line-up is: Mick Jagger (vocals), Keith Richards & Elmo Lewis [Brian Jones's pseudonym] (guitars), Dick Taylor (bass), Ian Stewart (piano), & Mick Avory (drums). A second group under Long John Baldry will also be there.'

In the event, Mick Avory, who later joined the Kinks, was not at the gig, which took place on 12 July 1962, and no one can seem to recall if there even was a drummer – it would be six months before Charlie was finally persuaded to join the band. And Elmo Lewis was of course Brian Jones's pseudonym in honour of his hero, Elmore James, and the Lewis being one of his middle names.

According to the handwritten set list, among the numbers they performed were songs by their heroes Jimmy Reed, Bo Diddley, Chuck Berry and Howlin' Wolf, including 'Kansas City', 'Confessin' The Blues', 'Bright Lights Big City', 'Down the Road A Piece', 'Dust My Broom' and 'Ride 'Em On Down', a song recorded by Eddie Taylor and included on the Stones' 2016 release, *Blue and Lonesome*.

A few weeks later, in August 1962, Mick decided to leave his comfortable home in leafy Dartford and he and Brian moved to a flat at 102 Edith Grove in Chelsea. Their rent was £16 per week. It was a scruffy place, lit by a single bulb in the living room; soon after, Keith moved in too.

The odd gig at the Ealing Club and the Marquee did little to enhance the Rollin' Stones' reputation, but according to Ian Stewart it had nothing to do with their ability. 'We had a job getting gigs, because there was this sort of Mafia thing. The trad thing had died and left a vacuum. Harold Pendleton, a guy called Bill Carey, and Alexis [Korner] tried to take over the R&B scene, and keep it very much a jazz thing. I went off to work for ICI as a clerk; the Stones sat around all day rehearsing and trying to get bookings.'

'God, we'd love that Charlie Watts if we could afford him – because we all thought Charlie was a God-given drummer.'

Keith Richards

The Stones made a demo record in later October 1962, and shortly afterwards they recruited Bill Wyman with his amplifiers and homemade bass guitar and secured a residency at the Flamingo Club in London's Soho. In December, Charlie left Blues Incorporated and the Stones set about trying to entice him to come over to what he still viewed as the dark side. Before they managed to convince Charlie, there were gigs in the first week of January 1963 at the Ealing Club. Hopes may or may not have been raised by the fact that Brian had written to the BBC asking for an audition for their band with 'an authentic Chicago R&B sound'.

ETROPOLITAN POLICE
NO
ARKI

1963
1964
1965
1966

1967
1968
1969

1963

Previous pages: The Stones in their matching houndstooth jackets

The UK's bestselling singles chart on New Year's Day 1963 was like a who's who of about-to-have-beens, at least that's what became apparent as the year unfolded. Month by month, throughout 1963 it was as though pop music accelerated from the sedate to the sensational at warp factor 10. Of the artists in the UK Top 20, all but three were solo singers – the exceptions being the Shadows and the Tornados (both of which had instrumental hits with a hint of a beat), while the other was veteran bandleader Joe Loss, whose 'Must Be Madison' celebrated a long-forgotten dance craze that momentarily swept the Mecca dance halls in Burnley, Rochdale and Stevenage.

The situation in America was barely any different, even though, on the surface, there appeared to be more groups pushing for success. Indeed, British band the Tornados occupied the top spot on the Hot 100 with 'Telstar', their homage to space exploration and global communication. There were a smattering of groups in the Top 20, including, the Excitors, the Tijuana Brass (before Herb Alpert gave himself star billing), the Cookies and the Four Seasons. The week's fastest climber on the top 20 was 'Pepino, The Italian Mouse' by 46-year-old Lou Monte ... It was a staid and respectable world that was about to change forever.

Eleven days into 1963 the Beatles released their second single in Britain. 'Please Please Me' made the charts a week later and peaked at No.2 in late February. It was as though someone had mobilized a teenage army of music fans who suddenly felt that this was music that was theirs, and theirs alone. By the end of the year the Beatles had held the top spot on the UK single's chart for 16 weeks with three monumental recordings – 'From Me To You', 'She Loves You' and 'I Want To Hold Your Hand'.

By late spring the Beatboom was fully underway, with fellow Liverpool bands, Gerry and the Pacemakers, The Searchers, and Billy J. Kramer with the Dakotas, all making No.1 on the charts. In America things were moving at a slightly slower pace, evidenced by the fact that for most of December the best-selling record was 'Dominique', performed by the Singing Nun – she was exactly as billed.

Change was faster in Britain, probably down to one simple fact: television was more national than regional. Programmes tended to be seen everywhere, roughly at the same time, which meant that *Thank Your Lucky Stars*, a weekly pop show on the commercial network rather than the BBC, could shape the musical mood very quickly. *TYLS* usually had 6 million viewers a week out of a population of just over 50 million, and most of them were young, record-buying fans. In August 1963 a second, even more teenager friendly TV show was launched. *Ready Steady Go!* was the epitome of what London was becoming, the swinging centre of the musical world.

On 2 January 1963, in a small, squalid flat not far from London's King's Road, the self-proclaimed leader of a London-based band calling themselves the Rollin' Stones was busy writing a letter to the BBC asking for an audition. The audacity of such a move is breathtaking. The band had hardly played any gigs, and those they had were at clubs around the capital where audiences were in the low hundreds at best. Their line-up was still somewhat fluid and naturally they didn't have a manager.

By April, the Stones had auditioned for the BBC and, a month later, they were rejected via a somewhat pompous letter. Meanwhile they had found managers, recorded their debut single and while they might not, in reality, have been on their way, it certainly felt like they were. In early July the Stones appeared on *Thank Your Lucky Stars* dressed in matching outfits, although they steadfastly refused to conform by having a haircut. More importantly, at the end of August they appeared on the third edition of *Ready Steady Go!* This time they wore their other set of matching clothes, although none of them appeared to have had a haircut.

Before the year was out, the Stones had made more TV appearances and performed live on *Saturday Club*, BBC radio's flagship pop programme, which broadcast every weekend. Thanks to all this media coverage the Stones' first two singles, the second of which was written by John Lennon and Paul McCartney, made the UK charts before 1963 ended.

The band, whose '... musical policy is simply to produce an authentic Chicago R&B sound', according to Brian Jones's letter to the BBC, was now very definitely on its way.

AUDITIONS AND RECOMMENDATIONS

As 1963 dawned, the Rollin' Stones were, in their view, on their way, even if they were unsure of exactly where they were going. Gigs during December had been none too plentiful, with a weekly residency at the Ealing Club their most regular opportunity to play in front of a paying audience.

What they needed was a break, so on 2 January Brian Jones, who very much saw himself as the leader of the band, took it upon himself to write to the BBC requesting an audition. If they were successful in securing one, it would mean they could be offered a chance of playing live on the BBC's Light Programme (the forerunner of Radio 2) – there was just the small question of passing the audition.

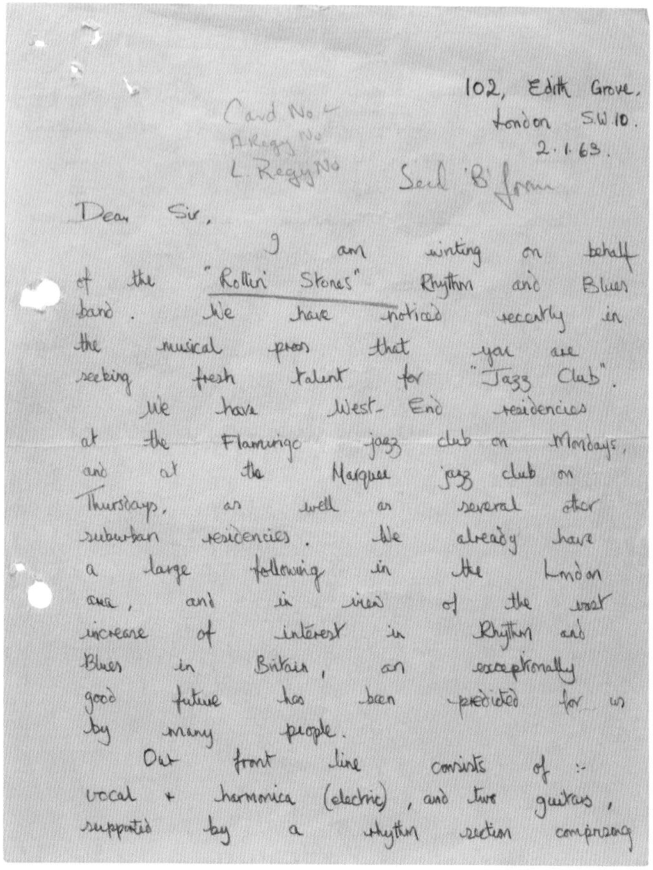
102, Edith Grove,
London S.W.10.
2.1.63.

Card No. ✓
A Regy No
L Regy No
Send 'B' form

Dear Sir,

I am writing on behalf of the "Rollin' Stones" Rhythm and Blues band. We have noticed recently in the musical press that you are seeking fresh talent for "Jazz Club".

We have West-End residencies at the Flamingo jazz club on Mondays, and at the Marquee jazz club on Thursdays, as well as several other suburban residencies. We already have a large following in the London area, and in view of the vast increase of interest in Rhythm and Blues in Britain, an exceptionally good future has been predicted for us by many people.

Our front line consists of :- vocal + harmonica (electric), and two guitars, supported by a rhythm section comprising

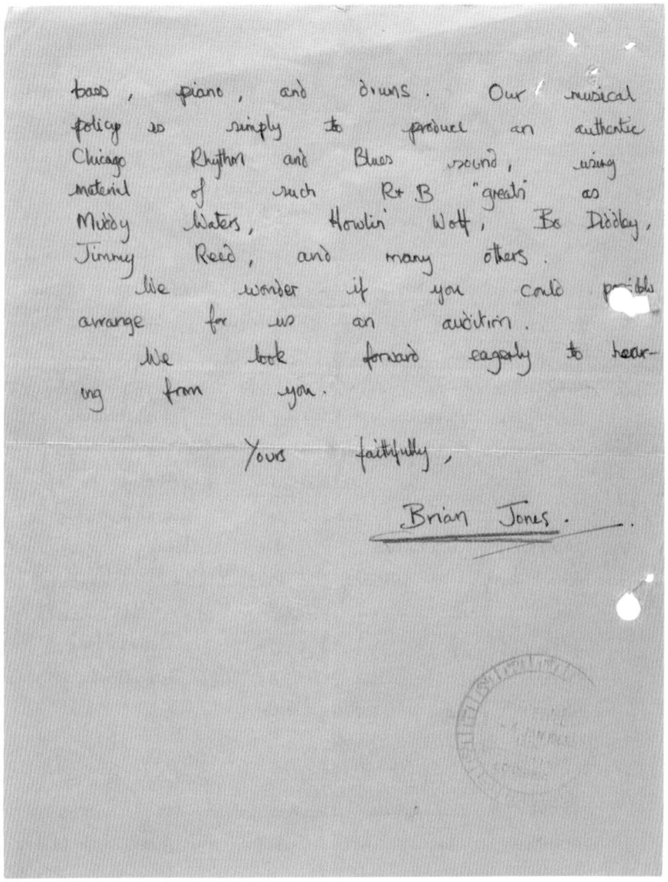
bass, piano, and drums. Our musical policy is simply to produce an authentic Chicago Rhythm and Blues sound, using material of such R+B "greats" as Muddy Waters, Howlin' Wolf, Bo Diddley, Jimmy Reed, and many others.

We wonder if you could possibly arrange for us an audition.

We look forward eagerly to hearing from you.

Yours faithfully,

Brian Jones.

Left and above: Brian Jones's letter to the BBC seeking an audition for the BBC's *Jazz Club* radio programme

In the music press the BBC had let it be known they were 'seeking fresh talent' to appear on their weekly Monday night programme, *Jazz Club*. In his letter to the BBC, Brian says, 'Our musical policy is simply to produce an authentic Chicago R&B sound, using material of such R&B greats as Muddy Waters, Howlin' Wolf, Bo Diddley, Jimmy Reed and many others.'

Brian also stated that 'The Rollin' Stones Rhythm and Blues Band' had 'West End residences at the Flamingo Jazz Club on Mondays, and at the Marquee Jazz Club on Thursdays, as well as several other suburban residences.' This was slightly disingenuous in that their gigs at both clubs had been sporadic, although the Stones were about to start appearing much more regularly at both. Three days after Brian's letter was written, adverts appeared in the *Melody Maker* for both the Marquee and the Flamingo Club promoting the Stones' appearances.

R & B • 1963 • MARQUEE
165 OXFORD STREET : GERard 8923

THURSDAYS	MONDAYS
CYRIL DAVIES ALL — STARS	BRIAN KNIGHT BLUES - BY - SIX

GUESTS INCLUDE VISITING R & B GROUPS
and THE ROLLIN' STONES group
COMPERE : BILL CAREY
THE LONDON HEADQUARTERS OF R & B
MEMBERS 4/- 11 p.m. : GUESTS 5/-

RHYTHM & BLUES EXCITEMENT
AT THE MARQUEE
EVERY MONDAY AND THURSDAY
THIS THURSDAY, 3rd JANUARY
CYRIL DAVIES R & B ALL STARS
WITH THE ROLLING STONES

JAZZ AT THE MARQUEE
165 OXFORD STREET, W.1 (Nr OXFORD CIRCUS)

Friday, January 4th
★ DICK CHARLESWORTH and his CITY GENTS
★ JACKIE LYNN
(Members 4/- Guests 5/-)
Saturday, January 5th
★ JOE HARRIOTT QUINTET
★ RONNIE ROSS QUARTET
(Members 6/- Guests 7/6)
Sunday, January 6th
★ Big Band Night
★ JOHN WILLIAMS BIG BAND
★ PETE SHADE QUARTET
(Members 4/- Guests 5/-)
Monday, January 7th
★ Rhythm and Blues Night
★ BLUES BY SIX
★ Pete Deuchar's
★ COUNTRY BLUES
(Members 4/- Guests 5/-)
Wednesday, January 9th
★ HUMPHREY LYTTELTON BAND
★ RUSTIX JUMPTET
(Members 5/- Guests 6/-)
Thursday, January 10th
★ Rhythm and Blues Night
★ CYRIL DAVIES' ALL-STAR
★ R & B GROUP
★ ROLLIN' STONES
(Members 4/- Guests 5/-)

Above: The Marquee was originally on Oxford Street, which is where the band played their first ever gig on 12 July 1962; they continued playing there in 1963 before it moved to Wardour Street in 1964

Below: The Stones played The Flamingo Club on Wardour Street in London's Soho prior to Bill and Charlie joining the band, and then regularly in early 1963 with the original line-up

Yet this was still the Rollin' Stones, without Charlie Watts; Bill Wyman's old band mate, Tony Chapman, from south-east London, was still occupying the drum stool ... just. He wasn't there for much longer: on Saturday 12 January, Charlie played his first gig with the band, somewhat appropriately at the Ealing Club.

Ten days after the Stones played with Charlie, and before appearing at the Red Lion pub in Sutton, Brian was busy filling in the audition form he'd received from the BBC. On the form the name of the group's leader was required and Brian filled in his own name. Underneath it listed the six members of the band as Brian Jones, guitar/harmonica; Keith Richards, guitar; Mick Jagger, vocal/harmonica; Ian Stewart, piano; Bill Perks [Wyman], bass; and Charles Watts, drums. Two days later the form was received by the BBC and initialled as 'checked'. The Rollin' Stones, as Brian was still calling the band, now just had to wait to be summoned for an audition.

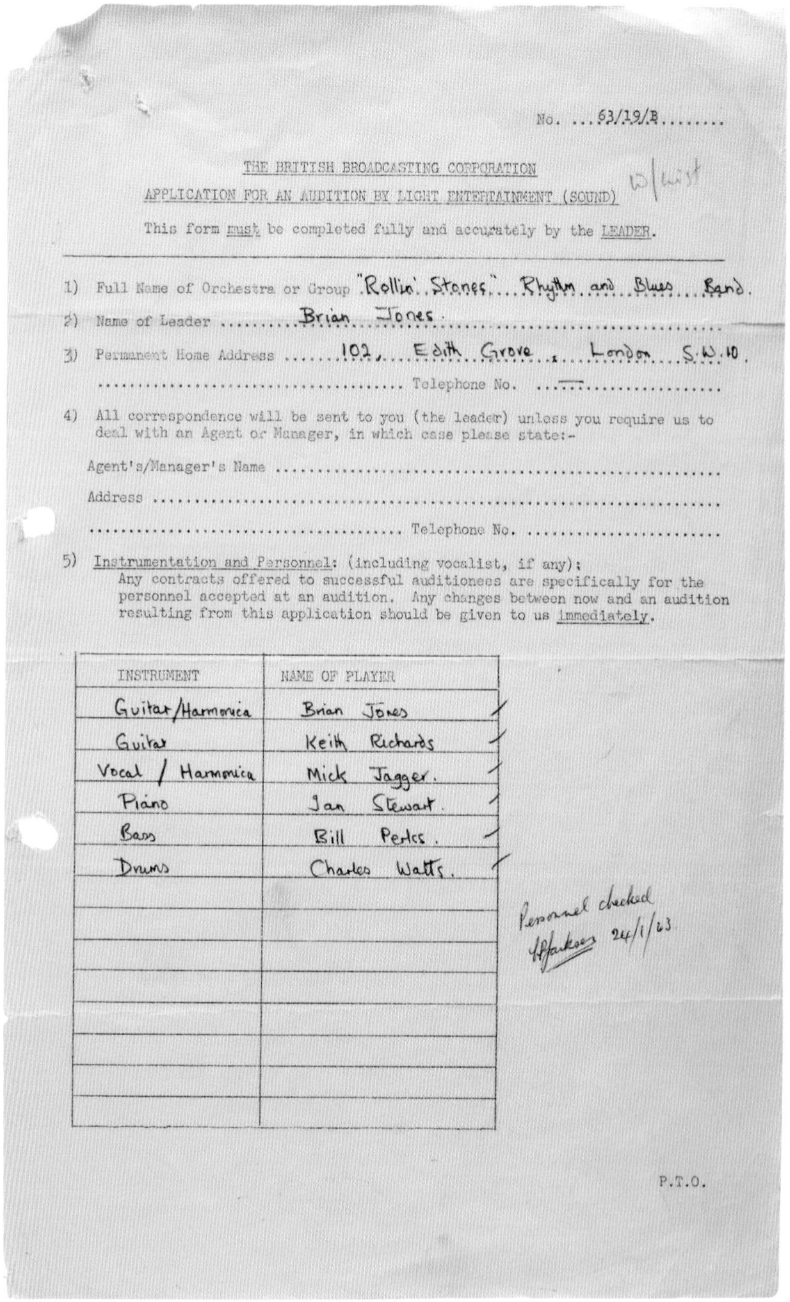

No. ...63/19/B........

THE BRITISH BROADCASTING CORPORATION

APPLICATION FOR AN AUDITION BY LIGHT ENTERTAINMENT (SOUND)

This form must be completed fully and accurately by the LEADER.

1) Full Name of Orchestra or Group "Rollin' Stones" ... Rhythm and Blues Band.

2) Name of Leader ....Brian Jones.

3) Permanent Home Address ......102, Edith Grove, London S.W.10.

.... Telephone No. ...—...

4) All correspondence will be sent to you (the leader) unless you require us to deal with an Agent or Manager, in which case please state:-

Agent's/Manager's Name ....

Address ....

.... Telephone No. ....

5) Instrumentation and Personnel: (including vocalist, if any):
Any contracts offered to successful auditionees are specifically for the personnel accepted at an audition. Any changes between now and an audition resulting from this application should be given to us immediately.

INSTRUMENT	NAME OF PLAYER
Guitar/Harmonica	Brian Jones
Guitar	Keith Richards
Vocal / Harmonica	Mick Jagger.
Piano	Ian Stewart.
Bass	Bill Perks.
Drums	Charles Watts.

Personnel checked 24/1/63.

P.T.O.

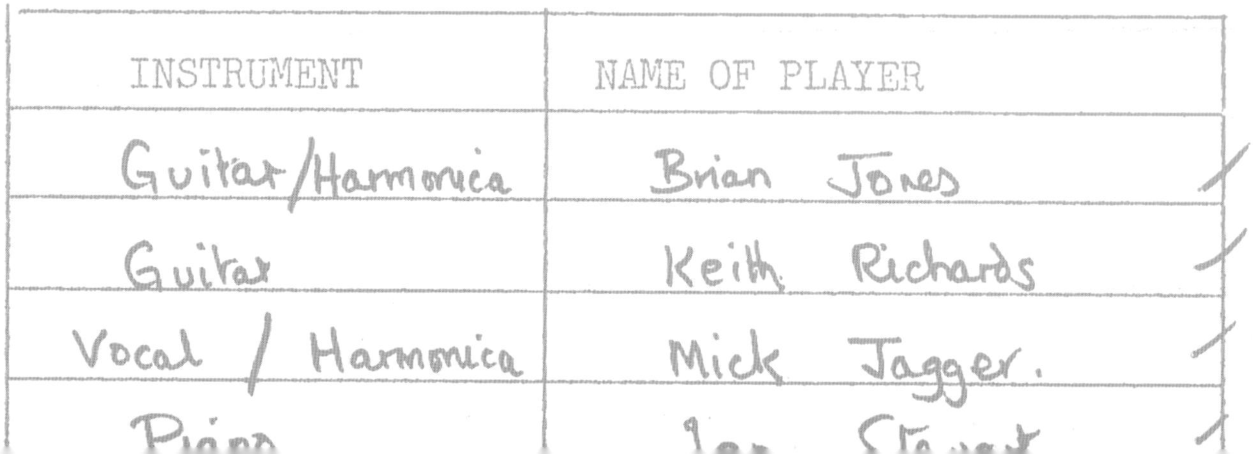

INSTRUMENT	NAME OF PLAYER
Guitar/Harmonica	Brian Jones
Guitar	Keith Richards
Vocal / Harmonica	Mick Jagger.

Piano	Ian Stewart.
Bass	Bill Perks.
Drums	Charles Watts.

- 2 -

6) Are all the members of the Group of British Nationality? ....YES........
If not, please give details ....

7) How long has the group existed with precisely this personnel? ...6 MONTHS.

7b) Is the group, in this form, in exclusively professional employment ...NO...

8) Has the group as at present constituted already had, or applied for, any kind of BBC audition? If 'YES' please give details:-

Date: Place: NO

9) Has the Group ever broadcast for the BBC? If 'YES' please give details:

Date: Place:

10) What experience has the group (in any field of public entertainment)?

We have played exclusively jazz clubs, including regular appearances at the MARQUEE + FLAMINGO jazz clubs in the West End of London. We have several suburban club residencies.

11) Please give details of last three engagements:-

Dates:	Places:
17.1.63	MARQUEE, Oxford Street. W.1.
19.1.63	EALING, Rhythm + Blues Club.
21.1.63	FLAMINGO, Wardour St. W.1.

12) Please describe the kind of music which the group features:-

The band's policy is to play authentic Chicago Rhythm and Blues music, using material of such outstanding exponents of this music as, Howling Wolf, Muddy Waters, Bo Diddley, Jimmy Reed etc. etc. Within our self-imposed limitations we have a large repertoire covering R + B styles from the P.T.O. early country blues-influenced R+B, to the few more commercial sound of Rhythm and Blues of the 1950's + 1960's.

- 3 -

13) Your performance will not be heard 'live' but will be recorded and assessed at a later stage. We should like to make it clear that the recording in question will be used for audition purposes only.

14) Any rehearsal time preceding an audition is exclusively for BBC use. To ensure, for example, that microphone balance is up to broadcasting standard.

NO STUDIO TIME CAN BE OFFERED FOR REHEARSAL OF THE PERFORMANCE.

Date: 22.1.63 Signature of Leader:: Brian Jones.

(FOR BBC USE)

Opposite and above: The BBC audition form, completed by Brian Jones, for the original six-piece band that included Ian Stewart and Bill Wyman before he changed his name from Perks

RICHMOND. Station Hotel, unrepressed **RHYTHM 'N' BLUES** with unmitigating, ebullient, perturbing **ROLLIN' STONES.**

Over the next few months the Stones began playing far more frequently, but always in and around London. Steadily they built a larger and larger following for their high-energy performances. In late February, the Stones played their first gig at the Station Hotel in Richmond, at the venue's Sunday blues night. This was run by Giorgio Gomelski, the son of a French mother and a Russian doctor, born in the Caucasian Mountains, whom Brian had met previously. Gomelski had been having problems with his resident band. Brian offered the perfect solution: 'Look, Giorgio, you can't run a club without knowing whether your band's going to turn up! Give us a break. We'll do it for nothing.'

And so it was that the Stones began appearing at what Gomelski soon renamed the Crawdaddy Club, its name derived from Bo Diddley's 1960 song 'Doing The Craw-Daddy'. It was around the time that the Stones met Gomelski that the BBC offered them the chance to audition, but not until 23 April, which to the band seemed like an awful long way off.

Nevertheless, in the meantime, the busy schedule of club gigs helped them to hone their playing together as they quickly became the best, and most authentic, R&B – with the accent on B – band in London and arguably the UK.

Besides giving the Stones the Sunday night residency, Gomelski did something that helped set in motion a sequence of events that played out over the coming months. At lunchtime on Easter Sunday, 14 April, Gomelski went to Teddington Studios where *Thank Your Lucky Stars*, the popular weekly TV show, was being recorded. Among the guests who were there to appear on the following Saturday's show were the Beatles. Ever the hustler, Gomelski invited the Beatles to stop off at the Crawdaddy later that evening, on their way back to central London, to see the Stones.

Opposite and above: The original 6-piece band at the Crawdaddy Club at the Station Hotel, Richmond

Top and above left: The Red Lion pub in Sutton, South London, where Bill first met the other Stones in late 1962

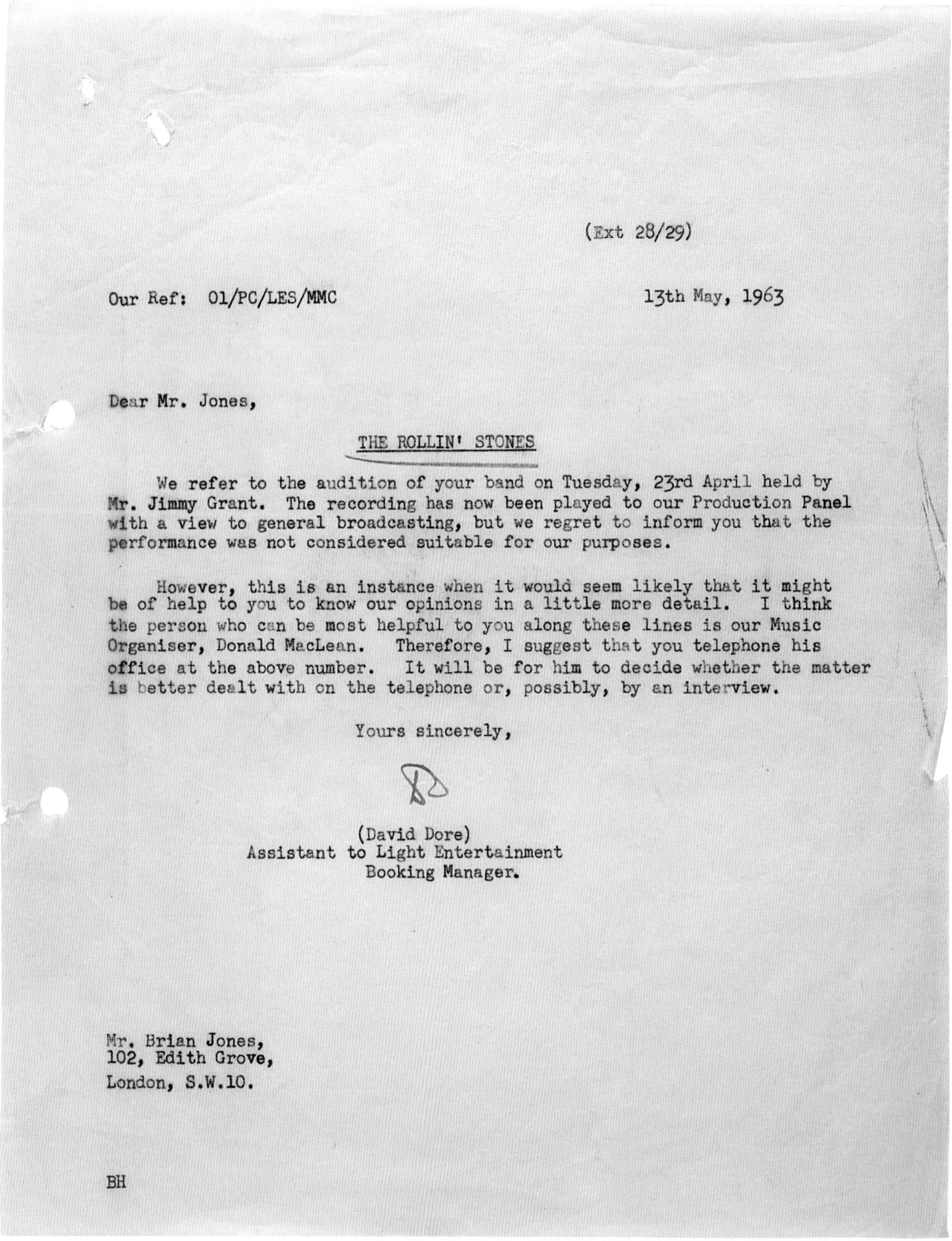

(Ext 28/29)

Our Ref: 01/PC/LES/MMC

13th May, 1963

Dear Mr. Jones,

THE ROLLIN' STONES

We refer to the audition of your band on Tuesday, 23rd April held by Mr. Jimmy Grant. The recording has now been played to our Production Panel with a view to general broadcasting, but we regret to inform you that the performance was not considered suitable for our purposes.

However, this is an instance when it would seem likely that it might be of help to you to know our opinions in a little more detail. I think the person who can be most helpful to you along these lines is our Music Organiser, Donald MacLean. Therefore, I suggest that you telephone his office at the above number. It will be for him to decide whether the matter is better dealt with on the telephone or, possibly, by an interview.

Yours sincerely,

(David Dore)
Assistant to Light Entertainment
Booking Manager.

Mr. Brian Jones,
102, Edith Grove,
London, S.W.10.

BH

On Easter Sunday, the Stones played their regular Sunday lunchtime gig at Studio 51 in Soho, before driving west along the A3 to Richmond. Early in their first set at the Crawdaddy, in walked the four Beatles with their roadie, Neil Aspinall. John, Paul, George and Ringo were dressed identically, in long black leather coats. According to Bill Wyman, 'I remember thinking, "Shit, that's the Beatles," and I got all nervous.'

Later, the Beatles went home with the Stones to Edith Grove, where they talked music into the early hours. They invited the Stones to what was to be the Beatles' first appearance at London's famed Royal Albert Hall a few days later. The Beatles were booked to appear on the BBC's *Swinging Sound '63*.

It was on Thursday 18 April that Mick, Keith and Brian went to see the Beatles at the Royal Albert Hall. To Mick, 'It was incredible for us to watch. I'd never seen hysteria on that level before. We were so turned on by those riots.'

The following Tuesday, 23 April, the three of them, along with Ian Stewart, were at the BBC for their long-awaited audition, which was held between 6.30 p.m. and 8 p.m. at the Aolian Hall in central London. Both Bill and Charlie were missing, the reason for which seems to have been lost in the mists of time; it's interesting that the BBC's internal feedback requests 'echo and a piano please'. It may have been because Brian had promised drummer Carlo Little and bass player Ricky Fensen that they could play at the audition. It may also have been because Bill and Charlie both had full-time jobs and couldn't get the time off work.

The Stones played, it's thought, Leiber and Stoller's 'I'm A Hog For You, Baby' and Hank Snow's 'I'm Moving On', among other things. Three weeks later, David Dore (assistant light entertainment booking manager at the BBC) wrote to Brian with the news that the Stones had failed the audition. Having become a tight band from playing with Bill and Charlie for close on four months, the substitution of Little and Fensen, who had been in Screaming Lord Sutch and the Savages, may have made them less like an 'authentic rhythm and blues' band.

Then again, the BBC may have simply not liked what they heard. They were, on the face of it, auditioning for a jazz programme, and the 'production panel' may have been confused by the relationship between blues and jazz … many people are.

However, by the time the Stones received the BBC's letter of rejection, events had moved on at quite a pace.

'It was incredible for us to watch. I'd never seen hysteria on that level before. We were so turned on by those riots'

Mick Jagger

Opposite: The BBC's letter of rejection following the band's audition
Above: The Stones first played Studio 51 Club in London's Soho in March 1963

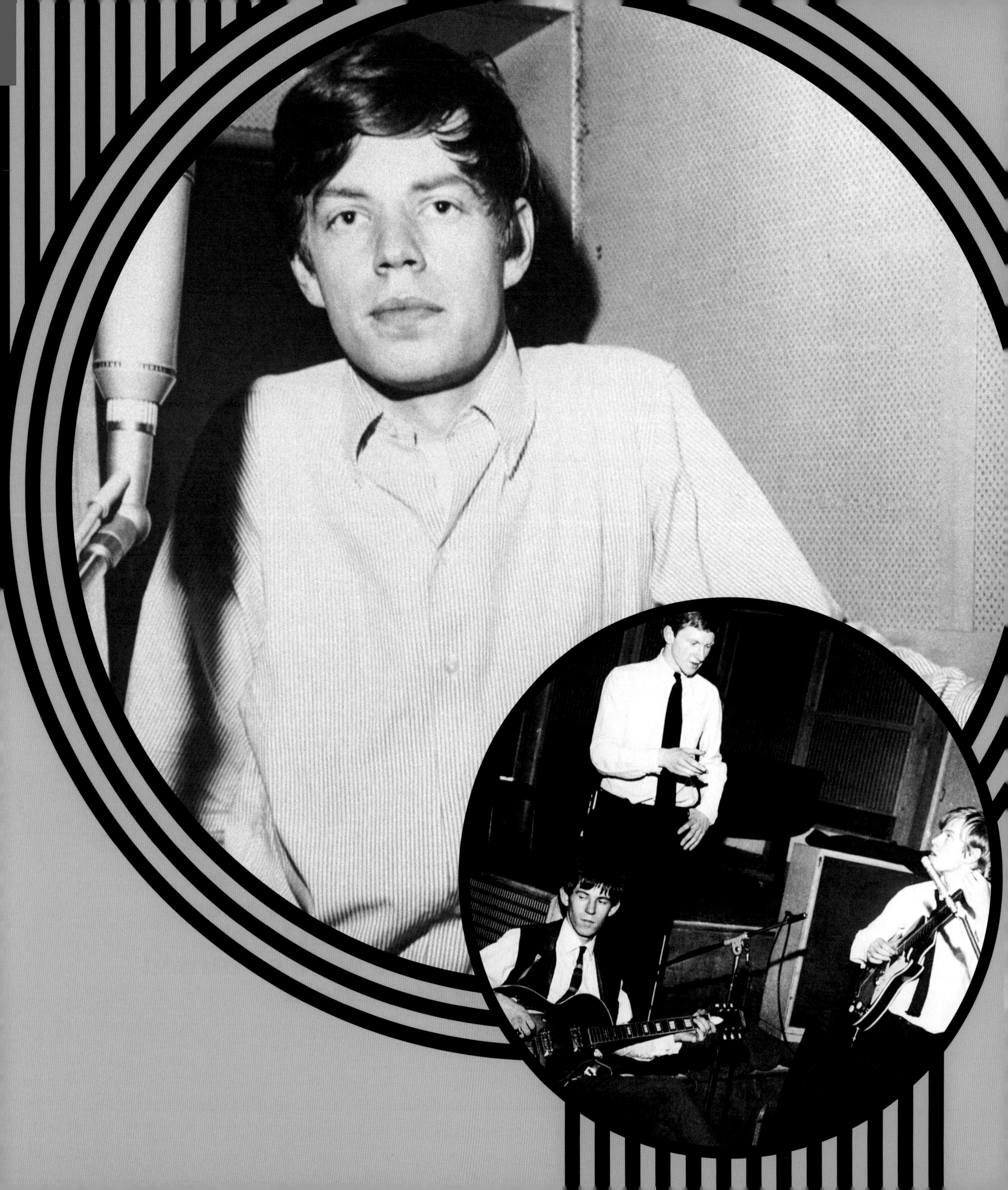

SIGNED, RECORDED AND TELEVISED

Opposite: The band record 'Come On' at Olympic Studios, Carlton Street, while manager Andrew Loog Oldham looks on

Two days before their BBC audition, Peter Jones, the editor of the influential *Record Mirror*, enters the story. Gomelski, with his missionary zeal when it came to promoting the band, invited Jones to the Crawdaddy on Sunday 21 April. Jones was impressed. So much so that the following day he got hold of Andrew Loog Oldham, a young hustler and PR man who had worked for Brian Epstein's NEMS company, to tell him that he should check out the Rollin' Stones.

According to Jones, '[Oldham] had this kind of public school image, and a basic feel for music. He was a very sharp boy. He agreed to take an interest. He had links with Eric Easton, who I have to say was one of the squarest guys on the fringe of the pop music industry in this country.' But Easton had the all-important contacts.

The following Sunday, Loog Oldham and Easton went to the Crawdaddy and both in their own way were amazed by what they saw. According to Loog Oldham, 'I'd never seen anything like it. You know when you're in a room with a fanatical audience. I was quite overpowered and a little taken aback. I was mesmerized.' Easton said, 'The Stones were just incredible, fantastic, fabulous. Communication was what was happening for them in a club setting. They got through to people.'

Two days later, on Tuesday 30 April, Brian Jones met with Loog Oldham and Easton at the latter's office in Regent's Street in London's West End. The day after, Brian, on behalf of the Stones, signed a management agreement with Loog Oldham and Easton's company, Impact Sound.

In the evening after signing their management deal, the Stones played their second ever gig at Eel Pie Island, in the middle of the River Thames between Richmond and Twickenham. Loog Oldham, who was a month younger than Keith Richards, the youngest of the Stones, came to see them and dropped a bombshell. He insisted that there should be only five men in the band, which meant that Ian Stewart was effectively sacked, something he took with good grace. Stu became the band's road manager, and forever after, to the rest of the Rolling Stones, he was always family.

From there, things moved fast. The following Sunday, 5 May, Dick Rowe from Decca Records was invited to the Crawdaddy by Andrew and, having famously turned down the Beatles, he was anxious not to miss out on 'the next big thing'. George Harrison also played a part. He and Dick had been judging a talent contest in Liverpool and according to his own account, Rowe said to George, '"You know, I really had my backside kicked over turning you lot down," and George said, "Well, I wouldn't worry too much about that, why don't you sign the Rolling Stones?"'

Five days later, the Stones were at the old Olympic Studio in Carlton Street in London's West End, to record what was to be their first single, a cover of Chuck Berry's 'Come On'– at one minute and forty-five seconds it was typical of so many beat group singles that were being made in the wake of the Beatles' success, and not at all like the kind of thing the Stones were playing around the London clubs.

DAILY MIRROR, Thursday, June 13, 1963 PAGE 25

TWITCHING THE NIGHT AWAY

ROLLING STONES

. . . from left to right: Keith Richard, Bill Wyman, Mick Jagger, Brian Jones, Charlie Watts. Five long-haired lads responsible for an extraordinary scene in suburban Surrey.

PATRICK DONCASTER
The Mirror's DJ

IN the half-darkness, the guitars and the drums started to twang and bang. A pulsating rhythm and blues. Shoulder to shoulder on the floor stood 500 youngsters, some in black leather, some in sweaters. You could have boiled an egg in the atmosphere.

They began to dance. And it was no place for Victor Silvester.

They just stood as they were. Their heads shook violently in what I can only describe as a paroxysm. "A sudden attack," says the dictionary of this word.

THRASHING

That's what it looked like in a sweating jazz club that meets in the Station Hotel at Richmond, Surrey.

Their feet stamped in tribal style. If they could, the dedicated occasionally put their hands above their heads and clapped in rhythm.

Suddenly there would be shaking figures above the rest of the on-the-spot dancers, held aloft by their colleagues, thrashing and yelling "Yeh, yehs."

No one needed a partner. It was simply shake, rattle and roll on your square foot of the floor.

In its fervour it was like a revivalist meeting in *America's Deep South.*

Responsible for this extraordinary scene in suburban Surrey are five long-haired lads known as the **Rolling Stones** — who roll out the rhythm and blues on guitars and drums.

Their names:

Mick Jagger, 19, studying at the London School of Economics; **Brian Jones,** 19, who used to be a lorry driver and lights up sixty smokes a day; **Keith Richard,** 19, who used to be a Post Office worker; **Bill Wyman,** 21, who likes poetry as well as rhythm, and drummer **Charlie Watts,** 21, an advertising agency man, who collects pocket handkerchiefs. He has 100.

TWITCH?

What do the fans call this dance? (I am told it happens nowhere else in Britain.) Nobody seems to know or care. They just do it.

It could well be the Parox . . . or the Twitch . . . or the Sudden Attack.

If you wish to try it out, all you need is a lot of people in a crowded room and the Rolling Stones' first record—"**Come On**" (Decca).

Or you might just like to listen. Which is quite exciting, anyway.

THE fanatics of the light fantastic—is it light any more? — are in considerable confusion.

There are so many dances that they are tripping over each other.

DECIDE!

So it is no surprise to have land on my desk a disc with the title: "**Us Kids Have Gotta Make Up Our Minds.**"

Make up their minds, that is, on what dance to do.

The disc might help you sort things out. Artist: American **Sonny Parks,** who warbles in on the Warner Bros' label.

P S: He hadn't caught up with the Twitch when he made this one.

LET'S take it a little easier and lend an ear to Mr. Bobby Darin and Mr. Acker Bilk.

Mr. Darin is most fetching with a cute number he wrote called "**Eighteen Yellow Roses**" (Capitol). It has leapt into the American charts, wistful as it is.

ROMANTIC

Mr. Acker Bilk, with the Leon Young Strings tugs gently at the eardrums, too, with the romantic "**Moonlight Tango**" (Columbia), a tune that might already be familiar to you.

Back on the rhythm kick there is **Joe Brown,** beating it along with a piece called "**Nature's Time for Love**" (Piccadilly).

Know what **Time** that is? The **same** old moonlight that enticed Mr. Bilk.

WE used to call **Bill Haley** the King of Rock 'n' Roll. He has long since abdicated. But here he comes again on Stateside with "**Tenor Man.**" And it still sounds like abdication music to me.

☆ I like the sound of **Bobby Sansom and the Giants** on Oriole. They come from Brighton, which is a change from Liverpool.

But who wrote the piece they spin along with, "**There's a Place**"?

Two members of Merseyside's talented Beatles . . .

POP 30

Britain's best-selling records—last week's figures in brackets.

1	(2)	DO YOU WANT TO KNOW A SECRET?—Billy J. Kramer with The Dakotas
2	(9)	I LIKE IT—Gerry and the Pacemakers
3	(1)	FROM ME TO YOU—Beatles
4	(6)	TAKE THESE CHAINS FROM MY HEART—Ray Charles
5	(12)	IF YOU GOTTA MAKE A FOOL OF SOMEBODY—Freddie and The Dreamers
6	(3)	SCARLETT O'HARA—Jet Harris and Tony Meehan
7	(4)	WHEN WILL YOU SAY I LOVE YOU?—Billy Fury
8	(10)	DECK OF CARDS—Wink Martindale
9	(5)	LUCKY LIPS—Cliff Richard and The Shadows
10	(23)	ATLANTIS—Shadows
11	(11)	IN DREAMS—Roy Orbison
12	(7)	TWO KINDS OF TEARDROPS—Del Shannon
13	(8)	CAN'T GET USED TO LOSING YOU—Andy Williams
14	(20)	FALLING—Roy Orbison
15	(13)	YOUNG LOVERS—Paul and Paula
16	(—)	BO DIDDLEY—Buddy Holly
17	(16)	PIPELINE—Chantays
18	(14)	NOBODY'S DARLIN' BUT MINE—Frank Ifield
19	(24)	FORGET HIM—Bobby Rydell
20	(15)	HOW DO YOU DO IT?—Gerry and the Pacemakers
21	(27)	THE ICE CREAM MAN—Tornados
22	(17)	FROM A JACK TO A KING—Ned Miller
23	(18)	LOSING YOU—Brenda Lee
24	(22)	THE HARVEST OF LOVE—Benny Hill
25	(19)	HE'S SO FINE—Chiffons
26	(21)	CASABLANCA—Kenny Ball
27	(—)	SHY GIRL—Mark Wynter
28	(30)	ANOTHER SATURDAY NIGHT—Sam Cooke
29	(26)	LITTLE BAND OF GOLD—James Gilreath
30	(29)	MY WAY—Eddie Cochran

Supplied by Melody Maker

Impact Sound did a deal with Decca Records and four weeks later, on 7 June, the first Stones' single was released. It was, according to the *New Musical Express*, 'A song and performance aimed straight at the current market for groups.' Significantly, printed on the Decca single were the words 'The Rolling Stones' – they were rollin' no more.

Two days after the single came out, the Stones were playing the Crawdaddy Club in Richmond again. In the audience was Patrick Doncaster, the *Daily Mirror*'s 46-year-old pop music columnist, who became the first national newspaper journalist to write about what he called 'five long-haired lads responsible for an extraordinary scene in suburban Surrey'.

Their single began to pick up some airplay on the BBC and, a few days before the end of the month, Eric Easton called Jimmy Grant at the BBC to discuss the possibility of the Stones having another audition, 'because of the growing impact of this group on the public'. Not that this impact was great enough to see 'Come On' make the charts, which may have been behind the BBC calling Easton a few days later to say that the Stones were being 'put on the waiting list for an audition'.

While BBC radio may have been unimpressed with the band, not so commercial television and in particular *Thank Your Lucky Stars*, at this time the most important pop programme on British television. They agreed to have the band come to Alpha Studios in Aston, Birmingham to record an appearance.

THANK YOUR LUCKY STARS

Opposite: The first ever mention of the Stones in a national newspaper

The show, made by ABC TV, first appeared on British television screens in 1961 and was produced by one of the companies that made up the ITV network that had launched in 1955. Whereas the BBC was, and still is, funded by the tax-payer, ITV's programmes were paid for by advertising, like the American television model.

The very first edition of *Thank Your Lucky Stars* aired on 1 April 1961 at 5.45 p.m., scheduled in direct competition with the BBC's pop programme, *Juke Box Jury*. The BBC's show was seen everywhere, while *TYLS* was initially only shown in the Midlands and North of England; viewers in London had to wait until February 1962 before it was aired in the capital. The show was initially hosted by DJ Pete Murray before Keith Fordyce took over, and by the time it was seen in London, Brian Matthew, the man most associated with *TYLS*, was the programme's host.

The format of *Thank Your Lucky Stars* was both predictable and safe. Each week, singers and bands were featured miming to their latest recordings on a set that was contrived and somewhat staid, even for the time. The show also featured a section called 'Spin-a-disc', in which a panel of young people gave their views and awarded points to new records. An early panellist was a girl from the Black Country, near Birmingham, named Janice Nicholls. She was so good that she became a regular on the show; if she liked a record she would award it top marks, announcing in her broad accent, 'Oi'll give it foive!'

By the time the Stones were asked to appear on *TYLS*, it was well-established and essential viewing for any self-respecting teenager. By the end of June there was no sign of 'Come On' making the charts, so if the record was to do anything it was essential that they got the kind of exposure that *TYLS* could bring.

The Stones were asked to appear on the episode that was to be broadcast on 13 July. There was just one problem, according to Loog Oldham. 'If they'd dressed the way they wanted, they wouldn't have been allowed inside the TV studios. They were asked to wear "uniforms" of some description.' His solution to this was to take them shopping in Soho on the weekend before their TV appearance.

According to Bill Wyman, 'During the afternoon of Saturday 29 June we went with Andrew to Carnaby Street, where we were measured for black trousers, and black and white dogtooth jackets with black velvet collars. We also bought blue shirts, black knit ties, and blue leather waistcoats. We then went to Anello and Davide and bought black Spanish boots with Cuban heels [later called "Beatle" boots].'

On Friday 5 July, the Stones played the Ricky Tick Club at the Star and Garter Hotel in Windsor, and because they needed to leave London early on Sunday morning to drive to Birmingham they cancelled a gig that they were due to play in King's Lynn, in Norfolk, on England's east coast. Among the other artists on *TYLS* in the week of the Stones' first TV

‘The Rolling Stones first burst into prominence as the long-haired London group with a twitch that was a kind of dance, who appeared on Thank Your Lucky Stars recently. From there the number they did, Chuck Berry’s “Come On”, progressed steadily and this week entered the NME chart.’

New Musical Express
2 August 1963

Opposite: The Stones at Alpha Studios, Aston, Birmingham, on 7 July to record their debut on *Thank Your Lucky Stars*

Top: The Stones pose with other guests on their first *Thank Your Lucky Stars* appearance, aired on 13 July

appearance were guest DJ Jimmy Henney, along with singers Helen Shapiro, Mickie Most, Johnny Cymbal, Patsy Ann Noble and two other groups, the Cadets (an Irish showband) and the Viscounts.

The set on which the Stones were placed, while miming to their single, looked like the veranda of a Wild West-style saloon; Mick, Keith, Brian, Bill and Charlie all wore their new dogtooth jackets and looked, by their standards, exceptionally smart, except for their hair. In fact, given what was soon to become the norm, the Stones’ hair was anything but long – it was at worst a little unkempt. Yet after they finished their spot, Pete Murray made some remarks about a delegation from the Hairdressers’ Union wanting to see the band because they hadn’t had a haircut since last year. And meanwhile a producer on the show pulled Loog Oldham to one side, saying that if he had any ambitions about the Stones ever amounting to anything, then he’d need to get rid of ‘the vile-looking singer with the tyre-tread lips’.

A little over two weeks after appearing on *Thank Your Lucky Stars*, ‘Come On’ finally made the charts, entering the UK Top 40 at No.32. No records exist as to the number of radio plays the band were getting on the BBC or on Radio Luxembourg, the other station much loved by British teenagers. It is likely, given the fact that they had appeared on TV, that Decca’s ‘pluggers’ were able to persuade radio producers and DJs to take a little more notice of the band. So without their TV debut it has to be said that ‘Come On’ may have sunk without trace. By the week ending 5 September, however, it was at No.24 on the chart, having been one place higher the week before.

'Things were quiet until we did an appearance on Thank Your Lucky Stars. Then the disc started to take off.'

Mick Jagger

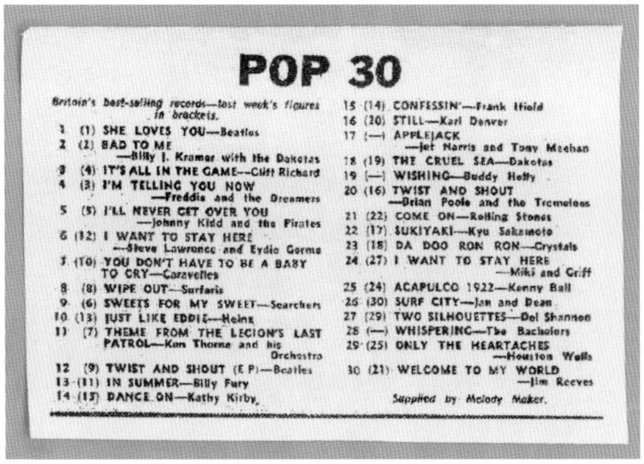

POP 30

Britain's best-selling records—last week's figures in brackets.

1 (1) SHE LOVES YOU—Beatles
2 (2) BAD TO ME —Billy J. Kramer with the Dakotas
3 (4) IT'S ALL IN THE GAME—Cliff Richard
4 (3) I'M TELLING YOU NOW —Freddie and the Dreamers
5 (5) I'LL NEVER GET OVER YOU —Johnny Kidd and the Pirates
6 (12) I WANT TO STAY HERE —Steve Lawrence and Eydie Gorme
7 (10) YOU DON'T HAVE TO BE A BABY TO CRY—Caravelles
8 (8) WIPE OUT—Surfaris
9 (6) SWEETS FOR MY SWEET—Searchers
10 (13) JUST LIKE EDDIE—Heinz
11 (7) THEME FROM THE LEGION'S LAST PATROL—Ken Thorne and his Orchestra
12 (9) TWIST AND SHOUT (E.P.)—Beatles
13 (11) IN SUMMER—Billy Fury
14 (15) DANCE ON—Kathy Kirby
15 (14) CONFESSIN'—Frank Ifield
16 (20) STILL—Karl Denver
17 (—) APPLEJACK —Jet Harris and Tony Meehan
18 (19) THE CRUEL SEA—Dakotas
19 (—) WISHING—Buddy Holly
20 (16) TWIST AND SHOUT —Brian Poole and the Tremeloes
21 (22) COME ON—Rolling Stones
22 (17) SUKIYAKI—Kyu Sakamoto
23 (18) DA DOO RON RON—Crystals
24 (27) I WANT TO STAY HERE —Miki and Griff
25 (24) ACAPULCO 1922—Kenny Ball
26 (30) SURF CITY—Jan and Dean
27 (29) TWO SILHOUETTES—Del Shannon
28 (—) WHISPERING—The Bachelors
29 (25) ONLY THE HEARTACHES —Houston Wells
30 (21) WELCOME TO MY WORLD —Jim Reeves

Supplied by Melody Maker.

Opposite: The band in the 'stage gear' bought in London's Carnaby Street a week before they recorded their *TYLS* debut

Above left: Decca released this *TYLS* tie-in LP that included two tracks by the Stones

Above right: The UK Top 30, including 'Come On'

A week after the release of the single, the *Melody Maker*, the UK's other major music weekly, featured 'Come On' as one of the records in its 'Blind Date' column, in which established stars were played records and then asked their opinion. This particular week's guest was singer Craig Douglas, who was unimpressed by the Stones' single: 'Very, very ordinary. Can't hear a word they're saying and I don't know what all this is about. If there was a Liverpool accent it might get somewhere, but this is definitely no hit. I dislike it, I'm afraid!'

On Sunday 8 September, the Stones again travelled to Birmingham to record an appearance on *TYLS* to be broadcast the following Saturday. This time they had played a gig on the Saturday night at King's Hall, Aberystwyth. Even today this would be a difficult cross-country drive but in 1963 the 120-mile journey in their beaten-up VW van took close to four hours, which meant that when they arrived at ABC TV's studio in Aston, they were without sleep and not at their best.

At the studio they found out that Craig Douglas was also to appear. This was an opportunity too good to miss for the band who decided to thank him for his ungenerous review of their single. It was well documented that Douglas had been a milkman before he became a singer and so the Stones collected every single milk bottle they could find around the studios and then put them outside Mr Douglas's dressing room, with a note saying '2 pints please'.

Douglas was furious and reported them to the *TYLS* production team who felt it necessary to give the Stones a telling-off. It would not be the last time they fell foul of authority in television and radio. Ironically, the song Douglas was promoting, 'I'm So Glad I Found Her', failed to make the chart.

In the week following their second *TYLS* appearance, 'Come On' managed to get to No.21 on the UK chart, its highest placing during its fourteen-week chart run.

In late September 1963, the Stones made their first ever appearance on a long-playing record, when 'Come On' was the last track on side two of *Thank Your Lucky Stars*, a TV tie-in released by Decca and featuring tracks from the label's artists that had appeared on the TV show.

CLUBS, BALLROOMS AND THE OCCASIONAL VILLAGE HALL

Below: Having signed their recording contract, the summer of 1963 was spent playing ballrooms throughout the UK, their more familiar clubs in London and the south-east of England, as well as the occasional village hall to honour earlier bookings

Right: The band played a Sunday afternoon gig at Studio 51 Club in London's Soho on 14 April before playing Richmond's Crawdaddy Club in the evening. It was that evening that the Beatles stopped in at the Crawdaddy to watch the Stones.

Two days after recording their TV debut for *Thank Your Lucky Stars*, the Stones were in north London at Decca Studios in West Hampstead to record a cover of Benny Spellman's 'Fortune Teller' as a potential follow-up to 'Come On'. The following Saturday, 13 July, Stu – Ian Stewart – drove the Stones 240 miles north of London to Middlesbrough to play the Alcove Club; it was their first gig away from the capital and the south east of England.

NELSONS SPORTS AND SOCIAL CLUB
presents by Public Request
TEEN·BEAT NIGHT '63
SIX HOURS NON-STOP DANCING FEATURING
FIRST TIME IN THE NORTH-WEST—BRITAIN'S TOP RHYTHM AND BLUES GROUP
THE ROLLING STONES
Decca Recording Stars—"Come On"
THE FAMOUS LIVERPOOL SOUND—DIRECT FROM THE "CAVERN," LIVERPOOL
THE MERSEYBEATS
Fontana Recording Stars—"It's Love That Really Counts"
DECCA RECORDING STARS—"TOSSING AND TURNING," "MEMPHIS, TENNESSEE"
DAVE BERRY & the CRUISERS
TWIST AND SHOUT TO THE EXCITING RHYTHM AND BLUES SOUND OF
THE DOODLE-BUGS
FLORAL HALL BALLROOM, MORECAMBE
FRIDAY, 27TH SEPTEMBER, 1963
8 p.m. to 2 a.m.
Tickets 5/-, at the door 6/-
BAR EXTENSION UNTIL 1 A.M. LATE TRANSPORT AVAILABLE
Tickets on sale from
Floral Hall Box Office; J. M. Harris, Westgate; John B. Barber and Son Ltd., New Street, Lancaster; S. E. Taverner, 18 Slyne Road, Torrisholme; Kenneth Gardner Ltd., all branches; Plough Hotel, Galgate; or any Member of the Committee
RECORDS OF THE ABOVE ARTISTS ARE OBTAINABLE FROM KENNETH GARDNER'S

There were growing signs that the Stones were making an impact when they made No. 10 in *Beat Monthly*'s regular monthly poll, although how genuine the poll was may be open to question. For the rest of July, the gigs were the usual round of London clubs, with a few in the counties adjacent to the capital. The band also went back to Decca Studios to record a version of the Coasters' American hit, 'Poison Ivy' – another attempt to record a second single.

With 'Come On' making the charts on 2 August, the Stones played their first gig of the month at the Wooden Bridge Hotel, near Guildford in Surrey. By the end of August they had played over thirty more, mainly at clubs, including the Crawdaddy, Eel Pie Island, the Ricky Tick, and Studio 51 in Soho along with a few ballrooms in Leicester, Margate, Woking and Dunstable, as well as Worplesdon Village Hall near Guildford and the Winter Gardens in Banbury, near Oxford. The Stones also appeared at the third Richmond Jazz Festival, held on the athletic ground adjoining the pavilion that was the new home of the Crawdaddy Club – albeit at the bottom of the bill.

On 8 August it was back to Decca Studios to record three more covers – Chuck Berry's 'Bye Bye Johnny', Barrett Strong's 'Money' and Arthur Alexander's 'You Better

KEN
COLYERS
JAZZMEN
WILL BE APPEARING
HERE
SATURDAY
SUNDAY

KEN
COLYERS
JAZZMEN

'I saw the Stones at the Richmond Jazz Festival playing in a tent; it was rocking. I was the last one out of the tent, looking at everybody packing up the gear.'

Ronnie Wood

Above: The Stones, along with almost every British jazz artist, played the National Jazz Festival on 11 August, watched by Ronnie Wood

Move On'. All three tracks were earmarked for an EP, and would all feature on various radio broadcasts over the coming nine months.

It was decided that 'Poison Ivy' with 'Fortune Teller' on the B-side was to be the follow-up to 'Come On', despite any reservations the band had. Its release date was set as 26 August, but at the last minute it was decided to withdraw the single as 'Come On' was still rising up the charts. The Stones had reason to be optimistic as they were about to go back on television to promote their debut, and this time it was an appearance on the hippest pop show on UK TV ... *Ready Steady Go!*

RSG! was not their only TV appearance during this time. At 7 a.m. on 29 August, Stu picked up the band to drive them back to Manchester, despite having played Eel Pie Island the previous evening. They were booked to appear on Granada TV's *Scene at 6.30*.

Granada was another of ITV's independent companies, this one based in Manchester, and *Scene at 6.30* was their weekday news and magazine programme, first broadcast in January 1963. The programme was presented by Mike Scott and frequently featured a musician or group miming to their latest record; the Beatles had already appeared on it twice in 1963, including one recording ten days prior to the Stones' appearance. In a neat twist, after the Stones were featured on 29 August miming to Chuck Berry's 'Come On', the American guitarist himself appeared on the programme a few weeks later, followed by another of the Stones' musical inspirations, Bo Diddley.

Scene at 6.30 was a live show broadcast from Granada Television Centre's Studio Four, and the band had left London so early in order to be in Manchester to rehearse by mid-afternoon. The show's producer was apparently somewhat shocked by their appearance. No footage exists of this performance and so we've no idea whether the band wore their 'street clothes' or were dressed identically. Given how early they had left London, it may have been asking too much for them to manage to get their 'uniforms' together.

After the TV appearance they drove to Liverpool and visited the Cavern Club where local band, the Big Three, were recording a live EP. According to the *New Musical Express*: 'The Rolling Stones dashed to Liverpool to watch the session as members of the audience and found themselves hailed as celebrities. The explanation for the Rolling Stones' widespread popularity in the North undoubtedly lies in their style – which is raw, exciting, down to earth, and strongly R&B flavoured.'

It sounds like Loog Oldham was behind the NME briefing on the Stones' northern popularity. But, there is no doubt that there was a real buzz building around the band.

READY STEADY GO!

Thursday 22 August 1963 was a rare day off for the Stones, after having played the sweaty Eelpiland Club at Eel Pie Island the previous night. All this work was bringing in much-needed extra money, which meant that the £10 a week each of the Stones had been paid in June and July had risen to £25, at a time when the average weekly earnings in Britain were about £15. As it turned out, September would be even busier for the band; they played live every day except two, and on one of those days they recorded an appearance on *Thank Your Lucky Stars* – the last occasion that 'Come On' would be performed on British television.

On Friday they were booked to play Worplesdon Village Hall, but instead they were in central London appearing on what was unquestionably the best British music show from the mid-Sixties – *Ready Steady Go!*

The importance of *Ready Steady Go!* to the beat band generation is impossible to over-emphasize. The show had been the brainchild of forty-something Elkan Allan, a former journalist and radio broadcaster and by 1962 the head of entertainment at Associated-Rediffusion, another one of the commercial TV companies in Britain.

Allan's idea was to create a music programme that had the minimum of production values, with no fake sets, just the artists, the kids and the energy that they could, together, produce. Allan involved another former journalist, Francis Hitching, as producer, with Robert Fleming as *RSG!*'s first director. This was a programme in the tradition of *Six-Five Special* and *Oh Boy!*, pioneering British 1950s music television shows that were the brainchild of producer Jack Good.

Above: Brian Poole and the Tremeloes on *Ready Steady Go!* in 1963

Opposite: The band's first appearance on *RSG!* on 23 August, wearing the leather waistcoats they bought in Carnaby Steet at the end of June

Left: Kathy Kirby

Bottom: The Caravelles: Andrea Simpson (l) and Lois Wilkinson (r) on *Ready Steady Go!* in 1963

The Stones appeared on the third edition of *RSG!*, two weeks after the first show that was broadcast on 8 August 1963. In all truth, the first *Ready Steady Go!* was a little lacking in the kind of dynamism for which it was soon famous. The principal guests, appearing in front of a studio audience of 200 kids, were Brian Poole and the Tremeloes, the band that Decca had signed instead of the Beatles, American folk singer Burl Ives plugging his single, 'The Ugly Bug Ball', Liverpool singer Billy Fury, more rock 'n' roll than beat, along with veteran bandleader Joe Loss judging a dance competition.

Both the first and second editions of *RSG!* were introduced by 35-year-old Cambridge law student, Keith Fordyce, along with David Gell, both of whom had previously worked on *Thank Your Lucky Stars*. Like the first *RSG!*, the second was also somewhat tame, with Shane Fenton, the Caravelles singing 'You Don't Have To Be A Baby To Cry', and Kathy Kirby – although Screaming Lord Sutch,

Right: Dusty Springfield presented some early episodes of *Ready Steady Go!* with Keith Fordyce

Below: Cathy McGowan

whose band, the Savages, included Carlo Little and Ricky Fenson and the aptly named pianist, Freddie 'Fingers' Lee, did help to give the programme a modicum of edge.

Broadcast at 7p.m. from TV House in London's Kingsway, *RSG!* used the Surfaris' 'Wipe Out' as its theme song, accompanied by its era-defining slogan, 'The Weekend Starts Here!' Perhaps conscious that weeks one and two had been a little less electrifying than had been hoped, the producers brought in 19-year-old Cathy McGowan as a co-presenter; she would quickly become a star in her own right and soon after earn the title 'Queen of the Mods'.

Through her appearances on *RSG!*, Cathy became an icon of pop culture, telling viewers what was in and hot, as well as what was out and not. Her meteoric rise – and it really was – somehow fitted the mood of the period, a time when it first became possible for ordinary people to 'make it', and make it big.

It was on Sunday 18 August that the Stones got their chance to appear on the show. Some of the production team went to the Crawdaddy Club looking for dancers to join the *RSG!* audience from among the crowd of 700 or so cramming the Richmond Athletic Club pavilion. They also liked the Stones, who had been playing there that night; after talking to them between sets they were invited to appear the following Friday.

The television audience, aside from showing off the latest dance crazes, was another very important facet of

‘I blundered my way through each show.’

Cathy McGowan

Ready Steady Go! They were selected not only for their dancing prowess, but also for their fashion sense and style. Given that these were London kids, they were at the epicentre of what was about to become the Swinging Sixties, so named by the *New York Times* in May 1966. Many of those in the audience of *RSG!* would shop in Carnaby Street.

John Stephen, the self-proclaimed King of Carnaby Street, opened the first of his shops, His Clothes, in 1963. This was soon followed by I Was Lord Kitchener's Valet, Lady Jane, Kleptomania, Mates, Ravel, and a string of others that all catered for pop stars and young people who wanted to look like pop stars. Designers like Mary Quant, Lord John, Merc and Irvine Sellar let everyone know that conformity was yesterday. Londoners wanted to dress differently, not just from the ‘squares’ who loved a dark suit or a sensible frock, but also from one another; individuality over the mode of the masses was everything. Soon the whole country, and then the whole world, wanted to dress like London dressed and listen to the music that London was listening to. And *RSG!*, in its role as Britain's weekly look at the ‘fab, happening scene’ in the capital, was there to shape the taste of the nation.

For the Stones' live debut on *RSG!* on 23 August, they were joined by the former bass player and drummer from the Shadows, Jet Harris and Tony Meehan, who performed ‘Applejack’, their third single, which was to be released a week later. The other guests included Little Peggy March, a 15-year-old American who had just become the youngest female singer ever to have had a No. 1 single on the *Billboard* charts.

While the show was broadcast live, the Stones, like the other artists, were miming to ‘Come On’, wearing their matching pale blue shirts and blue leather waistcoats; it is probably the last time they all dressed the same for a TV appearance.

McGowan's first real contribution to *RSG!* was to ask Brian Jones, ‘How do you cut your hair?’ Not an unreasonable enquiry given that the Stones had attracted as much attention about the length of their hair as they had about their music. Brian, in his posh Cheltenham accent, replied, ‘I cut my hair whenever necessary, with a pair of scissors and two mirrors.’ It was more a question of finances than anything else, although you can hardly blame him or any of the Stones for their aversion to traditional men's haircutting establishments, given their use of electric hair-clippers, designed primarily to produce a ‘short back and sides’ as favoured by everyone else.

As Cathy McGowan told *Rolling Stones Monthly* in November 1965, ‘The girls were really going mad. Mick did all that jumping around that made the girls scream. We had literally thousands of letters in the office, asking to see them again. The reaction to that first performance was so great that within three months they were regulars on the show.’ She was of course reflecting with the benefit of hindsight, but the Stones went on to appear on *RSG!* on over twenty separate occasions, both as a band and individually.

It was three months later, on 22 November, that the Stones appeared on *RSG!* for a second time. This time it was to promote their second single, 'I Wanna Be Your Man'; again the Stones were miming. Also appearing were Gerry and the Pacemakers, performing 'You'll Never Walk Alone', which was currently spending its fourth week at No.1 on the UK charts. The other acts were Freddie and the Dreamers with their single 'You Were Made For Me'; it was shooting up the charts before spending a number of weeks at No.3, kept from rising any higher by the Beatles. They were joined by singers Kathy Kirby and Kenny Lynch, and songwriter Mitch Murray, who had written Gerry and the Pacemakers' first hit, 'How Do You Do It?'

'I Wanna Be Your Man' had just entered the UK charts and so it was extremely current. Visually the Stones had by this time very definitely moved on. There were no matching jackets, waistcoats, or any attempt to wear a 'uniform', unlike the other groups on the show who all dressed identically.

On the same day as the Stones appeared on *RSG!*, the *New Musical Express* carried the news that 'Promoter Harry Dawson has set a series of concerts for the Ronettes headlining a package of British groups, including the Rolling Stones.'

Immediately after appearing live on TV, broadcast from central London, the band crossed over the Thames in their VW van heading to south-east London, where they played at Greenwich Town Hall. It was between these two appearances that they, like the rest of Britain, heard that President John F. Kennedy had been assassinated in Dallas, Texas.

A month earlier, in New York City, Bob Dylan had recorded a song that would be an anthem for the age. The times really were a changin'...

Right: 'Little' Stevie Wonder enjoys the Stones' performance on *RSG!* on 27 December

TOURING

Right: Package tours were developed in America during the 1950s to get the most artists on stage at a single venue to ensure a sell-out show. Just like in Britain, bands played two or three quick songs and then it was time for the next performer.

During their TV appearances in July and August, the Stones performed in the knowledge that there was another, significant, milestone on the horizon. It had been at the end of June that Eric Easton told them that he had managed to book them onto their first UK package tour. Easton had done a deal with the promoter Don Arden, a legend in the British music business and the future father-in-law of Ozzy Osbourne. Arden, known to drive a hard bargain, got the Stones for £42 per night, or £21 per show, as on every date on the tour there were two houses to play in cinemas from London to Glasgow and Taunton in the west to Ipswich in the east.

Package tours had been developed in America in the 1950s, having arguably started in the 1940s with the 'Jazz at the Philharmonic' tours that were started by Norman Granz. With the coming of rock 'n' roll, American DJ-turned-entrepreneur Alan Freed created his tours with a semi-revolving cast of stars, big and small, that could be added to as the tour went on, and as new artists made the best-seller lists.

In 1953, Freed was getting into his stride with his 'Rock 'n' Roll Holiday Show', which included Count Basie, LaVern Baker, the Heartbeats, the Cadillacs, the Wrens, Joe Williams, the Valentines and Fats Domino. Another package tour billed as the 'Rock and Roll Revue' featured Duke Ellington, Nat King Cole, Lionel Hampton and Dinah Washington among its almost exclusively jazz-playing entourage. But such was the selling power of rock 'n' roll, everyone wanted a slice of the action.

By the time the '1957 Biggest Show of Stars' came along, package tours in America were becoming enormous. Artists who took part included the Stones' favourite, Chuck Berry, as well as Eddie Cochran and the Everly Brothers. In January 1958, the Everly Brothers headlined a tour that also featured Danny and the Juniors and Buddy Holly and the Crickets.

In 1959, Buddy Holly, along with Ritchie Valens, Dion and the Belmonts and the Big Bopper, was one of the main attractions on the Winter Dance Party tour. It was while Holly, Valens and the Big Bopper were travelling between gigs on this tour that the plane on which they were flying crashed and all three stars were killed.

In Britain as well as Australia, and later on Europe too, the pattern of putting together a number of groups and artists on package tours became the normal way for singers and bands to be seen during the early to mid-1960s. The Beatles played on the package tour circuit, having first learned their craft in Hamburg. Naturally the Stones trod a similar path – not because they were imitating the Beatles or anyone else, it was just that this was the tried and tested way for artists to gain the maximum exposure.

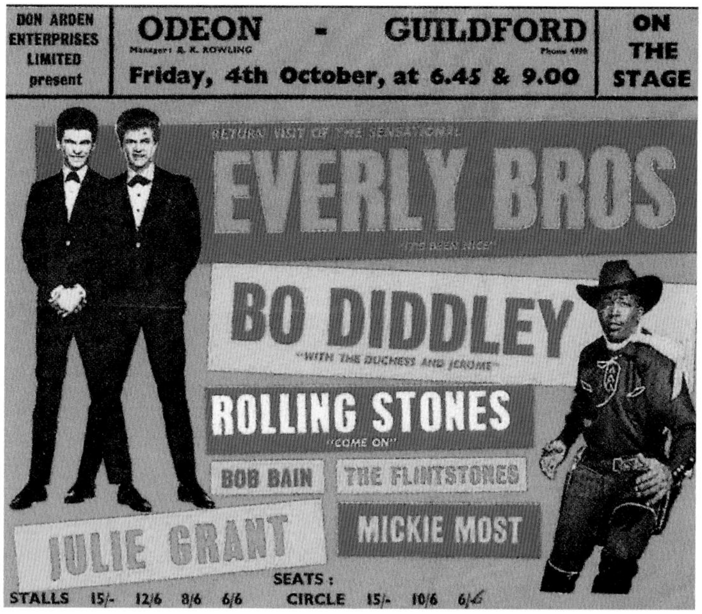

On the Stones' first package tour the headliners were the Everly Brothers, a duo who were vastly experienced at the whole game. It was to be a thirty-date tour lasting just thirty-six days, and the first show was at London's New Victoria Theatre on 29 September.

As Brian told the *NME* in the issue that hit the news stands on the day the Stones appeared on *Ready Steady Go!* for the first time, 'So far, we've raved only in clubs and dance halls, but now we're looking forward to raving on our first theatre tour with the Everly Brothers. For us, the big thrill is that Bo Diddley will be on the bill! He's been one of our great influences. It won't be a case of the pupils competing with the master, though. We're dropping from our act on the tour all the Bo Diddley numbers we sing.'

The Everly Brothers were genuine superstars, even if they were on the wane by this point, having chalked up four No.1s in both the UK and USA. Bo Diddley was, as Brian acknowledged, one of the band's heroes. Joining them were Lulu, Donovan, the Yardbirds, Jeff Beck and Julie Grant, who was managed by Eric Easton and Mickie Most. Most had had a minor hit earlier in the year but would later find fame as a producer, working with the Animals (including on their hit 'House Of The Rising Sun').

Prior to their first night at the New Victoria in London, the Stones were soundchecking when they met the stage manager, Peter Grant, who would later manage Led Zeppelin and become another legendary figure in the music business. According to Mick, shortly after the tour was announced, 'On the Everly Tour, we'll just go wild. We're having stage gear made but we don't know what it is yet. We've never worn a uniform in the clubs. It's going to be something really different, though.' In the event they wore their blue leather waistcoats on a few of the early shows, and they wore their dogtooth jackets, but most often as not they didn't all wear the same thing; all too soon they began appearing in whatever they happened to be wearing.

It was clear from even before the tour got underway that the Everly Brothers were not the draw they had once been and Arden decided to bring in the cavalry in the shape of Little Richard. According to the promoter: 'The Everly Brothers had definitely had it. I phoned up Little Richard and said, "Richard, you've gotta help me out." He said, "OK."' Little Richard joined the tour in Guildford on 4 October.

The package tour routine for the lesser bands on the bill was very much 'three quick songs and you're off'. True to their word, the Stones did no Bo Diddley numbers, but their songs were of course all covers and their ten-minute set was chosen from their debut single, 'Poison Ivy', 'Fortune Teller' and Barrett Strong's 'Money'. Later in the tour they added their new single, 'I Wanna Be Your Man', as well as 'Memphis Tennessee' and other assorted covers of blues and R&B tunes they had been playing in the clubs.

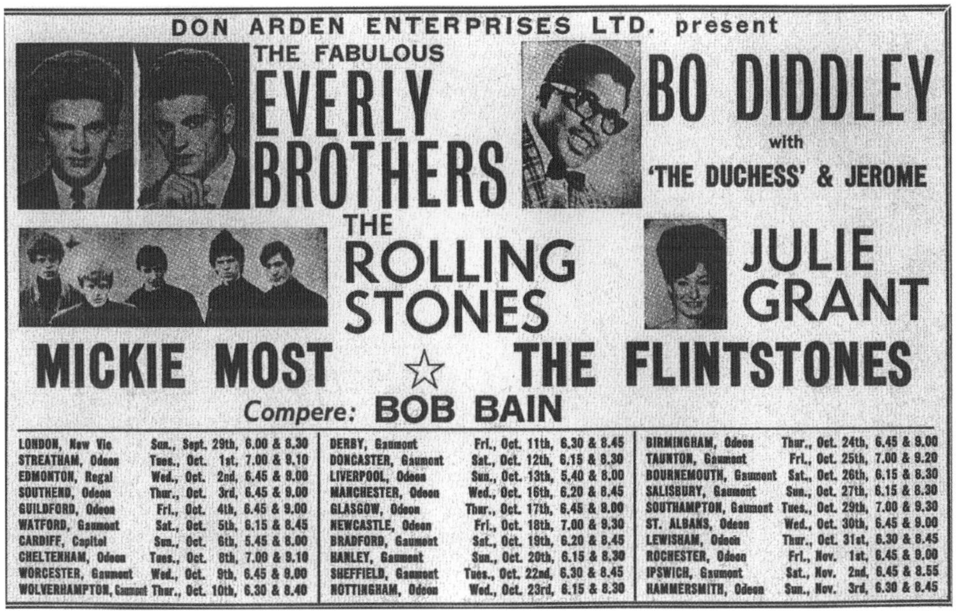
DON ARDEN ENTERPRISES LTD. present
THE FABULOUS
EVERLY BROTHERS
BO DIDDLEY
with
'THE DUCHESS' & JEROME
THE ROLLING STONES
JULIE GRANT
MICKIE MOST ☆ THE FLINTSTONES
Compere: BOB BAIN
LONDON, New Vic Sun., Sept. 29th, 6.00 & 8.30
STREATHAM, Odeon Tues., Oct. 1st, 7.00 & 9.10
EDMONTON, Regal Wed., Oct. 2nd, 6.45 & 9.00
SOUTHEND, Odeon Thur., Oct. 3rd, 6.45 & 9.00
GUILDFORD, Odeon Fri., Oct. 4th, 6.45 & 9.00
WATFORD, Gaumont Sat., Oct. 5th, 6.15 & 8.45
CARDIFF, Capitol Sun., Oct. 6th, 5.45 & 8.00
CHELTENHAM, Odeon Tues., Oct. 8th, 7.00 & 9.10
WORCESTER, Gaumont Wed., Oct. 9th, 6.45 & 9.00
WOLVERHAMPTON, Gaumont Thur., Oct. 10th, 6.30 & 8.40
DERBY, Gaumont Fri., Oct. 11th, 6.30 & 8.45
DONCASTER, Gaumont Sat., Oct. 12th, 6.15 & 8.30
LIVERPOOL, Odeon Sun., Oct. 13th, 5.40 & 8.00
MANCHESTER, Odeon Wed., Oct. 16th, 6.20 & 8.45
GLASGOW, Odeon Thur., Oct. 17th, 6.45 & 9.00
NEWCASTLE, Odeon Fri., Oct. 18th, 7.00 & 9.30
BRADFORD, Gaumont Sat., Oct. 19th, 6.20 & 8.45
HANLEY, Gaumont Sun., Oct. 20th, 6.15 & 8.30
SHEFFIELD, Gaumont Tues., Oct. 22nd, 6.30 & 8.45
NOTTINGHAM, Odeon Wed., Oct. 23rd, 6.15 & 8.30
BIRMINGHAM, Odeon Thur., Oct. 24th, 6.45 & 9.00
TAUNTON, Gaumont Fri., Oct. 25th, 7.00 & 9.20
BOURNEMOUTH, Gaumont Sat., Oct. 26th, 6.15 & 8.30
SALISBURY, Gaumont Sun., Oct. 27th, 6.15 & 8.30
SOUTHAMPTON, Gaumont Tues., Oct. 29th, 7.00 & 9.30
ST. ALBANS, Odeon Wed., Oct. 30th, 6.45 & 9.00
LEWISHAM, Odeon Thur., Oct. 31st, 6.30 & 8.45
ROCHESTER, Odeon Fri., Nov. 1st, 6.45 & 9.00
IPSWICH, Gaumont Sat., Nov. 2nd, 6.45 & 8.55
HAMMERSMITH, Odeon Sun., Nov. 3rd, 6.30 & 8.45

'So far, we've raved only in clubs and dance halls, but now we're looking forward to raving on our first theatre tour with the Everly Brothers. For us, the big thrill is that Bo Diddley will be on the bill!'

Brian Jones

Opposite left: Bo Diddley
Opposite right and above: The early dates for the Stones' first package tour did not include Little Richard, who was added when sales proved a little slow

VOX

On Tuesday 10 September, prior to beginning the Everly Brothers tour, the Stones were at Studio 51 in London's Soho, trying to come up with an A-side to record as a follow-up to 'Come On'. No one in the band or at Decca was keen on either 'Poison Ivy' or 'Fortune Teller'.

Midway through the afternoon, Andrew Loog Oldham left the rehearsal and, while walking along Charing Cross Road, spotted Paul McCartney and John Lennon getting out of a cab. The two Beatles had been to a Variety Club luncheon; Paul and John may even have had a drink or two, having cause to celebrate because 'She Loves You' was at No. 1 in the UK charts. Oldham hurried over to talk to them and soon all three were on their way back to the basement club. Less than half an hour after John and Paul's arrival, the Rolling Stones had their new single.

John and Paul played 'I Wanna Be Your Man' to their small audience of the Stones, Loog Oldham and Ian Stewart, amazing Bill Wyman because Paul, who was left-handed, played Bill's bass upside down. The Stones then began adapting the song for themselves, with Brian's slide guitar taking it in a very different direction to the Beatles' original.

What is interesting is that there had been no Beatles original recording at this point. It was not until the following day, 11 September, that the Beatles recorded their version at Abbey Road, with Ringo singing the lead vocal. This would appear on their *With The Beatles* album, which came out in the third week of November 1963.

On 4 October, when the Stones played in Southend in Essex, Ringo Starr was in the audience, and three nights later after having played in Cardiff the previous evening, the Stones returned to London on their 'day off' to record 'I Wanna Be Your Man' at De Lane Lea Studios in Soho, with Brian playing slide guitar. According to Keith, around the time the record was released, 'I dig that steel solo, Brian made that record with that bottleneck.'

'I Wanna Be Your Man' was released on 1 November, three days before the package tour ended, and two weeks later it made the UK singles chart, eventually climbing to No.12 by January 1964. This was despite the *New Musical Express* offering the opinion that it was: 'Not one of Lennon and McCartney's best numbers. Accent on beat, to the total exclusion of melody.'

The B-side of the single was a mostly instrumental number they called 'Stoned', which is credited to Nanker Phelge, the collective name for a group composition by the Rolling Stones in the first two years of their existence. It was Brian who suggested they use this moniker – Phelge comes from Jimmy Phelge, a guy who the band knew when they lived in Edith Grove in 1962, while a 'Nanker' was a revolting face that Brian was fond of pulling. 'Stoned' is an inversion of 'Green Onions', the classic Booker T and the MG's Stax recording.

Opposite: On stage for the opening night of the Everly Brothers' package tour on 29 September, possibly at London's new Victoria Theatre

Far left: Sheet music for 'I Wanna Be Your Man'; John Lennon and Paul McCartney 'gave' the band their second single after Andrew Loog Oldham bumped into the two Beatles in the street

Left: Backstage at the Mod Ball, Brian and Keith pulling a 'Nanker'

IT'S SATURDAY CLUB!

Clearly it was television that gave the Stones their broadcasting break, but BBC radio, once they got over their prejudices towards the band's music and the way they looked, soon caught up. It was on the morning after the Stones had played the Gaumont Cinema in Taunton, and before they played in Bournemouth on the Everly's tour, that they were first heard playing live on *Saturday Club*.

They had recorded their numbers, which were aired on the programme on 26 October, a month earlier, on the afternoon of Monday 23 September at the Playhouse Theatre in Northumberland Avenue, near London's Trafalgar Square. The BBC contract issued on 4 September said the Stones would appear on the 5 October programme, but they were moved to a subsequent show, possibly because the Beatles were added to the programme on what was *Saturday Club*'s fifth anniversary.

The Stones' debut on *Saturday Club* was one that featured live performances from Bo Diddley; Eden Kane; the Alan Elsdon Jazz Band; Tony Rivers and the Castaways, Essex's finest Beach Boys fanatics; and the Caravelles, the two British teenagers named after a French airliner, who at the time were on their way to a top 3 hit in America with 'You Don't Have To Be A Baby To Cry'.

The Stones played their current single, 'Come On', which had ironically dropped off the chart the week before their recording was broadcast. They also did three more Chuck Berry covers: 'Memphis Tennessee', which they played regularly on the Everlys' tour, 'Talkin' 'Bout You' and 'Roll Over Beethoven' – a staple of just about every beat band in Britain, including the Beatles who released it on *With The Beatles*. The Stones' final number was 'Money', which also featured most nights on the package tour.

Their basic appearance fee for *Saturday Club* was £36 plus various small amounts to be paid later, if the tracks were broadcast again, either in the UK or around the world on the BBC's Overseas Service. However, the size of the fee was unimportant; it was the exposure that counted.

In addition to appearing with the Stones, Brian, Bill and Charlie backed Bo Diddley on four numbers on the same edition of *Saturday Club*. This was recorded on the same day as the Stones played at the Playhouse Theatre, with Diddley's regular band members, Jerome Green on maracas and guitarist 'the Duchess', a.k.a. Norma-Jean Wofford, also appearing on the recording. Together they did 'Bo Diddley', 'Road Runner', 'Pretty Thing' and 'Hey! Bo Diddley' – all well known to the Stones as they had featured regularly in their club gigs since the early days.

For well over ten years, the go-to radio show for pop-mad teenagers in Britain was broadcast by the BBC on their 'Light' network. Every Saturday morning, straight after *Children's Favourites* at 10 a.m., *Saturday Club* broadcast both live music and records, catering to a younger audience that was fed on a controlled diet of pop music on the radio.

Today, Britain is used to every form of popular music getting airtime on radio (and in myriad other ways), but in the 1950s and 1960s, arcane rules were in force that governed how many hours of music could be broadcast by the BBC from records. It was all to do with the power of the Musicians' Union, which had an arrangement with the BBC designed to keep their many thousands of members in work, performing live on the radio and TV.

Prior to 1967, the BBC was allowed to play only five hours of music per day from 'gramophone records' during any twenty-four-hour period. This meant that during their normal eighteen-hour broadcasting day they were only permitted to play about seventeen minutes per hour of recorded music, or seven records. The BBC's solution was to have singers and groups of every kind, from jazz to beat, record 'sessions' for their programmes that allowed pop music in all its many forms to be heard.

Given that any self-respecting group, including the Stones, were used to performing, with none of the studio tricks that have become commonplace, it meant they had no difficulty in being in a BBC studio to play live or record a session for later broadcast.

Saturday Club started in June 1957 as *The Saturday Skiffle Club*, lasting for an hour. Regulars on the programme were Chas McDevitt, the Vipers Skiffle Group, Johnny Duncan and his Bluegrass Boys, and George Melly's Bubbling Over Four; Cliff Richard failed an audition for the show. Brian Matthew, a newsreader on the BBC who was charmingly referred to as 'the announcer', introduced the acts.

In October 1958, the programme was extended to two hours, from 10 a.m. to 12 noon, and the word 'skiffle' was dropped from the title. A wider variety of artists were booked to appear, including Chris Barber, Humphrey Lyttelton, Marty Wilde, Terry Dene, Vince Taylor, Johnny Kidd and Bert Weedon. It also became much more relaxed,

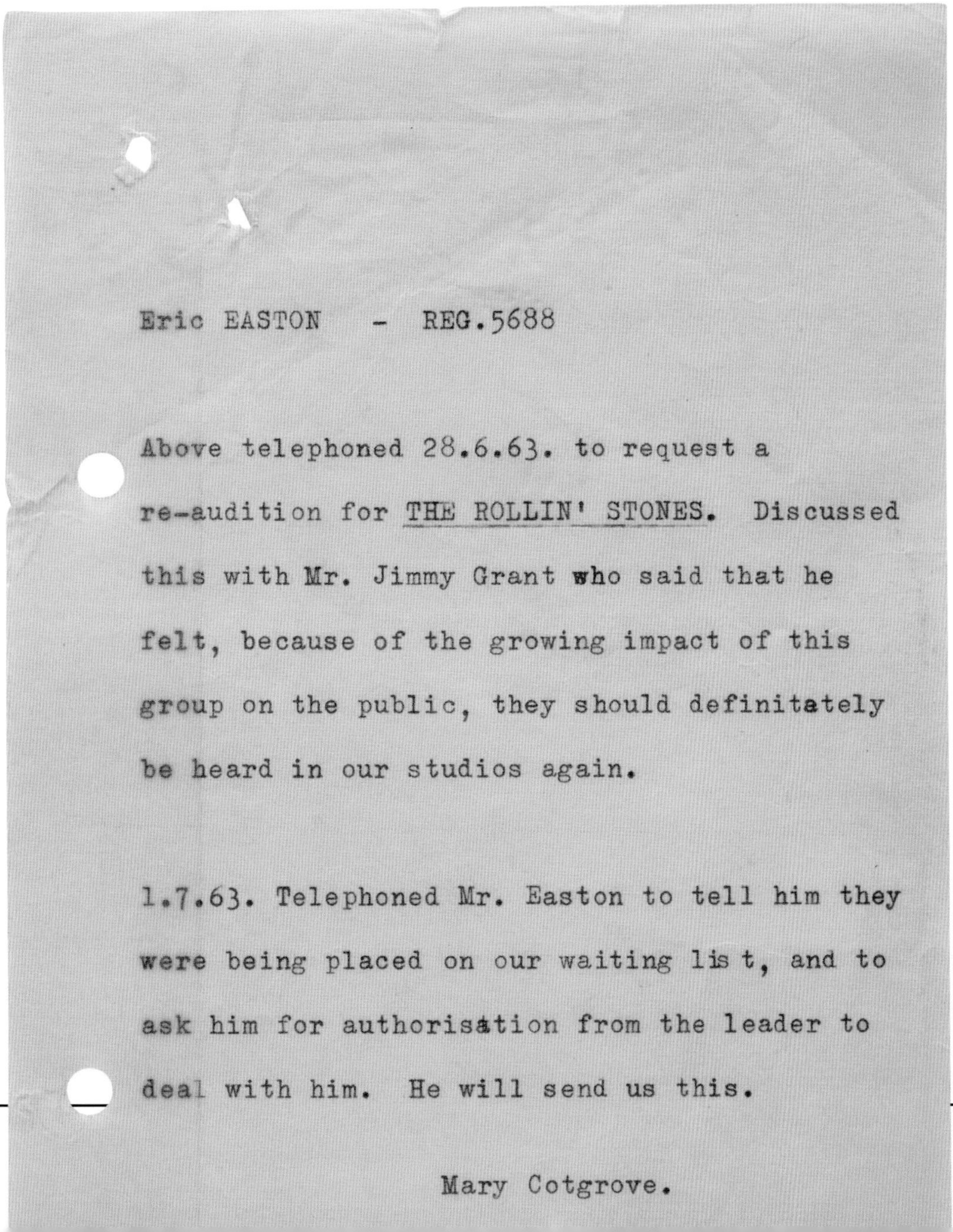

Eric EASTON - REG.5688

Above telephoned 28.6.63. to request a re-audition for THE ROLLIN' STONES. Discussed this with Mr. Jimmy Grant who said that he felt, because of the growing impact of this group on the public, they should definitately be heard in our studios again.

1.7.63. Telephoned Mr. Easton to tell him they were being placed on our waiting list, and to ask him for authorisation from the leader to deal with him. He will send us this.

Mary Cotgrove.

Left: Internal BBC memo regarding putting the Stones on the waiting list to appear on BBC radio.

(Ext 4329/2751)

Our Reference: 01/PC/LES/MMC 13th November, 1963.

Dear Mr. Jones,

THE ROLLIN' STONES

We are writing to inform you that the recording of your recent trial broadcast in 'Saturday Club' has now been played to our Production Panel, so that your work may be assessed for other programmes.

We are pleased to tell you that your performance received favourable reports, and your name has now been added to the list of artists available for broadcasting generally. This does not mean, of course, that offers of engagements will automatically follow, but simply that you may be considered for whatever opportunity to broadcast might occur.

Yours sincerely,

(David Dore)
Assistant to Light Entertainment
Booking Manager.

Mr. Brian Jones,
102, Edith Grove,
London, S.W.10.

JA

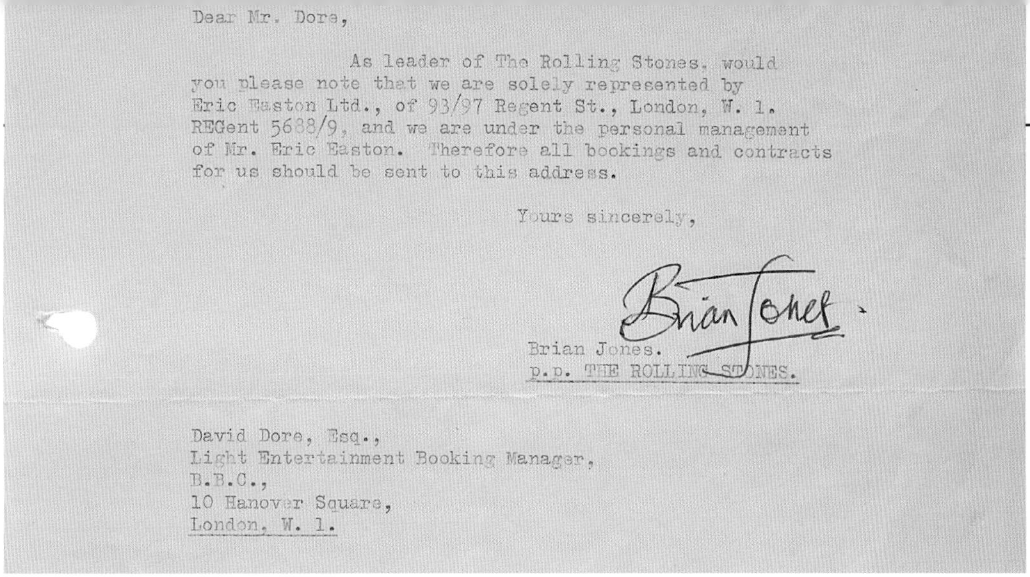

Dear Mr. Dore,

As leader of The Rolling Stones. would you please note that we are solely represented by Eric Easton Ltd., of 93/97 Regent St., London, W. 1. REGent 5688/9, and we are under the personal management of Mr. Eric Easton. Therefore all bookings and contracts for us should be sent to this address.

Yours sincerely,

Brian Jones

Brian Jones.
p.p. THE ROLLING STONES.

David Dore, Esq.,
Light Entertainment Booking Manager,
B.B.C.,
10 Hanover Square,
London, W. 1.

'Who knows whether or not anyone in the Stones' camp was aware, but the fact the BBC regarded their recording for Saturday Club as a trial has long since been forgotten. And the BBC still thought they were Rollin'.'

Opposite: The BBC inform Brian Jones that the Stones will be considered for future broadcasting

Above: Brian Jones confirms that Eric Easton is the Stones' manager

Right: Brian Matthew

with Brian Matthew adopting the style for which he became famous in both introducing and interviewing the artists that appeared on the show.

Programmes usually featured four live acts, a half dozen or so record requests and three new releases. By 1959, *Saturday Club* had a regular audience of 5 million listeners, and began to feature visiting American artists including Eddie Cochran, Gene Vincent, Duane Eddy, the Everly Brothers, Jerry Lee Lewis and Bobby Darin; this was only possible after a Musicians' Union ban on performances by non-British musicians ended.

The Beatles' first appearance on *Saturday Club* was in late January 1963 when they were heard playing their first and second singles, 'Love Me Do' and 'Please Please Me', along with three other songs from their live act, including 'Beautiful Dreamer', a nineteenth-century Stephen Foster song made famous by Bing Crosby. What the Beatles were doing was almost identical to what the Stones would do on their appearance on the show: play the hits and the road-honed numbers from their live shows.

JAGGER/ RICHARDS COMPOSITION

With the Everly's tour over by 3 November, the Stones went back to playing their London club gigs. Increasingly they also headed further afield to play ballrooms and cinemas, driving close to 5,000 miles in the two months before the year was over.

On 17 November, the night after playing Coventry's Matrix Ballroom, the Stones drove the few miles up the road to Alpha Studios in Aston, Birmingham, to record their last appearance of the year on *Thank Your Lucky Stars*. They mimed to their new single, 'I Wanna Be Your Man', which had made the UK singles chart a few days earlier. Also appearing on the show were Cliff Richard and the Shadows, Ronnie Carroll and, most significantly, American singer Gene Pitney.

Everything the Stones had performed on stage, on TV and on radio to this point was a cover of an American song; nothing had been written by anyone in the band because none of the Stones really knew how to write a song. Brian, despite his innate musical abilities, had no idea about how to start and neither Mick nor Keith had really thought much about it. That is until Loog Oldham decided it was high time Mick and Keith did try their hand at it. There's an often-repeated myth that Andrew locked them in a room at Edith Grove until they came up with a song, although the truth is less prosaic.

As Mick says, 'I think everyone got turned onto the idea of writing songs by the Beatles. It was like, if the Beatles can write, we can write.' According to Keith, 'It was Andrew that really forced Mick and I to sit down and try it, and get us through that initial period where you write absolute rubbish – things you've heard, and rewriting other people's songs – until you start coming up with songs of your own. Andrew made us persevere.'

Among the first songs that Mick and Keith wrote were 'It Should Be You' and 'Will You Be My Lover Tonight?', which were eventually recorded by George Bean in January 1964. They also wrote a song called 'My Only Girl' that they hustled Gene Pitney to record while they were rehearsing for their November *Thank Your Lucky Stars* appearance.

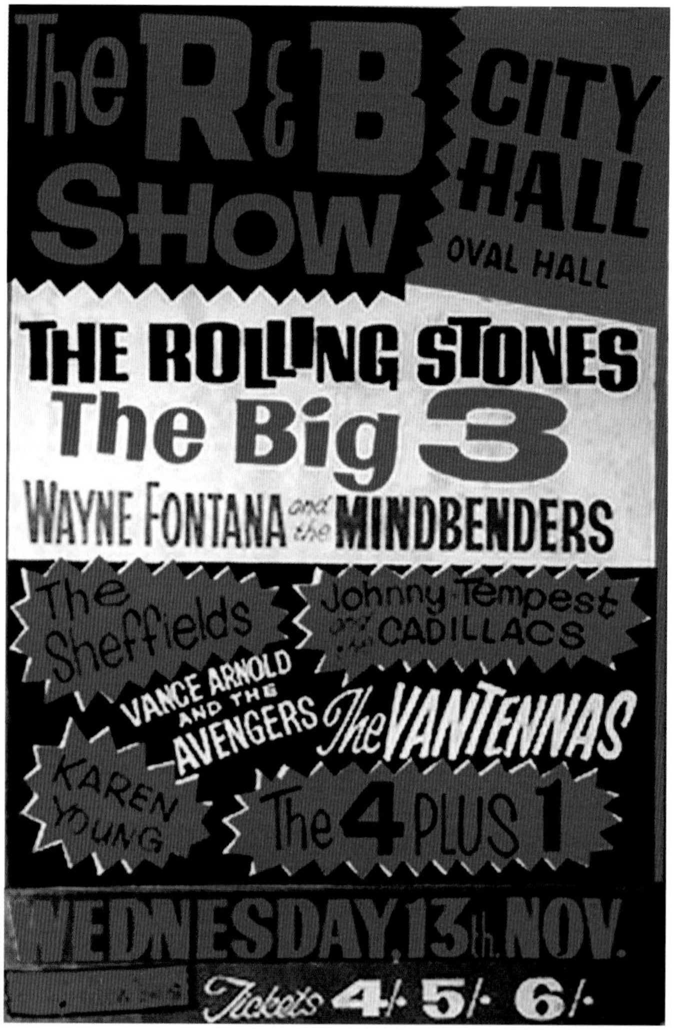

Above: As soon as the Everly Brothers tour was over it was back to one-night stands in pubs and clubs

Opposite: Waiting to go on stage at High Wycombe Town Hall, 12 November

PATRICK DONCASTER'S DISCS

If you can't beat 'em..

AMERICA'S Gene Pitney, a singing rage in the United States, where he is usually in top twenty and currently resides there with a song called "Twenty-four hours from Tulsa," surveyed the British pop scene and said:

"If you can't beat 'em, join 'em."

Gene, 22, dark-haired and neatly groomed, had been wondering why his US hits don't get off the ground here. So he took wing to London to do something about it

We looked at the chart.

EIGHT of the top TEN—British.

FOURTEEN of the top TWENTY—British.

TWENTY of the top THIRTY—British.

In London, Gene met five long-haired lads who will never figure in the list of Best Dressed Men—a group calling themselves the **Rolling Stones**, who this week join Pop Thirty and look like romping up the ladder.

Said Gene: "When I first saw them, I looked and gosh! I didn't know whether to say 'Hello' or bark.

"But then I got to know them. They are great. They are something, really something."

The Stones rolled into action with Mr. Pitney. Two of them wrote a song for him. And nothing like their own twistin' an' shoutin' rhythm and blues offerings. A dramatic beat ballad, instead, with the with-it title of "**That Girl Belongs to Yesterday.**"

HOPEFUL

What's more, Gene Pitney recorded it in London and the disc will be issued here and in the United States after Christmas.

The authors are Mick Jagger, 19, vocals and harmonica and ex-student of economics, and guitarist Keith Richard, 19, ex-Post Office worker.

Said Gene, whose "Tulsa" disc is out on United Artists here: "I hope we'll be able to crack the British market with the Rolling Stones' song."

It promises to be a good try.

Gene Pitney—"When I first saw the Rolling Stones, I didn't know whether to say 'Hello' or bark. . ."

Mick Jagger and Keith Richard—song for Pitney.

Shadows on the trail

THE SHADOWS are on the warpath again with "**Geronimo**" (Columbia), which romps along in "Apache" style. Of course, it's a hit.

☆ Like to see the **Orchids** hit with "**Love Hit Me**" (Decca). They are three Coventry schoolgirls, one 14, two 15, who sing as well as many a chart-bending American group.

★ A new ray of sunshine on Fontana—a little Jamaican girl of 15 just billed as **Millie**. She sings "**Don't You Know?**" And it's quite infectious.

☆ Young Steptoe, actor **Harry H. Corbett**, goes solo on Pye with a charmer called "**The Table and the Chair.**"

★ The versatile **Rolf Harris** has a laugh for all the family in "**I've Lost My Mummy**" (Columbia). Could be a Christmas hit.

☆ Liverpool's five-lad singing **Chants** group revives "**I Could Write A Book**" (Pye). I find it one of the most attractive spins of the week.

As Mick told the *NME* a couple of months later, 'Pitney was sitting in his dressing room, singing "If I Didn't Have A Dime", when we wandered in … Eventually we started fooling around with some of our numbers. One he particularly liked was one called "My Only Girl".' In the same paper, Pitney said, 'I couldn't wait to cut it. I asked Andrew to arrange a recording session for me. Later Charles Blackwell handled the session at a London recording studio, with a thirty-piece orchestra, which included guitarist Vic Flick and Arthur Greenslade.'

Three days after recording *TYLS*, the Stones went into Regent Sound Studios in Denmark Street with Andrew Loog Oldham to cut a demo version of 'My Only Girl', on which Pitney played piano, which almost immediately became known as 'That Girl Belongs To Yesterday'. As the *Daily Mirror* reported a week later, 'The Stones rolled into action with Mr Pitney. Two of them wrote a song for him. And nothing like their own twistin' an' hootin' rhythm and blues offerings. A dramatic beat ballad, instead, with the with-it title of "That Girl Belongs To Yesterday".'

Pitney's recording of 'That Girl Belongs To Yesterday' made the UK charts in early March, climbing to No.7; it was the follow-up to Pitney's big hit version of Burt Bacharach's 'Twenty-Four Hours From Tulsa', which he had promoted on his *TYLS* appearance with the Stones.

And so begins one of the greatest songwriting partnerships in rock music, even if their first effort was more of a romantic ballad than the kind of things that Mick and Keith eventually became famous for.

Left: Patrick Doncaster writing in the *Daily Mirror* about American singer Gene Pitney recording Mick and Keith's composition

1963 Selected TV & Radio Appearances

7 JULY 1963
(aired 13 July)

Thank Your Lucky Stars, Alpha Studios, Aston, Birmingham, UK

Come On (Chuck Berry) – playback

23 AUGUST 1963

Ready, Steady, Go!, TV House, Kingsway, London, UK

Come On (Chuck Berry) – playback

29 AUGUST 1963

Scene at 6.30, at Granada TV Studios, Manchester, UK

Come On (Chuck Berry) – playback

8 SEPTEMBER 1963
(aired 14 September)

Thank Your Lucky Stars, Alpha Studios, Aston, Birmingham, UK

Come On (Chuck Berry) – playback

23 SEPTEMBER 1963
(aired 26 October)

Saturday Club, Playhouse Theatre, Charing Cross, London, UK

BJ, BW and CW back Bo Diddley on five songs, along with Jerome Green and The Duchess: '**Bo Diddley**' (Ellas McDaniel), **Road Runner** (Ellas McDaniel), **Pretty Thing** (Willie Dixon) and **Hey! Bo Diddley** (Ellas McDaniel)

Saturday Club, Playhouse Theatre, Charing Cross, London, UK

Talkin' Bout You (Chuck Berry), **Money** (Berry Gordy Jr./Janie Bradford), **Come On** (Chuck Berry), **Memphis, Tennessee** (Chuck Berry) and **Roll Over Beethoven** (Chuck Berry)

17 NOVEMBER 1963
(aired 23 November)

Thank Your Lucky Stars, Alpha Studios, Aston, Birmingham, UK

I Wanna Be Your Man (John Lennon/Paul McCartney) – playback

22 NOVEMBER 1963

Ready, Steady, Go!, TV House, Kingsway, London, UK

I Wanna Be Your Man (John Lennon/Paul McCartney) – playback

19 DECEMBER 1963
(never aired)

Cops and Robbers, BBC TV pilot show, at St Michael's Hall, Sydenham Road, Sydenham, London, UK

Come On (Chuck Berry) – playback

27 DECEMBER 1963

Ready, Steady, Go!, TV House, Kingsway, London, UK

I Wanna Be Your Man (John Lennon/Paul McCartney) – playback

1963 1964 1965 1966

1967 1968 1969

1964

Previous pages: Appearing on *Juke Box Jury*. The BBC had to build a special desk to accomodate the five Rolling Stones as normally the *Juke Box Jury* panel consisted of just four people.

What a difference a year makes, or does it? When 1964 dawned, the UK singles chart was not quite awash with 'beat groups' but was certainly heavily infiltrated by them. The Beatles held two of the top three spots, with the Dave Clark Five at No.2, and the Rolling Stones at No.14, a position, or thereabouts, that they'd occupied since early December with their cover of John and Paul's 'I Wanna Be Your Man'; in fact it didn't drop out of the Top 40 until March, thanks to frequent radio and TV appearances.

But it was still a chart dominated by the less than hip, none more so than the Singing Nun, whose single 'Dominique' was in the Top 10, as were songs by Gene Pitney, Dusty Springfield, Kathy Kirby, Cliff and the Shadows and Los Indios Tabajaras, a pair of brothers from Brazil who were firmly stuck in the middle of the road.

Across the Atlantic, the *Billboard* Top 40 was just as uninspiring. The Singing Nun had just finished a four-week run at No.1 with barely a group in sight in the rest of the chart. The Kingsmen's 'Louie Louie' offered some hope, as did a number of Motown artists, including Martha and the Vandellas, Marvin Gaye, and the Supremes. There were just two British artists on the US Hot 100: the Caravelles and Cliff Richard, who was struggling to get into the Top 50. There was no sign of the Beatles, but all that was about to change, thanks to television.

The Beatles set foot on American soil, at New York's John F. Kennedy International Airport, on Friday 7 February 1964. It was the beginning of what has come to be called 'the British Invasion'. On 9 February, they appeared on *The Ed Sullivan Show* performing live to 73 million viewers in one of the most watched broadcasts in TV history. The following week, their second appearance on the show, broadcast from the Deauville Hotel in Miami, was watched by 70 million. The power of TV had been harnessed by pop music like never before.

In the week that the Beatles dominated American TV, the Stones were on BBC radio's *Saturday Club* and on TV's *Ready Steady Go!* They were also on a package tour of the UK with singer John Leyton, having only just finished another with American girl group the Ronettes. It epitomizes what aspiring groups and singers had to do in the early 1960s.

Soon the Beatles were ruling the American charts, as they did the British best-seller lists, which meant that turning on a radio you were guaranteed to hear the Fab Four. So great was their dominance in the US that in April their records took the top five places on the Hot 100, a feat that has never been and never will be repeated. The Beatles had another seven singles on the Hot 100 that same week, and there were others from the Dave Clark Five, the Searchers and the Swinging Blue Jeans. The British Invasion was now in full swing.

The Stones were late to the party; it wasn't until the first week of May that 'Not Fade Away' made the Hot 100 at a lowly No.98, although it eventually climbed to No.78 on 13 June, climbing a little higher each week until it reached No.48 in mid-July, by which time a second single, 'Tell Me', significantly a song written by Mick and Keith, was also on the charts. It had all happened after the Stones arrived in New York at the start of June to begin a short US tour and to appear on some TV shows, although notably not on *The Ed Sullivan Show*.

Back at home, 'Not Fade Away' made No.3 on the charts, and their follow-up, 'It's All Over Now', made No.1 in mid-July thanks to a non-stop round of TV and radio appearances and, of course, non-stop touring. The Stones' final UK single of 1964 was their cover of Howlin' Wolf's blues classic, 'Little Red Rooster', which topped the charts for a week in December, and may well have done better had the band not become embroiled in a row with the BBC, which saw them banned from TV and live radio appearances.

The Stones returned to America in October for their second US tour and this time they did appear on *The Ed Sullivan Show*, performing 'Time Is On My Side', which had made the Hot 100 ten days before they appeared. A week after the *Sullivan Show* it jumped twenty places to No.46 on the charts, and then climbed in a few short weeks to No.6.

It could not quite be said that the Stones had conquered America but they were, thanks to television, established as a British band like no other. Unconventional in dress, personality and presentation, this was not something American teens could garner from just listening to the band on the radio. This was a band that inspired so many American pop-wannabes in their dress and their hairstyles, playing music inspired by black American artists.

IT'S TOP OF THE POPS!

A new year and a new television show was how 1964 began for the Stones. 'I Wanna Be Your Man' had been on the charts since mid-November and, in the first few days of January, it was sitting at No.15 on the UK singles chart, having dropped one place since Christmas. It was the band's appearances on both *Thank Your Lucky Stars* and *Ready Steady Go!* that helped the song get into the Top 20 and kept it there throughout December.

In those somewhat more genteel times, the Stones, like many self-respecting and aspiring groups, were anxious to play as often as possible, wherever they could find an audience, and New Year's Eve 1963 was no exception. Having played a Monday-night gig at Studio 51 in Soho on 30 December, the following day they set off from London around lunchtime to drive the 160 miles north, to Lincoln, to play a New Year's Eve Dance at the Drill Hall in the centre of the city.

After the gig, they went to the fourteenth-century White Hart Hotel where they were to stay the night. Bill had retired to bed before the others and so the rest of the Stones decided to dress Brian up as a ghost and sent him off to knock on Bill's bedroom door in the early hours. A sleepy Bill opened the door and immediately said, 'Go to bed, Brian, and stop messing about!'

'You bastard!' said Brian. 'It's taken us an hour to get this together.'

The following day, after lunch at their hotel, Stu drove the Stones the 100 or so miles across country to the BBC's studios in Manchester to appear on the first ever edition of *Top of the Pops*.

The show was the broadcaster's response to the independent TV network's dominance of pop programmes. As the New Year's Day issue of the *Daily Mirror* announced: 'Teenagers get a new pop music show tonight – the BBC's *Top of the Pops* (6.35 p.m.). It is the Corporation's answer to ITV's *Ready Steady Go!* screened on Friday evenings.' It was televised immediately after the main 6 p.m. news and local news programme and before the 7 p.m. nightly magazine show, *Tonight*.

Opposite and below: The Stones backstage and on the set of *Top of the Pops* on 29 January

Right: The *Daily Mirror* previewing the BBC's new pop show on New Year's Day

PAGE 12 DAILY MIRROR, *Wednesday, January 1, 1964*

Hits on parade . .

TONIGHT'S VIEW

BY CLIFFORD DAVIS

TEENAGERS got a new pop music show tonight — the B B C's "Top of the Pops" (6.35).

It is the Corporation's answer to ITV's "Ready, Steady, Go!" screened on Friday evenings.

MIME

The B B C series will come from the Manchester studios, and a team of four disc jockeys have been booked as weekly hosts.

First to face the camera will be Jimmy Savile, followed by Alan Freeman, David Jacobs and Peter Murray.

For the first time the B B C are letting the performers mime their recordings—as they have done on I T V.

"We want viewers to hear the original discs," explains producer Johnnie Stewart.

"All the discs will be from the current hit parade and our audience will hear the exact sound that won the disc its popularity.

"Some of the artists will be booked at the very last moment, for our aim is to be as topical as the 'Top Twenty' itself."

For tonight's show, four acts are already taped on film. These include The Beatles.

ACTS

And standing by in the studios are half a dozen acts, including the **Dave Clark Five** (current big record: "Glad All Over"), **The Rolling Stones** ("I Wanna Be Your Man"), and **Dusty Springfield** ("I Only Want To Be With You").

"But we will not know the full line-up until a few hours before the show goes on the air," says Johnnie.

☆ **Ski-jumping comes to B B C viewers this afternoon (1.45) from Garmisch Partenkirchen, the German winter-sports centre in the Bavarian Alps, 40 miles from Innsbruck.**

★ The B B C launch a new "Animal Magic" series at 5.35 p.m. with Johnny Morris escorting a zebra called Alice from Bristol Zoo to Copenhagen.

☆ **Dr. Casey (Vincent Edwards) struggles to save the young and ambitious David Duncan (Robert Walker Jnr.) whose life is threatened by cancer of the brain in tonight's "Ben Casey" episode (London I T V, 8.0).**

★ In "Z Cars" (B B C, 8.0 p.m.), Sergeant Blackitt goes out of Newtown Police station on a

Top of the Pops was created by Johnnie Stewart, an in-house producer in his mid-forties who had been inspired by Radio Luxembourg's *Teen and Twenty Disc Club* in coming up with the idea for the TV show. *TOTP*'s format was simplicity itself, with artists miming to tracks from the week's Top 20 charts. At its climax, the presenter would use the now-immortal words – that never changed throughout five decades of the show being broadcast – 'It's No.1 ... It's Top of the Pops!' followed by the playing of the week's best-selling record.

The show changed in very few ways throughout its long-running existence. It grew slightly longer following its debut: it originally ran for twenty-five minutes, then it went up to thirty minutes in the following year, before being extended to forty-five minutes in the 1970s; it also extended its coverage up to the Top 40 singles. But in style and substance it barely altered. The set was quite basic, with several raised stages allowing a quick switch from one artist to another, and the space in between occupied by a studio audience who were encouraged to dance, clap and even swoon if the performer was right.

Johnnie Stewart, in coming up with the idea, devised a set of rules by which the show was effectively governed. Only an artist occupying the top spot was allowed to appear on consecutive weeks. Each edition included the week's highest new entry on the chart and, if it had not featured in the previous week's show, the week's highest climber. The one exception to the 'no repeat' formula was if a track had been used over the chart countdown or the closing credits. In that case, the artist would be allowed to appear in the following week's programme ... but only if they were in the studio. These rules stayed in place until the late 1990s when the changing nature of the Top 50 itself meant that the show was in flux.

Top of the Pops was originally only intended to run for a limited season but its success kept it going, and going, and going. By late 1964, it had moved from a Wednesday to a Thursday evening, where it stayed for most of its forty-two years on air. Four years before it ceased to be a weekly show in 2006, *Top of the Pops* reached its 2,000th performance, which means that there are few people alive in Britain today who have not seen it at least once.

The very first *Top of the Pops* was broadcast from Studio A on Dickenson Road in Rusholme, Manchester. This was the BBC's first television studio outside of London, and was situated in a converted church that the Corporation had acquired in 1954.

According to the *Daily Mirror*: 'The BBC series comes from the Manchester studios, and a team of four disc jockeys have been booked as weekly hosts. First to face the camera will be Jimmy Savile, followed by Alan Freeman, David Jacobs and Peter Murray.' Most significantly, perhaps, the BBC allowed artists to mime on the show, like they did on *Ready Steady Go!* and *Thank Your Lucky Stars*; on other variety programmes that featured pop music, the Corporation insisted on a live performance. According to Johnnie Stewart: 'We want viewers to hear the original discs. All the discs will be from the current hit parade and our audience will hear the exact sound that won the disc its popularity.'

Stewart went on to stress that acts would be booked at the very last minute to ensure the show be 'as topical as the Top 20'. It was a formula from which *TOTP* did not deviate and, given the huge audiences that it soon attracted, artists rarely refused to appear, as an appearance almost guaranteed a record climbed further up the charts. The Stones were no exception. Having dropped one place between Christmas and New Year, from 14 to 15, they climbed three places to

No.12 on the chart following their *TOTP* appearance. But it was a brief respite: the following week, their single was back down to No.14 again, as it began its slow descent, finally exiting the UK Top 40 on the first chart in March.

The Stones have the honour of being the first artist ever to appear on *Top of the Pops*. They were joined in the studio by Dusty Springfield singing, 'I Only Want To Be With You'. This was Dusty's first solo record since leaving the Springfields and it had dropped one place from No.5 to No.6 the week before her appearance. A week later, with the *TOTP* effect, it had climbed to No.4, where it stayed for the next three weeks.

In fact, *TOTP* had a remarkable effect on all the artists who appeared on this first show. The Dave Clark Five were at No.2 on the charts, with their second single, 'Glad All Over'; two weeks after *TOTP* they made it to No.1. Prior to appearing on the first *TOTP*, the Hollies' third single, 'Stay', had stalled at No.17 on the UK chart, but over the next few weeks it would climb to No.8. The highest new entry of the week was a Liverpool band, the Swinging Blue Jeans, whose version of 'Hippy Hippy Shake' had come in at No.13. It went on to make No.2 on the charts, kept from the top spot by the Dave Clark Five. Interestingly, 'Hippy Hippy Shake', a song written by Australian Chan Romero in 1959, had been performed live on BBC radio in the summer of 1963 by the Beatles.

Freddie and the Dreamers' 'You Were Made For Me' was used over the chart rundown, before the show climaxed with the week's No.1 record, which almost inevitably was by the Beatles; their fifth UK single, 'I Want To Hold Your Hand' was spending the fourth of five weeks on top.

'The songs were the best in the current hit parade, mimed from records to a bunch of serious-looking youngsters. I agree with the BBC's policy that the record itself should be heard, and not an on-the-spot "live" version. All artistes can't appear in the studio at the drop of a Beatle wig, but those who can't are going to suffer.'

Daily Mirror
2 January 1964

Opposite: The Dave Clark Five on *Top of the Pops* in 1964
Above: Johnnie Stewart
Following pages: A *Top of The Pops* appearance in 1964

PAGE 6   DAILY MIRROR, Thursday, January 2, 1964

After the Beatles, the Mersey beat and the Shake, PATRICK DONCASTER tunes in to the New Year

THE SOUND OF '64

The Rolling Stones—a young group who are catching on fast.

IT was a bumper year in Discland. As 1963 spun itself out, British record fans had hit a new all-time high note by spending around £25,000,000 during the twelve months.

This is some three millions more than in 1962. And most of it came in the second half of the year. And you know why

The Big, Big Beat—plus four lads from Liverpool with fringes.

But for at least two disc bosses it was a sad, sad year. They had both turned down the Beatles when they were offered them.

Complex

"Who can tell what is going to happen next in the complex field of pop music?" said one of the recording chiefs who has been kicking himself the year round.

"If any one person could tell, he'd be a millionaire in quick time."

Thus Discland goes into 1964 with the big question mark dangling over its head.

What comes next?

THAT'S the question I have been asking the shrewd and the successful, the music makers, the back room boys

They don't all agree, but through the cloud of uncertainty, there emerged this summing up: **It's going to be a Big Beat of a year again—with variations.**

First, over to the man who did say "yes" to the Beatles . . Parlophone boss George Martin, who produces all their hits

"I don't think there will be much of a change," he said. "The Beat mood will continue and will spread more widely to take in what we call the legitimate artists, people like Matt Monro.

"The trend towards Beat will make itself felt in other directions and become more part and parcel of the music scene. At the same time, there will still be the good ballads.

Good

"There will be more groups too—but only the good ones will break through."

LET'S move across to top guitarist Bert Weedon, 42, who has been one of the men responsible for the twang boom in Britain

The Shadows learned guitar via Bert's tutor that sells around the world. They also wrote a song for him called "Mr. Guitar."

"The Beatles told me they used my book, too," said Bert. "And they also wrote something for me but it got lost en route.

"Of course, the guitar boom is going to go on. Hundreds of thousands of kids have bought them and they are not going to put them aside.

"But I think a change in the mood is near. The rhythm will stay, but we will get sweeter — not syrupy—tunes.

The Dave Clark Five . . . brass with the twang.

Tremendous

"The public are ready to appreciate the tremendous repertoire of music and sounds one can get from the guitar."

Hence the lovely "Maria Elena" which twanged effortlessly and melodiously into the charts here and in America in the past few months

Hence Mr Weedon's first disc of 1964, out this week —a revival of the melodious oldie "It Happened in Monterey."

"I wanted to record this six months ago, because I felt the time was right then," he said. "Perhaps I was just too far ahead."

● **FACT:** One London instruments store alone is selling 6,000 guitars a month

PUBLICIST Les Perrin, who is Press Officer for Cliff Richard The Shadows, Frank Ifield the break-through Dave Clark Five and a score of other stars, thinks that the "powerhouse" group is going to score

Twang

Dave Clark is an illustration. In today's chart he is at number two with "Glad All Over," and second only to those Beatles. Dave uses brass with his twang. He has sold 750,000 records in the past few weeks.

"I think there will be a shift back to 'powerhouse,'" said Les Perrin. "The sax and other brass will return. After all, power is exciting, as Bill Haley proved years ago."

Agent and pianist Tommy Sanderson, who looks after the hit-parading Hollies group, doesn't think there will be much of a change either.

Comedy

"But I think comedy is about to get a better show," he said. "And a group that can combine comedy stands a chance of getting away."

Nearly all the groups that made headway in 1963 based their sounds on the Negro rhythm and blues —which has been around about as long as jazz itself.

Practically every group, from the Beatles on, have been inspired by America's R. and B. specialists, Chuck Berry and Bo Diddley

JACK HUTTON, editor of Britain's pop and jazz weekly "Melody Maker," had these thoughts about the 1964 sound.

"There will be more emphasis on rhythm and blues the American kind, a la Berry and Diddley—the stuff that is currently ousting Trad Jazz from Britain's clubs.

Relief

"There will be more and more groups," he said. "But as a relief a strong solo star is almost certain to emerge."

● **FACT:** R and B took its toll of one trad band this week. The Clyde Valley Stompers, founded eleven years ago, folded yesterday — ironically just as their new Ember L.P. "Stompin' at the Seaside," with Ian Menzies, goes into the shops.

Orchestra leader and ace arranger Harry Robinson—he used to be Lord Rockingham on discs — had rhythm and blues in mind too for 1964.

MS? I have to make the Big Beat hot favourite for another six months at least . . . with the accent on more melody.

The Beatles, at a fantastic peak, must continue to be big—but I see them settling down to a more leisurely pace before the year is out.

We will continue to get good ballads sprinkling the charts with or without a beat.

For bigger fame, I tip the Dave Clark Five and the shaggy-looking Rolling Stones group.

They are both catching on fast .

and here is the year's first

Pop 30

Britain's best-selling records—last week's figures in brackets.

1	(1)	I WANT TO HOLD YOUR HAND—Beatles
2	(3)	GLAD ALL OVER—Dave Clark Five
3	(2)	SHE LOVES YOU—Beatles
4	(6)	DOMINIQUE — Singing Nun
5	(4)	YOU WERE MADE FOR ME — Freddie and the Dreamers.
6	(19)	TWENTY - FOUR HOURS FROM TULSA—Gene Pitney
7	(7)	I ONLY WANT TO BE WITH YOU — Dusty Springfield
8	(8)	SECRET LOVE—Kathy Kirby
9	(18)	SWINGING ON A STAR—Big Dee Irwin
10	(15)	I WANNA BE YOUR MAN—Rolling Stones
11	(9)	MARIA ELENA — Los Indios Tabajaras
12	(25)	THE HIPPY HIPPY SHAKE — Swinging Blue Jeans
13	(12)	GERONIMO —Shadows
14	(5)	DON'T TALK TO HIM —Cliff Richard and the Shadows
15	(11)	YOU'LL NEVER WALK ALONE—Gerry and the Pacemakers
16	(13)	TWIST AND SHOUT (EP)—Beatles
17	(16)	MONEY—Bern Elliott
18	(22)	NOT TOO LITTLE, NOT TOO MUCH—Chris Sandford
19	(—)	KISS ME QUICK—Elvis Presley
20	(14)	I'LL KEEP YOU SATISFIED — Billy J. Kramer with the Dakotas
21	(21)	STAY—Hollies
22	(—)	WE ARE IN LOVE—Adam Faith
23	(20)	ALL I WANT FOR CHRISTMAS IS A BEATLE — Dora Bryan
24	(17)	THE BEATLES' HITS (EP)—Beatles
25	(26)	IT'S ALMOST TOMORROW — Mark Wynter
26	(27)	IF I RULED THE WORLD — Harry Secombe
27	(—)	WHAT TO DO—Buddy Holly
28	(23)	I (WHO HAVE NOTHING) — Shirley Bassey
29	(—)	DO YOU REALLY LOVE ME TOO?—Billy Fury
30	(24)	HUNGRY FOR LOVE—Johnny Kidd and the Pirates

Supplied by Melody Maker

Viewpoint

YOUR ANGLE ON EVENTS

● Many elderly, lonely people whose stories were told in the Mirror during Old Folks' Week last October, have found friends and happiness.

Johnny Gallagher, 87, of Liverpool, is one such person. He writes . . .

I WISH a very Happy New Year to all those kind people who made Christmas a very *happy time for me.* I had lots of cards sent from all over the country.

A kind friend gave me a transistor set, five little girls sent me a present and two ladies sent me some tobacco.

With a big fire, my pipe and my radio, I feel on top of the world.

God Bless everyone.

Resolutions

I WOULD like to see these resolutions kept in the New Year.

The end of blood sports.

The end of racial discrimination. —**V. Oakley, London, S.W.11.**

Childish?

I SEE that fifteen Europeans who attended a party to celebrate "the end of the white man's burden" are to be deported by the Uganda Government (Mirror, Saturday).

What a childish action for a Government to take. It makes you wonder if they are really ready for independence.—**Civil Servant, Portsmouth, Hants.**

Babies

SURELY too many willing adopters chasing too few babies is a happier state of affairs than too many unwanted babies chasing too few willing adopters. (Viewpoint, Tuesday.)

Most of the children in homes are not available for adoption. Their circumstances may be sad, but somebody is waiting for them when the situation improves. — **Philip Wright, Daily Mirror Readers' Service, London, E.C.1.**

Elsewhere in the same edition of the *Daily Mirror*, Patrick Doncaster, who six months earlier was the first national newspaperman to mention the Stones, described them as 'a young group who are catching on fast' in a feature headlined 'The Sound of '64'.

The day after appearing on *Top of the Pops*, the Stones were at Regent Sound Studios in Denmark Street, at the heart of London's Tin Pan Alley. The studio was established in the 1950s and in 1961 was sold to 22-year-old James Baring (of the Barings Bank family); he later became the 6th Baron Revelstoke, but in the Sixties his passion was music. From Andrew Loog Oldham's perspective, the studio had one overriding quality – it was cheap.

The Stones were at the studio to back a young singer by the name of Cleo Sylvester, Loog Oldham's newest protégée, as well as recording a song written by Oldham and Mike Leander entitled 'There Are But Five Rolling Stones', which was destined for the B-side of Sylvester's single and credited to the Andrew Oldham Orchestra. Ironically, given what had happened to Ian Stewart, the Orchestra consisted of the five Stones and Stu on piano. Over the next two days, the Stones recorded tracks for what would be their debut album. On 10 January, they worked on two more songs for the album and an early version of what would become their third single.

In the last few days of January, they recorded the final version of their next single, 'Not Fade Away'. Like everything else they had so far recorded for release, it was a cover, but it wasn't a straightforward blues or R&B tune. Buddy Holly, along with the Crickets, originally recorded it in 1957 in Clovis, New Mexico. What made the song both acceptable and appealing to the Stones was its rhythmical pattern, which is based on Bo Diddley's trademark beat.

Before January was over, the band were back in Manchester to record an appearance on the fifth edition of *TOTP*. It was not to promote a single but the Stones' first EP, which had been released on 10 January. Rather than asking them to drive the 200 or so miles north from London, the BBC splashed out £9 and 4 shillings for each of the five Stones to fly from Heathrow to Manchester on British European Airways. On top of this, they were paid 70 guineas (£73 10 shillings) to mime to their cover of Arthur Alexander's 'You Better Move On', one of the four tracks on the EP.

'We've been using "You Better Move On" in our act for ages and it has always gone down well; that's why we decided to record it'

Mick Jagger

Opposite: The Stones are the *Daily Mirror*'s tip for stardom in 1964
Left: The band's first UK EP and their first No.1

As writer Roy Carr said in the 1970s,'Without doubt it was"You Better Move On" alone that was responsible for catapulting this EP into the best-selling singles chart.' A week or so after the Stones appeared on *TOTP*, their EP went to No.1 on the UK EP charts, replacing the Beatles' second EP at the top. The Stones stayed there for a total of fourteen weeks. It was the extensive exposure that the Arthur Alexander cover received from TV and radio that helped the EP do so well.

On Friday 21 February, Decca released 'Not Fade Away' as the band's third UK single; during the one minute and forty-two seconds of this classic pop-rock record, Mick really sounds like Mick for the first time. Two weeks later, London Records released it, along with 'I Wanna Be Your Man' on the B-side, as the Stones' first US single.

The BBC was confident that this was going to be a hit and so the day after the single's release they arranged for the Stones to be filmed on the beach in Weymouth, Dorset, on England's south coast. Wearing big coats and scarves in the freezing cold, the Stones mimed to the song while the BBC crew filmed stones rolling down the cliffs.

This classic piece of pop video – 1964-style – did not air on the *TOTP* of 26 February, as some have said is the case, because Freddie and the Dreamers' 'Over You' was the week's highest new entry and the Stones entered the chart at No.29 – therefore failing to qualify under Johnnie Stewart's 'rules' for the programme.

The following week, though, 'Not Fade Away' jumped sixteen places to No.11 and on the show that aired on 4 March the band were featured live in the Manchester studio. By the end of the month, the single had climbed to No.3 on the UK chart, thanks in no small part to *TOTP*. The piece filmed on the beach at Weymouth did not go to waste, as it was used as the play-out number on the show on 11 March.

On 17 April, Decca released the Stones' first long-playing record in the UK. Like everything else they had so far recorded, this self-titled debut included cover versions – nine of them – along with one Mick and Keith original, as well as a group composition; what may seem odd nowadays is the fact that it included not one of their UK hit singles. It largely consisted of songs that the Stones performed on stage and it was steeped in the sound of blues and R&B.

By the end of the month, their album was No.1, which is why *TOTP* featured the Stones on 29 April, playing their version of 'I Just Want To Make Love To You', a Willie Dixon/Chess Records classic, originally made famous by Muddy Waters in 1954 as 'Just Make Love To Me'.

Above: The Stones' first UK album, released on 16 April 1964 on Decca Records, had neither the band's name nor the album's title on the cover
Opposite: The Stones make the front page of *Melody Maker*

'They're my boys. I like their version of "I Just Want To Make Love To You". They fade it out just like we did. One more trip and they'll have it. Believe me.'

Muddy Waters
Melody Maker
23 May 1964

Melody Maker

May 2, 1964 9d. weekly

PAGE ONE TOP TEN

1	DON'T THROW YOUR LOVE AWAY	Searchers
2	WORLD WITHOUT LOVE	Peter and Gordon
3	I BELIEVE	Bachelors
4	MY BOY LOLLIPOP	Millie
5	CAN'T BUY ME LOVE	Beatles
6	I LOVE YOU BECAUSE	Jim Reeves
7	EVERYTHING'S AL'RIGHT	Mojos
8	DON'T LET THE SUN CATCH YOU CRYING	Gerry and the Pacemakers
9	MOVE OVER DARLING	Doris Day
10	JULIET	Four Pennies

FULL POP 50 ON PAGE 2

Gerry — at 8

IT'S ROLLING IN FOR THE STONES!

THE Rolling Stones continued their march to popularity this week, as sales of their first LP soared past the 170,000 mark, and topped the album division of the hit parade.

Tomorrow (Thursday) and on Friday, the group visits the recording studios to plan material for its new single, an EP, and a future LP.

Their single, as a follow-up to "Not fade away" will probably be an original.

In July, the Stones make their film debut, and this autumn tour the country for six weeks as billtoppers.

Frank — after Continent

SINATRA SWINGS IN FOR SEPTEMBER TOUR

FRANK SINATRA is in line for a British tour.

He is expected to arrive here in September for concerts.

As well as London shows, Sinatra may do provincial dates.

Impresario Harold Davison told MM this week: "Frank would come in after Continental dates. Negotiations for the trip are well advanced."

He said Frank would be here for "a few days."

Sinatra was in London in June, 1962, for concerts during his world charity tour. The ticket stampede reached black-market scale.

Frank was so impressed by the organisation of his last British tour that he said he would return this year.

"It is not definitely fixed," added Davison, "but I am confident it will come off."

Cannonball coming PAGE 5

Blues Caravan in PAGE 6

Jeans Blind Date PAGE 11

* a bee in his bonnet – because the BBC don't use any of his artists. [initials]

Distribution:

1) Miss Myra Fleming, Ken. House. (for information)

2) Mr. Johnnie Stewart, 7007 T.C. [initials]

When I first booked this group they received 100 gns for a proper spot and I considered 70 gns very fair for T.O.P.s. There was no battle about the £12. What the agent in fact wanted was

AS/20/P

Nothing to be written or typed in t[he]

fares but as the group in any case had to go to Birkenhead for the following evening I did not consider it right that the Corporation should pay their transport – I did however give them a subsistence for the night they had to spend up there for us. The Agent really has *

Nothing to be written or typed

Licensed Annually by the L.C.C.

Phone Regent 5688-9

EE LIMITED

ERIC EASTON LIMITED

DIRECTORS: E. EASTON M. EASTON

Radnor House, 93-97 Regent Street, London, W.1.

IN ASSOCIATION WITH
ERIC EASTON (NORTHERN) LTD.
(MANAGING DIRECTOR: JOHN DELL)
11, FISHERGATE,
PRESTON, LANCS.
PHONE: PRESTON 3226

EE/jml

6th May, 1964.

Johnnie Stewart, Esq.,
B. B. C.,
Television Centre,
Wood Lane,
London, W. 12.

STONES The

Dear Johnnie,

Thank you for your letter and I am sorry The Stones arrived late for the rehearsal. I have had a chat with them and I hope that a similar situation will be avoided in the future.

I should mention that I am not getting along too well with your booking dept. at present. They are so mean about the money and, while I always bend over backwards to co-operate with B.B.C producers, the money they are prepared to pay the second-hottest group in the country is somewhat insulting.

For your show, the boys received £73. 10. 0d. and I had quite a battle to get about £12 expenses. I think this sort of offer is too bad and I have told booking department that I shall have to decline any other offers if the money cannot be a little more reasonable.

Such is life Johnnie - hope to see you soon.

All the best,

Sincerely,

Eric Easton.

ANY OFFER CONTAINED IN THIS LETTER DOES NOT CONSTITUTE A CONTRACT

Copies to:- Tel. Accounts (SU)
Tel. Accounts (PU)
Producer
Miss Brough
Index
~~Registry~~
File

ROLLING STONES

Ref: 35/MF

4th May, 1964.

Dear Eric Easton,

"TOP OF THE POPS" 12/1/4/0064
29th April, 1964.

Confirming our telephone conversation I am asking our Accounts Department to send you a cheque for £12. 10s. 0d. (twelve pounds, ten shillings) to cover one subsistence allowance for the 5 Rolling Stones.

Yours sincerely,

(Myra Fleming)
Artists' Bookings Department, Television.

Eric Easton Esq.,
93/97 Regent Street,
London, W.1.

RECEIVED
29 APR 1965
TELEVISION
ACCOUNTS

In May 1964 a lack of harmony between the BBC and the band was beginning to show. The BBC were unaccustomed to a band that had opinions and attitude.

Top ten LPs

1	(—)	**THE ROLLING STONES**	The Rolling Stones, Decca
2	(1)	**WITH THE BEATLES**	Beatles, Parlophone
3	(3)	**WEST SIDE STORY**	Soundtrack, CBS
4	(2)	**PLEASE PLEASE ME**	Beatles, Parlophone
5	(—)	**SESSION WITH THE DAVE CLARK FIVE**	Dave Clark Five, Columbia
6	(8)	**BLUE GENE**	Gene Pitney, United Artists
7	(4)	**STAY WITH THE HOLLIES**	Hollies, Parlophone
8	(5)	**MEET THE SEARCHERS**	Searchers, Pye
9	(—)	**A GIRL CALLED DUSTY**	Dusty Springfield, Philips
10	(7)	**IN DREAMS**	Roy Orbison, London

Left: The UK album chart for 2 May 1964

Once again, the Stones received the standard BBC appearance fee of 70 guineas but correspondence in the BBC archive reveals that they also received a further £12 10 shillings by way of 'subsistence'.

Having played Wallington Public Hall in south London the previous evening, the Stones had been driven to Manchester by Stu in their van, but for some reason the journey was slow, or they were delayed leaving London. In any event, they arrived late for rehearsals, which, as the BBC archives reveal, angered producer Johnnie Stewart, who wrote to Eric Easton to complain. Stewart's letter is no longer in existence but Easton's reply, dated 6 May, begins: 'Thank you for your letter and I am sorry the Stones arrived late for rehearsal, I have had a chat with them and I hope that a similar situation will be avoided in the future.' In the same letter Easton said he had 'quite a battle to get about £12 expenses'. It was the opening salvo in what was to become a fractious relationship between the band and BBC.

When the Stones arrived in America at the start of June 1964 to begin their first tour of the US, their first radio appearance was on *Murray the K's Swingin' Soiree* on WINS, the AM station located at 114 East 58th Street, New York. Murray Kaufman interviewed the Stones live and after they went off-air he played them a single by the Valentinos, Bobby Womack's group. Murray the K thought it would make a good song for the Stones to cover. As a result of this conversation, they recorded 'It's All Over Now' at Chess Studios in Chicago on 10 June.

Four days after the Stones returned from America on 22 June, 'It's All Over Now' was rush-released by Decca in the UK. On the following day, the Stones were recorded miming to the song: as the highest new entry of the week at No.25, it was featured on *TOTP* on 1 July. The following week they again appeared on the show, having jumped twenty-three places to No.2 on the charts – and by 16 July they were 'Top of the Pops'!

The song's success can be put down to several reasons. It was recorded in America and sounds so much more exciting than anything they had recorded in England. It sounds like a 'big' record, with an intro that makes it perfect for the radio; it grabs hold of the listener from the opening bars and never lets go.

'Having a No.1 hit's a good feeling, but we're not all mad about it. I like the sound on this new one more than I did on anything before. I'd hate everybody to think that just because we've made the top spot this time, we'll have to do it every time we have a single out.'

Keith Richards
Melody Maker
July 1964

On the same day that the Stones taped their appearance on *TOTP* (27 June), they had earlier recorded an appearance on another iconic BBC television programme, the long-running *Juke Box Jury*. First broadcast in June 1959, the show was hosted by David Jacobs and normally broadcast on a Saturday evening at around 5.30 p.m., in direct competition with *Thank Your Lucky Stars*.

The Stones appeared on the edition of the show that was broadcast at 7.10 p.m. on Saturday 4 July and this particular week it had many more viewers than normal, and not just because the Stones were on the programme. ITV's 3,500 technicians had been on strike for several days, and would remain so for three more days; the strike was only resolved with the intervention of the Prime Minister. This meant that the only television available on the evening of 4 July was on the BBC.

The format of *Juke Box Jury* was simple. Following the opening theme song, 'Hit or Miss', performed by the John Barry Seven Plus Four, David Jacobs introduced the four celebrity guests – around the time of the Stones' appearance, guest included actress Dorothy Dandridge, actor Lionel Jeffries and comedian Stubby Kaye. The guests were played a minute or so of a new record, after which they would give their comments and vote it either a 'Hit' or a 'Miss'; David Jacobs rang a bell for the former and played a klaxon-like sound for the latter.

The Beatles had been on the show in December 1963, but the Stones' appearance was very much a break with tradition as it was the first and only time there were five panellists. Each of the Stones was paid 30 guineas, and a special set was built to accommodate them. There were also problems getting the band into the BBC's Shepherd's Bush studio for an 8.15 p.m. recording because the venue was besieged by fans, delaying their arrival by two hours. According to Barry Longford, the show's producer, 'When they eventually reached the set they had to go on "cold" without any warm-up.'

Keith had this to say in the *Melody Maker* a few weeks later: 'I think the whole programme's very limited for a start. We all sat consciously knowing there were five of us, and we had a few seconds each after each record. We weren't great and that's a fact. But the records they played us! They were NOTHING! Don't misunderstand – they weren't bad

records, but there didn't seem anything to say about them.' He went on to say: 'We were all lost except for Charlie and maybe Mick. I agree we didn't come over well, but it wouldn't be much different if we did it again, quite honestly. I'll say one thing for our appearance on *Juke Box Jury*, though. I'm sure that's what helped us reach No.1. If nothing else, it kept our image up. People thought the worst of us before they saw us. When they finally saw us, it was a confirmation that we were a bunch of idiots. We don't care that much what people think. But I can tell you this: it's difficult to say anything sensible in a few seconds, especially with unspectacular records. But I could tell things were not going well on the show.'

According to the producer: 'I feel that more than a little of the criticism which has been levelled against the Rolling Stones' *Juke Box Jury* appearance is unjust. It has been suggested that they slated everything, but before they went on I gave them instructions to be completely honest and frank. They said, for instance, that they acknowledged Elvis as the greatest ever – but that they didn't like his present choice of material. Valid comment, surely. And it's significant that all their votes, hits and misses, have subsequently been proved right.'

The Elvis Presley song was 'There's Gold In The Mountains', and it failed to chart; the two numbers the Stones voted a hit were the Nashville Teens' 'Tobacco Road' and Dusty Springfield's 'I Just Don't Know What To Do With Myself'– both made the Top 10.

As one viewer wrote in a letter to the *NME*, 'The Rolling Stones on *Juke Box Jury?* To misquote Sir Winston Churchill – never in the course of human history has so much drivel been spouted by so few in front of so many!' However, despite the criticism, the fact that there were so many viewers that night undoubtedly did the band no harm at all. It all helped to grow their image as an alternative to the ever-popular Beatles.

By 1966, *Juke Box Jury* was beginning to feel like an outmoded format, but the BBC stuck with it, even introducing an all-DJ panel for a while. Come 1967 and the arrival of the BBC's Radio 1, the programme really had run its course and it was dropped, but not before a move to Wednesday evenings. There was a short revival of the programme in 1979 and again in 1989, but neither time did it remain on air for long. *Juke Box Jury* was of its time … a little like the jukebox itself.

For the Stones there were no more new *Top of the Pops* appearances until September 1964, and shortly after that the band had a row with the BBC … but more of that later.

Below: Fans in the *Juke Box Jury* audience

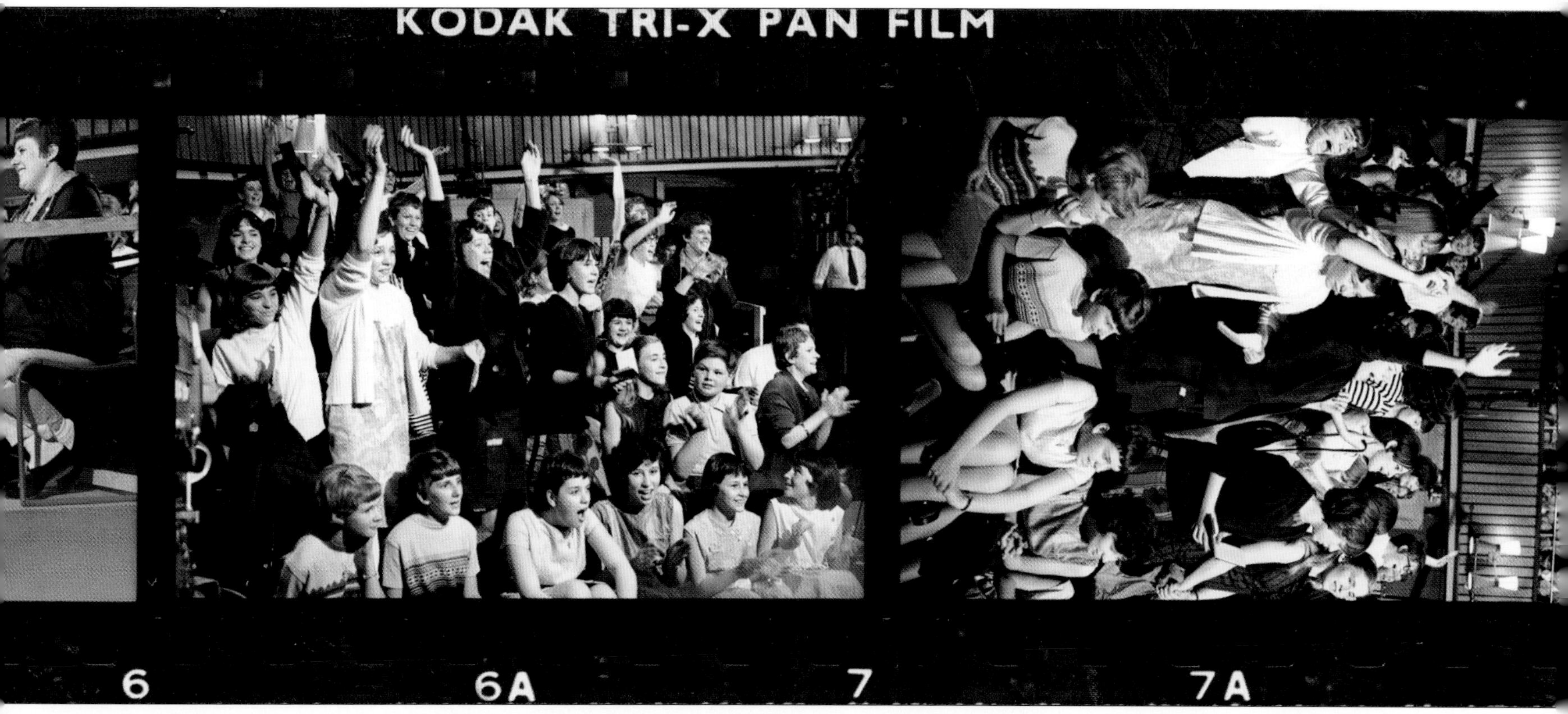

SNAP! CRACKLE! AND TOURING POP!

Below: An advert for the Stones' second UK package tour, which visited fourteen venues in twenty-two days, with two shows each night

Opposite: The Stones' third UK package tour: twenty-nine venues in twenty-nine days and two shows a night

The Stones really had got 1964 underway with a bang with their *Top of the Pops* appearance. Their second single was climbing to just outside the UK Top 10, which meant things were looking brighter than ever for the band.

'They may be the shape of things to come. Who would have thought that half of Britain's teenagers would end the year with heads like hairy pudding-basins? Millions of teenagers in 1964 may end up looking like them,' was the prediction of the *Daily Sketch*.

Following their recording sessions at the start of the year, the Stones were at the Granada Cinema in Harrow-on-the-Hill, north London, to begin another package tour. Dubbed 'The Group Scene 1964', it started on Monday 6 January and, by way of indication of the Stones' burgeoning reputation, they were the headliner with American girl group, the Ronettes, closing the first half of the show.

After Harrow-on-the-Hill's Granada, the tour visited thirteen other places in twenty-two days, not that the days in between were 'days off' for the band. The Stones also played other, mostly ballroom, gigs, including their second visit to Glasgow, where they played the infamous Barrowlands Ballroom. For their two shows each night on the tour, the Stones were paid £125.

The Ronettes had recently had a big hit in the UK with 'Be My Baby' and as the tour opened they charted another Phil Spector production, entitled 'Baby I Love You'. In her autobiography, Ronnie Bennett, who married Spector in 1968, remembers the tour:

'We couldn't get these guys to talk to us. I asked Andrew Oldham why the boys were ignoring us. "Darling, we'd all love to talk to you, but we got a telegram that forbids us to talk to you."

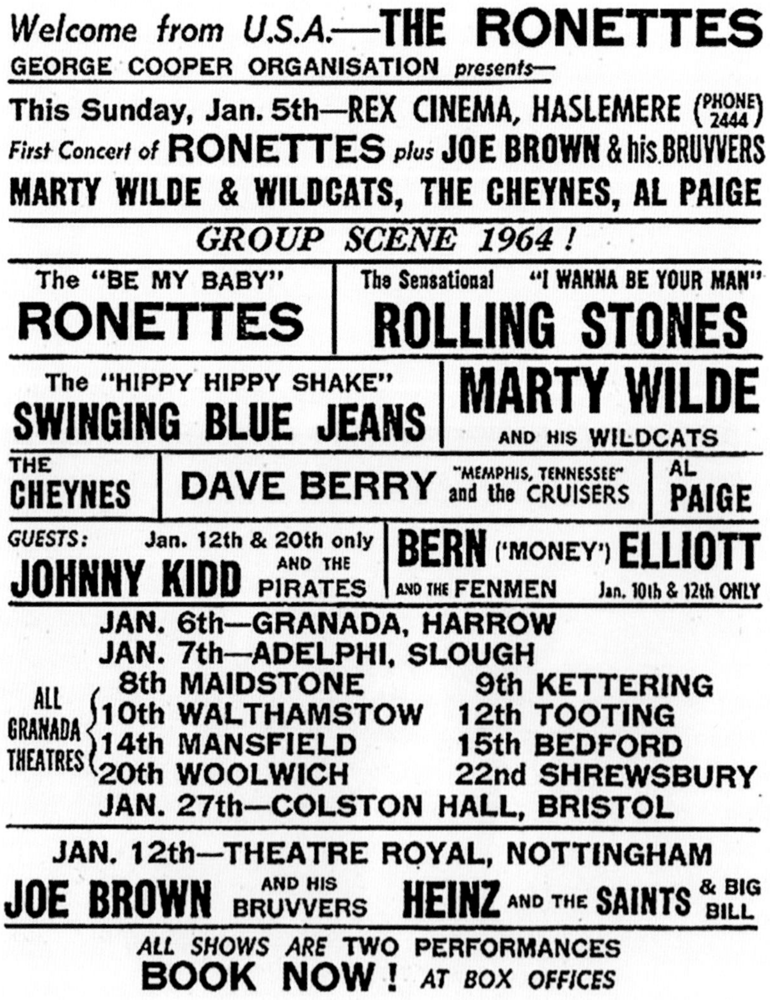
Welcome from U.S.A.—THE RONETTES
GEORGE COOPER ORGANISATION presents—
This Sunday, Jan. 5th—REX CINEMA, HASLEMERE (PHONE 2444)
First Concert of RONETTES plus JOE BROWN & his BRUVVERS
MARTY WILDE & WILDCATS, THE CHEYNES, AL PAIGE
GROUP SCENE 1964!
The "BE MY BABY" RONETTES
The Sensational "I WANNA BE YOUR MAN" ROLLING STONES
The "HIPPY HIPPY SHAKE" SWINGING BLUE JEANS
MARTY WILDE AND HIS WILDCATS
THE CHEYNES
DAVE BERRY "MEMPHIS, TENNESSEE" and the CRUISERS
AL PAIGE
GUESTS: Jan. 12th & 20th only JOHNNY KIDD AND THE PIRATES
BERN ('MONEY') ELLIOTT AND THE FENMEN Jan. 10th & 12th ONLY
JAN. 6th—GRANADA, HARROW
JAN. 7th—ADELPHI, SLOUGH
ALL GRANADA THEATRES
8th MAIDSTONE 9th KETTERING
10th WALTHAMSTOW 12th TOOTING
14th MANSFIELD 15th BEDFORD
20th WOOLWICH 22nd SHREWSBURY
JAN. 27th—COLSTON HALL, BRISTOL
JAN. 12th—THEATRE ROYAL, NOTTINGHAM
JOE BROWN AND HIS BRUVVERS HEINZ AND THE SAINTS & BIG BILL
ALL SHOWS ARE TWO PERFORMANCES
BOOK NOW! AT BOX OFFICES

'"Who from?" I asked.

'"From Phil, darling," he replied. "He said there would be dire consequences if we did."

'"That may be the way Phil feels but Phil's not here. You tell the Rolling Stones that if they don't start talking to us there'll be dire consequences from us."'

Other bands on the tour included the Cheynes (Mick Fleetwood's first group), Dave Berry and the Cruisers, and the Swinging Blue Jeans, while Johnny Kidd and the Pirates, along with Bern Elliott and the Fenmen, played some venues.

On Friday 24 January, Decca released a single by George Bean, former habitué of the Ealing Club. 'Will You Be My Lover Tonight?' with 'It Should Be You' on the B-side are both Jagger/Richard compositions, so the record holds the honour of being the first UK single to feature songs written by Mick and Keith. On the same day, the Stones were at the BBC's Maida Vale studio to record a radio appearance for the popular Light Programme show, *Go Man Go*, hosted by David Ede.

The Stones played six songs including 'I Wanna Be Your Man', two classic Willie Dixon compositions, two from Chuck Berry and Arthur Alexander's 'You Better Move On'. One of the Berry numbers was 'Bye, Bye Johnny', which featured on the Stones' first EP.

Also released on the same day as Bean's single was a Decca compilation LP called *Saturday Club*. It included both sides of the abortive Stones' single 'Poison Ivy', and 'Fortune Teller', along with a disparate selection of other tracks including one from Ted Heath and his Music, as well as Kathy Kirby, the Tornados and Brian Poole and the Tremeloes.

At the beginning of February at a recording session in Regent Sound Studios, the Stones were joined by Phil Spector and Gene Pitney, who had just flown in from America clutching a bottle of brandy (or two). They collectively recorded several tracks, most of which were unsuitable for release as the duty-free booze seems to have taken effect.

A few days later, on 6 February, the Stones were at Pye Studios, near London's Marble Arch, for another, somewhat unusual, recording session.

Nine years earlier, in the summer of 1955, British advertising agencies were just coming to terms with the concept of TV ads for the newly formed ITV network. The first agency to specially record a piece of music for an advert was the J. Walter Thompson company, for whom George Browne and his Calypso Mambo Band cut a one-minute song for use on a pilot commercial. Besides George, who played the guitar and sang, there was Curly Clayton who also played guitar, and Pat Ryan on the bongos.

Seven years later, on 27 October 1962 – two weeks after the Beatles' 'Love Me Do' entered the charts – the fledgling Rolling Stones recorded three songs at Curly Clayton's studio near Arsenal's football ground. The songs were made into a demo disc that was sent to EMI and Decca who, along with everyone else at the time, rejected the band.

The February 1964 Stones' session was to record a song in the style of Jimmy Reed, to be used on a TV advert for the popular breakfast cereal, Rice Krispies; again the ad was commissioned by J. Walter Thompson. Decades later, in August 1995, Microsoft used the Rolling Stones' 'Start Me Up' to launch their new operating system, Windows '95. The computer giant paid an undisclosed sum to use this track, but you better believe it was a great deal more than the £400 that Kellogg's paid the Stones, thirty-one years earlier.

Two days after recording the Rice Krispies advert, the Stones began another package tour, this one featuring John Leyton as the headline act. Despite being something of a fading recording artist at the time, Leyton still had great pulling power when it came to live appearances. His first record, the Joe Meek-produced 'Johnny Remember Me', had topped the UK charts in late 1961, and his last-ever hit made the charts for just one week during this tour. However, it was as an actor that Leyton was most appealing, having most recently starred in the 1962 film *The Great Escape*, alongside Steve McQueen.

The other artists on the tour included singer Billie Davis and bass-playing Jet Harris, who by this time had split from Tony Meehan. Harris was, apparently, drinking heavily and on some dates Billy Kuy of the Innocents played Jet's bass parts. To cap things off, on the last night of the tour, Billie Davis's poodle walked on stage during his set, cocked his leg against Harris's mic stand and relieved himself. Just another date on your average Sixties package tour, for which the Stones got paid £142 per night.

Left: The Stones with Gene Pitney and Phil Spector on 2 February at a recording session at Regent Sound Studios in London

Above: George Bean's Decca UK single is the first to carry a writing credit for Jagger/Richards

SATURDAY CLUB '64

On the morning of 8 February, the same day as the opening night of the John Leyton tour at Edmonton's Grenada in north London, the Stones made their second appearance on BBC radio's *Saturday Club*. They had recorded their numbers for the show five days earlier, at the Playhouse Theatre at Charing Cross in London, having been contracted by the BBC for this appearance on 20 December 1963; their fee was £36.

Yet again, Chuck Berry featured among the six songs they recorded, including, once again, 'Bye, Bye Johnny' from the first EP, but they also did 'Don't You Lie To Me', the first time it was recorded for radio. They also performed 'You Better Move On' and 'I Wanna Be Your Man', and then did two songs that featured on both the UK and US versions of their debut album – Bo Diddley's 'Mona', a regular from their days at the Crawdaddy, and Rufus Thomas's 'Walking The Dog'. Thomas's Stax classic had made No.5 on the US R&B chart and had peaked at No.10 on the Hot 100 just a month or so earlier; the Stones recorded their album version at Regent Sound Studios at their session early in January 1964.

It was an unusual *Saturday Club* in that it also featured an interview with the Beatles, who were in America for their first visit. The Beatles had arrived in New York the previous day and, following their *Saturday Club* interview – which was at a very early hour for the band given the time-change – they did a press photo-call in the city's Central Park. After lunch there were rehearsals for *The Ed Sullivan Show* that was to be broadcast live the following day to an estimated 73 million Americans in over 23 million homes; it remains one of the most-watched broadcasts in TV history. The British Invasion had begun … and the Stones would be joining it in a matter of months.

Brian Matthew, the host of the BBC's *Saturday Club*, was already thirty-six years old at the start of 1964, at a time when forty was considered middle-aged and past it. His approach was laconic and he always sounded like he was slightly detached from the artists he was talking with and introducing. He became a broadcasting legend, only retiring from hosting BBC Radio 2's *Sounds of the Sixties* aged 88 in 2017, less than two months before his death.

'I think perhaps a little bit mistakenly, I found their attitude in the studio, as apart from their music, extremely truculent.'

Brian Matthew
Saturday Club

DAILY MIRROR, Tuesday, May 12, 1964 PAGE 7

NO-TIE ROLLING STONE IS TOLD 'NO LUNCH'

Mick, centre, with Bill, left, and Keith.

By NED GRANT

MICK JAGGER, lead singer of the shaggy-haired Rolling Stones pop group, rolled to a sudden stop at a smart hotel yesterday.

He tried to walk into the hotel restaurant for lunch wearing sports shirt, sweater and jeans.

Concert

The restaurant was in the Grand Hotel, Bristol. Following a concert on Sunday night Mick, 19, stayed at the hotel with Rolling Stones Bill Wyman, 21, Keith Richard, 19, Brian Jones, 19, and Charlie Watts, 21.

They slept until nearly lunchtime.

Then the five, who have been called the ugliest group in show business, strolled down to the hotel's cocktail bar with their road manager, Ian Stewart.

Ian left the group and stepped into the restaurant.

Seconds later he stepped out and said: "We can't eat there unless we are togged up like city guys."

At this, Mick tried his luck. He did not get as far inside the restaurant as Ian.

The head waiter, in tail coat, stepped forward and said apologetically, but firmly:

"Sorry, sir. We cannot serve you unless you wear a tie and jacket."

Then, said Mick later, the head waiter offered him a tie and jacket.

Mick quipped: "But I didn't feel like a tie or jacket for lunch.

"So I told him to keep his fancy duds."

The group and Ian walked out of the hotel and ate elsewhere.

A hotel spokesman said: "We accept some modern vogues in male attire, but we draw the line at jeans and shirts."

Above: Typical coverage of the Stones' refusal to dress appropriately in hotel restaurants, showing that pop was increasingly tabloid news ... but not for the right reasons

Opposite left: Arthur Haynes

Opposite right: Singer Mark Wynter

Following pages: Appearing on *Ready Steady Go!* in February

Following the morning's broadcast of *Saturday Club* on 8 February, the Stones were back on British television screens that evening doing two numbers on ATV's *The Arthur Haynes Show*. The boys were scheduled to start rehearsals at 11 a.m. at Elstree Studios, Borehamwood, Hertfordshire, about forty minutes' drive from central London, but when the band met up with Stu and the van they decided to go clothes shopping in Carnaby Street instead and, to the annoyance of the show's producers, arrived over two hours late.

Not that any of this affected their performance, which is one of the best surviving TV appearances of the band from their very early days. It is so good because they play live in the studios, there's no miming; it's just pure unadulterated Stones, having a great time playing 'I Wanna Be Your Man' and 'You Better Move On'. The most significant moment on this appearance is when Brian plays slide guitar on the Lennon and McCartney composition. It was the first time that someone had played slide guitar on British television; in emulating his hero, Elmore James, Brian no doubt inspired others to do likewise.

Arthur Haynes was a fifty-something comedian whose sketch and variety show had been running on ATV since 1956. His appeal was the very antithesis of the Stones' and what makes their appearance so incongruous is the fact that it was the first time they played live on television.

The Stones' second *Saturday Club* appearance may have been some time in March. Recordings exist of 'Beautiful Delilah' and 'Roll Over Beethoven', both Chuck Berry songs, which some sources purport were recorded live on the John Leyton tour and then broadcast on the programme either early in the month or on 28 March. However, no direct reference can be found for this and no contract exists in the BBC archive. It may have happened, it may not ...

The band did, however, definitely appear on the programme on 18 April, when 'Not Fade Away' was still in the UK Top 10; it was one of six numbers they had recorded the previous Monday between 7p.m. and 10.30p.m. at the Playhouse Theatre. *The Saturday Club* appearance was nicely timed, as the previous day the band's debut album was released in the UK. The Stones featured three tracks from the LP: Chuck Berry's 'Carol', 'I Just Want To Make Love To You' and 'Walking The Dog'.

May proved to be something of a turning point for the band in respect of their growing anti-establishment reputation. Early in the month, they had played Bristol's Colston Hall on a bill that included rock 'n' roll star Gene Vincent; given the Stones' love of the blues it is ironic that the hall was named after Edward Colston, a seventeenth-century slave-trader. The following day, the Stones went to eat lunch in the main restaurant of the city's Grand Hotel, where they were staying, but were refused entry because they were inappropriately dressed, meaning they were not wearing jackets and ties. It was an incident that was covered by virtually every national newspaper and moved the Stones off the entertainment page and onto the news pages – a moment when everything changed.

Mick was quoted in one paper saying, 'I don't see why we were turned out. I had no intention of wearing borrowed clothes to eat in my hotel.' Keith said, 'We intended to buy lunch for some of our regular girl fans, who always turn up when we're in the West Country. We've stayed in plusher hotels than this, and there's never been any question of refusing to allow us into the dining-rooms.' A spokesman from the Grand was quoted as saying: 'One of the group looked so scruffy, he would have benefited from being put in a launderette.' It all divided opinion, with fans defending their heroes, while at least one person suggested that the Stones 'must learn to conform'. It never has happened ...

Two weeks later, on 25 May, the Stones were at the Playhouse Theatre once again to record for *Saturday Club*; it was a week before they were to leave London to fly to New York for their first US tour. They did two numbers from their debut album, 'You Can Make It If You Try' and 'Route 66' – a song made famous by Nat King Cole in the 1940s – while 'Down In The Bottom' had been a regular in the band's Crawdaddy days, although this was the first time it was played on air. Likewise 'Down The Road Apiece', a song the Stones would record at Chess Records in Chicago a fortnight later. 'Confessin' The Blues' is different again; it had not been played on the radio by the band until this edition of *Saturday Club*, and it too would be recorded in Chicago for inclusion as one of the five tracks on their 5 x 5 EP.

The dichotomy that was Sixties pop could be no better illustrated than this edition of *Saturday Club* that was broadcast on 6 June, a few hours after the Stones had come off stage at the Swing Auditorium in San Bernadino – their first ever concert on US soil. Appearing on the same BBC show were Dusty Springfield, backed by the Echoes, and the Hollies, as well as the British Sinatra-like Matt Monro and the pleasant but unchallenging Mark Wynter, along with BBC stalwarts, the Lorne Gibson Trio.

Throughout the summer, the Stones were absent from *Saturday Club*. They were scheduled to appear on 28 November, but due to a row with the BBC they missed the programme.

Rogers

5-4-3-2-1: READY STEADY GO! IN '64

Left and opposite:
Ready Steady Go!
13 April

The second *Ready Steady Go!* of 1964 aired on 10 January featuring a new band, the unusually named Manfred Mann. The group had its origins in the same London blues scene as the Stones, playing gigs at Ken Colyer's Jazz Club and the Marquee as the Mann-Hugg Blues. Manfred Mann was born Manfred Lubowitz in South Africa, moving to the UK in 1961, and he and drummer Mike Hugg formed their band in December 1962, recruiting Paul Jones as their singer. In mid-1963, they signed to HMV Records, who suggested they change their name to Manfred Mann.

Their first two singles released in the second half of 1963 flopped, but they got their break towards the end of the year when Francis Hitching, the producer of *RSG!*, invited them to write a theme song for the show. According to Manfred Mann: 'We recorded "5-4-3-2-1" at Abbey Road Studio 2. The record is built around a harmonica part, played by Paul Jones, which goes "chukka chukka chukka chukka", after which he sings "5-4-3-2-1".'

'On Ready Steady Go! we mime to the recording on Friday night. On Monday night at the Marquee club, while carrying our equipment down the stairs after the gig, someone says that "5-4-3-2-1" is No.29 in the New Musical Express chart after only two days' sales.'

Manfred Mann

3
RSG!

Thereafter, '5-4-3-2-1' introduced *RSG!* each week, and by the time that the Stones made their first appearance of 1964 on the show, Manfred Mann was at No.5 on the UK charts – the power of TV again.

For this first *RSG!* appearance of the year by the Stones, the band mimed to three songs. Somewhat appropriately, given it was also Valentine's Day, their first number was 'I Wanna Be Your Man', but they also, somewhat less appropriately, did 'You Better Move On', followed by the television debut of 'Not Fade Away', which was to be released the following week in the UK. The week after 'Not Fade Away' came out, it entered the chart at No.29, the third highest new entry, behind Jim Reeves and Freddie and the Dreamers.

Also on the show was the ever-present Dusty Springfield, American girl-group the Crystals, singer Kenny Lynch, Heinz and the Woodpeckers, and former member of the Echoes, the drummer Laurie Jay and his Combo, whose drum kit Charlie sat behind, miming his drum part during the three Stones' numbers. Keith Fordyce interviewed Mick and some of the other Stones during the programme.

With 'Not Fade Away' having peaked at No.3 on the charts the previous week, the Stones were back on *RSG!* on 3 April, miming to their current hit and also doing 'I Just Want To Make Love To You'. The song was recorded by the Stones for their debut album that was released in the UK two weeks later; it also became the B-side of their second American single, 'Tell Me'.

A look behind the scenes at *RSG!* was provided by Penny Valentine, a 'pop columnist' on *Disc*, a weekly paper. 'Sitting in the dressing room was like being in the middle of a mad railway station. Keith was huddled in the corner with a sketch-pad, drawing Bill, and muttering under his breath, making noises like an angry bull, concentrating. Brian was popping in and out, looking for Mick, who was rushing around wild-eyed. Nobody knew why. In the confusion, sad-eyed Charlie sat patiently ignoring everyone. Andrew arrived with their week's money, which was £201 ... Charlie and Keith said they were hungry, and we all went to the canteen, to eat fish and chips with sauce.'

Among the other guests on this show were Billy J. Kramer with the Dakotas, Manfred Mann, Sounds Incorporated and former Dusty Springfield backing singer Madeline Bell, miming to her second UK release, 'Don't Cross To My Side'; five years later Madeline would sing backing vocals on 'You Can't Always Get What You Want'. After appearing on *RSG!*, the evening's work was far from over as the Stones played a gig in south-west London at Wimbledon Palais.

After this, the band started gearing up to another *RSG!* recording in just five days' time: the Mod Ball.

So what exactly were Mods? They have their roots in 1950s modern jazz, when people listening to the kind of music released by Blue Note Records were dubbed Modernists – or Mods. The Mod movement had its origins in London and by late 1963 and 1964 these men and women, who revered smart clothes, particularly Italian suits for men, Italian-made scooters – Lambrettas and Vespas – and dancing at all-nighters in clubs, were being seen all over Britain.

While a love of fashion was key to all things Mod, music formed a vital part of the culture. It was black music that Mods danced to in clubs like the Marquee, La Discothèque, the Flamingo and their spiritual home, the hottest of the hot, the Scene Club in London's Ham Yard. Today most people see the Who as synonymous with Mod culture, but before the Who hit the headlines, *RSG!* championed the scene, if not always the kind of music that your average Mod liked to listen to.

Mods' love of black music included Motown, Stax Records, recordings on obscure American labels from the South and Jamaican ska. Motown's tours of the UK and their early assault on the British charts with the Supremes, Martha and the Vandellas and Marvin Gaye – the sharpest dresser among Motown's sharpest dressers – was given impetus by Mod record buyers. The Stones were influenced by Motown and Stax and all forms of black music and, above any other white band in Britain in April 1964, they could be said to have a strong streak of Mod running through them.

Ready Steady Go! was mandated viewing for every self-respecting Mod, as well as those who just pretended they were Mods but were too young to have a scooter – sixteen was the minimum age for acquiring a licence. From its earliest days, *RSG!*'s producers trawled the clubs and ballrooms in the London area, such as Purley's legendary Orchid Ballroom, recruiting the best dancers – all of whom were fans of the latest sounds from America's black R&B and soul artists.

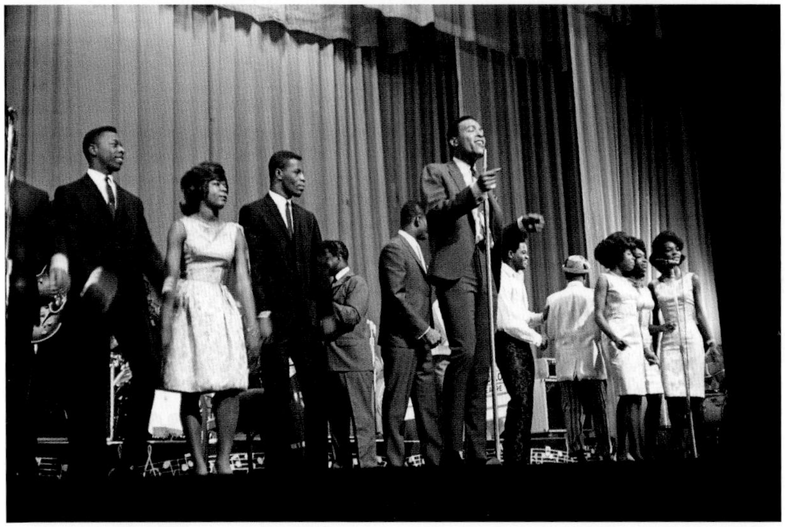

Opposite: *RSG!* 13 April
Top: The Supremes
Middle: Marvin Gaye (centre), Martha and the Vandellas, Joe Tex and others at the Apollo Theater in Harlem, New York in 1964
Right: Mods revered smart clothes, particularly Italian suits for men, Italian-made scooters and dancing to soul music at all-nighters in clubs

The Mod Ball was held on Wednesday 8 April at Wembley's Empire Pool, and was organized by *Ready Steady Go!* and the Variety Club of Great Britain, a showbiz charity. As the day dawned, newspapers were asking 'the big question. Will the Rockers try and infiltrate this event for their rivals, the Mods?' The Rockers were the antithesis of all things Mod – they were motorbike-riding, leather jacket-wearing greasers who liked rock 'n' roll, Chuck Berry records and fighting with their rivals.

According to newspaper reports, Mods thought that Rockers had secretly bought tickets. A Wembley official said, 'We will have more than 100 security men on duty. We realise Rockers may try to get in on the act.'

Joining the Stones to play to an ecstatic and excitable crowd of over 8,000 were Billy J. Kramer with the Dakotas, the Fourmost, the Merseybeats, Sounds Incorporated, the Searchers, Cilla Black, Kathy Kirby, Freddie and the Dreamers, Kenny Lynch and Manfred Mann. The Stones appeared on a circular rostrum, which had to be accessed through the crowd. This proved a nightmare; they also had to share the same drum kit with the Fourmost and the Dakotas. They mimed to 'Not Fade Away', 'Walking The Dog', 'Hi-Heel Sneakers' and Bo Diddley's 'I'm Alright'.

The Mod Ball was broadcast later that same evening at 9.50 p.m. on ITV for an hour, but it is unclear which of the songs performed by the Stones were actually shown on the television. What was clear from the following day's newspaper reports is that officials had every right to be concerned about the Rockers and Mods. As the *Daily Mirror* said, 'More than a dozen teenagers were arrested last night outside the Mod Ball. A police spokesman said, "They are likely to be charged with insulting behaviour and causing an obstruction." Those arrested were either roaring about on motorcycles or fighting among themselves.'

As it turned out, this was just a warm-up for the massed fights at seaside resorts on the south coast of England during the Whitsun Bank Holiday at the end of May 1964, when there were hundreds of arrests and some serious injuries during running battles between huge rival gangs of Mods and Rockers.

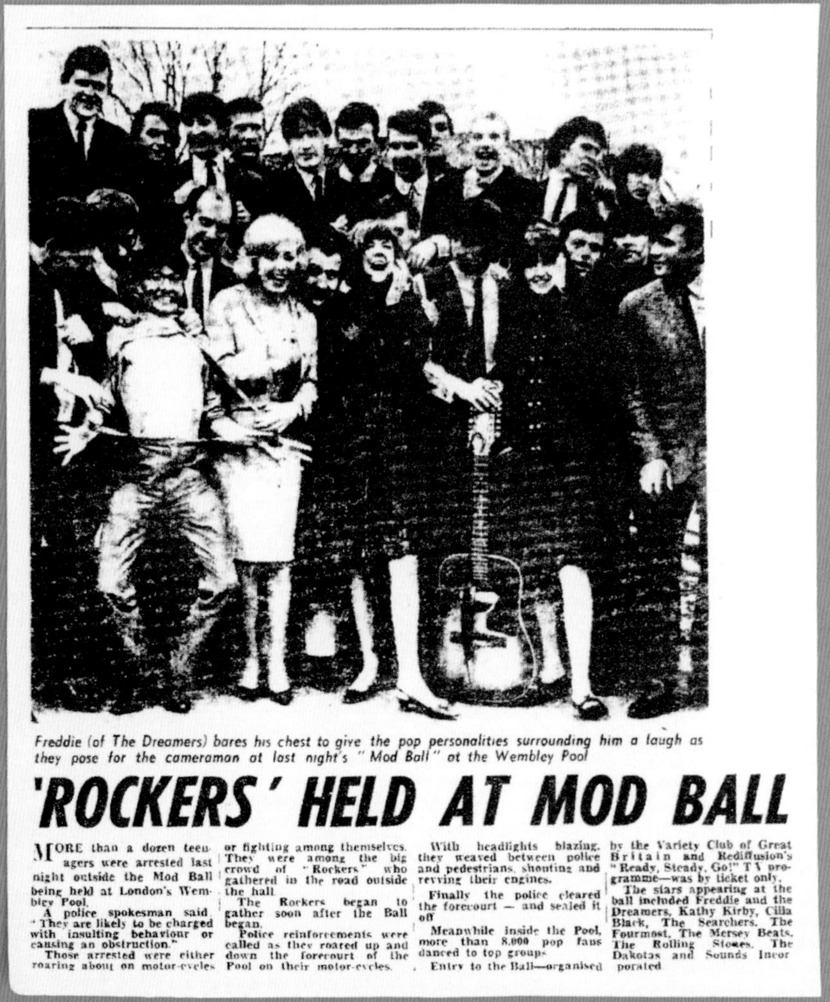

Freddie (of The Dreamers) bares his chest to give the pop personalities surrounding him a laugh as they pose for the cameraman at last night's "Mod Ball" at the Wembley Pool

'ROCKERS' HELD AT MOD BALL

MORE than a dozen teenagers were arrested last night outside the Mod Ball being held at London's Wembley Pool.

A police spokesman said "They are likely to be charged with insulting behaviour or causing an obstruction."

Those arrested were either roaring about on motor-cycles or fighting among themselves. They were among the big crowd of "Rockers" who gathered in the road outside the hall.

The Rockers began to gather soon after the Ball began.

Police reinforcements were called as they roared up and down the forecourt of the Pool on their motor-cycles.

With headlights blazing, they weaved between police and pedestrians, shouting and revving their engines.

Finally the police cleared the forecourt — and sealed it off.

Meanwhile inside the Pool, more than 8,000 pop fans danced to top groups.

Entry to the Ball—organised by the Variety Club of Great Britain and Rediffusion's "Ready, Steady, Go!" TV programme—was by ticket only.

The stars appearing at the ball included Freddie and the Dreamers, Kathy Kirby, Cilla Black, The Searchers, The Fourmost, The Mersey Beats, The Rolling Stones, The Dakotas and Sounds Incorporated.

Below: The *Daily Mirror* reports on the Rockers arrested outside the Mod Ball

Opposite: On stage at the Mod Ball

Having featured the Stones twice in five days, *Ready Steady Go!* gave them a bit of a break during the remainder of spring and into the early days of summer. It was not until four days after they returned from their first trip to America that they were back on the programme, to debut both sides of their brand-new single on British TV. They mimed to 'It's All Over Now' and 'Good Times, Bad Times'; the latter song was the first Jagger/Richards composition to be performed by the band on British television. Before the month was over, the Stones were back on *RSG!* in the week that the Beatles' 'A Hard Day's Night' replaced them at No.1 in the UK.

The Stones' growing status as something more than just recording artists was evident in July when Brian Jones was asked to be a judge on an episode of a new spin-off show from *Ready Steady Go!* called *Ready Steady Win*, a competition to find the next big thing; a month or so later, Mick, along with Lulu and Alan Freeman, were the judges. The competition was won by a Mod band from Harrow called the Bo Street Runners, whose prize was a recording contract with Decca. One of the bands that they beat was another Mod group, west London's Birds, which featured a certain Ron Wood on guitar and vocals.

On 7 August, the Stones were back on *RSG!* for the first anniversary show – and not just playing, as Brian and Bill were the guest hosts on this special edition; the pair of them also mimed to a parody of 'A Hard Day's Night'. Aside from playing their current hit, the Stones also did Chuck Berry's 'Around and Around' and Wilson Pickett's 'If You Need Me', both of which they had recorded at Chess Records in June and were included on the 5 x 5 EP that came out in the UK the following week.

It would be three months before the Stones returned to *RSG!* because they were away in Europe and America for most of October and only got back to the UK the day before their 20 November appearance on the show. They opened with 'Off The Hook', the B-side of their new single that had come out a week earlier, and then gave the A-side, 'Little Red Rooster', its TV debut, before 'Around And Around' was used over the closing credits.

Both Brian and Mick were interviewed by Keith Fordyce before they played 'Little Red Rooster'; Brian talked about being hospitalized in America with a virus and Mick discussed a book about the band written by George Tremlett – it was the first of many.

Marvin Gaye was on the same edition of the show, as was Van Morrison's band, Them, playing their single 'Baby, Please Don't Go'. Just after the Stones finished miming, Keith collapsed, having not slept for five nights. Fortunately, he quickly recovered, as they had to drive from central London to Wembley to appear at the Glad Rag Ball, along with the Animals, Long John Baldry and Ginger Johnson and his African Drummers, who would appear with the Stones at Hyde Park in July 1969. According to the *Daily Mirror*, 'There was a near riot by 7,000 screaming teenagers as the Stones took the stage. When the group had finished, Brian, in checked shirt, was mobbed as he was leaving. Mick escaped through a side door.' The 45-minute programme aired five days later on the ITV network.

While they were at Wembley, Charlie was confronted by a reporter from the *Daily Express* asking if he and his girlfriend, Shirley, were married. Charlie had not even told the Stones they had married in Bradford a month earlier because he thought the band would be angry.

'I emphatically deny I am married. It would do a great deal of harm to my career, if the story got around.'

Charlie Watts

Right: Brian is mobbed by the crowd at the Glad Rag Ball

Following pages: On stage at the Glad Rag Ball

THANK YOUR LUCKY STARS '64

Opposite and following pages: Rehearsing for an appearance on *Thank Your Lucky Stars*, possibly on 29 November

Nineteen sixty-four was a leap year, a fact that had somehow eluded the Stones' manager Andrew Loog Oldham. At a recording session at the beginning of the year, the Stones played on an instrumental written by Loog Oldham and Mike Leander called '365 Rolling Stones'. In April, it became a single credited to the Andrew Oldham Orchestra on Decca. It was on 29 February, as if to make the point, that the Stones made their first appearance of the year on *Thank Your Lucky Stars.*

The band were recorded miming to 'Not Fade Away' on the afternoon of 23 February at Alpha Studios in Birmingham, having broken down on the way from Bournemouth where they had played the previous night, causing them to be over two hours late. Later in the evening, the Stones played two shows at Birmingham's Hippodrome Theatre on the John Leyton tour. As soon as the show was over, they drove home to London via the M1, the UK's first motorway, stopping at the Blue Boar, an all-night café near Birmingham. The next day the Leyton tour played Southend, but not before the Stones went to Regent Sound Studios to record some tracks for their first album. It really was all go ... It would be three months before the Stones were back on *TYLS*, yet when they did so they were still miming to 'Not Fade Away', just as it was making its chart exit; they also did 'I Just Want To Make Love To You'. Both numbers were in stark contrast to the rest of the performances on the programme, emphasizing the gulf between *TYLS*, recorded in Birmingham and reeking of provincialism, and *Ready Steady Go!*, which was recorded in London with a far hipper, sassier outlook. The line-up on this edition of *TYLS* included a string of Britain's finest middle-of-the-road performers – Jackie Trent (wife of songwriter Tony Hatch, who together wrote the theme to the hit TV show *Neighbours*), Adam Faith, Mark Wynter, Kenny Ball and his Jazzmen, local band the Strangers with Mike Shannon, and the Eagles – not THE Eagles, but a group from Bristol that specialized in Shadows-like instrumentals. There was one visiting American artist who also appeared – Miss Dionne Warwick, who was riding high on the charts with her definitive version of 'Walk On By'.

STONES

VOX

Top: Dionne Warwick
Bottom: Adam Faith and the Roulettes
Opposite and following pages: Appearing on *Thank Your Lucky Stars* in 1964

The Stones recorded their 30 May appearance six days earlier while they were in the midst of a headlining tour of the UK that also featured a bunch of fairly pedestrian bands, including the Barron Knights, the Overlanders, David John and the Mood, Julie Grant and the Caravelles.

The band left for America two days after this *TYLS* edition aired and, following their return from the US, they were back on the programme on 8 August, miming to 'It's All Over Now'. Fortunately, they were saved a round trip to Birmingham as this was recorded in Teddington, to the west of London.

In late September, while on tour with American brother-and-sister R&B duo, Inez and Charlie Foxx, the Stones were due to record an appearance on *Thank Your Lucky Stars* that was to be broadcast on 3 October, shortly before they were due to head off to Europe and then America to tour. The Stones were once again playing Birmingham's Hippodrome Theatre. Somehow there was a mix-up in arrangements and they failed to get to Alpha Studios to record their appearance. According to a spokesman for ATV: 'Because of the timings of their shows at Birmingham Hippodrome, it was impossible for us to pre-record the Stones. We therefore cancelled their appearance at the last moment. In all probability we shall be presenting a special *Lucky Stars* on the Stones next month.'

Given their touring commitments, it wouldn't be until the end of November that the band were able to get back to Birmingham in order to record four songs for the *Lucky Stars Special* that was broadcast on 5 December. Extended to forty-five minutes, the show was to accommodate four numbers from the Stones – both sides of their current single, 'Little Red Rooster' and 'Off The Hook', which was at No.1 in the UK charts; 'Around And Around'; and something of a rarity, 'Empty Heart', one of the tracks on *5 x 5* and the only number from the record that they had so far not performed on TV or radio. In fact this was its only known airing.

As usual, the Stones courted controversy by failing to conform to the accepted way of doing things on this type of TV show. They were asked to pose for photographs and invited to a 'backstage reception' to meet up with the other stars of *TYLS*, including Petula Clark, Sandie Shaw, Herman's Hermits, Clinton Ford, and the ubiquitous Mark Wynter. They refused both offers and instead headed home to London straight after their recording, taking something of a lambasting in the press and from ATV as a result.

THE STATION OF THE STARS

If you are of a certain age, and British, then the mere mention of the words Radio Luxembourg will cause a wave of nostalgia to flow over you, along with the memory of the immense sense of frustration at having to listen to an AM radio station on which the volume and quality of the sound went up and down like the proverbial yo-yo.

It was in 1944 that the English-language service of Radio Luxembourg became the first commercial station to broadcast to the UK and Ireland. It allowed advertisers to bypass UK laws that prevented anyone broadcasting legally to the UK prior to 1973, other than the BBC. Radio Luxembourg, which called itself 'The Station of the Stars', had what was purported to be the most powerful transmitter in the world, boasting an impressive 1,300 kW, but it was a long way from the Grand Duchy to the UK and it was only in the north of England that reception was acceptable at best.

Broadcast on 208 metres on the medium wave, Radio Luxembourg's programmes in the early 1950s were a mix of music as well as some series, such as *The Adventures of Dan Dare* and *Perry Mason*. Later in the 1950s, the station's evening and night-time broadcasts included *The Capitol Records Show*, playing purely new releases on the American record label, and *Rockin' to Dreamland*, presented by Keith Fordyce. Among the other DJs who were heard on the station were Alan Freeman, David Gell, Tony Hall, Jack Jackson, David Jacobs, Brian Matthew, Don Moss, Pete Murray, Shaw Taylor, Jimmy Young and Muriel Young. All of the DJs gave the impression that they were in the Grand Duchy broadcasting live to Britain, despite the fact that many shows were pre-recorded from their London studios at 38 Hertford Street.

Radio Luxembourg had latched onto the Stones, like the BBC, and in February 1964 the commercial station invited the band to record several tracks that would be used in a series of sponsored programmes, entitled *Nestlé's Top Swinging Groups*. Shortly after lunch on 18 March, the Stones, who the previous

..AND RADIO

LIGHT

6.30 a.m. Weather; News; Music. 8.55 Metcast. 9.0 Housewives' Choice. 9.55 Five to Ten. 10.0 Clinton's Cakewalk. 10.31 Music While You Work. 11.0 Story. 11.15 The Dales. 11.31 Latin-American Music. 12.0 Twelve O'Clock Spin. 12.31 Music-Hall. 1.30 News. 1.35 Cricket. 1.45 Listen With Mother. 2.0 Woman's Hour. 3.0 Music for Dancing. 3.31 Music While You Work.

4.15 The Dales. 4.31 Racing; Cricket. 4.35 Playtime. 5.0 Roundabout. 6.33 Sport. 6.45 The Archers. 7.0 News; Newsreel. 7.25 Sport. 7.31 PETER GOODWRIGHT SHOW. 8.0 Mister Mayor. 8.30 News; Topic. 8.40 Rhapsody. 9.30 Hey There. 10.0 Music to Midnight. 11.55 News.

HOME

6.40 a.m. Farm. 6.50 Thought. 6.55 Weather. 7.0 News. 7.10 South-East News. 7.15 Today. 7.45 Papers. 7.50 Lift Up Your Hearts. 7.55 Weather. 8.0 News. 8.10 South-East News. 8.15 Today. 8.40 Papers. 8.45 A World of Sound. 9.0 News. 9.5 Letter From America. 9.20 Talking About Music. 9.55 Schools. 10.15 Service. 10.30 Schools. 11.20 It Takes All Sorts. 11.40 Schools.

12.0 Cricket. 12.10 Concert. 12.55 Weather. 1.0 News. 1.10 DESERT ISLAND DISCS: David Kossoff. 1.40 The Storyteller. 2.0 Schools. 3.0 Afternoon Theatre: Love and Mr. Lewisham. 4.15 Cricket. 4.45 Home This Afternoon. 5.25 Music Club. 5.55 Weather. 6.0 News. 6.10 South-East. 6.32 Markets. 6.35 Music on the Move. 7.0 Piano at Seven. 7.30 Ring Up The Curtain. 8.30 Expedition: Play. 10.0 News; Comment. 10.30 My Lords, Ladies, and Gentlemen. 10.45 Parliament. 10.59 Weather. 11.0 News. 11.2 A Book at Bedtime. 11.15-11.45 Music at Night.

THIRD NETWORK

6.30 p.m. Facts in Focus. 6.35 French. 6.40 Spanish. 7.5 Forgetting. 7.30 Jazz Session. 8.0 Beethoven. 8.45 How Much Common Ground? 9.15 Beethoven: Part 2. 9.55 Michael Ayrton. 10.25 Palestrina. 11.0 News. 11.15-11.20 Markets.

LUXEMBOURG

7.0 p.m. The World Tomorrow. 7.30 Disc Break. 7.45 Let's Take A Spin. 8.0 Don Moss. 8.30 Record Choice. 9.0 The Merseybeats versus The Rolling Stones. 9.15 Jim Dale. 9.30 Topical Tunes. 9.45 Swinging USA. 10.0 TOP POPS. 10.30 Hit Parade. 11.0 Monday Night Special. 11.15 Peter Aldersley. 11.30 Ray's On. 12.0-3.0 a.m. Music In The Night.

AFN

7.0 p.m. News; Music. 8.0 Report from Europe; Local Service. 8.30 Connotation. 9.0 News; EUCOM Report. 9.30 Evening In Paris. 9.50 On the Scene. 10.0 News; Music-Hall. 10.55 Sports. 11.0 News; Requests. 12.0 News; Midnight In Europe.

Above: The radio listings for 11 May 1964, with a Battle of the Bands on Radio Luxembourg featuring the Stones vs The Merseybeats: the Stones won

Below: Jack Jackson
Bottom left: Muriel Young
Bottom right: Shaw Taylor
Following pages: Performing 'High Heel Sneakers' on TV's *Open House* at Riverside Studios, Hammersmith, London, 9 May

night had played the Assembly Rooms in Tunbridge Wells, were in the studio in London (possibly Pye Studios in Marble Arch) to record fourteen numbers.

Aside from their two most recent singles, 'I Wanna Be Your Man' and 'Not Fade Away', they did 'Bye, Bye Johnny', 'Diddley Daddy', 'Little By Little', 'Look What You Done', 'Mona (I Need You Baby)', 'Now I've Got A Witness', 'Pretty Thing', 'Walking The Dog', 'You Better Move On', 'Reelin' and Rockin'', 'Roll Over Beethoven' and 'Route 66'. The fourteen songs were broadcast over four fifteen-minute programmes, starting on 17 April and ending on 6 May. Besides being a reflection of the kind of things they were playing live, especially at ballroom and club gigs, as well as their two singles, five of the songs featured on their first UK album, which was released the day before the first show was broadcast.

In July, the Stones featured on another show on Radio Luxembourg, *This Is Your Life*. Broadcast at 8 p.m. on a Sunday evening, it gave a rundown of the band's career thus far. On Sunday 12 July in the *Sunday Mirror*, Andrew Loog Oldham was bemoaning the Stones' lack of earnings. 'After the manager, agent, publicity, fan club and tax have been paid, plus other deductions, the Stones get about one-twelfth each of their gross earnings, sometimes working out as little as around £70 per week. In America most chart acts work five months and retire for the other seven. That's why I'm setting up shop in the States as soon as possible.'

In another of Luxembourg's somewhat contrived, but no less popular, shows, the Stones were pitted against the Animals in *The Battle of the Giants*, which aired over two parts in October. The Stones won. Three days after Christmas in another edition of the same show, the Stones went head to head with Gene Pitney, which seems somewhat bizarre, and they again won, based on listeners' votes – although in those pre-scrutiny days it's possible that voting may have been neither prolific nor entirely accurately counted.

VOX

THE STONES IN STEREO

Opposite: The Stones pre-record the BBC's experimental stereo radio show at the Camden Theatre, London, while Long John Baldry reads his script

In the first week of March, the *Melody Maker* had this to say: 'They call them the ugliest pop group in Britain – the group parents detest. They have their biggest hit "Not Fade Away". It's sparked off international interest in the five dishevelled young men. America wants them, and they're off there next month. France is bidding for them, and they're in line for a season at the Olympia. Britain has accepted them – at least the young fans have. They revel in their rebellious image. Because adults hate their scruffiness, young people react to the hate campaign by rallying round them. Three film companies have offered them screen debuts.'

The weekly music paper was a little premature, as organising an American tour so quickly would have been difficult to say the least. However, in mid-March, on the day the Stones played Chatham's Invicta Ballroom in Kent – without Charlie who was on holiday, and with Micky Waller sitting in on drums – they chatted backstage with a young guitarist, Jimmy Page, about their forthcoming American tour, which was set for June.

Four days later on Thursday 19 March, the day after recording the fourteen tracks for Radio Luxembourg, the band went to the Camden Theatre, to the east of Regent's Park in London, to record a thirty-minute BBC radio show.

The show itself was part of a series called *Rhythm & Blues*, but this was a very special experimental radio broadcast. Advertised in the newspapers as *Stereophony* and broadcast at 9.30 in the morning of Saturday 9 May, it was one of the first transmissions designed to be listened to in stereo.

According to the show's producer, Ian Grant: 'They had to broadcast on two separate channels, that was the only way ... you had to move your radio near to your television and place them eight feet apart at the suitable angles and sit in the middle and you got this stereo image. Before the broadcast they put out this little announcement saying, "Just to qualify the system: have you got your television sound? This is the left speaker, this is the right speaker – so if you've got your left and right it's great!" And they played the tape.' Essentially, the BBC's Third Programme carried one channel on the radio, while the television broadcast the other channel.

The first half of the broadcast was given over to Georgie Fame and the Blue Flames and the whole thing was compered by singer Long John Baldry, who introduced the Stones as 'those charming deviationists'. They performed 'Route 66', 'Cops And Robbers', 'You Better Move On', and 'Mona' in front of an audience that had been imported from the Flamingo Jazz Club where the Stones had last performed in January 1963.

The BBC stereo recordings really are superb – Keith's guitar cuts through, and Mick is on fine form. 'Mona', first recorded in January 1964 and released on their debut UK album, is taken at a faster pace on the BBC recording than the studio version. This is the only known Stones recording of Kent Harris's song 'Cops And Robbers', which was recorded by Bo Diddley for his 1960 album, *Have Guitar Will Travel*.

'Route 66' appeared on both the first UK and American albums and is a number that the Stones performed often in these early days; it's played with the familiarity that you'd expect. Bill's bass thunders and growls, Brian plays the guitar solo and Charlie's drumming is tight.

These are among the most exciting tracks recorded by the Stones in their first year or so together, sounding, as they do, so crisp and clear. The Stones received a standard BBC fee of £36, with a further £18 for 'mechanical reproduction' rights. There were some other small amounts ranging from £9 to £18 for broadcast in the British Commonwealth, the USA and the rest of the world, should the BBC sell the recordings to other broadcasters.

Little did they or any of us know that we would be hearing a great deal more of the Stones in stereo.

Publ. Stereophony s/c

THE BRITISH BROADCASTING CORPORATION

EXPERIMENTAL STEREOPHONIC SOUND TRANSMISSIONS

It is impossible for various reasons to reproduce in the home precisely the sounds that would be heard in a concert hall, broadcasting or recording studio. The aim is, therefore, to provide the most pleasing reproduction avoiding any annoying distortions. Modern equipment can provide such reproduction - especially that having controls with which the listener can adjust the response of the equipment to suit personal taste and the acoustics of the room. Stereophonic sound reproduction is an additional aid to the pleasure of listening. Its aim is to enable the listener to locate the relative positions and movement of the various sources of sound and also to give a general effect of spaciousness.

The experiments now being carried out by the BBC are to explore the possibilities of stereophonic broadcasting, and to give listeners an opportunity of hearing for themselves the stereophonic effects that may be achieved.

The experimental transmissions of stereophonic sound will be broadcast on alternate Saturday mornings from 10.15 a.m. to 11.15 a.m. Any changes in the times or dates, together with information about the programme will be found in the current issue of the RADIO TIMES. To hear these broadcasts stereophonically a sound receiver and a television receiver are required. Listeners should sit and face the two loudspeakers with the sound receiver on the left, tuned to Network Three preferably on VHF, and the television receiver on the right, tuned to BBC television sound. The receiver loudspeakers should be about the same height from the floor and spaced about six to ten feet apart. The best listening positions will be found by experiment and are usually in a small area situated at approximately equal distances from the two loudspeakers and at a similar distance from the loudspeakers as they are from each other. If the television set has its loudspeaker mounted on the side it may be better to turn the set round so that the loudspeaker is facing towards the front; sometimes a better effect can be obtained if the two loudspeakers are turned towards the central listening area.

Before the experimental broadcast a short period of music will be transmitted (but not stereophonically) on both channels. This period may be used to adjust volume and tone controls so as to make the reproduction from each loudspeaker sound as alike as possible. After the music there will be two minutes of stereophonic test speech during which the relative volume of the two sets should be adjusted as far as possible to make the speaker's voice appear to come from a point mid-way between the loudspeakers. This adjustment is easier if carried out by one person (standing clear of the loudspeaker) while another checks the results in the listening area. Increasing the volume of one loudspeaker will tend to move the apparent source of sound towards it and vice versa.

If the test speech cannot be satisfactorily centralised one of the loudspeakers may not be operating in correct phase; i.e. the movement of the loudspeaker cones is not in sympathy. In this case the loudspeaker connections in one of the receivers will have to be reversed. In many sound receivers the loudspeaker is connected by means of plugs and sockets at the back of the set and all that need be done is to reverse the positions of the plugs in the sockets. Other receivers will have soldered connections and the modification will require more skill. It is not advisable for anyone who is not an expert to remove the back of the set to make alterations, but if this is done, the receiver <u>must first be switched off and disconnected entirely from the mains supply</u>. This is most important because of the high and possibly lethal voltages that may be present, particularly in television receivers. A radio dealer or technician would easily be able to make the simple modification quickly and should be consulted if there is any doubt.

P.T.O.

Listeners receiving the transmissions from stations more than about 100 miles from London may not obtain a true stereophonic effect because of differences in the characteristics of the programme lines connecting the transmitters with the London studio. This has the effect of putting the loudspeakers partially out of step and this is one of the problems that needs to be overcome in stereophonic broadcasting. However, even under these conditions an effect of spaciousness and greater realism will be obtained than is possible with reception of normal transmissions.

The transmission of stereophonic sound requires two or more channels from programme source to listening room. The present experiments are a basic arrangement of two channels each consisting of separate microphones, programme lines, transmitters on different wavelengths, receivers, and loudspeakers. It has, however, a number of disadvantages and could not be used for a regular stereophonic broadcasting service. It is not compatible; i.e. properly balanced reproduction cannot be obtained when listening with one receiver to either channel alone, and it uses additional wavelengths which are not normally available. For these reasons the experimental transmissions have to be made outside the regular programme times. The only practicable period is during Saturday morning when the Network Three and Television Sound channels are usually free. Various systems offering promise of overcoming these disadvantages are being studied for possible adoption in a future stereophonic broadcasting service.

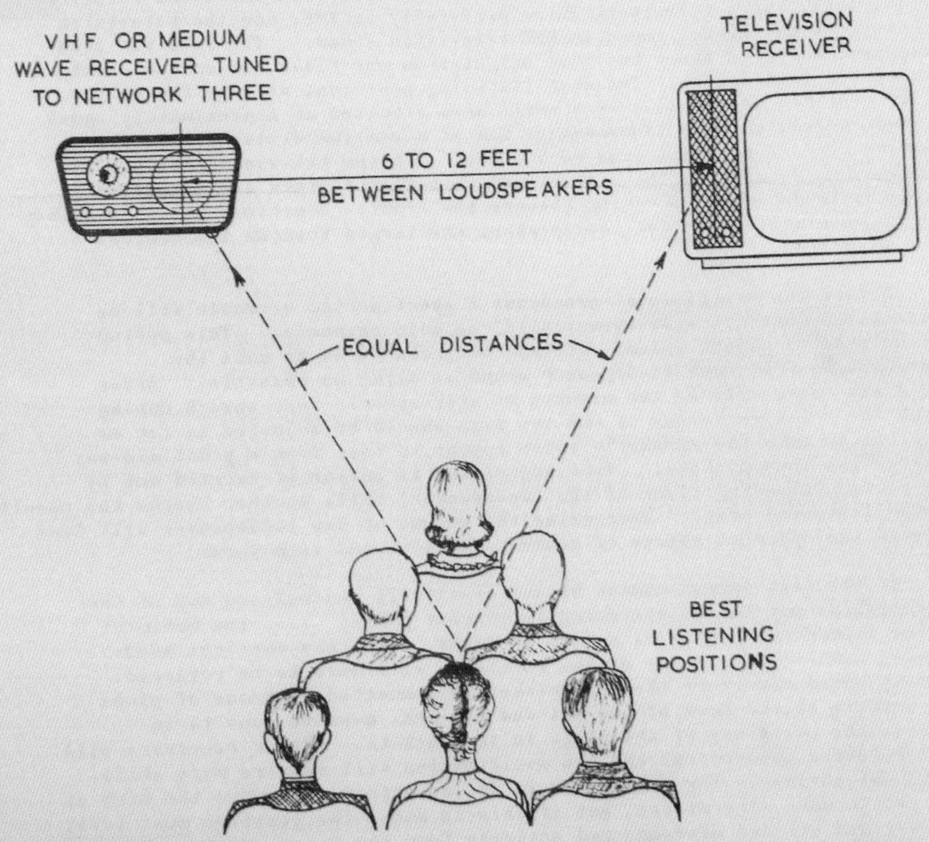

Leaflet No. EID/F/6a

Engineering Information Department,
The British Broadcasting Corporation,
Broadcasting House, London, W.1.

Left and opposite: Technical notes from the BBC's engineering information department on how to position a radio and a TV set to get the full 'stereo effect' for their experimental broadcast and 'give the general effect of spaciousness'.

RADIO WAVES

Above: DJ Alan Freeman

Opposite: Appearing on the BBC Light Programme's *Go Man Go*, hosted by David Ede, on 24 January

Television broadened the reach of the Stones, as it did for every other artist that featured on British TV screens, not just via the big three dedicated pop programmes but also through the variety shows and regional programmes like *Scene at 6.30*. However, it was the day-to-day exposure on radio that kept the band ringing in teenage ears.

That said, the opportunities for BBC radio coverage of the band were somewhat limited. In 1964, the BBC's main pop channel was the Light Programme, which did pretty much what it says on the tin. But it was a network that only broadcast to younger people for a fraction of its daily output, and in fact it didn't broadcast much music at all. It featured everything from radio soaps, like *The Archers* and *The Dales*, to *Listen With Mother*, *Woman's Hour*, quiz shows and even a light-hearted panel show called *Does the Team Think?* What was clear is that the BBC did not think much of pop music.

On any given weekday in early 1964, the opportunities for hearing a Rolling Stones record were limited to programmes like *The Beat Show*, broadcast at lunchtime on certain days of the week, or *Housewives' Choice*, a request show on which you were more likely to hear Matt Monro and Kathy Kirby than any beat band.

On 18 February, the Stones' new single, 'Not Fade Away', was played and they were interviewed by Keith Fordyce on *Pop Inn*, a lunchtime magazine and music show aimed at a younger audience that was broadcast from Paris Studios, a former cinema on Lower Regent Street in London. The studio held an audience of around 400 and the stage was very low, which gave the whole place a feeling of intimacy. Straight after their appearance, for which they were played 10 guineas, the Stones drove to Colchester in Essex to play two shows at the Rank Cinema for another stop on the John Leyton tour.

This limited radio coverage is why *Saturday Club* was so important to every beat band and pop artist during this time. And Saturday was the day of the week when records could get heard on other younger-focused shows like *Children's Favourites*. Although you were more likely to hear Tommy Steele singing about a 'Little White Bull' or Lonnie Donegan asking the question, 'Does Your Chewing Gum Lose Its Flavour (On The Bedpost Overnight)?', it did occasionally play something a little more current.

For any pop-mad British teenager, aside from *Saturday Club*, the highlight of the week was the chart rundown *Pick of the Pops*, which in early 1964 was broadcast at 4 p.m. every Sunday. The programme was presented by DJ Alan Freeman, a (late) thirty-something, former accountant from Melbourne, whose dulcet Aussie tones began each show with the immortal words, 'Greetings, Pop Pickers.' It was unique in that it played wall-to-wall records, with no live recordings or any other adulterations brought about by 'needle-time' restrictions.

It was a show on which the Stones had regularly appeared, given their relatively long chart run for 'I Wanna Be Your Man'. Now they were about to be regulars once again, thanks to 'Not Fade Away', which was played on *Pick of the Pops* for the first time on Sunday 5 March.

is is "GO
MAN
RADIO SHOW
WITH THE MOST
DAVID EDE &
THE RABIN
FAVOURITE POP MUSIC

At 12.31 p.m. on Friday 10 April, the Stones appeared on another of those random BBC Light Programme shows to feature pop music, *The Joe Loss Pop Show*. Loss had been a dance bandleader in Britain since the Second World War and by the early Sixties was also a successful recording artist making LPs of 'pop hits' in a dance-band style, much like James Last would do in Germany. Loss also had minor success on the singles charts with some dance tunes and later in 1964 his cash-in single, 'The March Of The Mods', became his most memorable hit, if not his most successful. For twenty years or more afterwards, there was not a British wedding disco that didn't play it, where it was danced to by ageing relatives who still thought it the height of hip.

For *The Joe Loss Pop Show*, the Stones played live to a very appreciative audience at the Playhouse Theatre in London. Among the songs they performed were 'Little By Little', the first time it had been heard on radio, and Hank Snow's 'I'm Moving On', which they had played at their original audition – the one they failed. They also did their current hit, 'Not Fade Away', which had dropped from No.4 to No.6 on the previous day's *Pick of the Pops*.

The paucity of BBC shows that featured pop music only goes to emphasize the huge part that Radio Luxembourg played in promoting pop careers. But two weeks before the Stones appeared on *The Joe Loss Pop Show*, something happened to UK radio that would have far-reaching consequences – something that affected, in a positive way, the Stones and every other pop artist of the era. Radio Caroline began broadcasting, illegally, from a converted Danish passenger ferry anchored in international waters off the east coast of Britain; it was therefore, technically, outside the control of the UK government. From the outset it played the Stones, and underserved British teenagers could listen to pop music twenty-four hours a day with none of the arcane needle-time regulations.

It's fair to say that pirate radio in Britain, as stations proliferated, changed the face of popular music, and for a time the pirates ruled the airwaves while riding the ocean waves of the North Sea ... But they would prove to be choppy waters as the BBC and the British government got around to fighting back.

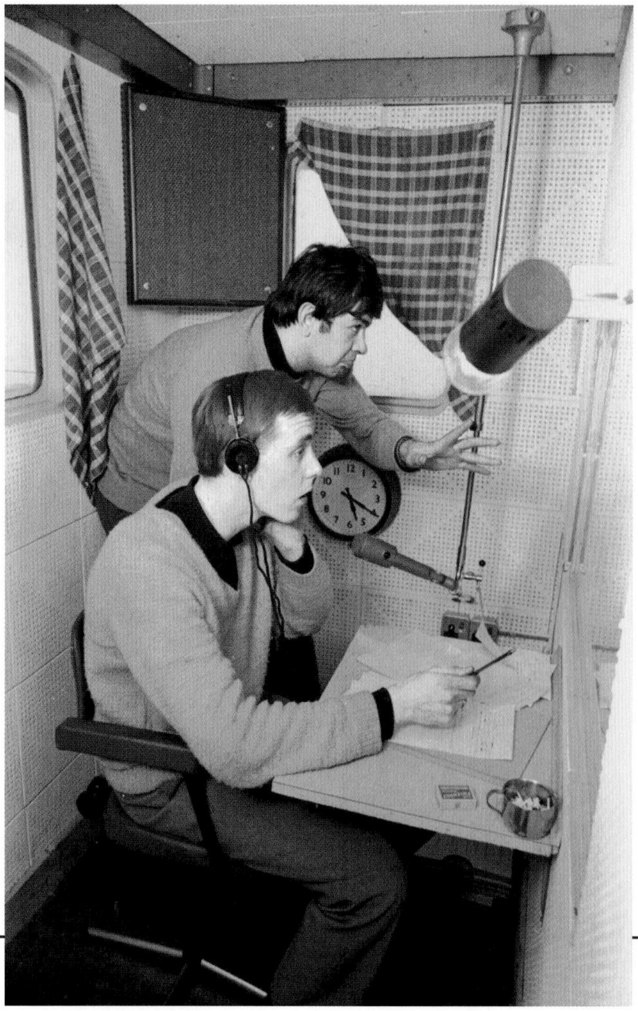

Left: Bandleader and broadcaster Joe Loss
Bottom: On board Radio Caroline with DJ Simon Dee seated at the microphone

CUCKOO-CLOCK LAND

On the day the band's first UK album was unleashed upon the British public, the Stones played Coventry's Locarno Ballroom; 2,000 wild fans turned up, causing something of a small-scale riot. So frenetic were the fans that the ballroom's management used fire extinguishers to quieten the crowd so the band could play their two half-hour sets. The following day, a Saturday, it was a gig at the Royalty Theatre in Chester; immediately after coming off stage and loading their equipment they drove south to London, because on Sunday they were due to fly to Switzerland for what was the band's first overseas gig.

Ready Steady Go! was one of the British entries for the Golden Rose TV Awards, with the Stones as one of the stars of the show. At London's Heathrow Airport, around 200 fans were there to see off the performers, presenters and producers, along with forty of the show's regular teenage audience, as they left on a charter flight to Geneva. The other performer leaving from London was Kenny Lynch, and also present were Andrew Loog Oldham and the show's hosts, Cathy McGowan and Michael Aldred. Footage of them all leaving Heathrow was shown on the ITN evening news, one of the first occasions the Stones would feature on a non-music programme and far from the last time they would make the national news.

'The Rolling Stones are the worst, one of them looks as if he has got a feather duster on his head.'

Fifty-year-old Wallace Scowcroft
President of the National Federation of Hairdressers, who offered free haircuts to the next group to top the charts

Right: Performing at the Golden Rose TV Awards on 21 April

Above: Singer Adamo
Above right: Popular in France, les Surfs originated in Madagascar

Following their arrival in Geneva, the party transferred to a large steamer for a five-hour boat trip on Lake Geneva to Montreux. Loog Oldham – it's worth remembering he was still only twenty years old – took with him his brand-new portable record player on which he proceeded to loudly play 45s throughout the journey.

The whole party checked into the Montreux Place Hotel and the Stones, along with everyone else, rehearsed on Monday afternoon, before the show was recorded later that evening at the casino. It was all performed in front of the imported teenagers from London who were joined by around 800 specially invited Swiss kids to make up the rest of the audience; also watching were the judges for the competition. The Stones performed Bo Diddley's 'Mona', 'Route 66' and their latest single, 'Not Fade Away'.

The fifty-minute *RSG! Special* was broadcast in the UK on Friday 24 April at 6.10 p.m., straight after the main evening news. It featured not only the Stones and Kenny Lynch, but also Petula Clark, who had left Britain and married a Frenchman in 1961. She was a huge star in France and in much of mainland Europe so it was a shrewd move to add the 31-year-old to the bill. While Clark's career in the UK had floundered somewhat, she was on the cusp of international stardom; her record, 'Downtown', a song written by her producer, Tony Hatch, would become a worldwide hit and top the American charts a couple of months later.

Also on the bill were Adamo, an Italian/Belgian singer who recorded mainly in French and who had recently had a string of big hits in France; les Surfs, a family group consisting of four brothers and two sisters born in Madagascar whose single, 'Reviens Vite Et Oublie' (a cover of the Ronettes' 'Be My Baby'), had recently topped the French charts for three months; and les Missiles, an Algerian group who were also having success in France.

'Here in cuckoo-clock land, the mountains are still echoing to the sound and impact of the British teenager. The climax of ITV's pop invasion was the Stones. The show was a roaring success, but the sight of Beatle haircuts and hipster jeans on the staid streets has caused the Swiss to stop and stare in amazement. When the judges announced their awards, there was no mention of British beat shows.'

Richard Sear
Daily Mirror
25 April 1964

Given the quality and carefully thought-out guests for the show, expectations were high before the results show was broadcast at 10.55 p.m. on 24 April on BBC 1. The winner turned out to be a Swiss programme called *Happy End*, a 'romantic fantasy'. *RSG!* was not the only disappointed British entry. *Thank Your Lucky Stars* was also up for the award – their edition featured the Beatles – as was *Beat City*, an ITV programme about the Liverpool beat boom, along with a show about Little Richard. By way of contrast, the BBC entered an edition of *The Good Old Days*, a variety show in the style of an old-time musical hall with audience and performers dressed in Edwardian costume. According to a BBC spokesman, the independent television companies' entries created the impression that 'no one in Britain gets their hair cut'.

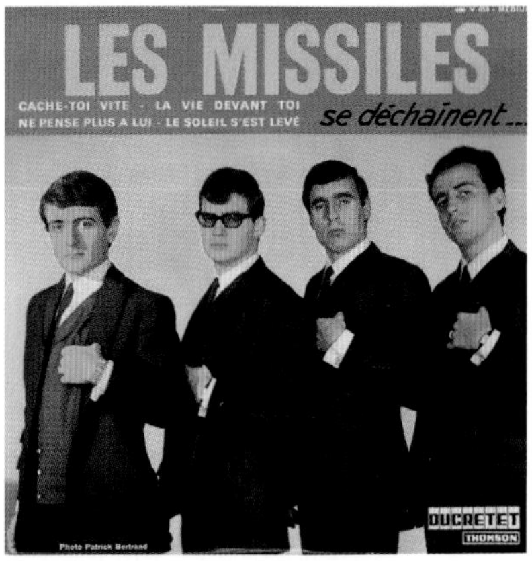

DAILY MIRROR, Saturday, April 25, 1964 PAGE 13

magazine MIRROR

TV Town—where beer is 10s a glass and they don't give 2d for the Beatles

From RICHARD SEAR
Montreux, Switzerland, Friday

HERE in cuckoo-clock-land, where time ticks past slowly, the mountains are still echoing to the sound of the Mersey beat and the impact of the British teenagers.

For this sleepy, lakeside resort, host to 400 world delegates gathered to watch the "Golden Rose of Montreux TV Contest" has been woken up by a barrage of British pop shows.

But the critics have given these shows a lukewarm reception.

Climax of ITV's pop invasion of Montreux was the visit of the Rolling Stones accompanied by forty teenagers.

They flew in last Sunday and recorded "Ready Steady, Go!" at the local casino.

The show was a roaring success with the Swiss teenagers who were invited to watch the recording.

Jeans

But the sight of Beatle haircuts and hipster jeans along the staid streets of this town, has caused the Swiss to stop and stare in amazement.

By the luck of the draw, ITV's entry "Thank Your Lucky Stars," was shown on the first day of the Festival, and top of the line-up of Liverpool stars was the Beatles.

The following day Rediffusion's unofficial entry "Beat City," with Dan Farson meeting some of the top Liverpool groups, was screened.

This was followed by Granada TV's "Little Richard," another beat show

Delegates and journalists from all over the world gave these programmes a cool reception—even the Beatles failed to raise much enthusiasm.

BBC Light Entertainment Chief Tom Sloane summed up: "Everybody has the impression that we don't get our hair cut."

The BBC's entry "The Good Old Days," with Jimmy Edwards, helped to change this image.

The old fashioned music-hall style had more impact than all Merseyside on the assembled TV experts.

Ideas

This seven-day Festival costing £100,000 and now in its fourth year attracted 24 entries from 21 countries, including Russia and America.

The impression I got however is that the world is rapidly running out of ideas for television entertainment.

There have been five shows with the theme of producers scratching their heads for something new, before putting on a programme.

There has been no shortage of publicity stunts.

ABC TV took journalists out on the new Swiss hydrofoil over Lake Geneva, to announce a change of programmes.

This £160,000 launch on stilts is the latest attraction to this millionaires' playground, where you can pay 10s. for a glass of beer—but where they don't seem to give tuppence for the Beatles.

In fact, when the judges announced their awards today there was no mention of British beat shows.

The top award went to Switzerland with "Happy End," a romantic fantasy which, ironically, included a regiment of guitar players.

Above: Les Missiles
Left: The *Daily Mirror* were typically shocked, this time by the price of drinks abroad

WINNERS AND TOP BEAT BANDS

Below: The annual *NME* Poll Winners Concert was one of the biggest events on the musical calendar in the first half of the 60s

Opposite: The stars perform at the concert (clockwise from top left): Gerry Marsden of Gerry and the Pacemakers; Freddie of Freddie and the Dreamers; the Beatles; Cliff Richard and the Shadows; Mick Jagger

Any disappointment felt by the band – and it's doubtful whether there was any – over failing to win the Golden Rose was subsumed by appearances in Norwich and Luton on the All Stars '64 Tour on the Friday and Saturday night after they returned to the UK. This was followed by a Sunday appearance at London's Empire Pool, Wembley, where the Stones were included in the annual *New Musical Express* Poll Winners' Concert.

Much had changed in the last twelve months. Only a year earlier, Mick, Keith and Brian were at the Royal Albert Hall as guests of the Beatles; here, for the first time, the Stones were on the same bill as the Liverpool band, and giving them a run for their money. In fact, on the exact same date in 1963, the Rolling Stones were playing to a few hundred people at the Ricky Tick Club in Windsor, without even a record deal to their name, nor one in sight. Now, on Sunday 26 April 1964, they were playing to 10,000 wildly enthusiastic fans.

The Poll Winners' Concert got underway at 2.30 p.m. with Derek Johnson, the features editor of the NME, introducing the Joe Loss Band. They were followed by the Swinging Blue Jeans, Joe Brown and the Bruvvers, the Dave Clark Five, Big Dee Irwin, the Shadows – who then backed Cliff Richard – Manfred Mann, Brian Poole and the Tremeloes, and Billy J. Kramer with the Dakotas, before it was time for the Stones, who were introduced by Jimmy Savile.

Led out by Brian, the Stones tore into a frantic version of 'Not Fade Away', with Brian on harmonica, Keith playing his 1959 Harmony Meteor guitar and Mick with his maracas. Watching footage of the concert, it's amazing to see that Jagger already has his moves down pat, with many of the

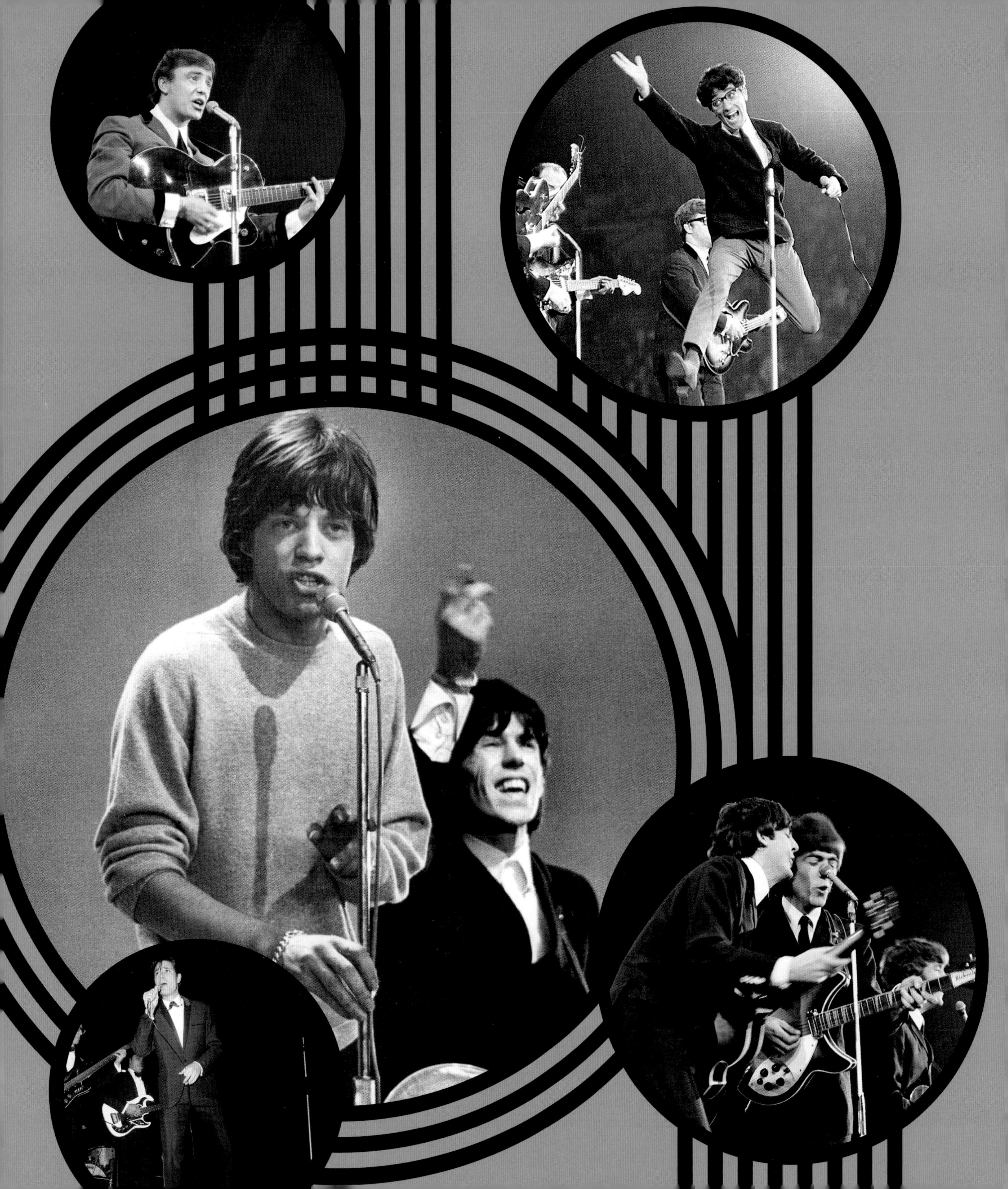

mannerisms that still pervade his performances fully in place. They then played 'I Just Want To Make Love To You', with Mick wringing every ounce of suggestiveness from the lyrics; once again, Brian plays harmonica and superbly too.

'This is Charlie Boy, and as you don't get to see as much of him as the rest of us we're going to get him to introduce the next one,' says Mick.

'Thank you, we'd like to play a Bo Diddley number, "I'm Alright"... I hope you are,' Charlie replies. On this song, Brian plays his Gretsch 6118 and as they rip into the Diddley classic it's hard not to be reminded of what it must have been like at the Crawdaddy when they would stretch out on this number, and others like it, making them last way longer than on these truncated package tours, TV and radio performances.

'The Stones received the second biggest ovation ... they were a fantastic sight, with hip-movements and wear-what-you-like clothes, which included a shiny blue leather waistcoat, a striped waistcoat, a shortie jacket, and a blue roll-neck sweater. I was sitting two rows from the rostrum and couldn't hear any of it, through the screams.'

Graeme Andrews
New Musical Express
2 May 1964

The Stones were followed by Gerry and the Pacemakers, the Searchers and the Beatles – who were presented with their awards by actor Roger Moore, the star of TV's *The Saint* and who would later play James Bond – before finally the Merseybeats closed the show.

The broadcast was split into two halves with the Stones in the first show that was aired on Sunday 3 May and the Beatles and others in the second show a week later. Also at the concert was the American DJ Murray the K, who secured an audiotape of the show, which he used to help promote the band on his New York City radio programme.

The following night, so as not to be outdone by ITV, the BBC were at the Royal Albert Hall to record the Top Beat Pop Prom for both TV and radio, compered by Alan Freeman. Aside from the Stones, this felt way more conservative than the Poll Winners' Concert, as could be witnessed by much of the country when it was broadcast at 9.20 p.m. on Monday 25 May for forty-five minutes. It featured Kenny Ball and his Jazzmen, Freddie and the Dreamers, Billy J. Kramer with the Dakotas and Brian Poole and the Tremeloes. At both the matinee and evening shows, the Stones played 'Not Fade Away', 'Hi-Heel Sneakers' and 'I'm Alright', although it's unclear which of these songs were broadcast on television and radio.

Above: Backstage at the Top Beat Pop Prom, Royal Albert Hall, London 27 April
Opposite: Decca Records promoting their success in the *NME* polls

'Parents do not like the Rolling Stones ... They do not want their sons to grow up like them; they do not want their daughters to marry them. Mother and daughter cannot worship at the same shrine. The moment that the mothers, and fathers, and politicians, and employers, and foreigners, and Ella Fitzgerald, and crowned heads grew to love the Beatles, the floating fan went over to the Stones.'

Maureen Cleave
Evening Standard
11 May 1964

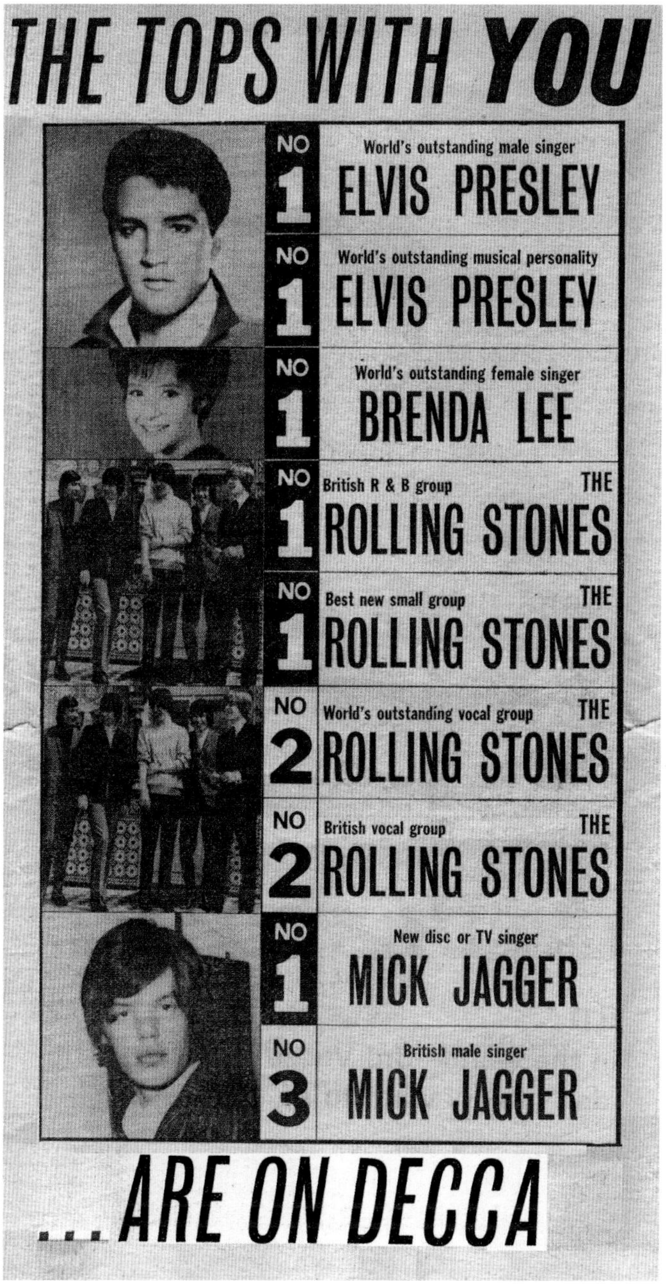

With May taken up with ballroom gigs, some more dates on the All-Star '64 Tour, a little recording and TV and radio work, it meant that the Stones had worked every day but two during the month. It culminated with another big show at Wembley's Empire Pool: the Pop Hit Parade, which also featured Wayne Fontana and the Mindbenders, the Hollies, the Swinging Blue Jeans, the Merseybeats, the McKinleys, the Undertakers, Julie Grant and Adam Faith. This show was not filmed.

The following day, the Rolling Stones flew to America ... and nothing would ever quite be the same again – either for them or for the rest of us.

MONKEYS, ELEPHANTS, NEANDERTHALS AND THE ROLLING STONES

Nineteen sixty-four was the year that British groups grabbed Americans by their ears, practically forcing them to take notice of what pop music could, and should, sound like. It's not that American artists were making bad records, it's in part a reflection of the fact that America was still a polarised nation, with segregation a crippling cancer, particularly in the Southern states.

Tamla Motown, the record company started by Berry Gordy in Detroit, was beginning to find its feet and some of the label's fabulous records had already influenced both the Beatles and the Stones, as well as other British bands. By covering records by black artists, British bands somehow made them more acceptable to American radio in the first instance and American teenagers soon afterwards.

The Stones covered Marvin Gaye's 'Can I Get A Witness' on their first LP, while the Beatles covered three Motown hits on their second album: Smokey Robinson's 'You Really Got A Hold On Me', Barrett Strong's 'Money' and the Marvelettes' 'Please Mr Postman'. America was waking up to the magic of Motown and in the middle of May, the label had its first No. 1 record when Mary Wells' 'My Guy' topped the Hot 100. As the Stones landed in New York at Kennedy Airport on board BOAC flight 505 at 3.30 p.m. on 1 June, the Beatles were topping the American charts with 'Love Me Do'. The reason their first UK single, released in 1962, had become their fourth US No. 1 was down to the fact that Capitol Records, EMI's company in America, initially refused to release the Beatles' records, deeming them unsellable.

Left: The shaggy haired Old English Sheepdog brought to the press conference at the airport

Below: The Stones surrounded by fans on Broadway

Opposite: A London Records promotional postcard to celebrate the arrival of the Stones in America

DAILY MIRROR, Tuesday, June 9, 1964 PAGE 17

DISC GUEST COLUMN

by JACK HUTTON, Editor of 'Melody Maker', now touring America with the Rolling Stones

Stones stir up the fans—and the sniggers

The Rolling Stones as seen by Sallon . . . (from the left) Charlie Watts, Brian Jones, Keith Richard, Bill Wyman, Mick Jagger.

San Antonio, Texas, Monday.

BRITAIN'S Rolling Stones group are being treated as freaks in America. People gasp in amazement when they appear at airports, in hotel lobbies and in the streets.

Shouts of "Where are your razors?" and "Get your hair cut" are commonplace. Men have whistled at Mick Jagger and Co., and one girl asked: "Do they wear lipstick and eye make-up and carry purses?" When I assured her they didn't she seemed disappointed!

On the famed Hollywood Palace TV show—the "Sunday Night at the London Palladium" of the West Coast—Donald O'Connor said to Dean Martin after watching the Stones perform: "I didn't know whether to applaud them, or set traps!"

'Five More Freaks'

In New York, Hollywood and here in Texas, no one really takes the Stones seriously. In a country that dotes on freaks, the Stones are just five more.

But the boys are not allowing the atmosphere to get them down. They are swimming and sunbathing, making friends with American fans, and giving as good as they get in the verbal exchanges.

In America the popularity of British groups is patchy. Some areas of this vast country don't dig them. Others go wild.

San Bernardino, 62 miles from Hollywood, California, is a Stones stronghold. They could get the freedom of the place. We knew something was afoot when screaming girls met the Stones' bus at the Swing Auditorium.

It became more obvious with nearly 5,000 squealing girls in the auditorium.

Girls, dressed in tight shorts, some with bare feet and bare midriffs, went wild and threw jelly-babies and love-letters at the boys. They hoisted banners saying: "We love the Stones," and then started invading the stage like dive-bombers, one at a time.

Guns

Huge policemen with white skidlids and low-slung revolvers climbed on to the stage and brandished truncheons.

Still the girls got through. One grabbed singer Mick Jagger round the waist and dragged him 15ft. across the stage. Three 6ft. policemen ripped her off.

Guitarist Keith Richard kept on playing with a girl round his neck.

Brian Jones nearly had his harmonica pushed down his throat.

The boys beamed happily as they tumbled off the stage. "Just like home," they said.

HERE in Texas the boys are starring with American singer Bobby Vee.

Stetson-hatted locals can hardly believe their eyes as the Stones amble about with their shoulder-length hair. And when they went swimming in the pool at their hotel, residents came to the windows to stare.

Frights!

One man was heard to say: "Shucks, I thought they were girls wearing one-piece bathing suits."

How do the Stones reply to all these cracks? As if by a pre-arranged signal, all five simultaneously pull down the skin under their eyes and push up their noses. Believe me, it's frightening.

STOP PRESS TOP TEN

Last week's figures in brackets

1 (1) YOU'RE MY WORLD—Cilla Black
2 (3) IT'S OVER—Roy Orbison
3 (7) HERE I GO AGAIN—Hollies
4 (5) THE RISE AND FALL OF FLINGEL BUNT—Shadows
5 (12) SOMEONE, SOMEONE—Brian Poole and the Tremeloes
6 (4) CONSTANTLY—Cliff Richard
7 (11) MY GUY—Mary Wells
8 (6) NO PARTICULAR PLACE TO GO—Chuck Berry
9 (2) JULIET—Four Pennies
10 (17) SHOUT—Lulu and the Luvers

By arrangement with Melody Maker

Above: Back home in Britain the *Daily Mirror* is suitably shocked at the coverage the Stones receive in America

In the first week of June 1964, the US charts were dominated by Britain's beat groups. On the Hot 100 when the Stones arrived in New York, aside from four Beatles' singles, were Peter and Gordon (No.7), Billy J. Kramer (No.8 and No.71), the Dave Clark Five (No.12 and No.54), the Bachelors (No.20), the Swinging Blue Jeans (No.46), Gerry and the Pacemakers (No.47), and the Searchers (No.50 and No.68) – all of which were currently rising up the charts. Trailing in their wake were the Stones, whose 'Not Fade Away' had entered the charts on 2 May at No.96 and by 30 May had crawled its way to No.82. It was thanks, in no small measure, to Murray the K that it had got even that high; he was one of the band's few supporters in the US.

Waiting to greet the Stones at JFK were 500 screaming fans, yet they were also met with cries of 'Get your hair cut!' and 'Are you the Beatles?' – not from the fans, of course, but from passengers and airport staff. A press conference for about a hundred newsmen was presided over by Murray the K and a PR man from London Records, who had had arranged for an Old English Sheepdog to be there for the obligatory photos. The dog naturally drew comparisons over its hairstyle and those of the band.

Elizabeth Monger and a friend from Ozone Park, Queens, a suburb of New York, were there to give the Stones bunches of flowers. When a reporter asked what prompted them to wear their hair so long, the Stones' reply was simply,

‘Why, this is the style set by Charles I.’ Listening and watching interviews from this time, full of their deadpan humour, is really very amusing. Like the Beatles a few months before them, the Stones generally befuddled American journalists, especially those of middle to advancing years … which was most of them.

From the airport, limos took the Stones to Manhattan, where they were booked into the Hotel Astor on Times Square. There was mayhem at the hotel; fans invaded the lobby and the band had great difficulty even getting to their rooms on the third floor, which they were sharing. Mick and Keith were in one, Bill and Brian in another, Charlie shared with Loog Oldham and Stu with Eric Easton.

Later, the Stones went to WINS to appear on *Murray the K's Swinging Soiree* for what was their first live interview on American radio. It included the revelation that on the following day Charlie would be twenty-three years old, not twenty-two as all the band's press releases had to this point stated (it took years for the press to get Charlie's age correct). Their appearance on the show lasted for three hours, after which they went to the city's famed Peppermint Lounge until the early hours. When the show was over and before they left, Murray the K played them the Valentinos' version of ‘It's All Over Now’, which would prove to be a pivotal moment in early Stones history.

Top: Keith signs autographs on Broadway
Above: Times Square in 1964

'Murray the K gave us "It's All Over Now" which was great because ... he turned us on to something good. It was a great record by the Valentinos but it wasn't a hit.'

Mick Jagger
October 1968

After breakfast the next day, the Stones went to WMCA radio at 10 a.m. This was another influential Top 40 station, and home to 'The Good Guys' – 'Dandy' Dan Daniel, Harry Harrison, Gary Stevens, Frankie Crocker, Dean Anthony, B. Mitchel Reed, Jack Spector, Ed Baer and Frank Stickel. They were among the earliest personality jocks on American radio.

Following an afternoon of sightseeing and then dinner, the Stones went to WABC-TV at around 11.30 p.m. to tape an appearance on *The Les Crane Show*. Their debut on American television was an hour-long phone in which the band answered questions, not all of them relevant or even nice.

Opposite: Posing with DJ Murray 'The K' Kaufman in New York

On 3 June, the band flew to Los Angeles, where they stayed at the Beverly Hilton. Having checked in, they then went to the Hollywood Playhouse, on Hollywood and Vine, to record a segment for ABC TV's *Hollywood Palace*, compered by Dean Martin. According to Bob Bonis, the American tour manager for this first Stones visit, 'Dean Martin was a little out of it and made an awful lot of fun of the band. The producer gave them money to go out and buy themselves uniforms. We said, "They don't wear uniforms." Dean Martin and I got into an argument, and Keith was about to pop him one with his guitar.'

The *Hollywood Palace* appearance was broadcast on 13 June, on the night that the Stones were playing the Music Hall Auditorium in Omaha, Nebraska, to a crowd of 650 people, on the fifth date of their tour. All that America saw of the two songs the Stones recorded for *Hollywood Palace* was forty-five seconds of 'I Just Want To Make Love To You', along with the wise-cracking Martin: 'Their hair isn't long, it's just smaller foreheads and higher eyebrows.' The show featured a baby elephant, and separately a trampoline artist who Martin introduced by saying, 'That's the father of the Rolling Stones. He's been trying to kill himself ever since.' Three months later on 25 September, a short clip of 'Not Fade Away', recorded on 3 June, was broadcast on another edition of *Hollywood Palace*. The following day, after shopping for clothes at Beau Gentry on North Vine Street in Hollywood, there was a trip to Malibu Beach and then in the evening a visit to RCA Recording Studios, where they would soon record some of their definitive 1960s hits. On Friday 5 June, a bus took the band to San Bernardino, where the Stones played for 4,500 roaring fans at their first-ever concert on American soil.

On 6 June, they flew to San Antonio to play the State Fair. This was the biggest crowd of the whole tour, but they were not there to see the Rolling Stones – country singer George Jones, a Texan favourite, along with singer Bobby Vee, were a bigger draw. The Stones spent the night in San Antonio, as they were back at the State Fair for another matinee and evening performance the following day; yet again they followed some performing monkeys on to the stage.

On the weekend they spent in San Antonio, 'Not Fade Away' had stalled at No.82 on Billboard's Hot 100, having not had the benefit of any gigs or TV, and very little radio to move it along any further. Even after the small amount of TV, it only climbed four places the following week, not helped by the fact that their only network TV show, *Hollywood Palace*, had failed to feature the single.

'The Stones are a serious threat to the Beatles' worldwide popularity. The American people are going to go absolutely wild for them. Their appearance will create the initial interest, just as it did with the Beatles. But when it sinks in that the Stones are a completely different kettle of fish, their popularity will sky-rocket.'

Murray the K

'NBC, CBS and Ed Sullivan turned the Stones down. They could appear on the Hollywood Palace show, on condition that they could not perform on another TV show for twenty-one days before or after their appearance. Besides terrible treatment at the hands of Dean Martin, who literally vilified and degraded them in a vindictive manner, for some reason, their hit record "Not Fade Away" was cut out completely.'

Jackie Kallen
Teenbeat magazine

Opposite top: Posing with the elephants that also starred on *Hollywood Palace*, a typically cheesy variety show; bottom: host Dean Martin
Following pages: On the roof of WHK Radio, Pittsburgh where the Stones appeared on the *Clark Race Show*

Probably on 2 June, when the band were still in New York, they went to WPIX's studios at Second Avenue and East 42nd Street in Midtown Manhattan to record an appearance on *The Clay Cole Teen Show*. It was a local New York station with limited reach outside the metropolitan area.

It is thought that the Stones made their musical debut on American TV on 6 June when they did 'Tell Me', Mick and Keith's song that was to be released as the band's second US single, followed by Chuck Berry's 'Carol' and, of course, 'Not Fade Away'; it is possible that one or all of these songs were shown again on 20 June when the Stones were back in New York City, but no one is entirely certain and none of the TV listings in newspapers show either appearance.

Cole, who was just a couple of years older than Mick and Keith and younger than Bill, was later referred to by Loog Oldham as 'a stagger-brained, lacquered pimp, with a smile and demeanour so cut-out and fake that we all thought we'd stopped off on the wrong set and were in *Hogan's Heroes* meets *The Twilight Zone*'. He was, like most people they encountered on their first US tour, somewhat incredulous, and mostly just downright rude.

Cole described Brian Jones's 'Prince Valiant' hairdo and kept pressing Mick to make comparisons between the Stones and the Beatles; all the while referring to the Stones as 'that other British group'. They were asked the dumbest of dumb questions: 'You guys all dress different – how come?' to which Mick proffered the reply, 'Because we are all different persons.'

From San Antonio, the Stones flew to Chicago, and upon arrival in the Windy City, arguably the home of the blues, they checked into the Water Tower Inn. The following day, they were at WMAQ for an appearance on *The Jack Eigen Show*, which broadcast live from Studio G in downtown Chicago.

The 50-year-old Eigen was yet another unsympathetic radio interviewer, constantly plugging himself and trying, vainly, to send up the Stones. After they left the studio they carried on listening to Eigen's show on the car radio and he carried on making sarcastic comments. A woman called the station, accusing the Stones of being 'dirty and not combing their hair'; Eigan's reply was, 'They may have more in their group than they think' – the implication being that the band had such dirty hair they probably had fleas.

The Stones were in the car on their way to Chess Records, the home to many of their heroes, including Muddy Waters, Chuck Berry, Bo Diddley and Howlin' Wolf. For Mick and Keith, still both just twenty years old, this was like going to church, especially as it was not that long ago that both of them had been writing to Chicago record shops to buy hard-to-get Chess Record releases.

It was the band who wanted to record at Chess, along with their house engineer, Ron Malo, somewhat against Loog Oldham's wishes. The Stones immediately set up their equipment and as soon as Malo began working his magic they started turning out some great-sounding records. 'It's All Over Now' was first up, followed by Muddy Waters' 'I Can't Be Satisfied', an early version of Irma Thomas's 'Time Is On My Side' and a band composition, 'Stewed and Keefed', an instrumental featuring Stu on piano.

The following day they were back at Chess, recording more songs, including tracks for 5 x 5 along with some songs that appeared on the band's second album. Willie Dixon, whose compositions the Stones had already recorded, visited them at Chess and they recorded 'Down In The Bottom', a song he'd written that was initially made famous by Howlin' Wolf. While they were at Chess, Brian Jones talked to Bo Diddley on the phone and the contents of their conversation was reported in the *Chicago Daily News* a few days later: 'We joked a bit about America, and then he got very serious and sad about how hard it is for the Negro to make it here in the States, unless he's in jazz.'

Prior to playing Omaha on 13 June, the Stones played Minneapolis, and on Sunday 14 June they were at Detroit Olympia Stadium. The 40-year-old building had been the third largest stadium of its kind when it was built, but the Stones could muster only a thousand fans in the 15,000 capacity building. It seems likely that WXYZ Channel 7 in the city broadcast some or all of a Stones song on a news programme.

Three days later and it was Pittsburgh's Westview Park in the evening, but during the day there was a recording for an appearance on a TV show hosted by Clark Race, a local DJ whose *Dance Party* aired on KDKA on Saturday afternoons; it's been suggested that they performed 'Route 66' as well as being interviewed. The following day it was Cleveland, Ohio, although they were not there to play a gig, but to appear on KYW-TV's *Mike Douglas Show*.

Unusually, the Stones mimed to two songs and played two songs live. Both 'Carol' and 'Not Fade Away' were performed in front of 200 or so teenagers with the band miming to 'Tell Me' and 'I Just Want To Make Love To You'. The latter two numbers were both A- and B-side of their new US single, released a couple of days earlier. 'Tell Me' would eventually climb to No.24 on the Hot 100.

On Friday night, the Stones played Harrisburg, Pennsylvania's Farm Show arena; the capacity was 7,500 but there were only 1,000 fans at the gig. The previous evening they were due to play New Haven Arena, but there was so little interest in buying tickets that the show was called off. Back home in England, the *Melody Maker* reported Mick Jagger as saying, 'I give the Stones about another two years. I'm saving for my future. I bank all my song royalties.'

However, things looked up again on their final day of touring in America, Saturday 20 June, when they played New York's prestigious Carnegie Hall. Having arrived in New York's Park Sheraton Hotel at 870 Seventh Avenue in the early hours of the morning, the Stones went to the venue around lunchtime, in time for an afternoon matinee show that also featured Cathy Carr, the Counts, a doo-wop group, and Jay and the Americans; they played again that evening and both shows were very nearly sold out.

Above: Chuck Berry on stage at the Star Club in Hamburg, Germany, June 1964

Right: Howlin' Wolf

Opposite: Muddy Waters at Fairfield Halls in Croydon in 1964

The Stones' first US album was released two days before they arrived in America, and was dubbed *England's Newest Hit Makers* by London Records. It was essentially the UK album with 'Not Fade Away' substituted for Bo Diddley's 'Mona'; it was different because the Decca LP, with no name or title on the cover, was just too risky an option. A week after the Stones' Carnegie Hall concerts, *England's Newest Hit Makers* crept into the *Billboard* album charts at No.104. London Records were quoted in the same magazine on 27 June, the day the album charted, reporting that the band's album was 'pushing the 100,000 sales mark'. Elsewhere in the same issue, a review of 'Tell Me' was clear: 'Neanderthal music at its best. The British group offers a crude chant and the rockiest sound around.'

Today, many people claim to have seen the Stones on their first ever US tour, but the truth is they are probably confused and it was either on their second or even third tour that they saw them. The band did just nine shows in eight cities, and there were probably less than 20,000 people in total who saw them perform on this first American trip.

Just like in Britain, American TV and radio were slow to catch on to them, but there is no doubting the part both played in establishing the band and paving the way for a second, much bigger, tour just four months later.

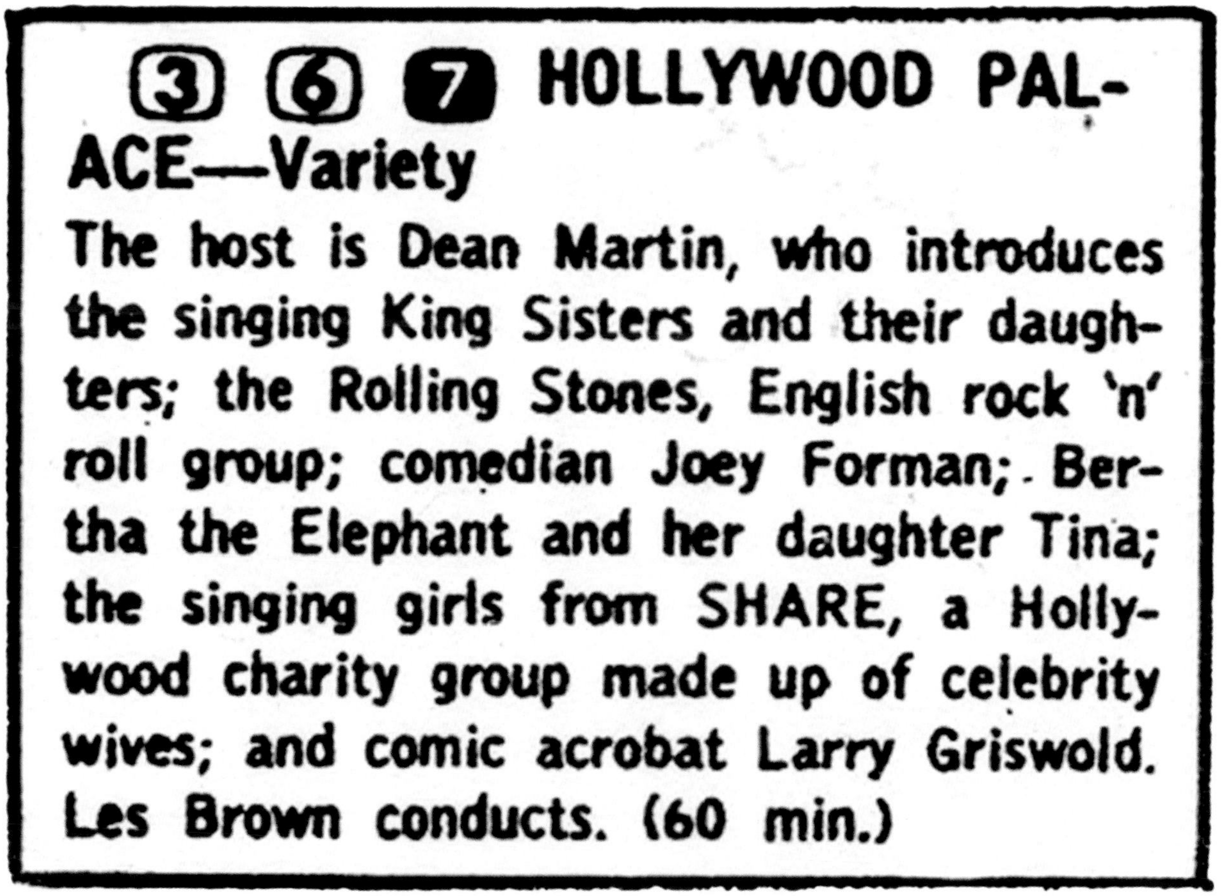

3 6 7 HOLLYWOOD PALACE—Variety

The host is Dean Martin, who introduces the singing King Sisters and their daughters; the Rolling Stones, English rock 'n' roll group; comedian Joey Forman; Bertha the Elephant and her daughter Tina; the singing girls from SHARE, a Hollywood charity group made up of celebrity wives; and comic acrobat Larry Griswold. Les Brown conducts. (60 min.)

WHEN TOP GEAR REALLY WAS TOP GEAR

With 'It's All Over Now' debuting on the UK charts during the first week of July at No.25, it then climbed to the No.2 spot the following week, kept from the top by the Animals with their take on the traditional blues song, 'The House Of The Rising Sun'. However, by 18 July, 'It's All Over Now' became the first Rolling Stones single to top the charts in Britain.

Two days earlier, on the afternoon of Thursday 16 July, the Stones were back at Pye Studios, close to London's Marble Arch, to record another Radio Luxembourg show – *The Teen and Twenty Disc Club*. Hosted by Jimmy Savile, it was broadcast at 10 p.m. each Wednesday, so it seems likely that the edition featuring the Stones went out the following week on 23 July.

On Radio Luxembourg, the Stones were plugging 'It's All Over Now', just as they were the following day when they made their second appearance on *The Joe Loss Pop Show* on the BBC's Light Programme. They were at the BBC's Playhouse Theatre in Charing Cross, which had been a studio since 1951, having previously been a regular theatre. In 1934, Alec Guinness had made his debut there on the London stage. During its time as a BBC studio, the 650-seat theatre played host to the recording of some classic BBC radio comedy shows, among them *The Goon Show*, *Steptoe and Son* and *Hancock's Half Hour*.

For *The Joe Loss Pop Show*, the Stones played five songs, including the UK radio debut of 'If You Need Me'. The song, along with 'Confessin' The Blues', which they also performed live on the show, was included on their EP, 5 x 5, that was due for release in the middle of August.

At the end of June, the BBC contracted the Stones to appear on a new Light Programme show, one that was to be presented by the host of *Saturday Club*. It still had not been given a name and on the contract it's simply called '*The Brian Matthew Show* (working title)'. The contract was also made out

Above and right: Rehearsals for a BBC radio broadcast at the Playhouse Theatre

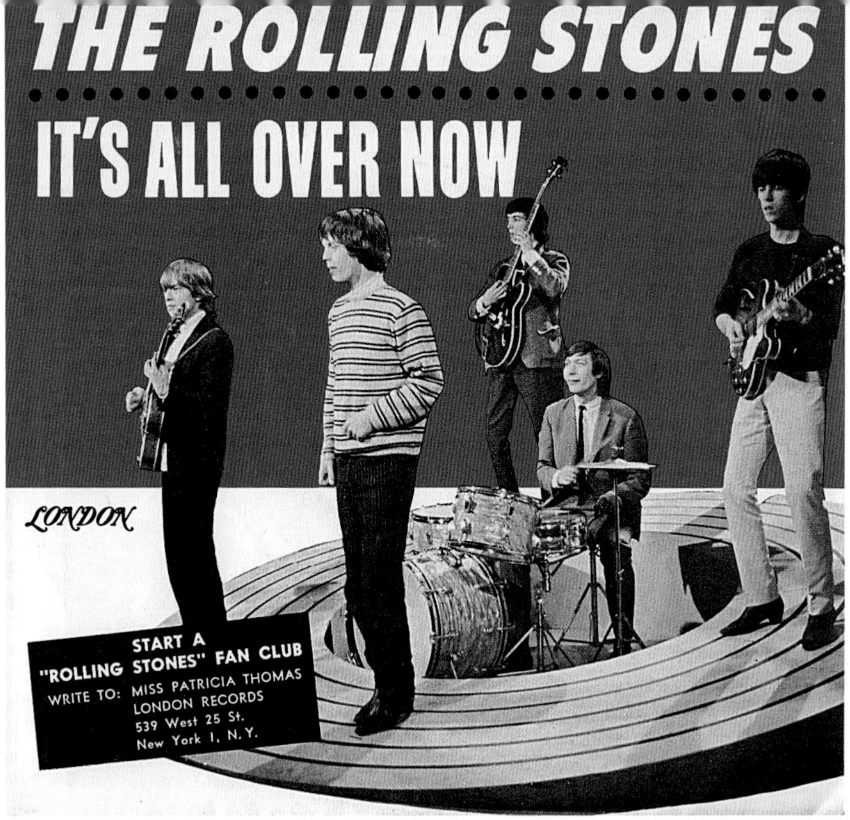

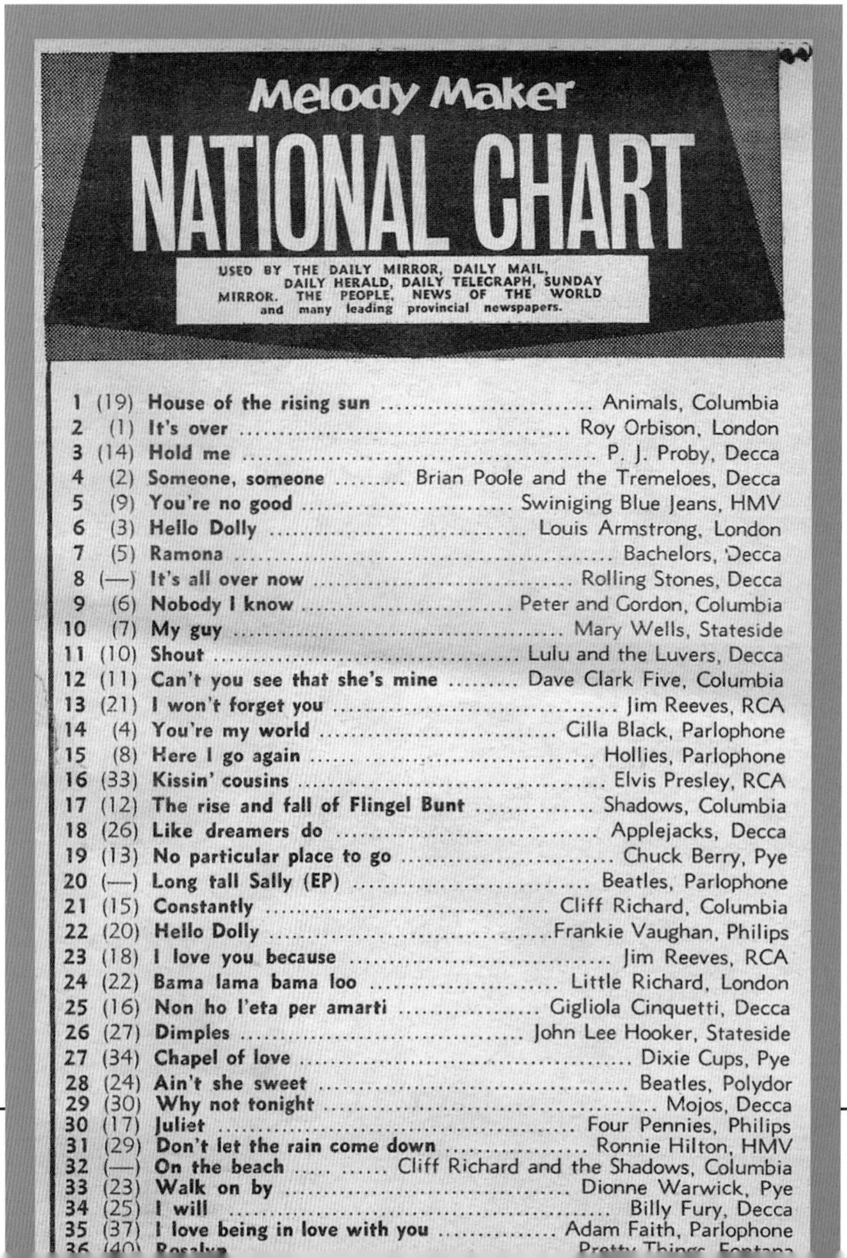

Melody Maker

NATIONAL CHART

USED BY THE DAILY MIRROR, DAILY MAIL, DAILY HERALD, DAILY TELEGRAPH, SUNDAY MIRROR, THE PEOPLE, NEWS OF THE WORLD and many leading provincial newspapers.

1	(19)	House of the rising sun	Animals, Columbia
2	(1)	It's over	Roy Orbison, London
3	(14)	Hold me	P. J. Proby, Decca
4	(2)	Someone, someone	Brian Poole and the Tremeloes, Decca
5	(9)	You're no good	Swiniging Blue Jeans, HMV
6	(3)	Hello Dolly	Louis Armstrong, London
7	(5)	Ramona	Bachelors, Decca
8	(—)	It's all over now	Rolling Stones, Decca
9	(6)	Nobody I know	Peter and Gordon, Columbia
10	(7)	My guy	Mary Wells, Stateside
11	(10)	Shout	Lulu and the Luvers, Decca
12	(11)	Can't you see that she's mine	Dave Clark Five, Columbia
13	(21)	I won't forget you	Jim Reeves, RCA
14	(4)	You're my world	Cilla Black, Parlophone
15	(8)	Here I go again	Hollies, Parlophone
16	(33)	Kissin' cousins	Elvis Presley, RCA
17	(12)	The rise and fall of Flingel Bunt	Shadows, Columbia
18	(26)	Like dreamers do	Applejacks, Decca
19	(13)	No particular place to go	Chuck Berry, Pye
20	(—)	Long tall Sally (EP)	Beatles, Parlophone
21	(15)	Constantly	Cliff Richard, Columbia
22	(20)	Hello Dolly	Frankie Vaughan, Philips
23	(18)	I love you because	Jim Reeves, RCA
24	(22)	Bama lama bama loo	Little Richard, London
25	(16)	Non ho l'eta per amarti	Gigliola Cinquetti, Decca
26	(27)	Dimples	John Lee Hooker, Stateside
27	(34)	Chapel of love	Dixie Cups, Pye
28	(24)	Ain't she sweet	Beatles, Polydor
29	(30)	Why not tonight	Mojos, Decca
30	(17)	Juliet	Four Pennies, Philips
31	(29)	Don't let the rain come down	Ronnie Hilton, HMV
32	(—)	On the beach	Cliff Richard and the Shadows, Columbia
33	(23)	Walk on by	Dionne Warwick, Pye
34	(25)	I will	Billy Fury, Decca
35	(37)	I love being in love with you	Adam Faith, Parlophone
36	(40)	Rosalyn	Pretty Things, Fontana

Above left: The US single release of 'It's All Over Now'

Above right: An American advert for the single's release

Right: Weekly charts were supplied to UK record shops to display in their windows

Opposite: The *Daily Mirror* celebrates the Stones' first UK No.1 single

PAGE 2 DAILY MIRROR, Tuesday, July 7, 1964

TOPS! THE STONES ROLL UP TO No 1

By PATRICK DONCASTER

THE five shaggy-haired Rolling Stones rolled to the top of the Melody Maker pop chart for the first time last night. But only one of them was around to hear the big news.

He was the longest-haired Stone of them all, Brian Jones, 19, who plays guitar and harmonica. He had postponed a holiday trip to New York because of "business interests."

THE LONELY ONE

Brian Jones . . .. on his own in London. The other Rolling Stones were on holiday.

Lead singer Mick Jagger, 20, was on holiday at Ibiza, a Mediterranean island off Spain, with drummer Charlie Watts, 22.

Keith Richard, 20, and Bill Wyman, 22, were "around the South Coast somewhere."

The record that did the trick was their fourth single, "It's All Over Now," recorded in Chicago last month and issued only ten days ago.

Eclipsed

Brian was delighted at the news. He said: "I didn't like the number when I heard it on a radio. But I like it now."

Last week's chart-topping Animals group slip to No. 2 with "House of the Rising Sun."

Both groups are likely to be eclipsed by the Beatles next week with their film single "A Hard Day's Night," due for issue on Friday with 500,000 advance orders.

Top Ten Stop Press—Centre Pages

with the name Bill Perks; it would be the last BBC radio show before Bill changed his name officially, by deed poll, to Bill Wyman – he hated the name Perks!

By the time the Stones were back at the Playhouse Theatre, on the evening of 17 July, a few hours after they recorded *The Joe Loss Pop Show*, the BBC had come up with a title for Matthew's new show, naming it *Top Gear*. The title was actually the result of a national competition that was won by Susan Warne. The first edition of *Top Gear* was broadcast the night before the Stones recorded their appearance and had featured the Beatles, Dusty Springfield and Mark Wynter.

The Stones, naturally, did 'It's All Over Now', as well as 'Around And Around' and 'If You Need Me'. They also did two songs that they had not previously played on radio or TV. The first was a cast-iron blues classic, Muddy Waters' 'I Can't Be Satisfied', a song that the Stones had recorded at Chess in June that would be included on their second album.

Muddy had left the Delta in 1943 and a couple of years later, having lived in Chicago, he switched from acoustic to electric guitar, a move that galvanized his career. While continuing to play traditional Delta bottleneck, using the neck of a bottle to slide along the neck of the guitar, the electric guitar transformed his sound and helped 'invent' post-war Chicago blues.

In 1948, Leonard Chess – the co-founder of Chess Records – released Muddy Waters' 'I Feel Like Going Home' coupled with 'I Can't Be Satisfied'; the latter was a reworking of 'I Be's Troubled', a song Muddy recorded for Alan Lomax at Stovall's Plantation, where Muddy worked, in 1941. The record sold out in Chicago on the day of release; Muddy later recalled that he even had trouble buying a copy. This was truly the Stones paying homage.

British Broadcasting Corporation Confidential

AN AUDIENCE RESEARCH REPORT 6

(Week 30). LR/64/1269

TOP GEAR

With Brian Matthew

Producer: Bernard Andrews

Thursday, 23rd July, 1964. 10.00-11.55 pm, Light Programme.

1. Size of audience (based on results of the Survey of Listening and Viewing shown in full on the daily audience Barometer).

The estimated audiences for each half hour was 1.5%, 1.2%, 0.8% and 0.7% (including 6%, 4%, 3%, and 3% of the Sound only public).

2. Reaction of audience (based on questionnaires completed by a sample of the audience. This sample, 83 in number, is the 5% of the B Division of the Listening Panel who heard all or most of the broadcast).

The reactions of thes sample of the audience were distributed as follows:-

A+	A	B	C	C-
%	%	%	%	%
11	22	38	17	12

giving an APPRECIATION INDEX of 51. Last week's Top Gear gained 53.

3. About two thirds of the sample audience seem to have been dissatisfied with Top Gear this week. Apparently it was not so much the standard of performance or the manner of the compere, Brian Matthew, or even, really, the music in itself, as that it was all on at the wrong time: 'Must we have this sort of music at this time of night?'; 'Far too restless at this time of night'; 'The wrong sort of music for a late hour'. Several admitted that what they called 'trashy pop' was not in their line, but did not want it banned altogether. They just felt that the last couple of hours in the day might be devoted to the sort of soothing and melodious music they themselves enjoy - Joe Loss and Nat King Cole were specified, for instance. There were a few other complaints - Brian Matthew is 'a model of insincerity' and is heard too often, none of the performers who were there sounded 'as good as on their records', both Elkie Brooks and The Rolling Stones were 'terrible', Arthur Greenslade and the Gee Men provided too loud a backing, especially for P.J. Proby, and the predominance of just a few groups during the two hours made it all a bit boring. But the main trouble for most, evidently, was just that, not caring for 'this kind of music', they were the more irritated to find it on for two hours at night.

4. The smaller proportion who did like the programme were apparently very pleased with it, however. It all added up to what one called 'real entertainment', and, though a few said they only liked parts of it, most who praised it seem to have had few reservations: 'The best pop programme done by the BBC'; 'A marvellous change from that dreary Music to Midnight. Three hearty cheers'; 'The most fab music'. Joe Brown and his Bruvvers were called exceptionally good by a few, the Frank Ifield record was popular, apparently, and so was Louis Armstrong's Moon River. 'Lively and encouraging' one listener called it all and Brian Matthew evidently added to the gay and pleasant atmosphere with his keeness and easy manner; he does not gush or talk too much, it was said, but still 'keeps everything going with a swing': 'An expert at this kind of programme and quite irreplaceable'. Virtues such as these, however, evidently did not make much impression on the comparatively large proportion who seemed to want to be soothed at bedtime and did not think this programme filled the bill.

Audience Research Department.
14th August, 1964.

NE/GM

PAGE 14 DAILY MIRROR, Tuesday, June 30, 1964

PATRICK DONCASTER'S DISCS

The heat's on for a record '64 summer..

IT'S ring-a-ding-ding time on the Discland cash registers . . . even though July is just coming into view and holidays are swinging in.

A few years back there used to be a let-up in the platter parade around this time of the year.

Disc bosses planned their autumn onslaught while Britain holidayed—and they started looking at pretty, pretty Santa Claus songs for Christmas. But not today. It's boom, boom, boom.

Consider the Geordie Fivesome, the Animals—today's No. 1. Their four-minute-plus disc of "The House of the Rising Sun" sold more than 250,000 in a week.

The Rolling Stones have racked up the same for their lively "It's All Over Now" (Decca) in the past few days.

No wonder the longest-haired Stone of them all, Brian Jones, standing resplendant before me in striped Californian sports coat, was considering a flat in Mayfair.

"I used to live in Belgravia," he said with the solemnity of the successful.

He was considering a holiday, too. "I think I'll go to New York," he said, "and visit some friends I found there during our recent tour. . . ."

Brian Jones

The Searchers, hardly off the plane from the States, rushed quickly into the Pye studios to record "Some Day We're Gonna Love Again"—a song they found in America. I will be surprised if another quarter of a million disc fans don't buy it. . . .

Somebody's holiday money is taking a real thrashing. . . . Cliff Richard and the Shadows' double-sider—"On the Beach" and "A Matter of Moments," from their film—was around the 200,000 mark yesterday.

Meantime, orders were piling in for the Beatles' film single "A Hard Day's Night." Nearing a half-million was last night's report . . . with more than a week to go.

Freddie and the Dreamers leap on to the scene again with their sprightly film song "Just For You" (Columbia), out this Friday. The Mersey Beats, with another tuneful piece, come in on Fontana with "Wishin' and Hopin'."

And next week, the chart topping Four Pennies will be having another go with their follow-up to "Juliet."

Label lookout

THE German Polydor label, first company to record the Beatles back in their Hamburg days, is going to make discs in Britain—for the first time for seven years.

But they are not looking for groups. They are looking for girls. Girls who look good—and CAN sing. "The group market seems to be saturated," said a Polydor spokesman, "and there are six girls in the current top thirty."

Cheesed off

BEFORE (if you are a girl) you rush to volunteer, listen to some words of advice from Decca's new thrush—little Miss Barry St. John, 20, a 4ft. 11in. green-eyed blonde from Glasgow.

"It's a hard life," says this veteran of three years as a singer, who first came to London with a group.

The other number the Stones did was a version of Bo Diddley's 'Crackin' Up'; it was the one and only time the Stones ever played this number on air and it dates back to their earliest gigs at the Crawdaddy and around London's clubs. On this slow beat number, the Stones sound totally comfortable and faithful to the original, just as they do when they revisited it at El Mocambo Tavern in Toronto in 1977, as captured on their *Love You Live* album.

Top Gear, for which they received £50 – rather than the £36 they were previously being paid for radio appearances – went out on 23 July at 10 p.m. and ran for two hours. Alongside the Stones, this second edition of the programme featured Cilla Black and the Animals. The broadcast coincided with the birth of Brian Jones's fourth illegitimate child.

Today, *Top Gear* is more readily recognized as the BBC's flagship programme about cars and driving that has been franchised around the world. However, back in 1964, the title was in keeping with the mood of the moment in which all things great were referred to as 'fab gear'. From its tentative beginnings, the original *Top Gear* was specifically designed to compete with the kind of output heard on pirate radio stations, but it soon grew into one of the most significant programmes on BBC radio.

By 1967, and the coming of Radio 1, *Top Gear* took on a different tone, featuring 'progressive' music and hosted by a roster of DJs that included Pete Drummond, Tommy Vance and most especially John Peel, who over the years became synonymous with the show as he took on the role of sole presenter. Peel had been a DJ on pirate radio station Radio London and his late-night *Perfumed Garden* programme there was very much the model for what *Top Gear* became.

Opposite: The BBC carried out constant audience research on their programmes during the 1960s, with opinions generally polarized

Left: The UK mainstream media shows its obsession with how much young pop stars are earning

THERE'S A RIOT GOIN' ON

Following their return from the US tour, the Stones were not only engaged in TV and radio appearances, they were also back out on the road. But, having played around 120 gigs between January and May 1964, their schedule in late June and throughout July was comparatively light – less than a dozen gigs.

Two days after their appearance on *Top Gear,* both Mick and Bill appeared on TV, but not performing: they had made the main evening news. The previous night, the Stones played at the Empress Ballroom in Blackpool, where they were paid £750 to appear, one of the highest fees the Stones had so far received. They were booked to play two twenty-five-minute sets and there were over 7,000 people crammed into the venue when the Stones took to the stage. Among the large crowd were many Scots, mostly Glaswegians, who were in Blackpool for their annual 'Trade's Week' holiday – the Scottish equivalent of Wakes Week. During the band's second set, fighting broke out, with some in the drink fuelled crowd taking exception to others among the watching fans. Pretty soon it escalated into a full-scale riot, particularly after some of the crowd began spitting at the band on stage.

According to Stu, 'It was very nearly the date on my gravestone. Keith still thought he was God, and that he could kick one of these guys and get away with it. The rest of the band already turned, realising they'd got to get off stage. I just pushed Keith, and said, "For fuck's sake, get out of here while you're still alive." We could hear cymbals going through the air, thumps as all the amps got smashed up, and then there was the most glorious crash of all time – there'd been a grand piano on the stage. The cops waited and sent for reinforcements. When there were about fifty of them, they went in with truncheons. Charlie wasn't using his drums. He'd borrowed a kit from this guy, who was sitting there crying over his lovely Ludwig kit.'

'I certainly didn't hit anybody. I simply made an aggressive movement with my guitar.'

Keith Richards
Daily Express
25 July 1964

Opposite: Keith Fordyce interviewing Bill and Brian on *Ready Steady Go!* on 26 June

RSG!

As Mick said at the time, 'We were scared stiff. Nothing like this has ever happened before. You cannot expect people to put up with having their property smashed up like that.' Brian commented: 'Everyone seems to think that we are always out to be antagonistic, and to put their backs up. It just isn't true! All we want is for people to accept us and our music. Not to look on us as freaks.'

A couple of months earlier, Maureen Cleave, a journalist who was extremely fond of the Beatles, had this to say in the London *Evening Standard*: 'Never have the middle-class virtues of neatness, obedience and punctuality been so conspicuously lacking as they are in the Rolling Stones. The Rolling Stones are not the people you build empires with; they are not the people who always remember to wash their hands before lunch. Parents feel cheated. Just when the Beatles had taught them that pop music was respectable. Just when they were beginning to understand. What happens? Their children develop a passion beyond the comprehension of everybody for these five young men.'

It seemed to be all coming so very true.

On the same day as the Blackpool riot, the Stones were busy plugging 'It's All Over Now' on *Ready Steady Go!*, despite the single having now been overtaken at the top of the charts by the Beatles, with the theme song for their first feature film, *A Hard Day's Night*. The Stones had recorded their appearance the previous day, along with the Animals, the Mojos, Sandie Shaw, the Fourmost, Kingsize Taylor and the Dominoes and the Paramounts, a band from Southend that included Gary Brooker, who would later morph into Procol Harum. Keith Fordyce interviewed Brian and Bill.

The promotion of the new single continued with a recording for *Thank Your Lucky Stars*, a couple of days before the Stones took a lunchtime flight to Belfast on the last day of July to go to the BBC's Ulster Studio at Ormeau Avenue to record an interview. Keith overslept and missed the flight, but arrived in time for some more interviews recorded for the BBC's *6.10 Show* backstage at the city's Usher Hall.

As well as recording interviews with all five of the band, the cameras also catch them playing through a slow blues number that is an early manifestation of 'Little Red Rooster', which they would record a month later at Regent Sound Studios. On this, their first visit to Northern Ireland, their early evening show at the Usher Hall also came close to ending in a riot, but they escaped without incident to play at their 11 p.m. concert at the Flamingo Ballroom in Ballymena.

STONE FANS IN A RIOT

A ROLLING STONES concert ended in pandemonium last night after twelve minutes.

Police tried to stop the show after four minutes when girls in the 4,000 audience started to faint.

Fans were packed so tight at Belfast's Ulster Hall that there was only one place to take the fainting girls—on to the stage.

After four numbers from the shaggy - haired pop group one hundred people had fainted.

Head Constable William Seay, fearing that fainting girls would die of suffocation in the screaming mob walked on stage to try to stop the show.

His words were drowned by the fans. And when a couple of the Rolling Stones appeared to argue with the police the crowd went berserk.

At one point there were seventy people on stage—including fans, policemen, ambulance men and the Stones. Hysterical girls had to be strapped on to stretchers.

As they scuffled about the Stones tried to continue their performance. Eventually they walked off.

When the show was over fights continued outside and three people were taken to hospital with leg injuries after the Stones' car suddenly reversed.

2 SAVED IN SEA FIRE

A Trinity House boat rescued Mr. and Mrs. Michael Hawkins, of Stoke Gabriel, Devon, when their 21ft. cabin cruiser caught fire off the Needles, Isle of Wight, yesterday.

Two days after returning from Belfast, the Stones were playing for the nobility, in the shape of Lord Bath at his stately home, Longleat House, not far from the town of Warminster in Wiltshire. With somewhere between 15,000 and 20,000 fans turning up, the police were concerned that it might be another situation that could get out of hand. Lord Bath had no such worries, with the benefit of hindsight, as he told the *Daily Mirror*: 'I don't see what the police are bellyaching about. I thought the show went off in an orderly way.' The Stones were interviewed for a local ITV news show to publicize the gig. Their collateral was rapidly changing; they were not just musicians, but a part of a new wave of stars that were re-shaping the face of pop.

Before August was over, things became a little busier for the band on the touring front, with a trip to the Channel Islands of Guernsey and Jersey, as well as their first trip to Europe for a proper gig, rather than the TV special recorded in Montreux. The Stones flew to Holland on the morning of 8 August, to play at the Kurhaus club in Scheveningen, The Hague.

Prior to their appearance, the Stones did interviews for various Dutch TV and radio companies and they were also filmed on stage at the Kurhaus where they played many of their Crawdaddy favourites, including 'Beautiful Delilah', 'Walking The Dog', 'Mona', 'Susie Q' and 'Hi-Heel Sneakers.' Yet again there was a riot that was extensively reported by the media, and especially so on Dutch TV news.

Their Channel Islands gigs were also well-covered by the local ITV company on their evening magazine programme, *Here Today*, which featured concert footage and an interview with Mick. For once, it was not a problem of rioting fans – other than some nutcase pelting the band with rotten fruit and eggs – but an incident with an air hostess on the flight home from Jersey that garnered the most controversy on the trip. She said to the band, 'Well, boys, have you washed today?' It got progressively nastier, with the airline insisting via the press that the Stones would never be allowed to fly with them again. To date they have never returned to the Channel Islands for any gigs.

Meanwhile in the *Daily Mirror*, the Stones were summed up as follows: 'About 200 screaming, yelling, teenage girls fainted as fights broke out at a Rolling Stones show in New Brighton, on Monday night [10 August] ... These performers are a menace to law and order, as a result of their formula of vocal laryngitis, cranial fur and sex, the police are diverted from bank robbers, murders and other forms of mayhem to quell the mob violence they generate.'

The Yowlers

ABOUT 200 screaming, yelling, teen-age girls fainted as fights broke out at a Rolling Stones show at New Brighton on Monday night. Fifty youths were chucked out from the hall and so was one young Boadicea who brandished a knife at the stewards.

The night before about 2,000 teenagers got taken mad at Manchester where the same pop group was a-yowling and a-twanging. Only 100 girls fainted this time. The police were called and the usual semi-riot took place.

These performers and, of course, their competitors, ranging from adenoidal striplings in frowsy night clubs to the millionaire Beatles, are a menace to law and order and, as a result of their formula of vocal laryngitis, cranial fur and sex, the police are diverted from bank robberies, murders and other forms of mayhem to quell the mob violence that they generate.

Contrast these mob scenes with the Leicester Square buskers who call themselves the Road Stars, led by Bert Hollis.

They seem pretty harmless troubadours to me. And indeed they are. No one gets hurt, no one feels compelled to draw a flick-knife to express his or her musical criticism.

Yet the police have arrested the Road Stars over 300 times and the magistrates have threatened to throw them in prison.

It's all a bit odd.

Opposite and right: The papers report on riots at gigs in Belfast and New Brighton
Above and top: The Stones' open-air concert at Longleat

THE RED SKELTON HOUR

Top: The Stones record their appearance on *The Red Skelton Hour* for American TV at The London Palladium on 5 August
Above: Red Skelton

This American TV show was the last occasion that the Stones appeared on a show that was so totally inappropriate for what they were all about. Their appearance on Red Skelton's show was booked in anticipation of a second American tour that was arranged for later in the year; someone, somewhere, thought that some additional exposure on US television would not go amiss. But *The Red Skelton Hour* was just the worst fit imaginable.

Skelton was a veteran of 1920s medicine shows and 1930s vaudeville theatre, a performer rooted in the back roads of America with a hayseed comedic style that struggled to make any self-respecting 1960s teenager laugh – today it just looks bizarre.

'Here we are at the London Palladium where the Rolling Stones are appearing; they're even shaggier than the Beatles,' says a voice-over as the segment of the show featuring the Stones begins. The footage reveals the marquee of the Palladium decorated with posters announcing that the band were appearing at the theatre; truth was they had never even been to the iconic London venue before and it would be a year before their first concert-proper at the famous theatre.

'Ain't those Rolling Stones really something? That hair, they make the Beatles look like Yul Brynner.'

Red Skelton

On the television show, Skelton enters the foyer, where there are about forty screaming fans, while the Stones mime to 'Tell Me', Carol' and 'It's All Over Now' from the steps inside leading into the theatre. Even by their standards of sometimes appearing detached while on TV, the Stones look remarkably bored. Meanwhile, the camera keeps cutting to Skelton, who makes faces and puts his fingers in his ears and generally hams it up. As was still the norm, Brian, playing his month-old Vox Teardrop guitar, is standing out front alongside Mick.

By the time the programme first aired on 22 September, 'It's All Over Now' was at its peak chart position of No.26 on the *Billboard* chart. It slipped eleven places the following week, while 'Tell Me' had dropped off the American charts several weeks earlier, having reached No.24. It was still the best performing of their first three American singles.

FROM CARLISLE TO PARIS

Early in September, the Stones embarked upon yet another UK package tour, this one with brother and sister soul duo, Inez and Charlie Foxx, as the other interesting draw for fans. The Foxx siblings came from Greensboro, North Carolina, and in the summer of 1963 they had had a Top 10 hit in America with their classic song, 'Mockingbird'– although it didn't make the UK singles chart until 1969.

This was another typical tour, with two shows a night at thirty-two different locations in thirty-seven days, although the economics for the Stones were somewhat different this time. Eric Easton had done a deal to split the profits with promoter Robert Stigwood (who would later manage Eric Clapton), three ways – with Stigwood and the Stones taking 40 per cent each, and Easton receiving 20 per cent. The Stones were paid a paltry £50 per week in anticipation of a big profit share, but things ended acrimoniously in the High Court in 1965 with the Stones suing Stigwood for £12,000 – a small fortune back then – that they attested to be their 40 per cent share.

The tour began on 5 September at Finsbury Park's Astoria Cinema in north London, ending on 11 October on England's south coast at Brighton's Hippodrome Theatre. Other artists on the bill included Mike Berry, backed by the Innocents; the Mojos; and Stigwood protégé, Simon Scott and the LeRoys, who had just had a minor hit on Parlophone and would never be heard of again.

Right: Inez and Charlie Foxx had a big American hit with 'Mockingbird', but it failed to chart in the UK until 1969, despite their tour with the Stones

‘This tour is the biggest thing the Stones have done yet. Our repertoire for the tour consists of about twenty numbers, from which we choose eight every night.’

Mick Jagger
Melody Maker
12 September 1964

With the band’s reputation preceding them, local police forces the length and breadth of Britain were forewarned and available in large numbers to keep the rabid fans at bay. At one venue, the band had to make their escape by scaling a ten-foot wall and then hitching a ride in a police van to avoid a throng of fanatics.

On 16 September, Andrew Loog Oldham married art student Sheila Klein in Scotland, after spending two weeks north of the border to qualify for a marriage licence. The following night, the Stones played the ABC Cinema in Carlisle, just south of the border between England and Scotland; the local ITV company, Border Television, covered the event, most likely in anticipation of a fracas. In other matters relating to affairs of the heart, another of Brian’s girlfriends gave birth to what was his fifth illegitimate child while he was on tour. It was a son.

Half way through the tour, on the day the Stones played Hull on the east coast of England, they were filmed by Pathé News for a six-minute ‘short’ to be shown in cinemas between the main movies. Unimaginatively titled – and certainly not for the last time – *Rolling Stones Gather Moss*, the film showed the band pretending to hitchhike on their way to the gig and later miming to ‘Around And Around’. A few days later, the BBC’s *World in Action* featured the Stones playing ‘Hi-Heel Sneakers’ and ‘Not Fade Away’ at an appearance they had made at Bridlington’s Spa Hall back in July. Despite being short, it’s fabulous footage, showing the kind of mayhem that the Stones were conjuring up wherever they played.

On 14 October, Charlie secretly married his girlfriend, Shirley, in Bradford and four days later the band flew from Heathrow to Brussels to start what was to be their first, albeit mini, tour of the Continent. It was with apposite timing, as ‘It’s All Over Now’ had recently topped the German charts as well as being a Top 10 hit in France, Sweden and Holland. By now, whenever the Stones arrived in any country, there seemed to be an obligatory airport press conference and Belgium proved no different. This was followed by more TV and radio interviews in the city centre.

The band’s Brussels concert was at the Amerikaans Theatre located in the grounds of the 1958 World Fair. This was also the studios of VRT, the Flemish radio and television organization, which recorded the Stones concert and arranged for the band to be interviewed by ‘Uncle Bob’ and ‘Aunt Terry’ for *Tienerklanken*, a Belgian music and chat show for teenagers. Their set was typical of what the Stones were playing live during their recent UK tour, including their last

Right: *Disc* report on the Stones' trip to Paris, where they appeared on French TV

Below: A US review is somewhat of a backhanded compliment

Following pages: The Stones on French television, backed by scenes of a foggy London

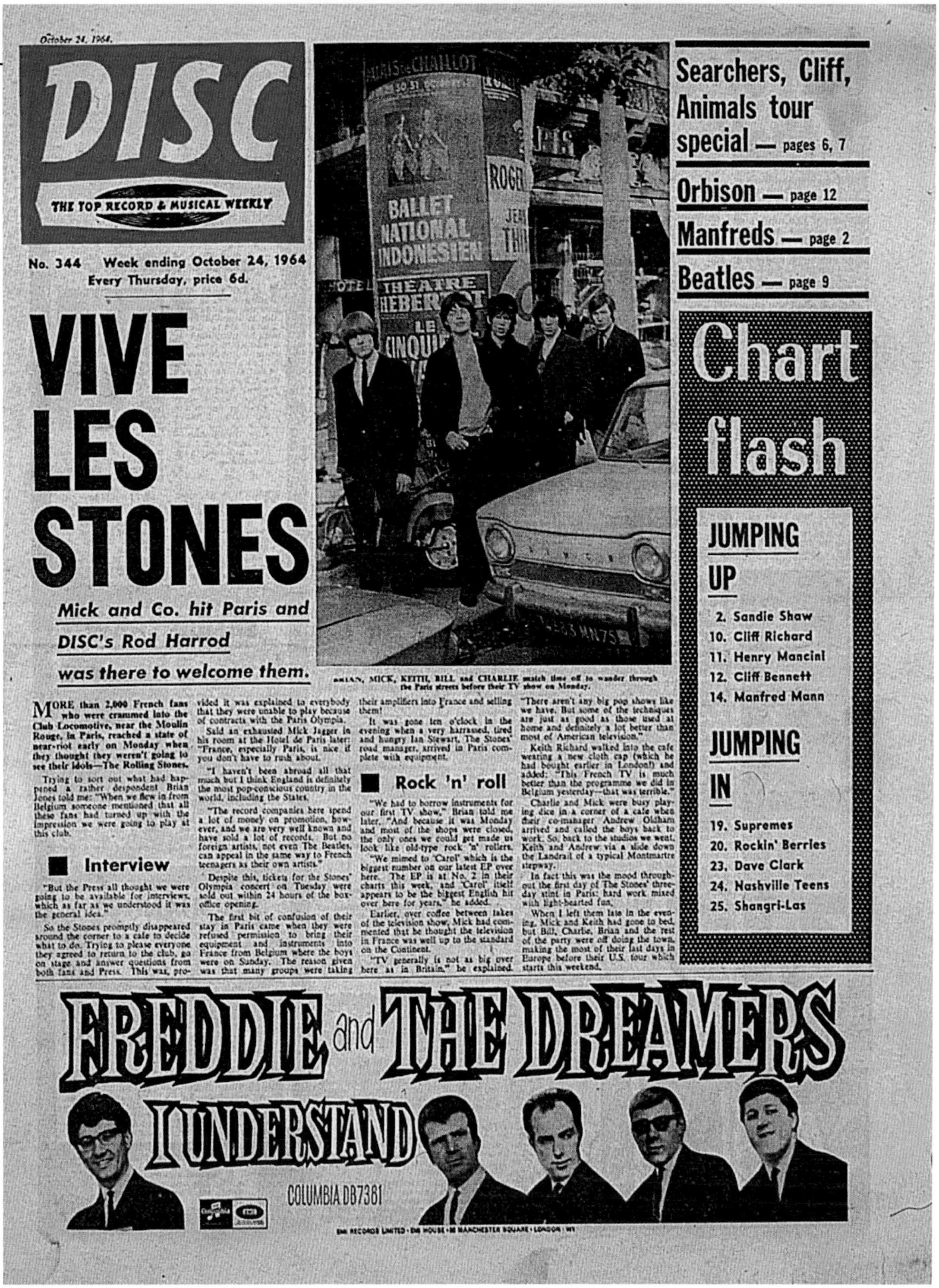

October 24, 1964.

DISC

THE TOP RECORD & MUSICAL WEEKLY

No. 344 Week ending October 24, 1964
Every Thursday, price 6d.

Searchers, Cliff, Animals tour special — pages 6, 7

Orbison — page 12

Manfreds — page 2

Beatles — page 9

VIVE LES STONES

Mick and Co. hit Paris and DISC's Rod Harrod was there to welcome them.

BRIAN, MICK, KEITH, BILL and CHARLIE snatch time off to wander through the Paris streets before their TV show on Monday.

MORE than 2,000 French fans who were crammed into the Club Locomotive, near the Moulin Rouge, in Paris, reached a state of near-riot early on Monday when they thought they weren't going to see their idols—The Rolling Stones.

Trying to sort out what had happened a rather despondent Brian Jones told me: "When we flew in from Belgium someone mentioned that all these fans had turned up with the impression we were going to play at this club.

Interview

"But the Press all thought we were going to be available for interviews, which as far as we understood it was the general idea."

So the Stones promptly disappeared around the corner to a cafe to decide what to do. Trying to please everyone they agreed to return to the club, go on stage and answer questions from both fans and Press. This was, provided it was explained to everybody that they were unable to play because of contracts with the Paris Olympia.

Said an exhausted Mick Jagger in his room at the Hotel de Paris later: "France, especially Paris, is nice if you don't have to rush about.

"I haven't been abroad all that much but I think England is definitely the most pop-conscious country in the world, including the States.

"The record companies here spend a lot of money on promotion, however, and we are very well known and have sold a lot of records. But no foreign artists, not even The Beatles, can appeal in the same way to French teenagers as their own artists."

Despite this, tickets for the Stones' Olympia concert on Tuesday were sold out within 24 hours of the box-office opening.

The first bit of confusion of their stay in Paris came when they were refused permission to bring their equipment and instruments into France from Belgium where the boys were on Sunday. The reason given was that many groups were taking their amplifiers into France and selling them!

It was gone ten o'clock in the evening when a very harrassed, tired and hungry Ian Stewart, The Stones' road manager, arrived in Paris complete with equipment.

Rock 'n' roll

"We had to borrow instruments for our first TV show," Brian told me later. "And because it was Monday and most of the shops were closed, the only ones we could get made us look like old-type rock 'n' rollers.

"We mimed to 'Carol' which is the biggest number on our latest EP over here. The EP is at No. 2 in their charts this week, and 'Carol' itself appears to be the biggest English hit over here for years," he added.

Earlier, over coffee between takes of the television show, Mick had commented that he thought the television in France was well up to the standard on the Continent.

"TV generally is not as big over here as in Britain," he explained. "There aren't any big pop shows like we have. But some of the techniques are just as good as those used at home and definitely a lot better than most of American television."

Keith Richard walked into the cafe wearing a new cloth cap (which he had bought earlier in London!) and added: "This French TV is much better than the programme we did in Belgium yesterday—that was terrible."

Charlie and Mick were busy playing dice in a corner of a cafe when their co-manager Andrew Oldham arrived and called the boys back to work. So, back to the studios we went, Keith and Andrew via a slide down the handrail of a typical Montmartre stepway.

In fact this was the mood throughout the first day of The Stones' three-day stint in Paris: hard work mixed with light-hearted fun.

When I left them late in the evening, Mick and Keith had gone to bed, but Bill, Charlie, Brian and the rest of the party were off doing the town, making the most of their last days in Europe before their U.S. tour which starts this weekend.

Chart flash

JUMPING UP

2. Sandie Shaw
10. Cliff Richard
11. Henry Mancini
12. Cliff Bennett
14. Manfred Mann

JUMPING IN

19. Supremes
20. Rockin' Berries
23. Dave Clark
24. Nashville Teens
25. Shangri-Las

ROLLING STONES—TELL ME (Southern, ASCAP) (2:35) — I JUST WANT TO MAKE LOVE TO YOU (Arc, BMI) (2:15)—Neanderthal music at its best. The British group offers a crude chant and the rockiest sound around. Flip features lead in r&b groove. Sustained guitars beat with hand-clappin' makes it r&b with British accent.
London 9682

two singles and 'Tell Me', a couple of Chuck Berry covers and other covers featured on their first album and their EPs. They also did 'Time Is On My Side', which they had recorded at Chess and which had been released as a single in the US at the end of September.

From Brussels, they flew to Paris for their first ever appearance in the French capital. Stu and the band's equipment was delayed on the drive south and when the band arrived at French TV channel ORTF2 for their appearance on *Quoi De Neuf* ('What's New'), they had to borrow equipment. However, as there was no bass guitar, Bill is seen miming with a regular guitar, playing 'Carol', their most popular song in France, and 'It's All Over Now'.

The next day they played at L'Olympia, Paris's most prestigious venue for visiting bands and major French pop artists. After a rehearsal in the afternoon, the Stones played live, recorded by Europe No. 1 radio and broadcast simultaneously across France. Also on the bill in Paris was British rock 'n' roller Vince Taylor, who had moved from Middlesex to Paris by way of Hollywood and had achieved something approaching legendary status as a rock god for the French.

ANGRY FANS RIOT AT 'STONES' SHOW

Paris, Wednesday

From AUBREY THOMAS

HUNDREDS of stampeding teenagers smashed seats and broke windows at a Paris theatre today at the end of a show given by Britain's Rolling Stones beat group.

Two thousand shrieking, whistling fans had expected the Stones to play a dozen numbers.

When the curtain at the Olympia Theatre stayed down, about 200 youths started to smash seats.

The police were called. They hustled the audience out of the theatre.

As they went, some of the youths yelled insults at the police and smashed windows in the foyer. The stage manager was injured by flying glass.

In the street, scores of youths were bundled into police vans.

But many others dodged the police and went down the boulevard. They tore down posters, broke windows and slashed the fronts of newspaper kiosks.

At a cafe, the youths overturned tables and threw customers on to the pavement.

Altogether, 150 youths were arrested. A theatre spokesman said that about £1,400 worth of damage had been done at the Olympia.

Mike Dorsey, the Stones' production manager told me later:

"A Black Maria was driven up to the stage door and the police helped us to scramble into it.

"We then drove around Paris sitting on riot-squad machine-guns for ninety minutes before the police thought it was safe for us to return to our hotel."

Mr. Dorsey said that the Stones had given eleven numbers, including three encores.

Prior to their appearance, the Stones were spirited into the theatre in a police van, but once again trouble was not too far away, as after the show forty fans staged a mini riot in the foyer of L'Olympia and a number of them were arrested by police. Later, another hundred or so teenagers were arrested after upsetting tables at cafés and staging what was becoming an all-too-familiar scene at Stones' concerts.

What's particularly interesting is that both these Continental shows were based around TV (and radio) appearances. The Stones and other bands were becoming more keenly aware of the opportunities that the media presented and, for their part, television and radio were very aware of the value of presenting pop music for an increasingly affluent and engaged younger audience.

'The police van was all right, I suppose, but when I noticed a rack of Sten guns above my head, I began to wonder what sort of trouble they were expecting.'

Mick Jagger
Record Mirror
31 October 1964

Left: Yet more riots
Opposite: The L'Olympia concert on 20 October, supported by a leather-clad Vince Taylor, was broadcast on French radio

AMERICA SECOND TIME AROUND

While the Stones were on their UK tour with Inez and Charlie Foxx, the band's fourth US single was released. None of their three earlier singles had made the Top 20 in America, and so London Records were anxious for a breakthrough on the charts that would put the Stones on the same kind of level as other British Invasion bands.

On the *Billboard* chart of 26 September 1964, the same week as the release of 'Time Is On My Side', the Animals had just slipped to No.3, having spent three weeks at the top of the Hot 100 with their bluesy 'House of the Rising Sun'. Manfred Mann were in the Top 10, and the Dave Clark Five, Billy J. Kramer and, naturally, the Beatles were all there in the Top 30.

Three weeks later, on the day before the Stones played in Brussels, 'Time Is On My Side' broke into the Hot 100 at No.80, one place below Herman's Hermits and seven places ahead of the Zombies' 'She's Not There'.

Five days later, the Stones arrived at JFK to begin their second US tour and the following day, Bill Wyman's twenty-eighth birthday, the band's second US album, *12 x 5*, came out. The single had also jumped twenty-five places, but they were still lagging behind Herman and had been overtaken by the Zombies.

Recorded at Chess Records during their first US tour, Jerry Ragovoy's 'Time Is On My Side', originally recorded by Irma Thomas, is classic early period Stones. As the *NME* said in November 1964, 'It begins with Stu playing organ as though he were in church. Then what seems to be a whole chorus of voices crashes in. The song is taken at a very slow pace, but is to me one of the best things the Stones have ever done. Keith takes a great guitar solo.'

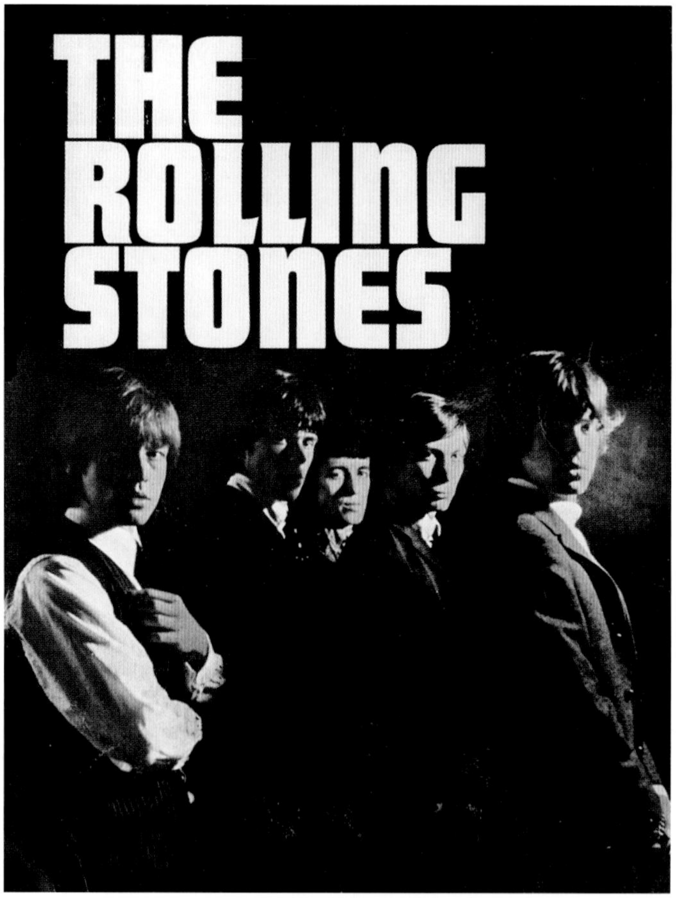

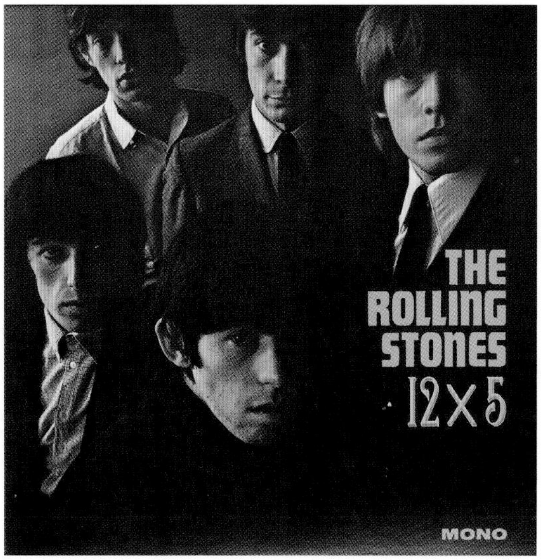

Opposite: The official programme for the band's second US tour uses the same photo as the band's debut album, taken by Nicholas Wright

Above right: The second US album release.

Above left and bottom: This is the US release that became the band's first Top 10 hit on the Hot 100. Originally recorded by jazz trumpeter Kai Winding, it became the B-side of a minor R&B hit by Irma Thomas after lyrics were added

The Stones' US arrival, according to the *Daily Mail* in New York, was to be kept low-key. 'Receptions at Kennedy Airport will be banned and the actual arrival time of the Stones is to be kept as precious a secret as the combination on the vaults at Fort Knox.' Nevertheless, when they arrived, just before 2 p.m. local time, there were 500 screaming, yelling fans who were so loud they almost drowned out some of DJ Ed Rudy's commentary at the airport.

'Believe it or not, that is the sound of an invasion,' he reported. 'The most controversial of invading British balladeers is a quintet called the Rolling Stones. And while they may not gather any moss, they certainly are raking in a lot of good green American money, and gathering hundreds of thousands of teenage fans in the process. The Stones are different. Not only from the American groups, but even very different from their own countrymen. They are not really very neat in appearance, and one of them has been known to appear onstage in grease-stained slacks, and another customarily sings in a sweatshirt.'

Shock, horror! Yet another middle-aged radio presenter who really didn't get the Stones – but Rudy was important, because he worked for Radio Pulsebeat News and INS Radio News and his coverage was syndicated to hundreds of stations across the country. He reached places that the Stones had no chance of visiting on their twelve-date tour of the country – four of which were in California, and the majority of the rest in the north-eastern part of America.

As well as covering the Stones' arrival at the airport, Rudy did interviews with all five of the band, along with Eric Easton, in a private room in Kennedy Airport. Among the questions he asked Easton was, 'How do you account for the Stones' phenomenal success?' To which Easton replied: 'In England they're the next biggest to the Beatles, in fact they're equal with the Beatles and I think, before we've finished this tour of the States, I think they'll be just as big here. The Stones have to be seen, and heard, to be believed. They didn't become popular as a result of the record plugs on radio or television. When the young people see them in the flesh, that's it. They're the most exciting group in the world, and if the Stones are going to appear anywhere near where any American teenagers are living, they should go and see them, because they are fantastic.'

Easton was somewhat over-optimistic in his predictions. Even on their second US tour, the number of fans who saw the band in concert was limited, compared to those who heard their records on radio, saw them on TV and heard them interviewed.

However, the band were making steady progress Stateside, and their second day in America was a busy one. They had rehearsed the previous evening for *The Ed Sullivan Show* and did so again in the late morning of 24 October. This was followed by a live appearance on Murray the K's radio show, which was an opportunity for fans to besiege the radio station, WINS. A few weeks later in the *NME*, Mike Dorsey, the Stones' assistant road manager at the time,

THE ROLLING STONES—TIME IS ON MY SIDE (Rittenhouse-Maygar, BMI) (2:50)—Old r&b classic is given distinctive English accent, tambourine preachin' and all. Flip: "Congratulations" (Hollis, BMI) (2:25). **London 9708**

reported what happened: 'As it went out live, this was the signal for all the teenagers to gather round the radio station. As a result, we couldn't get out. Finally the police cleared a way through the crowd and we made a mad dash to the two Cadillacs we were using. When we had got away, we discovered Bill wasn't with us. The police toured the city looking for him, and found he had gone back inside the radio station, and was OK.'

From WINS they went to WPIX TV to tape their second appearance on *The Clay Cole Show*. They mimed to their new single as well as 'If You Need Me', 'It's All Over Now', 'Around And Around' and 'Confessin' The Blues'. Cole also interviewed the band and they answered questions from members of the audience. They then played the first of two shows at the Academy of Music, at 126 East 14th Street and Broadway.

The following day, having partied until very early morning, the band went to *The Ed Sullivan Show* shortly after lunch to rehearse one last time before their evening appearance that was broadcast live. Towards the end of the first half of the show they played 'Around And Around', which was the opening track on side one of *12 x 5*; towards the end of the show they did 'Time Is On My Side'.

However, it seems Mr Sullivan may have spoken with a forked tongue, or at least that's what Dennis Braithwaite implied in the *Toronto Globe and Mail* in November 1964. 'Ed Sullivan wrote to say that he agreed with my description of the Stones as a grubby lot, and to pledge that he won't have them back. I am bucked up by Ed's promise that "So help me, the untidy Stones will never again darken our portals."'

The day after their *Ed Sullivan* appearance, the Stones flew west to Los Angeles where they played Sacramento on 26 October, before playing San Bernardino on 31 October and both Long Beach and San Diego the following day. During their time in California there were numerous radio interviews including one with Gary Mack on KRLA as well as at least one TV interview.

Between their Sacramento show and their return to San Bernardino the Stones appeared at the Santa Monica Civic Auditorium, but not for a concert as such. Instead it was to perform for a film that was dubbed *The Teen Age Music International Awards*, or *The TAMI Show* as it has come to be known.

On that Wednesday and Thursday, 28 and 29 October, the *TAMI Show* was the hottest ticket in town – although no one actually paid for one, as they were distributed to local high school students, for free.

The house band was under the direction of Jack Nitzsche and it featured the cream of LA session musicians who worked collectively as 'The Wrecking Crew', including drummer Hal Blaine, guitarists Tommy Tedesco and Glen Campbell, Sonny Bono on percussion and pianist Leon Russell. Also appearing at the concert were the Beach Boys, Chuck Berry, James Brown and the Famous Flames, Lesley

'Ed told us that it was the wildest, most enthusiastic audience he'd seen any artiste get in the history of his show. We got a message from him a few days later, saying, "Received hundreds of letters from parents complaining about you, but thousands from teenagers saying how much they enjoyed your performance."'

Mick Jagger
Rolling Stone
December 1964

Opposite: Performing on *The Ed Sullivan Show* in October

Gore, and Jan and Dean, along with a trio of Motown stars: Smokey Robinson and the Miracles, the Supremes and Marvin Gaye.

The Stones, two gigs into their US tour, were told they would be closing the show – this despite the fact that James Brown thought he should be top of the bill. After a day spent rehearsing, the main concert was to be filmed in a new technique called Electronovision (much like video) on the Thursday. The opening act was Chuck Berry, who along with Marvin Gaye was sharing a dressing room with the Stones. Both were encouraging towards the Stones, who were somewhat fazed at the prospect of having to follow James Brown, especially Mick. Marvin Gaye told them, 'People love you because of what you do on stage, so just go out there and do it and forget about James Brown. Go do your thing – that's what I do.'

Once Chuck Berry, Gerry and the Pacemakers, Smokey Robinson, Marvin Gaye and Lesley Gore had played, it was time for Jan and Dean, who also compered the show, followed by the Beach Boys. This was very much a hometown gig for both bands and their sets were a homage to California's national sport of surfing. The Beach Boys did 'Surfin' USA', 'I Get Around', 'Surfer Girl' and closed with 'Dance, Dance, Dance'. After this it was Billy J. Kramer and then the Supremes did four numbers.

Finally it was time for the Godfather himself, James Brown. His high-energy, four-song set featured 'Out Of Sight', 'Prisoner Of Love', 'Please, Please, Please' and 'Night Train'. When the Stones got back to England, Mick told *Disc*: 'James Brown was probably the best thing about our trip. He is a fantastic artist. When you've seen him, you've seen the act to end all acts. We appeared with him on the *TAMI Show* and we had to follow him. It was a disaster in a way, because nobody can follow James Brown, it's impossible.'

But follow him they did. The Stones' four songs were very much a reflection of what they were playing on their US tour – 'Around And Around', 'Off The Hook', 'Time Is On My Side' and 'It's All Over Now'. After this the Stones began 'I'm Alright' as they were joined on stage by the rest of the performers, before they also all did 'Let's Get Together' by way of a finale.

As the Stones left the stage, James Brown came over and shook all their hands; it was the beginning of a friendship that was rekindled frequently over the years when their paths crossed on tour. The film had its initial release on 29 December 1964 and a limited release in the UK under the less-than-inspiring title of *Gather No Moss*.

After their San Diego show, the Stones went to RCA's Hollywood studio where they recorded with engineer Dave Hassinger. They laid down a number of tracks that featured on various albums, as well as 'Heart Of Stone'. Joining them in the studio was Jack Nitzsche, whom they had met at the *TAMI Show*, who played piano on several numbers.

Opposite: The poster for the US cinema release of *The First Annual TAMI Show*

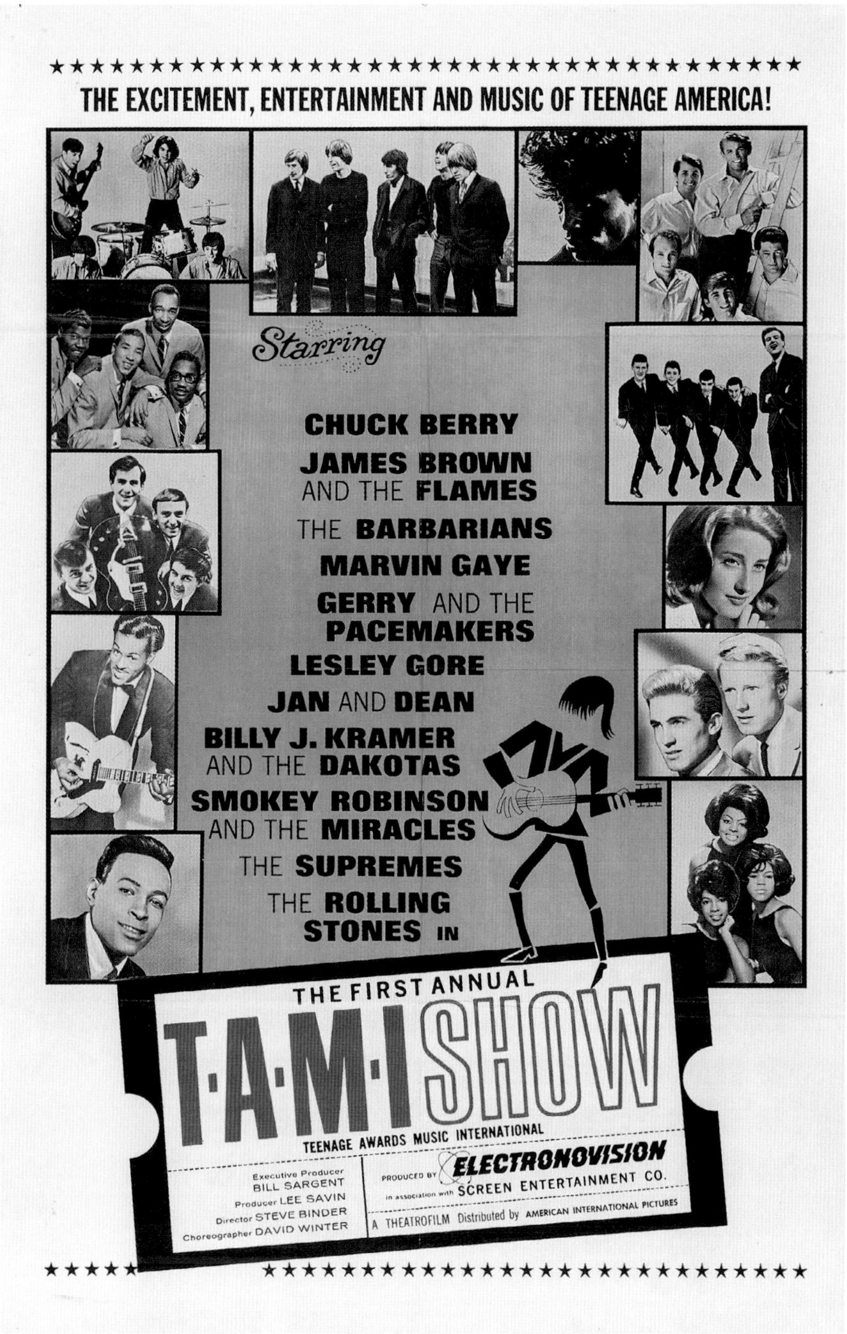

'They were the first rock and roll band I met that were intelligent. There was no guidance at all on those records, and very little need for it. They changed my whole idea of recording. Nobody had the big ego thing about keeping a song a certain way. That changed me. That was the first really free feeling I had in the studio.'

Jack Nitzsche

Between shows at Providence, Rhode Island on 4 November and Milwaukee, Wisconsin on 11 November, the Stones returned to Chess Records in Chicago for another session where they recorded a number of tracks, including a reworked 'Time Is On My Side'. It's the version that appears on *The Rolling Stones No. 2*, their second UK album.

The Stones played their last show of this second US tour on 15 November at Chicago's Arie Crown Theater. At the time it was one of the city's largest indoor venues with 5,000 seats and every one was filled to help give the band an amazing reception. They had well and truly cracked America at last. As Mick told the *Melody Maker* in November, 'I wouldn't mind going back, provided they keep me away from those stupid questions about hair.'

A ROW WITH THE BBC

The first glimmer of the Stones exercising some kind of control over their own destiny came on 2 September 1964 when they recorded what would become their fifth UK single. A couple of months later they flexed their collective muscle in a different way, much to the annoyance of the British Broadcasting Corporation.

Their new single was no R&B cover, no beat record with a tinge of blues, it was an out and out blues classic ... Howlin' Wolf's 'The Red Rooster', a song written by Willie Dixon. In the best traditions of the blues this was a farmyard song, strong on metaphor and coded sexual innuendo, but subtle enough to get played on the radio – although everyone who heard it knew what it was all about. It was closer to their hearts than anything they had so far recorded.

Given that the Stones had topped the UK charts in July with 'It's All Over Now', hopes were high when Decca released 'Little Red Rooster' on Friday 13 November. On the day the single came out the *NME*'s Derek Johnson, reviewing it, said, 'If it wasn't the Stones, I wouldn't give it much hope, because it's not all that commercial, but advance orders already guarantee a massive hit.'

It immediately caught on. Audiences were beguiled by Mick's purring vocals – the very antithesis of those on Howlin' Wolf's original, 'The Red Rooster', written by Willie Dixon and recorded for Chess Records back in 1961. Much of the credit for its success must also go to Brian Jones, whose slide guitar emulates Wolf's playing, accompanied by the wonderful Hubert Sumlin, on the original.

'People say "Little Red Rooster" is too slow. I don't see why we should have to conform to any pattern. We thought just for a change, we'd do a nice, straight blues on a single. What's wrong with that? It's suitable for dancing. It just depends who you're dancing with. Charlie's drumming makes it good for dancing.'

Mick Jagger
Melody Maker
28 November 1964

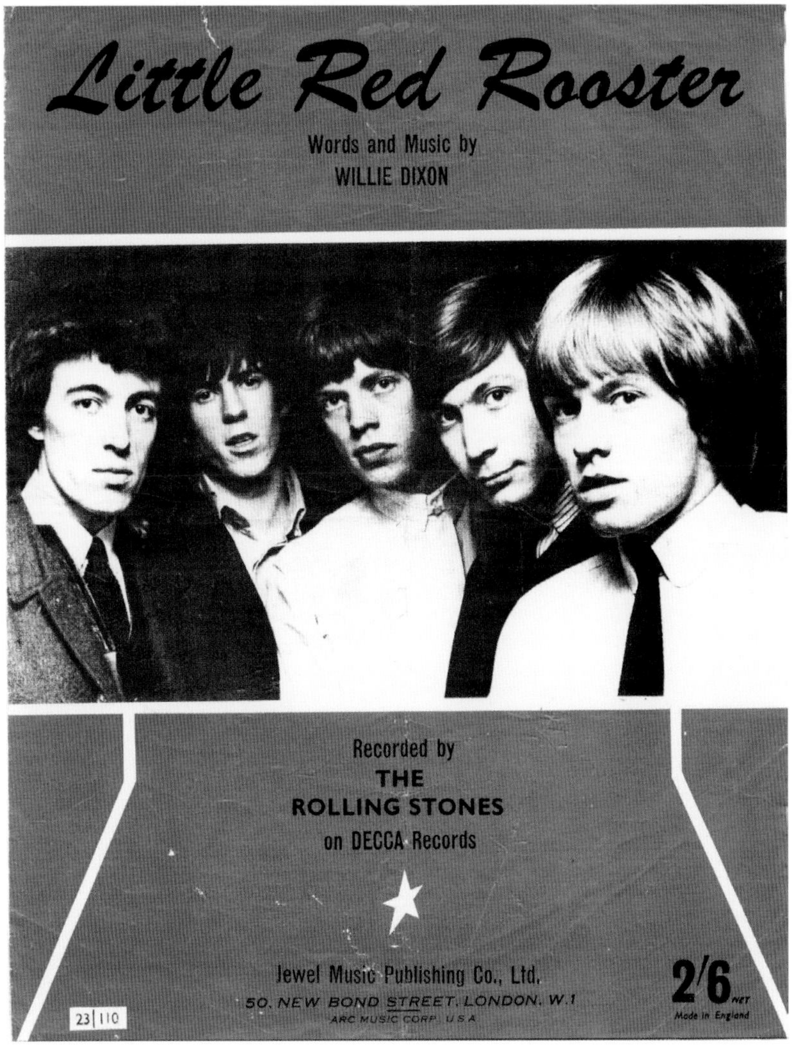

Despite what some people thought of its chances, it became the first bona fide blues song to top the UK charts. However, 'Little Red Rooster' spent just a week at No.1 and might have done better had not the Stones been embroiled in an argument with the BBC, who refused to have them appear on *Top of the Pops* in the week it reached the top of the charts – nor did they even play the single.

A week earlier, on 28 November, according to the *Radio Times*, the band were booked to appear on *Saturday Club* but failed to show up for the recording, leaving Britain's teenagers distraught and the BBC fuming. Well before the *Saturday Club* broadcast, Eric Easton had written Patrick Newman, the BBC's light entertainment booking manager, a grovelling apology. The letter on 24 November, the day after they had been scheduled to record their slot on the programme, said, 'The blame lies entirely with me because the Sones [sic] had intimated some two or three weeks ago that they would rather not accept these engagements, but as I was very keen that they should appear on these programmes I endeavoured right up to the last minute to get them to record as arranged.'

Above: 'Little Red Rooster' sheet music
Right: Eric Easton with Mick

Easton called the BBC's chief producer, Jimmy Grant, on 22 November to say they would not be appearing on *Saturday Club* (28 November), *Top Gear* (3 December) and *The Joe Loss Pop Show* (14 December), all of which he had contracted with the Corporation. The day after Easton's apology, the BBC's Patrick Newman wrote a long, detailed memorandum going over the events. On 23 November Newman had called Easton at home where he was recovering from pneumonia and, following that call, according to BBC's memo, Newman spoke 'to one of the group (Charles Watts) at his home and he told me many weeks previously the group had told Easton that they did not want any more engagements … as they wished to take a holiday'. According to Newman, 'I told him that it would be in their best interests to try and get them to the studio and he referred me back to the office.'

Despite what Easton wrote in his letter of 24 November, Newman went on to say in his internal BBC memo, 'Easton is extremely upset by their behaviour and would think us justified in taking whatever action we see fit.' It's an extraordinary turn of events for a manager to take such a stance, especially as he was by his own admission in the wrong. Newman then writes, 'I myself would dearly love to impose sanctions of some sort… it would be a salutary lesson not only to the group in question, but to the whole industry.'

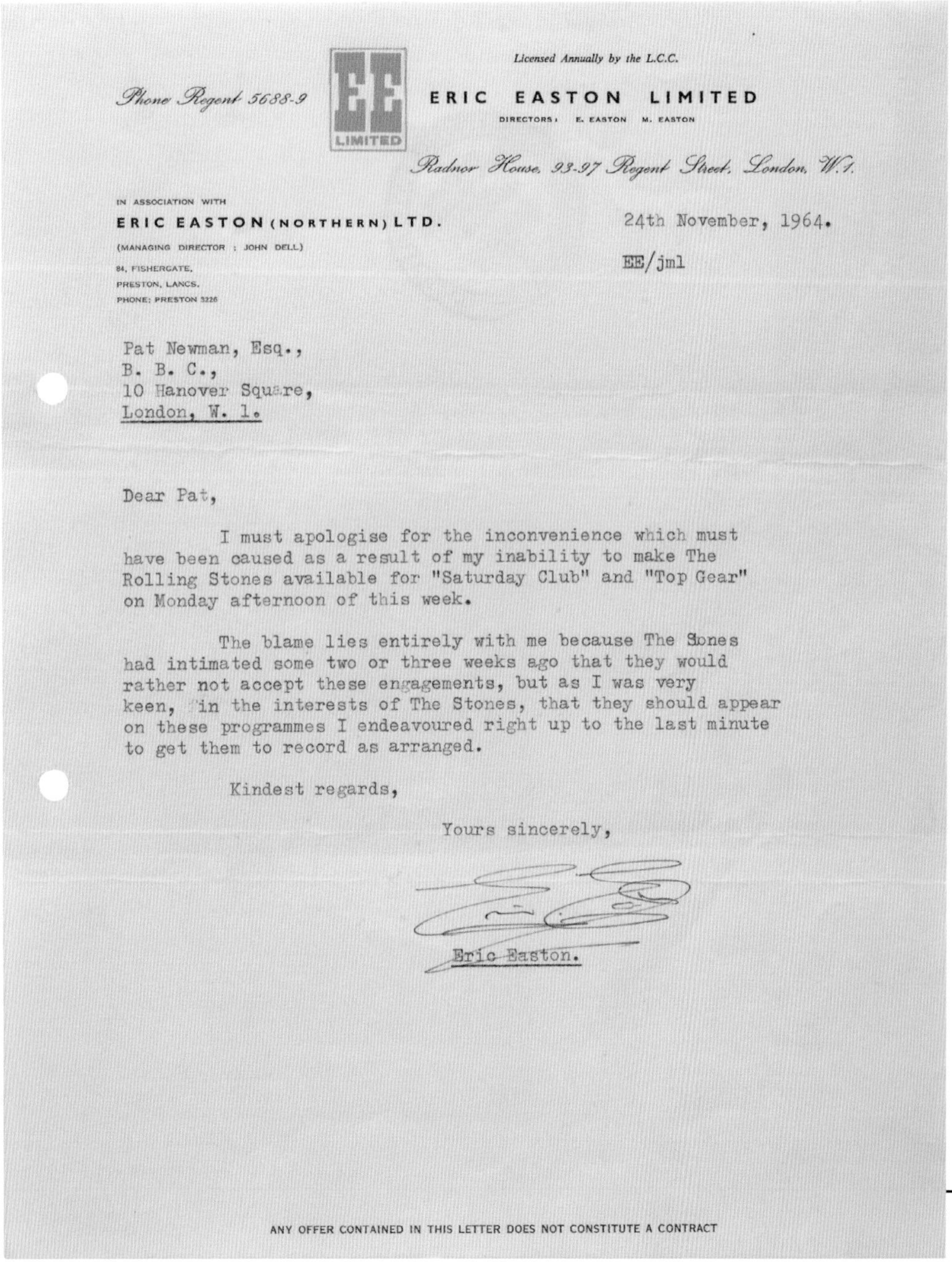

Licensed Annually by the L.C.C.

Phone Regent 5688-9

EE LIMITED

ERIC EASTON LIMITED

DIRECTORS: E. EASTON M. EASTON

Radnor House, 93-97 Regent Street, London, W.1.

IN ASSOCIATION WITH
ERIC EASTON (NORTHERN) LTD.
(MANAGING DIRECTOR : JOHN DELL)
84, FISHERGATE,
PRESTON, LANCS.
PHONE: PRESTON 3226

24th November, 1964.

EE/jml

Pat Newman, Esq.,
B. B. C.,
10 Hanover Square,
London, W. 1.

Dear Pat,

I must apologise for the inconvenience which must have been caused as a result of my inability to make The Rolling Stones available for "Saturday Club" and "Top Gear" on Monday afternoon of this week.

The blame lies entirely with me because The Stones had intimated some two or three weeks ago that they would rather not accept these engagements, but as I was very keen, in the interests of The Stones, that they should appear on these programmes I endeavoured right up to the last minute to get them to record as arranged.

Kindest regards,

Yours sincerely,

Eric Easton.

ANY OFFER CONTAINED IN THIS LETTER DOES NOT CONSTITUTE A CONTRACT

Left and opposite: Eric Easton takes the blame for the Stones

Following pages: The BBC consider sanctions against the band

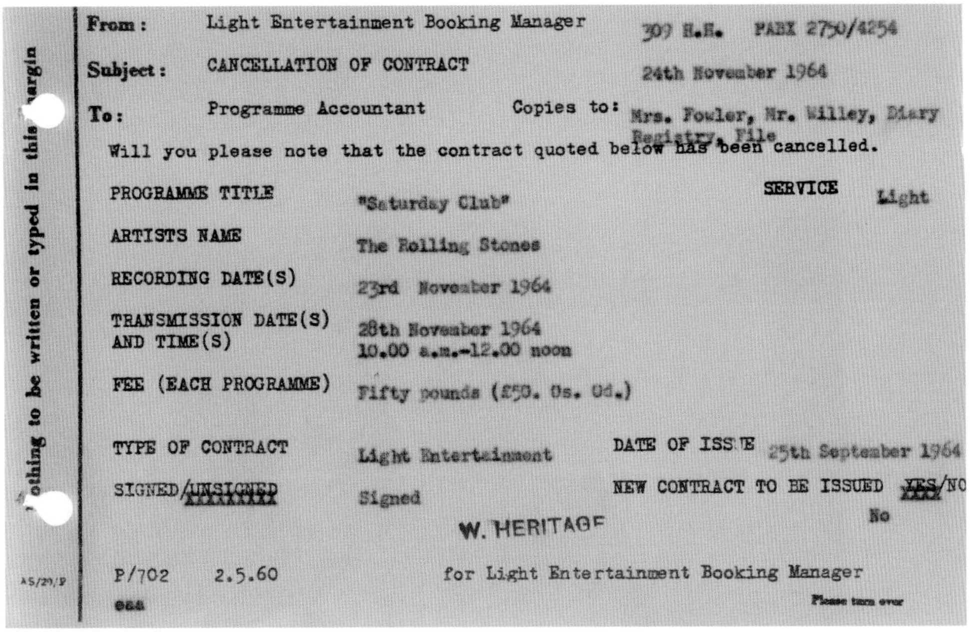

Nothing to be written or typed in this margin

From: Light Entertainment Booking Manager 309 H.H. PABX 2750/4254

Subject: CANCELLATION OF CONTRACT 24th November 1964

To: Programme Accountant Copies to: Mrs. Fowler, Mr. Willey, Diary Registry, File

Will you please note that the contract quoted below has been cancelled.

PROGRAMME TITLE	"Saturday Club"	SERVICE	Light
ARTISTS NAME	The Rolling Stones		
RECORDING DATE(S)	23rd November 1964		
TRANSMISSION DATE(S) AND TIME(S)	28th November 1964 10.00 a.m.-12.00 noon		
FEE (EACH PROGRAMME)	Fifty pounds (£50. 0s. 0d.)		
TYPE OF CONTRACT	Light Entertainment	DATE OF ISSUE	25th September 1964
SIGNED/~~UNSIGNED~~	Signed	NEW CONTRACT TO BE ISSUED ~~YES~~/NO	No

W. HERITAGE

for Light Entertainment Booking Manager

AS/29/P P/702 2.5.60

esa

Please turn over

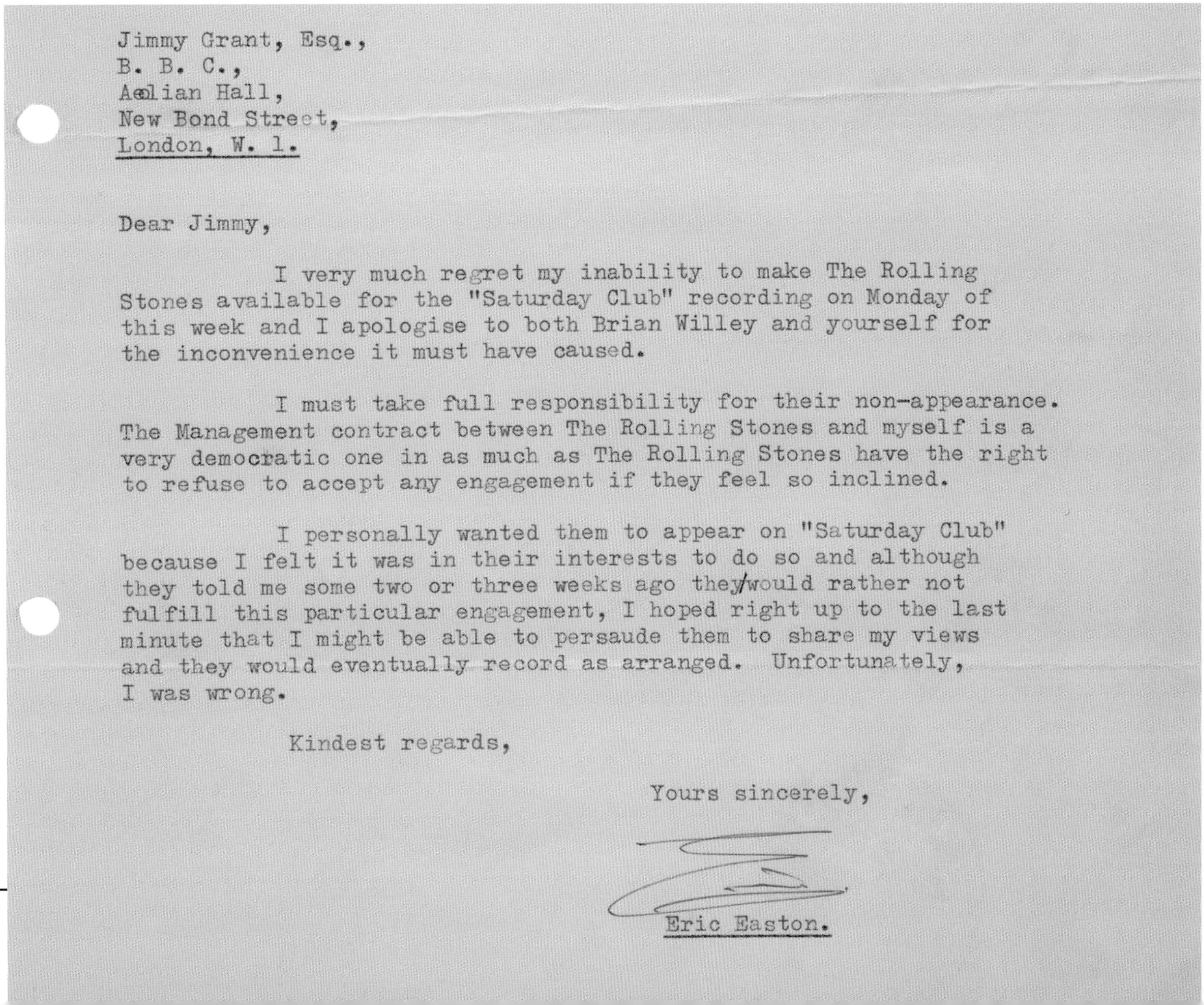

Jimmy Grant, Esq.,
B. B. C.,
Aeolian Hall,
New Bond Street,
London, W. 1.

Dear Jimmy,

I very much regret my inability to make The Rolling Stones available for the "Saturday Club" recording on Monday of this week and I apologise to both Brian Willey and yourself for the inconvenience it must have caused.

I must take full responsibility for their non-appearance. The Management contract between The Rolling Stones and myself is a very democratic one in as much as The Rolling Stones have the right to refuse to accept any engagement if they feel so inclined.

I personally wanted them to appear on "Saturday Club" because I felt it was in their interests to do so and although they told me some two or three weeks ago they would rather not fulfill this particular engagement, I hoped right up to the last minute that I might be able to persaude them to share my views and they would eventually record as arranged. Unfortunately, I was wrong.

Kindest regards,

Yours sincerely,

Eric Easton.

From: Light Entertainment Booking Manager. 305 H.H. PABX 2684/4250

Subject: THE ROLLING STONES

To: H.P.C. 25th November 1964

On the 25th September a contract was issued for the engagement of the above group to appear in "Saturday Club", (transmission date 28th November - pre-recorded at The Playhouse on the 23rd November). The contract was received back, signed, on the 20th October. (See November 28th edition of Radio Times, Page 9 - wryly amusing - and Page 15.) On 5th October contract issued for "Top Gear", (transmission 3rd December, pre-recorded at The Playhouse on 23rd November). The contract was received back, signed, on the 20th October.

(The planning of the pre-recording of the above two programmes on the same afternoon was done in the interests of the artists.)

On 22nd October contract issued for "The Joe Loss Pop Show" (transmission 11th December, pre-recorded at The Playhouse, 4th December). Contract unsigned.

In all three cases contracts were issued following a verbal acceptance from the agent.

On Sunday, the 22nd November, agent Eric Easton rang Chief Producer, Jimmy Grant, to say that the artists had told him they would not be appearing on any of the aforementioned three programmes. Grant spoke to me on the morning of Monday, the 23rd and I spoke to the Easton office and then to Easton himself (at home recovering from pneumonia). I also spoke to one of the group (Charles Watts) at his home and he told me that many weeks previously the group had told Easton that they did not want any more engagements for some time as they wished to take a holiday. I told him that I thought it would be in his own interests to try and get them to the studio and he referred me back to the office. There I spoke to a Bob Knight who said he would do his best, but he didn't think they'd appear.

They did not, in fact, put in an appearance that afternoon and subsequently Knight rang me to re-iterate that they would not appear for the 4th December recording of "The Joe Loss Pop Show". Easton is extremely upset about their behaviour and would think us justified in taking whatever action we think fit. I myself (possibly still smarting with the memory of The Animals) would dearly love to impose sanctions of some sort. And I am to say that H.P.M.(S). feels likewise. It seems to me that it would be a salutary lesson not only for the group in question, but for the whole industry.

Are we or are we not in a position to proceed against either the artists or the agent?

If we are, and we do so ..... well and good. If we are and we do not do so because, for example, it is a decision from on high that it is perhaps "beneath"

/Continued............

the Corporation, well, though I think this would not be very satisfactory, at least all concerned would accept some such top-level pronouncement and we would simply learn to relax and slowly thicken our skins against such cavalier treatment.

If we are not in a position to take action does the fault lie with the Booking Section, or with the wording of our contracts? If the fault lies with me, then I would like some legal observation as to where is the weak link in the chain so that I can take some corrective action to make sure it does not happen again. (This is why I attach herewith a history of our dealings with this group up to the moment of default. It sets out in details such matters as authorisation from artists, per pro signatures where a limited company is concerned, etc. etc.) If the fault lies with the wording of the contract can something be done on this score? (I am here reminded of your note of the 11th September 1964 - subject "The Animals" - which so astonished, and depressed, me that I had the temerity to write as I did on the 17th September, only to get back nothing more encouraging than your 23rd September comment.)

You may know that these gentlemen (sic) are (for a transient moment one rather hopes) third in the Top Ten or the "charts" which is a sort of thermometer of this world which these days even rates regular mention in the august (?) columns of The Daily Telegraph. For my part I am a firm believer in noses being very occasionally cut off to spite one's face. So - if we cannot get somebody into court and mulct them of some money (if only as recompense for wear and tear of a Booking Manager if you like) can we not have someone at nigh unto D.G. level denying them any "exposure" at all ..... this of course would include the playing of their commercial gramophone records?

Pat Newman

(Patrick Newman)

P.S.: I've a hunch they are treating BBC-TV the same way.

P.P.S.: I have (personally) agreed with Publicity the use of the words "failed to appear" as suitable for a Press statement. The producer has not yet approached me for advice as to what announcement we make at the microphone.

VM
Enc.

Nothing to be written or typed in this margin

From : Light Entertainment Booking Manager. 305 H.H. PABX 2684/4250

Subject : THE ROLLING STONES 26th November 1964

To : H.P.C.

As a follow-up to my memo of yesterday's date I attach herewith two letters which we have received from the agent together with a copy of my reply. (I understand that he has written letters in similar vein to the producers concerned.)

It now looks as though the agent is to blame. In the previous case (The Animals) it also eventually transpired that the agent was at fault. The tiresome thing is that the agent of The Rolling Stones (Eric Easton) is a jolly nice helpful fellow (who appears to have bitten off more than he can chew in handling this group), whereas the agent for The Animals (Don Arden) is a thoroughly naughty man who at the moment is, amongst other things, in trouble with the Agents' Association.

To sum up it is still my feeling that we should take some action against someone. If it can be against the group of artists that's fine. However, it we can only proceed against the agent then I fear I think we should do so.

(Patrick Newman)

VM/Enc.

AS/20/P

Please turn over

Nothing to be written or typed in this margin

From : Light Entertainment Booking Manager. 305 H.H. PABX 2684/4250

Subject : THE ROLLING STONES

To : H.P.C. 27th November 1964

As a follow-up to my note of yesterday's date I can say (though I do not think that it helps things much) that if we are to take any legal action (successfully that is) the person who will suffer will be the agent, Eric Easton. He tells me that if we were to proceed against The Rolling Stones Ltd. and if we were to win, and if the law said that the five performers themselves were the ones to pay up, then he, Easton, would still feel morally bound to re-imburse them.

One would like to think that we could totally ban this group for a period of, say, six months; that is to say, they would not be seen on television, nor would they be heard on sound radio either live, or by means of the playing of commercial gramophone records. One problem here would be that "Pick of the Pops" (which comes under the aegis of Gramophone Department) is a programme specifically alluding to the current rating (in terms of the sale of gramophone records) of this type of artist, and we could hardly leave them out if that particular week they were No. 1. on the list.

(Patrick Newman)

VM

AS/20/P

Please turn over

Left: Internal BBC memos continue the debate

Opposite: Patrick Newman writes to Eric Easton

Reference: 01/PC/PN 26th November 1964

Dear Eric,

<u>The Rolling Stones</u>

Thank you for your letter of the 24th November ..... you can also take this as an acknowledgement of your letter of the same date addressed to David Dore.

I must say I am a little concerned to see you shouldering the blame for this extraordinarily unsatisfactory situation. Also it puzzles me a little if only because, when I spoke to you on the phone on Monday, you were not quite so forthcoming.

I must tell you that it is my opinion that the Corporation should really take some action over this particular case ..... otherwise it makes a nonsense of our contracts. I imagine you must agree with me on this score.

Anyhow, the position is that I have set out the entire sequence of events in detail and my notes have been sent over to the Head of our Programme Contracts Department. I do not know, at the moment, what action the Corporation will decide to take.

Yours sincerely,

PATRICK NEWMAN

(Patrick Newman)
Light Entertainment Booking Manager

Eric Easton, Esq.,
Eric Easton, Ltd.,
Radnor House,
93-97 Regent Street,
London, W. 1.

VM

Licensed Annually by the L.C.C.

Phone Regent 5688-9

ERIC EASTON LIMITED

DIRECTORS: E. EASTON M. EASTON

Radnor House, 93-97 Regent Street, London, W.1.

IN ASSOCIATION WITH

ERIC EASTON (NORTHERN) LTD.

(MANAGING DIRECTOR : JOHN DELL)

84, FISHERGATE,
PRESTON, LANCS.
PHONE: PRESTON 3226

EE/jml

30th November, 1964.

Patrick Newman, Esq.,
Light Entertainment Booking Manager,
B. B. C.,
Broadcasting House,
London, W. 1.

Dear Pat,

Thank you for your letter of the 26th instant. I thought I had made it quite plain on the telephone that it was I who had accepted the two radio dates in question for The Rolling Stones and I am sorry if I did not make it quite clear.

I do hope that this situation will resolve itself in the near future because I dislike there being misunderstandings of any sort.

Best wishes,

Yours sincerely,

Eric Easton.

Reference: 01/PC/PN 2nd December 1964

Rolling Stones

Dear Eric,

Thank you for your further letter of the 30th November. Of course I knew perfectly well that it was you (or at any rate your office) who had accepted the dates in question. But it does not seem to me automatically to follow that the responsibility for their not turning up was yours.

I am enchanted at the - if you will forgive my saying so - naive tone of your final paragraph. Frankly, I cannot quite see how, at this juncture, the situation will "resolve itself"; although you can certainly take it that the Corporation dislikes misunderstandings of this sort every bit as much as you do ...... rather as I myself disliked the traffic on my telephone from our Press Office over the week-end.

Consideration is now being given to what - if any - action we shall take and I expect I shall be back to you again later.

Yours sincerely,

PATRICK NEWMAN
(Patrick Newman)
Light Entertainment Booking Manager

Eric Easton Esq.,
Eric Easton Ltd.,
Radnor House,
93-97 Regent Street,
London, W. 1.

H.PC To add to the pile, please.

VM

Following pages:
The debate rumbles on

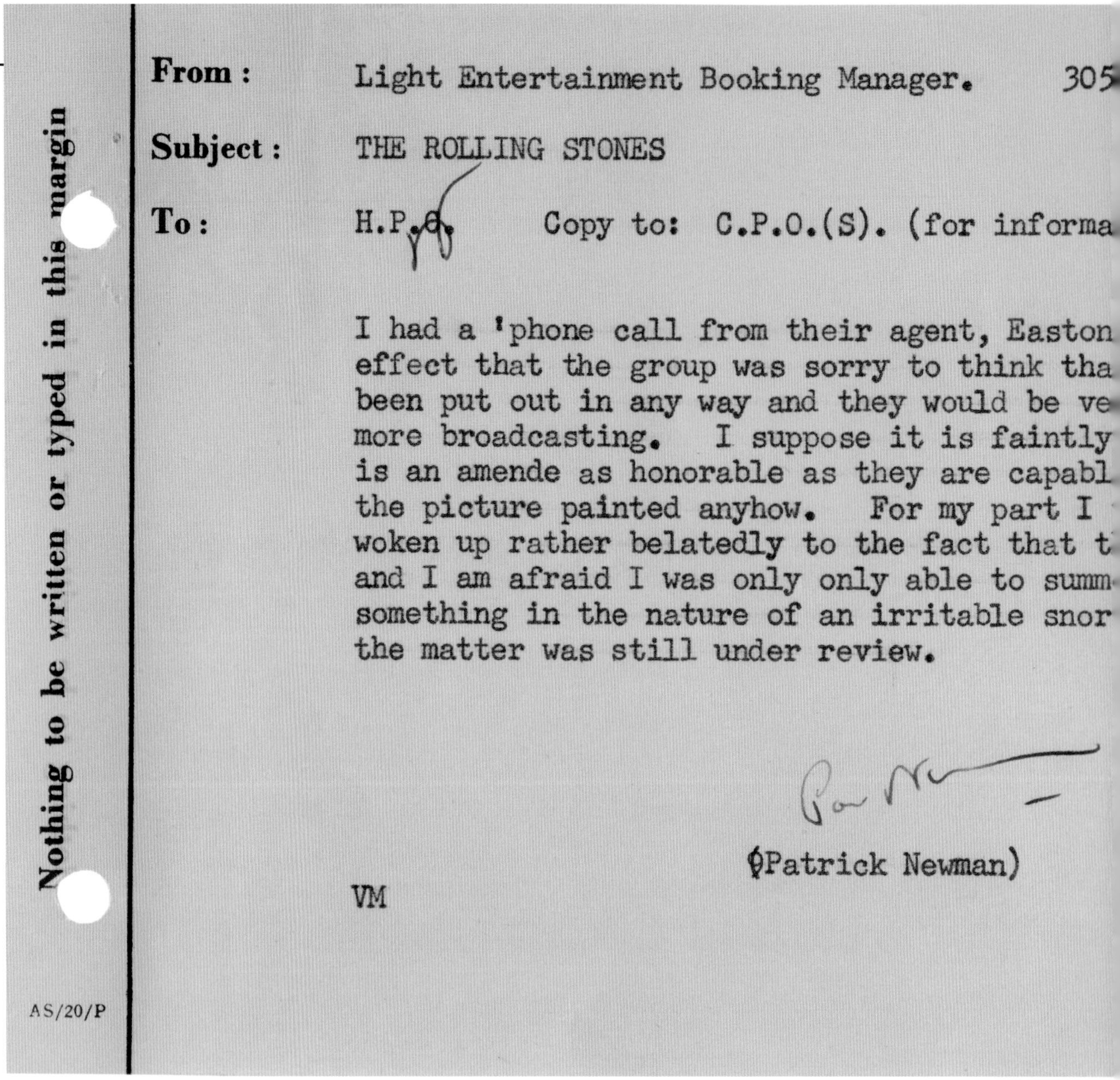

Nothing to be written or typed in this margin

From : Light Entertainment Booking Manager. 305

Subject : THE ROLLING STONES

To : H.P.G. Copy to: C.P.O.(S). (for informa

I had a 'phone call from their agent, Easton
effect that the group was sorry to think tha
been put out in any way and they would be ve
more broadcasting. I suppose it is faintly
is an amende as honorable as they are capabl
the picture painted anyhow. For my part I
woken up rather belatedly to the fact that t
and I am afraid I was only only able to summ
something in the nature of an irritable snor
the matter was still under review.

(Patrick Newman)

VM

AS/20/P

The bitter row rumbled on for several more weeks, with the music press in particular having a field day with what they perceived as the BBC's high-handed attitude and the only losers in the row being the fans. In the week following the Stones' non-appearance on *Top of the Pops*, one angry reader wrote in to the *Record Mirror* to complain: 'I think this is a direct snub to the Stones and their fans,' while another wrote: 'Fans want an explanation, an apology and rolling BBC-type heads. Fast!'

None of this unduly troubled the executives at the BBC. The programme controller (Sound) wrote a memo saying, 'I don't think as a reprisal for these breaches of contract we can bar the records of the Rolling Stones from the air ... partly because of our monopoly position and partly because of innocent parties, i.e. the gramophone company, the composers and music publishers [who] would be penalized thereby.' However, he went on to say that the BBC must not give the impression that 'we are ready to lie down under this kind of treatment'. Fundamental to the BBC's approach was enlisting the help of Decca to get their artist to 'respect undertakings on their behalf'.

Earlier in December, Andrew Loog Oldham had gone to the BBC to appear on their *Teen Scene* programme only to be told, ten minutes before he was due to go on air, that he would not be appearing. *The Melody Maker* asked the BBC to comment on the 'Stones ban' and they responded by saying, 'As there has been some misunderstanding with the Rolling Stones it was thought inadvisable for their manager to appear.' They went on to add, 'It is not known if there is any question of legal action.'

Maybe it was the spirit of Christmas that finally brought about a thaw in relations. On 18 December G. M.

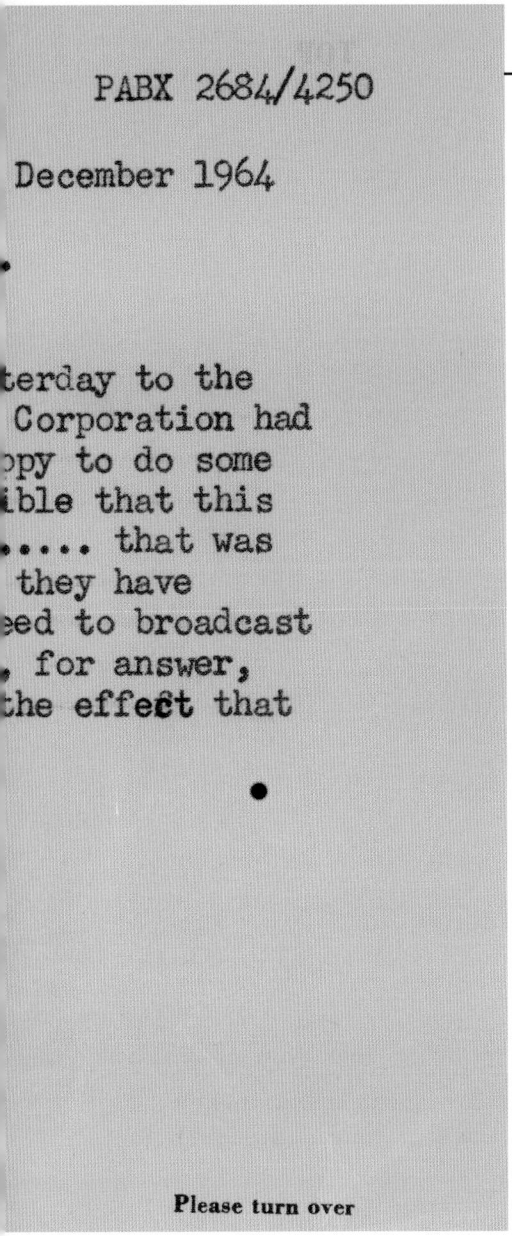

PABX 2684/4250

December 1964

terday to the
Corporation had
ppy to do some
ible that this
..... that was
they have
eed to broadcast
, for answer,
the effect that

Please turn over

Turnell, head of programme contracts, wrote to Eric Easton saying, 'While we do not propose to take any further action on this occasion, if the Rolling Stones fail to honour any further commitment we shall cease to offer them engagements in radio.'

However the television people were not quite so forgiving. Having not played the Stones' No.1 record earlier in the month, the assistant controller for television programme services, a Mr Leonard Maill, wrote a memo saying, 'Light Entertainment Group have undertaken not to make any approaches to the Rolling Stones without checking first with Artists Bookings, Television who in turn, have arranged to check with Programme Contracts before offering an engagement ... When the need for special precautions has passed would you please let us know.' It was on 20 January 1965 that the head of programme contracts wrote to what seemed like every department head in the BBC, saying: 'We have had a reasonable reply from the Rolling Stones' manager and that the need for special precautions has passed.'

In the Orwellian world of the BBC it would be 1 March 1965 before the Stones again appeared in person on BBC radio and three days later they were on *Top of the Pops*.

Meanwhile, in America, London Records had passed on releasing 'Rooster', which displeased the band. Executives at London thought the sexual undertones of the lyrics were too blatant and felt there was every chance that American radio stations would refuse to play it and so they released 'Heart Of Stone' instead.

FROM: Controller, Programme Organisation (Sound)

SUBJECT: THE ROLLING STONES 15th December 1964

TO: H.P.C. Copy to: A.D.S.B., C.P.S.Tel., H.P.M.(S)
Light Ent. Booking Manager
Ch.L.P. (for information)

I don't think that as a reprisal for these breaches of contract we can bar the records of 'The Rolling Stones' from the air. I have discussed this possibility with A.D.S.B. and he is against it partly because of our monopoly position and partly because other quite innocent parties, i.e. the Gramophone Company, the composers and Music Publishers would be penalised thereby.

On the other hand we certainly must not give the impression that we are ready to lie down under this kind of treatment. The situation in this particular case is affected by the belated apology that we have since received on behalf of 'The Rolling Stones' and since, as Light Ent. Booking Manager puts it, this is possibly the most honourable amende of which they are capable we had better accept it as that an not impose a stop on further bookings.

But we must make our attitude clear for the future and I think that we should write to their agent in forthright terms saying:

(a) that whatever arrangement he may have with them if he accepts a booking on their behalf we shall and must regard this as a commitment. If he has not authority to commit his artists and yet elects to do so we cannot do business with him and moreover we shall bring this matter before the Agents' Association;

(b) if the Rolling Stones fail to honour any future commitment we shall cease to offer them any further engagements in radio.

I hope and believe that our Television Service would in such circumstances fall in line with us. Perhaps C.P.S.Tel. will let you know. It need not at this stage be mentioned to the agent.

I think that H.G.P. should get hold of the appropriate person in the Gramophone Company which issues their records and let him know what has happened i.e. 3 contractual commitments dishonoured and what steps we intend to take if it happens again. Radio appearances are far too valuable for the Gramophone Company to ignore their importance, and I am pretty sure that this will be another means of bringing effective pressure on these artists to respect undertakings on their behalf. H.G.P. should not threaten that we will ban their records and in fact the word 'ban' is best avoided in the context altogether. The Gramophone Company can draw their own conclusions as to the effect which the situation might have on our use of their records, and so far as our discontinuing to book them for live performances this would simply be because we could not depend upon their turning up.

As to the 'Animals' who have seemingly proffered no apology, I think we should write to their agent and say that unless we can have an undertaking that they will honour commitments we shall discontinue making them any offers for radio. Again I think that H.G.P. should make the position known to the Gramophone Company concerned i.e. that pending an apology we shall offer no further dates.

All this now needs to be done as soon as possible.

M. Standing

PJS (M.F.C. Standing)

Copies inadvertently kept by C.P.O.(S)'s office

It's [illegible] way [illegible] J.D. 16/12/64

CONFIDENTIAL

FROM: Assistant Controller, Programme Services, Television 6034 T.C.
2119-2944

SUBJECT: THE ROLLING STONES 29th December 1964

TO: C.P.O.(S.) Copy to: A.D.S.B., C.P.S.Tel., H.P.C., H.P.M.(S.),
Light Entertainment Booking Manager,
Ch.L.P.

H.A.B.Tel., A.H.A.B.Tel.,
Senior Booking Manager, Television

H.L.E.G.Tel., A.H.L.E.G.Tel.(Variety),
A.H.L.E.G.Tel.(Comedy), C.A.(Gen.) L.E.

In the absence of C.P.S.Tel. on leave I am writing to let you know that the Television Service was alerted before Christmas to the situation with regard to The Rolling Stones and is prepared to back you up if you need to apply sanctions.

Light Entertainment Group has undertaken not to make anyapproaches to The Rolling Stones without checking first with Artists Bookings, Television who, in turn, have arranged to check with Programme Contracts before offering an engagement.

We will keep this matter confidential.

When the need for special precautions has passed would you please let us know.

LEONARD MIALL

jrc (Leonard Miall)

x well – according to HPC's letter of 18/12 (of which C.P.S. Tel. had a copy) we're not applying "special precautions"

[initials]

Below: The matter is finally wrapped up, much to Eric Easton's relief

---

Licensed Annually by the L.C.C.

Phone Regent 4536 ERIC EASTON LIMITED

DIRECTORS: E. EASTON M. EASTON

1 Little Argyll St., ~~Radnor House 93-97~~ Regent Street, London, W.1.

IN ASSOCIATION WITH

ERIC EASTON (NORTHERN) LTD.

(MANAGING DIRECTOR : JOHN DELL)

84, FISHERGATE,
PRESTON, LANCS.
PHONE: PRESTON 3226

EE/jml

30th December, 1964.

G. M. Turnell, Esq.,
Head of Programme Contracts,
B. B. C.,
Broadcasting House,
London, W. 1.

Dear Mr. Turnell,

Thank you for your letter dated 18th December regarding The Rolling Stones. Your comments are noted and I would like to thank you for the very reasonable way in which the B.B.C. have treated this matter and I must again apologise for any inconvenience which was caused.

Yours sincerely,

Eric Easton.

RETURN OF THE CONQUERING HEROES

The Stones' need for a break from the constant round of gigs, radio and TV shows was inevitable, which resulted in December 1964 being the least busy month for the band for two years. They played just one concert during the month on Friday 4 December in South London at the Fairfield Halls, with support from Cliff Bennett and the Rebel Rousers and Twinkle among others.

Three days later they recorded their first appearance for US TV show, *Shindig*, and that was it until New Year's Eve when the band starred on *RSG!'s The New Year Starts Here*, which aired from 11.05 p.m. until half past midnight. Joining the Stones were the Dave Clark Five, the Animals, Dusty Springfield and a few other minor stars. Given the BBC ban, the Corporation comforted themselves with two programmes in direct competition. On BBC 1 was the traditional *New Year Party* broadcast live from Scotland, this year from Perth's City Hall, starring Jimmy Shand and Andy Stewart, while BBC 2 had *Beat in the New* featuring Billy J. Kramer, the Kinks and P. J. Proby.

In a revealing interview given by Keith to *Disc* in the dressing room of *RSG!*, he said, 'The thing is, you get used to living with Mick. He isn't a great organizer, but he has to be, with me around. I'm terrible. I forget everything. Mick's very good at getting up in the morning. He comes in and wakes me up, and I go back to sleep again. He brings me cups of tea.'

With two gold records and 2 million sellers, two US tours, concerts in Europe, four US hit singles, two British No.1 singles, a No.1 British album and an album that got to No.11 in the USA, the band had been rewarded for their hard work, having gained the support of radio and TV… and they were about to go global.

1964 SELECTED TV & RADIO APPEARANCES

1 JANUARY 1964
Top of the Pops, Studio A, Dickenson Road, Rusholme, Manchester, UK
I Wanna Be Your Man (John Lennon/Paul McCartney) – playback

24 JANUARY 1964
Go Man Go, BBC Maida Vale, London, UK
I Wanna Be Your Man (John Lennon/Paul McCartney), **Pretty Thing** (Willie Dixon), **Bye Bye Johnny** (Chuck Berry), **You Better Move On** (Arthur Alexander), **I Want To Be Loved** (Willie Dixon) and **Roll Over Beethoven** (Chuck Berry)

29 JANUARY 1964
Top of the Pops, Studio A, Dickenson Road, Rusholme, Manchester, UK
You Better Move On (Arthur Alexander) – playback

3 FEBRUARY 1964
(aired 8 February)
Saturday Club, Playhouse Theatre, Charing Cross Road, London, UK
Don't Lie To Me (Chuck Berry), **You Better Move On** (Arthur Alexander), **I Wanna Be Your Man** (John Lennon/Paul McCartney), **Mona** (Ellas McDaniel), **Walking The Dog** (Rufus Thomas) and **Bye Bye Johnny** (Chuck Berry)

7 FEBRUARY 1964
(aired 8 February)
The Arthur Haynes Show, Elstree Studios, Borehamwood, Hertfordshire, UK
I Wanna Be Your Man (John Lennon/Paul McCartney) and **You Better Move On** (Arthur Alexander)

14 FEBRUARY 1964
Ready Steady Go!, TV House, Kingsway, London, UK
Not Fade Away (Norman Petty/Charles Hardin Holly), **I Wanna Be Your Man** (John Lennon/Paul McCartney) – playback, and **You Better Move On** (Arthur Alexander) – playback

18 FEBRUARY 1964
Pop Inn, Paris Theatre, Lower Regent Street, London, UK
Not Fade Away (Norman Petty/Charles Hardin Holly)

22 FEBRUARY 1964
(probably aired 27 February, possibly repeated 12 March)
Top of the Pops, filmed on Weymouth Beach, Dorset, UK
Not Fade Away (Norman Petty/Charles Hardin Holly)

23 FEBRUARY 1964
(aired 29 February)
Thank Your Lucky Stars, Alpha Studios, Aston, Birmingham, UK
Not Fade Away (Norman Petty/Charles Hardin Holly) – playback

4 MARCH 1964
(aired 5 March)
Scene at 6.30, ITV Studios, Manchester, UK
Not Fade Away (Norman Petty/Charles Hardin Holly) – playback
(aired probably 5 March, possibly 12 March and 8 April)
Top of the Pops, Studio A, Dickenson Road, Rusholme, Manchester, UK
Not Fade Away (Norman Petty/Charles Hardin Holly) – playback

18 MARCH 1964
(aired 17 April, 24 April, 1 May and 8 May)
Pre-recorded 14 tracks for 4 x 15 minute radio shows for Radio Luxembourg in London
Bye Bye Johnny (Chuck Berry), **Diddley Daddy** (Ellas McDaniel/Harvey Fuqua), **I Wanna Be Your Man** (John Lennon/Paul McCartney), **Little By Little** (Nanker Phelge/Phil Spector), **Look What You've Done** (McKinley Morganfield), **Mona** (Ellas McDaniel), **Not Fade Away** (Norman Petty/Charles Hardin Holly), **Now I've Got A Witness** (Nanker Phelge), **Pretty Thing** (Willie Dixon), **Reelin' And Rockin** (Chuck Berry), **Roll Over Beethoven** (Chuck Berry), **Route 66** (Bobby Troup), **Walking The Dog** (Rufus Thomas) and **You Better Move On** (Arthur Alexander)
All unverified

19 MARCH 1963
(aired 9 May)
Blues in Rhythm, stereo radio show, Camden Theatre, London, UK
Route 66 (Bobby Troup), **Cops and Robbers** (Kent L. Harris), **You Better Move On** (Arthur Alexander) and **Mona** (Ellas McDaniel)

3 APRIL 1964
Ready, Steady, Go!, TV House, Kingsway, London, UK
Not Fade Away (Norman Petty/Charles Hardin Holly) – playback, and **I Just Want to Make Love To You** (Willie Dixon)

8 APRIL 1964
(aired 8 April)
Ready Steady Go Mod Ball, Empire Pool Wembley, UK
Not Fade Away (Norman Petty/Charles Hardin Holly) – playback, **Walking The Dog** (Rufus Thomas) – playback, **Hi-Heel Sneakers** (Robert Higginbotham) – playback, and **I'm Alright** (Ellas McDaniel)

10 APRIL 1964
The Joe Loss Show, Playhouse Theatre, Charing Cross Road, London, UK
Not Fade Away (Norman Petty/Charles Hardin Holly), **Hi-Heel Sneakers** (Robert Higginbotham), **Little By Little** (Nanker Phelge/Phil Spector), **I Just Want To Make Love To You** (Willie Dixon) and **I'm Moving On** (Hank Snow)

13 APRIL 1964
(aired 18 April)
Saturday Club, Playhouse Theatre, Charing Cross Road, London, UK
I Just Want To Make Love To You (Willie Dixon), **Walking The Dog** (Rufus Thomas), **Not Fade Away** (Norman Petty/Charles Hardin Holly), **Beautiful Delilah** (Chuck Berry), **Hi-Heel Sneakers** (Robert Higginbotham) and **Carol** (Chuck Berry)

20 APRIL 1964
(aired 24 April)
International Golden Rose TV Awards, Montreux, Switzerland
Mona (Ellas McDaniel), **Route 66** (Bobby Troup) and **Not Fade Away** (Norman Petty/Charles Hardin Holly)

26 APRIL 1964
(aired 3 May, repeated 1 November)
NME Poll Winners Concert, Empire Pool, Wembley, UK
Taped by WINS Radio, New York, for **The Murray the K Show** (one or more of the tracks were broadcast in late April)
Not Fade Away (Norman Petty/Charles Hardin Holly), **I Just Want To Make Love To You** (Willie Dixon) and **I'm Alright** (Ellas McDaniel)

27 APRIL 1964
(aired 25 May)
Top Beat Pop Prom, Royal Albert Hall, London, UK
Not Fade Away (Norman Petty/Charles Hardin Holly), **Hi-Heel Sneakers** (Robert Higginbotham) and **I'm Alright** (Ellas McDaniel)

29 APRIL 1964
(aired 30 April, possibly repeated November/December 1965)
Top of the Pops, Studio A, Dickenson Road in Rusholme, Manchester, UK
I Just Want To Make Love To You (Willie Dixon)

6 MAY 1964
(probably aired the same day)
Two Go Round, Southampton, Hampshire, UK
Not Fade Away (Norman Petty/Charles Hardin Holly)

9 MAY 1964
Open House, Riverside Studios, Hammersmith, London, UK
Hi-Heel Sneakers (Robert Higginbotham)

15 MAY 1964
(aired 6 June)

Saturday Club, Playhouse Theatre, Charing Cross Road, London, UK

Down In The Bottom (Willie Dixon), **You Can Make It If You Try** (Ted Jarrett), **Route 66** (Bobby Troup), **Confessin' The Blues** (Walter Brown/Jay McShann) and **Down The Road Apiece** (Don Raye)

1 JUNE 1964

Murray The K's Swinging Soiree, WINS Radio, New York, USA – interviews

2 JUNE 1964

WMCA Good Guys, WMCA Radio, New York, USA – live Interview

The Les Crane Show, WABC TV, New York, USA – interview

(aired 7 June, probably repeated 20 June)

The Clay Cole Teen Show, WPIX TV, New York, USA (probably pre-recorded)

Tell Me (MJ/KR), **Carol** (Chuck Berry) and **Not Fade Away** (Norman Petty/Charles Hardin Holly)

3 JUNE 1964

The Hollywood Palace Show, ABC TV, Hollywood Playhouse, Hollywood and Vine, CA, USA

(aired 13 June)

I Just Want To Make Love To You (Willie Dixon)

(aired 26 September)

Not Fade Away (Norman Petty/Charles Hardin Holly)

18 JUNE 1964
(probably aired the same day)

The Mike Douglas Show, KYW-TV3, Cleveland, Ohio, USA

Carol (Chuck Berry), **Tell Me** (MJ/KR) – playback, **Not Fade Away** (Norman Petty/Charles Hardin Holly) and **I Just Want To Make Love To You** (Willie Dixon) –playback

26 JUNE 1964

Ready, Steady, Go!, TV House, Kingsway, London, UK

It's All Over Now (Bobby and Shirley Womack) and **Good Times, Bad Times** (MJ/KR) – both playback

27 JUNE 1964
(aired 1, 8 and 29 July)

Top of the Pops, BBC Television Centre, White City, London, UK

It's All Over Now (Bobby and Shirley Womack) – playback

(aired 4 July)

Juke Box Jury, BBC, Shepherd's Bush TV Studios, London, UK

16 JULY 1964
(probably aired 24 July)

Teen and Twenty Disc Club, Radio Luxembourg, Pye Studios, Marble Arch, London, UK or Greenford, London, UK

17 JULY 1964

The Joe Loss Show, Playhouse Theatre, Charing Cross Road, London, UK

It's All Over Now (Bobby and Shirley Womack), **If You Need Me** (Wilson Pickett/Robert Bateman), **Confessin' The Blues** (Walter Brown/Jay McShann), **Carol** (Chuck Berry) and **Mona** (Ellas McDaniel)

(aired 23 July)

Top Gear, Playhouse Theatre, Charing Cross Road, London, UK

It's All Over Now (Bobby and Shirley Womack), **Around And Around** (Chuck Berry), **If You Need Me** (Wilson Pickett/Robert Bateman), **I Can't Be Satisfied** (McKinley Morganfield) and **Crackin' Up** (Ellas McDaniel)

31 JULY 1964

6.10 Show, Ulster Hall, Belfast, Northern Ireland – interview

5 AUGUST 1964
(aired 22 September, 10 November)

The Red Skelton Hour, London Palladium, London, UK

Tell Me (MJ/KR), **Carol** (Chuck Berry) and **It's All Over Now** (Bobby and Shirley Womack) – all playback

7 AUGUST 1964

Ready, Steady, Go! (1st Anniversary Show), TV House, Kingsway, London, UK

Around And Around (Chuck Berry), **If You Need Me** (Wilson Pickett/Robert Bateman) and **It's All Over Now** (Bobby and Shirley Womack) – playback

8 OCTOBER 1964
(aired 31 October)

Rhythm and Blues, BBC General Overseas Service, Playhouse Theatre, Charing Cross Road, London, UK

Dust My Pyramids (KR/BJ), **Around And Around** (Chuck Berry), **If You Need Me** (Wilson Pickett/Robert Bateman), **Ain't That Lovin' You, Baby** (Jimmy Reed), **Mona** (Ellas McDaniel) and **2120 South Michigan Avenue** (Nanker Phelge)

18 OCTOBER 1964
(aired 16 November)

Tienerklanken, The Amerikaans Theatre, World Fair Grounds, Brussels, Belgium

Not Fade Away (Norman Petty/Charles Hardin Holly), **Walking The Dog** (Rufus Thomas), **If You Need Me** (Wilson Pickett/Robert Bateman), **I'm Alright** (Ellas McDaniel), **Carol** (Chuck Berry), **Time Is On My Side** (Jerry Ragovoy/Jimmy Norman), **Tell Me** (MJ/KR), **It's All Over Now** (Bobby and Shirley Womack) and **Around And Around** (Chuck Berry)

19 OCTOBER 1964
(aired 5 November)

Quoi De Neuf, Paris, France

Carol (Chuck Berry), **Mona** (Ellas McDaniel) and **It's All Over Now** (Bobby and Shirley Womack) – playback

20 OCTOBER 1964

Europe No. 1 Radio – featured live broadcast of Stones gig at l'Olympia Theatre, Paris, France

24 OCTOBER 1964
(aired 31 October and 7 November)

The Clay Cole Teen Show, WPIX TV, New York, USA

If You Need Me (Wilson Pickett/Robert Bateman), **Time Is On My Side** (Jerry Ragovoy/Jimmy Norman), **It's All Over Now** (Bobby and Shirley Womack), **Around And Around'** (Chuck Berry) and **Confessin' The Blues** (Walter Brown/Jay McShann) –playback plus **Tell Me** (MJ/KR) – all playback; repeat from 20 June

25 OCTOBER 1964

The Ed Sullivan Show, New York, USA

Around And Around (Chuck Berry) and **Time Is On My Side** (Jerry Ragovoy/Jimmy Norman) – playback

20 NOVEMBER 1964
(aired same day and repeated on 31 December, New Year's Eve special)

Ready, Steady, Go!, TV House, Kingsway, London, UK

Off The Hook (MJ/KR), **Little Red Rooster** (Willie Dixon) and **Around And Around** (Chuck Berry)

(aired 25 November)

Glad Rag Ball, Empire Pool, Wembley, London, UK

Off The Hook (Nanker Phelge), **Little Red Rooster** (Willie Dixon) and **Around And Around** (Chuck Berry). Televised without **Off The Hook**

22 NOVEMBER 1964
(aired 27 November)

Teen Scene, BBC Broadcasting House, London, UK

15 DECEMBER 1964
(some tracks aired 20 January and 3 March 1965)

Shindig!, ABC TV Centre, Halliford Studios, Shepperton, UK

Oh Baby (Barbara Lynn Ozen), **Down The Road Apiece** (Don Raye), **Heart Of Stone** (MJ/KR) and **Susie Q** (Stanley Lewis/Dale Hawkins/Eleanor Broadwater) – playback

1963
1964
1965
1966

1967
1968
1969

1965

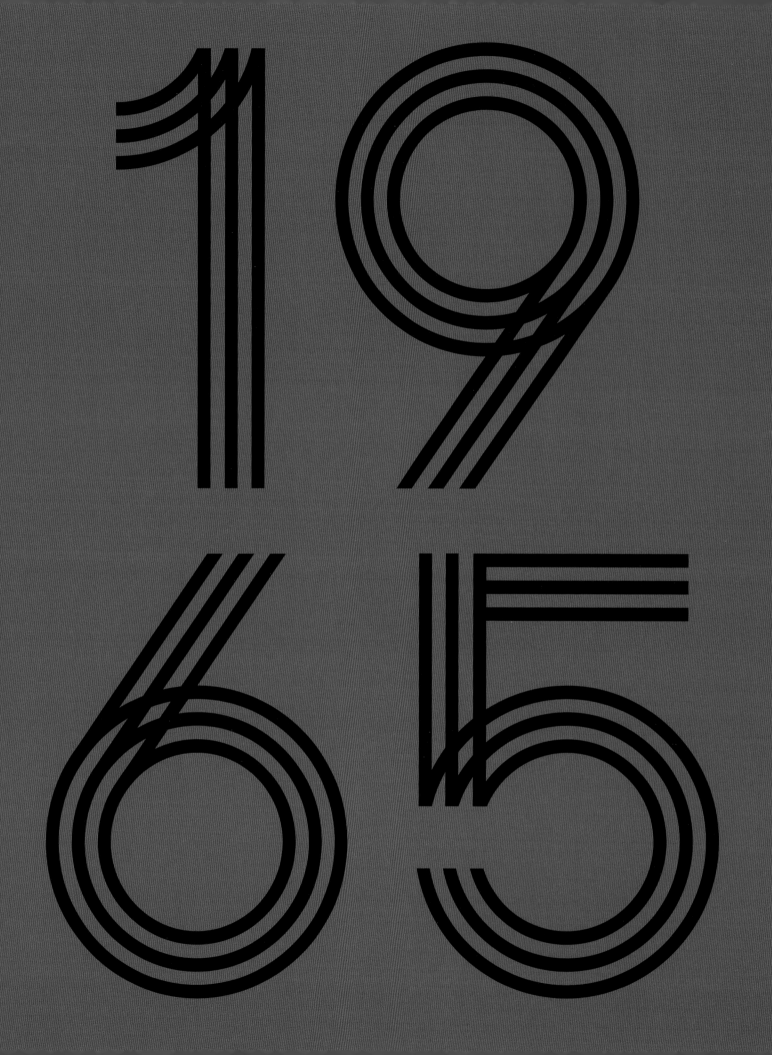

Previous pages: Recording an appearance on *Scene at 6.30* on 11 March, performing 'The Last Time'

The UK pop charts in the mid-1960s – and for that matter for much of the decade – were a veritable potpourri, although it would be another decade before having bowls of dried flowers around the house became chic.

In the first week of January 1965, the Beatles were, as usual or so it seemed, at No.1, but there was only one other group in the UK Top 10 – the Moody Blues. The other eight places were occupied by Twinkle, Petula Clark, Val Doonican, Gene Pitney, Sandie Shaw, P.J. Proby, Cliff Richard and Georgie Fame, with only the latter offering some real musical credibility.

In America, it was marginally better, with the Beatles occupying two of the top five spots, including the top spot, along with Bobby Vinton, the Searchers and the Supremes. A week later, the Stones made the Hot 100 with 'Heart Of Stone', a single released by London Records in America that was just an album track in the UK. London, in their wisdom, decided not to release 'Little Red Rooster', even though it had been No.1 in the UK the previous month and was still on the UK Top 20.

America and Britain were more than just 'two countries separated by the same language' as George Bernard Shaw had so eloquently put it. They were, and are, divided by the North Atlantic, which meant that during this time it was very much the Dark Ages of communications. Telephone calls had to be booked between the two countries, you couldn't just dial an overseas number; telegrams and cables were the speediest, if confusing, means of communication. Everything took a while to make the Atlantic crossing, and when musicians did they were often treated with a degree of wonderment because of being 'different', and none more so than the Stones.

Two US tours in 1964 had given the Stones a toehold with American teenagers, but it was in 1965 that the band turned it into a full-scale assault. They also made their first appearance on *Shindig!*, although it was taped in the UK. Their third US tour was in April and May, a far bigger affair than their second at the tail end of 1964; come October, their fourth US tour was a huge affair, playing thirty-seven venues in thirty-eight days.

In and around these American tours were television appearances and unprecedented radio coverage. All this resulted in the Stones securing their first US No.1 in June 1965 with '(I Can't Get No) Satisfaction', followed by a second in November with 'Get Off Of My Cloud'. Both songs also topped the UK charts, as did 'The Last Time', earlier in the year. It all added up to the fact that by year-end the Stones were more successful on the UK singles chart than the Beatles, and they certainly pushed them hard in America, where 'Satisfaction' was the 'top hit' of the year, according to *Billboard* magazine.

This was also the year that the Stones became a worldwide success. In January, they toured Australia and New Zealand. In March their first, albeit short, European tour to Denmark and Sweden was followed by another mini-tour to Scandinavia in June. Prior to heading to the USA for their fourth tour, the Stones went to West Germany and Austria and, aside from their music being a sensation, it was on news programmes that the band was most often seen, as riots broke out at almost every show on the six-city tour. In amongst it all there were UK tours which resulted in the band barely having time to catch their breath between gigs, TV, radio, recording and media access that seemed to be on a twenty-four-hour non-stop basis.

Come the end of 1965 and there was a subtle shift in pop music. The LP had become something else, something other than a hastily cobbled-together collection of tracks that were designed to cash in on an artist's latest hit single. The Beatles released *Rubber Soul* in December and this was a clear sign of the changing times. As the Stones' fourth US tour came to an end, they went into RCA Studios to record tracks that would appear on *Aftermath*, which, like *Rubber Soul*, was something very different from what other artists were doing. One of the tracks the Stones recorded in December was 'Goin' Home', which ran for over eleven minutes on *Aftermath*, the longest rock song to appear on an album up until this point.

And the key word is 'rock'. This was the beginning of a subtle shift away from the disposability of pop to the more credible, more thoughtful undertones of rock music. And to put it all into perspective, on 18 December Keith celebrated his twenty-second birthday, just as Mick had done a few months earlier.

HOME AND AWAY

When the Stones taped what was to be their debut for the American TV show, *Shindig!* on 15 December 1964, hosted by Los Angeles DJ Jimmy O'Neill, it had only been on the air for three months. It was O'Neill and his wife, Sharon Sheeley, who came up with the original concept for the show; Sheeley, as an 18-year-old, had written Ricky Nelson's first No.1 record, 'Poor Little Fool'. Later she became Eddie Cochran's girlfriend, writing 'Somethin' Else' for him, and she had been with him when he was killed in a car crash in England in April 1960.

Shindig! was devised for ABC as a replacement for their short-lived series, *Hootenanny*, which rode on the back of the folk craze in America, a trend killed off by the 'British Invasion'. When *Shindig!* first aired it was a half-hour show every Wednesday evening, but by the time the Stones appeared on 20 January 1965 it had expanded to an hour.

This was the first of half a dozen appearances by the Stones on the show, recorded at Halliford Studios in Shepperton, to the west of London. Despite miming to four songs, it was just their latest American single 'Heart Of Stone' that was used on the programme; when it aired the single was sitting at No.47 on the *Billboard* Hot 100 having entered the chart two weeks earlier at No.77. The song was included on the band's second UK album, *The Rolling Stones No. 2*, which was released five days before their *Shindig!* appearance. It was also included on their third US LP, *The Rolling Stones, Now!* that went on sale a month later.

Possibly as a result of some of the criticism of the band's dress on earlier American TV shows, all of them are wearing jackets for their *Shindig!* appearance, with Brian and Charlie both sporting ties.

Appearing alongside the Stones on the show was Petula Clark, whose latest single, 'Downtown', was about to spend two weeks at No.1. Fellow Brits the Kinks played two songs including 'All Day And All Of The Night', which was just going Top 20, as did the Dave Clark Five and Gerry and the Pacemakers. The episode also featured the Walker

Above: Jimmy O'Neill (3rd from left) with the Animals (l-r: Eric Burdon, Charles Chandler, Hilton Valentine, John Steel and Alan Price) and Donna Loren

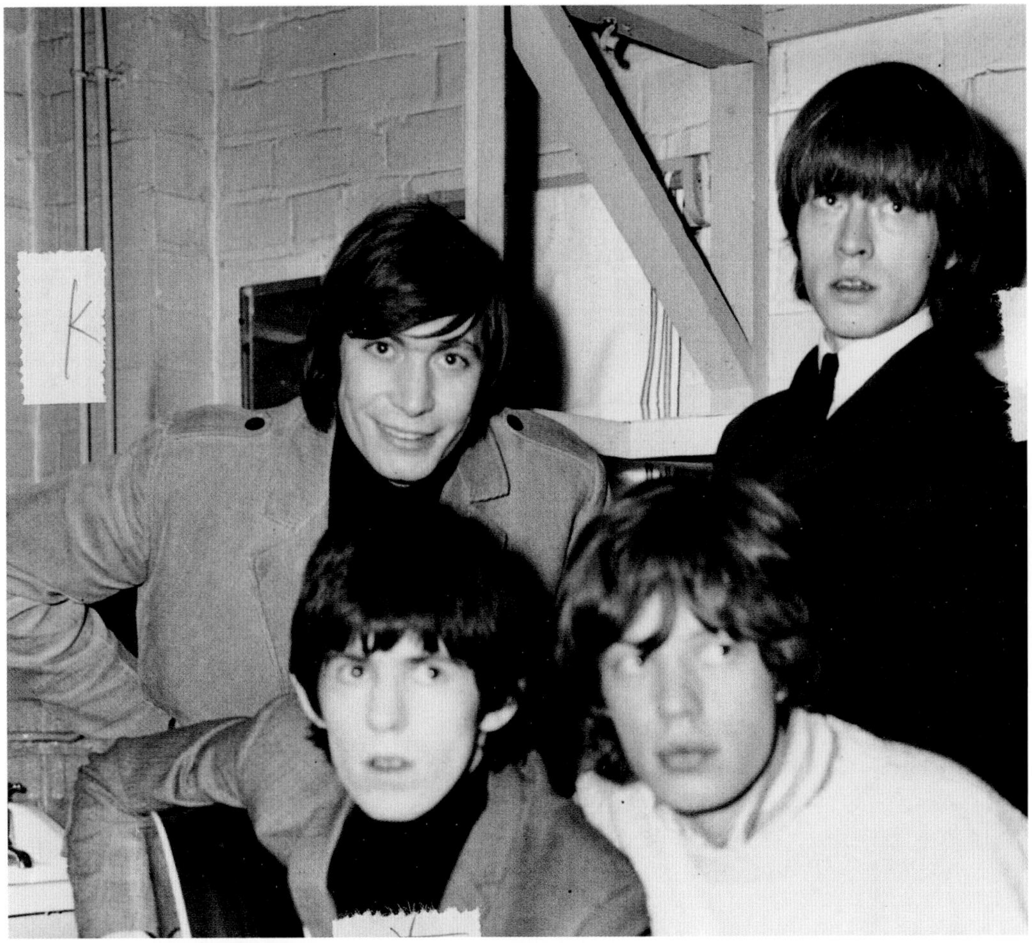

Left and below: Appearing at the ABC Theatre, Belfast, on 6 January to film BBC Northern Ireland's *Six-Five Show*

Brothers on what was probably their US TV debut, shortly before they crossed the Atlantic to mount a US invasion of the UK charts.

For the Stones, 1965 began with a three-date Irish tour, with shows in Belfast, Dublin and Cork, as well as an appearance on the BBC's Northern Ireland-only *Six-Five Show* where they were seen playing some of 'Little Red Rooster', while rehearsing on stage at the ABC Cinema in Belfast where they appeared later that evening.

Home from Ireland they were in Teddington recording an appearance on *Thank Your Lucky Stars*, which aired on 30 January and featured three songs from the band's new album – 'Down Home Girl', 'Under The Boardwalk' and 'Susie Q'. Two days later and it was another appearance on *Ready Steady Go!*, this one coinciding with the release of their second UK album. This too featured three tracks from the LP, but different ones from *TYLS* – 'Time Is On My Side', 'Everybody Needs Somebody To Love' and 'Down The Road Apiece', the latter over the closing credits. It was the last time the Stones appeared on television in the 1960s without performing at least one of Mick and Keith's compositions.

'Every generation brings a fresh wave of ideas, and if this was stifled, society and culture would be doomed. Our children will be rebelling against us in twenty years' time.'

Brian Jones
Melody Maker at RSG!
15 January 1965

Opposite: Appearing on *Ready Steady Go!* 15 January

On Sunday 17 January they left London's Heathrow for Los Angeles, their first stop en route to Australia and a tour Down Under. The following day was spent in RCA's studio recording what would become both sides of their next single – 'The Last Time' and 'Play With Fire'. According to Keith in the April 1965 edition of *Beat Monthly*, 'We've decided that the sound we get in the US recording studios is better ... In the UK the sound engineers spend far too much time looking at all those dials, instead of worrying about the most important thing of all, which is the sound that they're taping on their machines. In the US it's completely different ... the sound they get is terrific. What else counts when you're making a record?'

The next day they flew to Australia via Hawaii and Fiji, arriving in Sydney on the morning of Thursday 21 January, having 'lost' a day crossing the International Date Line. Their reception was the kind that they had grown used to. According to the Australian *TV Times* magazine, 'At 8.27a.m. the Stones raced down the gangway of their aircraft onto Australian soil. They neither paused nor waved to 2,500 squealing fans. Long thin legs pumping like pistons, they dashed to the customs shed. A few fans caught a glimpse. The great majority saw nothing. It was over in seconds.' The *Sydney Morning Herald* added: 'Weeping teenage girls and police were trampled under foot as 300 fans crowded behind a section of a crash barrier surged forward. A straining human chain of police almost lost the battle with the hysterical crowd and three baggage trolleys and a tractor were used to force the mob back.'

At the airport there were the obligatory TV and press interviews, followed by yet more at the Chevron Hilton Hotel in the Kings Cross area of the city, overlooking the famous harbour and the Sydney Opera House, which was still under construction. Over fifty reporters, photographers and cameramen were there to capture their every utterance. The TV news reports followed in the same vein as the press, and the interviews were of the shocked incredulity type.

The following day the Stones played the first of twenty-two Australian shows, and in between they travelled to New Zealand for another eleven shows in five different cities. There were TV and radio interviews wherever they went, including a half-hour special that aired on Melbourne's GMV-6 TV on 17 February. Also while in Melbourne they taped *The Rolling Stones Special Big Beat Show* for ATV-O Channel 10 at their studios in the city. The Stones had to be smuggled into the rear entrance as large crowds of girls followed their every move around the city; once inside they recorded four numbers, including 'Little Red Rooster'. The TV special recorded on 29 January also starred Roy Orbison who supported the Stones throughout the Australasian tour; it was also Andrew Loog Oldham's twenty-first birthday. It's often forgotten in the retelling of the Stones' story just how young he was – a year younger than Keith, the youngest member of the band.

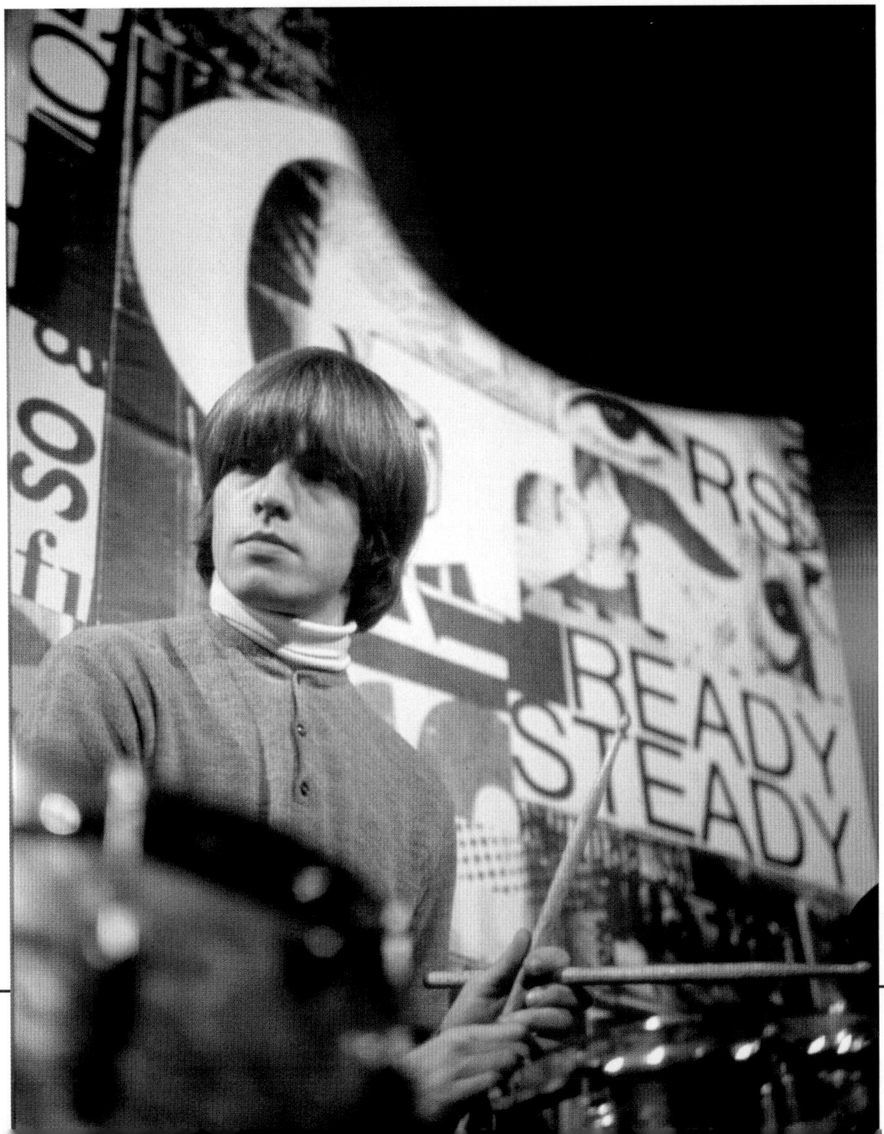

'Invercargill [in New Zealand] is the end of the earth. There are twenty-eight rooms in this hotel, and only two baths between everybody. The last meal you can get is supper, and that finishes at 7 p.m.'

Mick Jagger

The Stones in Australia.
Opposite: Backstage at the Agricultural Hall, Sydney Showground
Above: With Stan Rofe for KZ Talk radio at Essendon Airport, Melbourne
Right: With Roy Orbison at the Chevron Hilton Hotel in Sydney

‘How many times do you wash your hair?’ ‘About twice a week.’ ‘And who cuts it for you?’ ‘Usually Keith...’

Mick Jagger
interviewed by
Cathy McGowan
on *RSG!*

Opposite: Appearing on *Ready Steady Go!* in 1965 with presenter Cathy McGowan

From Perth, Western Australia, they flew with Qantas to Singapore, on the day after Valentine’s, to play two shows at the city’s Badminton Hall, on Guillemard Road in Geylang. The following day after a brief layover in Hong Kong the band visited Tokyo, but not to appear in concert. Instead they just gave a press conference at the airport for the awaiting TV, radio and newspaper reporters. Then it was homeward bound via Los Angeles where Mick redid his vocals for ‘The Last Time’ at RCA Studios.

Back in the UK they had no work for a week but got back to the day job on Friday 26 February in the familiar surroundings of *Ready Steady Go!* to promote their new single. It coincided with the release of ‘The Last Time’ and ‘Play With Fire’ and – not wanting to risk any kind of issues with playing these new songs live – it was decided that they should mime to the B-side first, after which Mick was interviewed by the host, Cathy McGowan; they then mimed to ‘The Last Time’.

Cathy’s interview with Mick was a classic example of her slightly excitable style, but delivered in such an endearing way that it was impossible not to like her. In fact part of what made her so popular with the show’s audience was that she asked the kind of questions they would ask, in a way they would have asked them.

‘How did you enjoy the tour?’ asks Cathy.

‘Very much actually.’

‘You know when you’re going to come on, we get hundreds of letters from girls, asking me if I’d give them to you, and the kind of things they want to know is, how many times do you wash your hair?’

‘About twice a week.’

‘And who cuts it for you?’

‘Usually Keith, but sometimes other people.’

‘And who cuts Keith’s?’

‘Keith cuts his with a mirror.’

‘And mums write in to me and say, how many times do they take a bath?’

‘If it’s a hot country, every day.’

‘That’s a super answer, Mick. And do you think if you got married, it would affect you as a person, and your popularity?’

‘It might do; I only fancy unmarried people, so why should anyone fancy a married me?’

‘That’s quite true. Anyway, let’s hear the A-side of the new record . . .’

Following 'The Last Time', the other compere on the show, Keith Fordyce, introduced them, saying: 'Let's round off with a great live number from the Stones, called "Everybody Needs Somebody To Love".'

As they played live, and the credits began to roll, Mick was pulled into the crowd. According to one newspaper report, 'Mick was hurt when screaming girls dragged him from a rostrum. Later he nursed a twisted ankle. Millions of viewers saw the girls break through a safety barrier of studio staff and drag the singer from the dais.'

'I had a haircut three days ago that saved me from worse injuries. Otherwise the girls would have used my long hair for a hand-hold and I would never have got back on the rostrum. I thudded down on the floor and a mass of girls smothered me. I was stamped on by scores of stiletto heels.'

Mick Jagger

While shows like *Top of the Pops, Ready Steady Go!* and *Thank Your Lucky Stars* were the weekly must-see programmes for UK teens and music lovers, variety shows were also an opportunity to promote a new record, as well as in some cases the chance for singers and bands to have their say. *The Eamonn Andrews Show* was a forty-five-minute late-night chat and music programme on the ITV network that ran from October 1964 to 1969. The Stones appeared on the show on the last day of February and mimed to 'The Last Time'. Also appearing was American singer Keely Smith, British singer Keith Michell and politician and the leader of the Liberal Party, Jeremy Thorpe.

Mick was interviewed by Andrews about the life that he now found himself leading and for this first interview it was all somewhat pedestrian stuff – two years later it would be very different. The show was recorded in the early evening and went out at 11 p.m. Meanwhile most of the other Stones – including Brian, whose twenty-third birthday it was – were at a party in Kensington hosted by *Disc*.

Right: Performing on *Ready Steady Go!*, 26 February

TOURING AND TV

Having had a week off, following their return from Australasia and the Far East, the Stones were fully focused on promoting their new single. With their 'misunderstanding' with the BBC now fully resolved, their first BBC radio appearance in over four months was recorded on 1 March – despite the earlier ban, BBC radio continued to play the Stones' records. Brian Matthew also interviewed Mick and Brian on *Top Gear* and it aired five days later.

The following day Mick and Brian were again interviewed for another BBC Light Programme show, *Pop Inn*; this weekly lunchtime show, hosted by Keith Fordyce, went out on a Tuesday and featured a mix of interviews and records. The series, which first aired in October 1962, was normally based in the studio, but this week it broadcast live from the Ideal Home Exhibition at London's Olympia, a somewhat incongruous place for the Stones to be. However, it served its purpose of getting them back on the radio – all part of the gentle art of promotion.

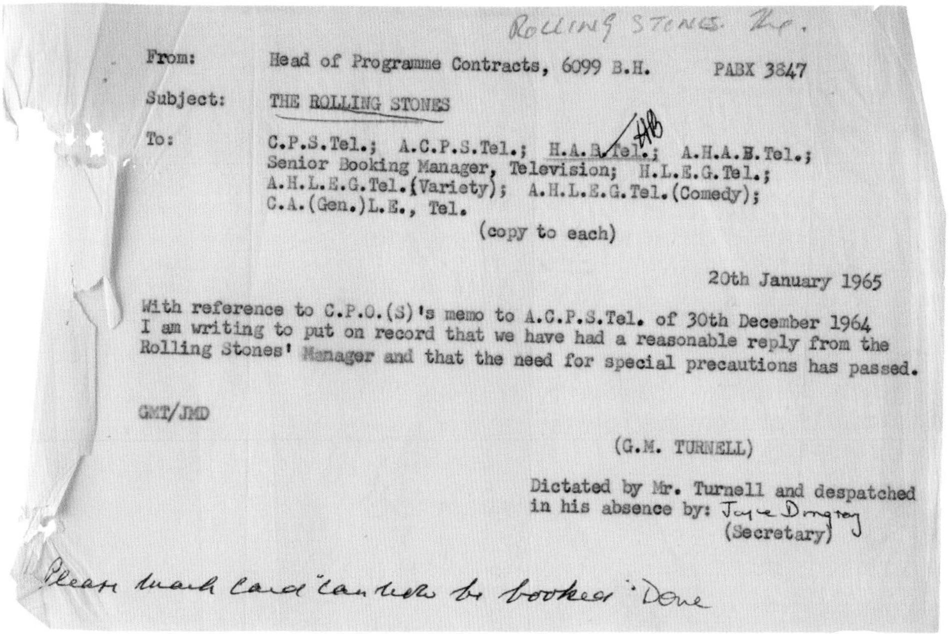

ROLLING STONES

From: Head of Programme Contracts, 6099 B.H. PABX 3847

Subject: THE ROLLING STONES

To: C.P.S.Tel.; A.C.P.S.Tel.; H.A.B.Tel.; A.H.A.B.Tel.; Senior Booking Manager, Television; H.L.E.G.Tel.; A.H.L.E.G.Tel.(Variety); A.H.L.E.G.Tel.(Comedy); C.A.(Gen.)L.E., Tel.

(copy to each)

20th January 1965

With reference to C.P.O.(S)'s memo to A.C.P.S.Tel. of 30th December 1964 I am writing to put on record that we have had a reasonable reply from the Rolling Stones' Manager and that the need for special precautions has passed.

GMT/JMD

(G.M. TURNELL)

Dictated by Mr. Turnell and despatched in his absence by: Joyce Dongray (Secretary)

Please mark card "can now be booked". Done

Top: Another appearance for UK TV
Right: The BBC row comes to an end

Rolling Stones man talks of a BBC rumpus

By JACK BELL

POP group manager Andrew Oldham, 22, talked last night about a rumpus at the BBC's Lime Grove Studios, in London — after he switched one of the studio TV sets to the Independent channel.

Oldham, manager of the Rolling Stones, said that after the recording of "Juke Box Jury" for the BBC, he and his wife watched the programme in the viewing room.

"Then I switched to ITV's 'Lucky Stars,'" Oldham said.

Shout

"And a BBC man shouted 'We don't watch that here!'"

Oldham said he was told that the other man was Billy Cotton, Junior — assistant head of BBC light entertainment.

"I told him who I was," Oldham added. "There was another row outside the viewing room."

Billy Cotton Junior commented last night: "It's all very petty.

The next day the band's rehabilitation with the BBC was complete when they flew from London to Manchester to appear on *Top of the Pops*. Following a quick afternoon rehearsal they mimed to 'The Last Time', which had entered the UK chart at No.31 that very same day. The following week it climbed to No.6 on the bestseller list and a week later it replaced Tom Jones's 'It's Not Unusual' at the top – their third UK No.1 in a row.

While TV and radio were important there is no underestimating the power of the package tour to help sales of singles and albums and on Friday 5 March the Stones began their fifth UK tour. It was a two-shows-a-night tour that ran until 18 March featuring the Hollies as second on the bill, along with Dave Berry and the Cruisers, the Original Checkmates, Goldie and the Gingerbreads and the Konrads – the band that once included a young David Bowie, although by this time he had gone his own way.

Left: The *Daily Mirror* report on the row with the BBC

Above: One of the earliest photographs of Mick playing the guitar, taken during rehearsals for *Ready Steady Go!*

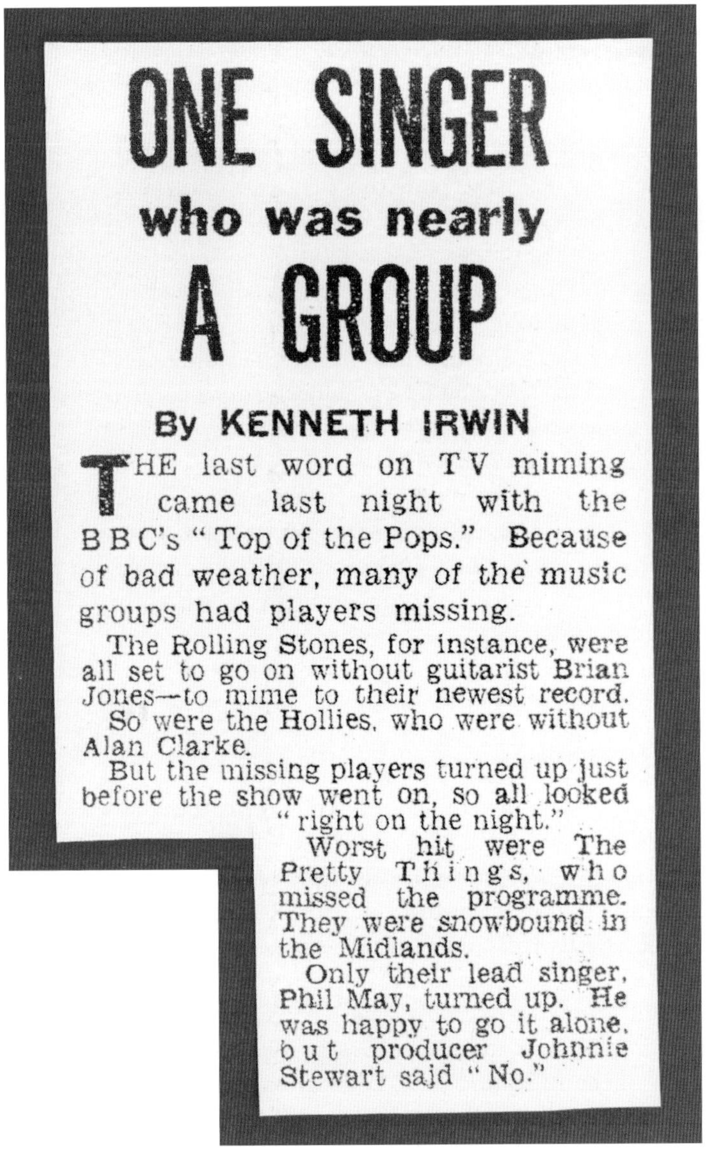

ONE SINGER who was nearly A GROUP

By KENNETH IRWIN

THE last word on TV miming came last night with the B B C's "Top of the Pops." Because of bad weather, many of the music groups had players missing.

The Rolling Stones, for instance, were all set to go on without guitarist Brian Jones—to mime to their newest record.

So were the Hollies, who were without Alan Clarke.

But the missing players turned up just before the show went on, so all looked "right on the night."

Worst hit were The Pretty Things, who missed the programme. They were snowbound in the Midlands.

Only their lead singer, Phil May, turned up. He was happy to go it alone, but producer Johnnie Stewart said "No."

Left: The previous night's *Top of the Pops*, blighted by bad weather, gets a mention in the *Daily Mirror*

'There was an incredible difference between the depth of emotion expressed for the Stones and for us. We could certainly drive them crazy but then it went to a brand new level when the Stones came on – it was somehow deeper and darker than Beatlemania.'

Graham Nash
The Hollies

The tour's opening night was in London at Edmonton's Regal Cinema and by 11 March they were in Sheffield for their two evening shows. Earlier in the day they taped an appearance on Granada TV's *Scene at 6.30*. The same team that was responsible for *Scene at 6.30* also produced *Granada in the North*, a late-night chat show. This was presented by 29-year-old Michael Parkinson, a journalist who would later become the most famous of all British TV interviewers.

In the course of his interview with Mick, Parkinson asks him what he would like to do in the future. 'I never thought I'd be doing this for two years, [but] we'll probably be doing it for another year,' replied Mick. 'I'll try and write songs and produce records and I'd also like to appear in films, but that's something I'd have to work hard at.' Parkinson raised the issue of a hotel in the north of England complaining about the band's behaviour, and especially the fact that they trod biscuits into the carpet, to which Mick replied, 'I accidentally trod on a biscuit I'd dropped the night before when I got out of bed; I'm sure commercial travellers sometimes tread on biscuits.'

With 'The Last Time' at No.1 there were appearances on *Thank Your Lucky Stars* and another on *Top of the Pops*; for the BBC show the record was played with stills of the band on screen. *TYLS* was a recording done on 21 March because by this time the Stones were already in Denmark for what was their very first European tour.

Some 2,000 fans were at Copenhagen's main airport to greet them, as well as Danish TV and the obligatory press corps. The following day the Stones flew to Odense for their first concert of the tour – two shows at Fyns Forum. At the soundcheck both Bill and Mick suffered electric shocks. According to Mick, 'What happened was that I touched two microphones simultaneously, and couldn't let go of them. I was knocked back, I can tell you. I felt like I had just been in a fight. Bill was knocked unconscious by the shock but, like us, carried on afterwards.'

On 31 March there was the fourth date in Gothenburg, following four shows over two days in Copenhagen. In Stockholm, Swedish radio recorded interviews with the band, backstage between shows at the city's Kungliga Tennishallen. Prior to their second day at the same venue they were in Stockholm's Cirkus building to record an appearance on Swedish TV's *Popside*. They did six songs, including 'Little Red Rooster' and 'The Last Time', which aired in Sweden, Denmark, Norway and Finland at various times in April.

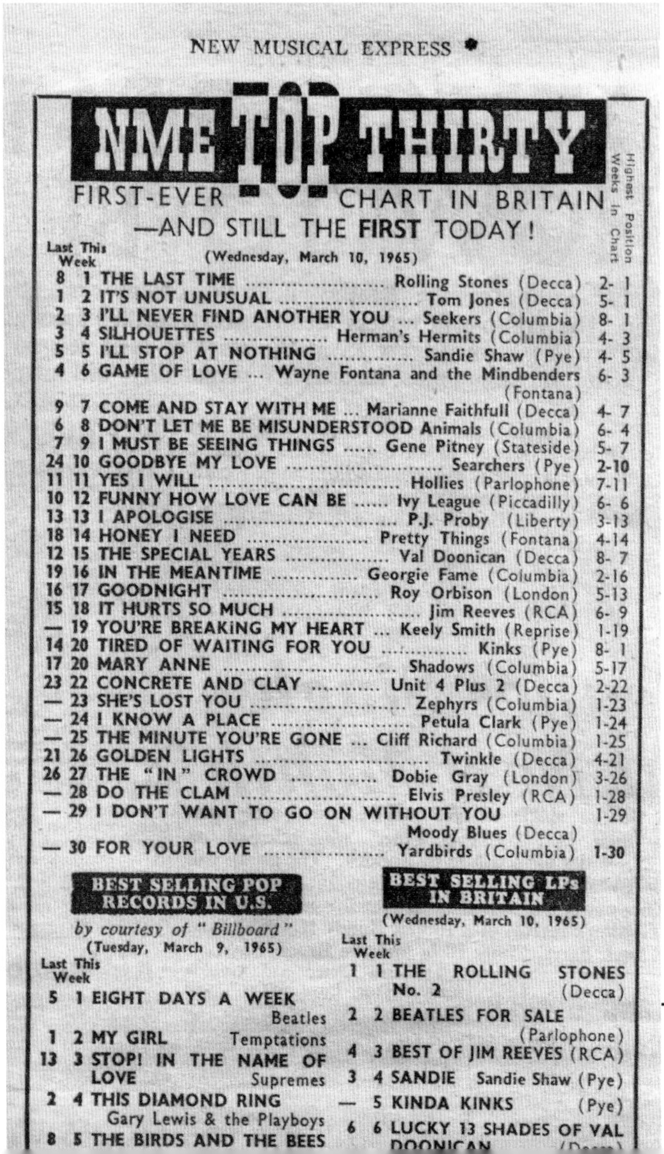
NEW MUSICAL EXPRESS

NME TOP THIRTY

FIRST-EVER CHART IN BRITAIN —AND STILL THE FIRST TODAY!

(Wednesday, March 10, 1965)

Last Week	This Week	Title	Artist (Label)	Weeks in Chart – Highest Position
8	1	THE LAST TIME	Rolling Stones (Decca)	2- 1
1	2	IT'S NOT UNUSUAL	Tom Jones (Decca)	5- 1
2	3	I'LL NEVER FIND ANOTHER YOU	Seekers (Columbia)	8- 1
3	4	SILHOUETTES	Herman's Hermits (Columbia)	4- 3
5	5	I'LL STOP AT NOTHING	Sandie Shaw (Pye)	4- 5
4	6	GAME OF LOVE	Wayne Fontana and the Mindbenders (Fontana)	6- 3
9	7	COME AND STAY WITH ME	Marianne Faithfull (Decca)	4- 7
6	8	DON'T LET ME BE MISUNDERSTOOD	Animals (Columbia)	6- 4
7	9	I MUST BE SEEING THINGS	Gene Pitney (Stateside)	5- 7
24	10	GOODBYE MY LOVE	Searchers (Pye)	2-10
11	11	YES I WILL	Hollies (Parlophone)	7-11
10	12	FUNNY HOW LOVE CAN BE	Ivy League (Piccadilly)	6- 6
13	13	I APOLOGISE	P.J. Proby (Liberty)	3-13
18	14	HONEY I NEED	Pretty Things (Fontana)	4-14
12	15	THE SPECIAL YEARS	Val Doonican (Decca)	8- 7
19	16	IN THE MEANTIME	Georgie Fame (Columbia)	2-16
16	17	GOODNIGHT	Roy Orbison (London)	5-13
15	18	IT HURTS SO MUCH	Jim Reeves (RCA)	6- 9
—	19	YOU'RE BREAKING MY HEART	Keely Smith (Reprise)	1-19
14	20	TIRED OF WAITING FOR YOU	Kinks (Pye)	8- 1
17	20	MARY ANNE	Shadows (Columbia)	5-17
23	22	CONCRETE AND CLAY	Unit 4 Plus 2 (Decca)	2-22
—	23	SHE'S LOST YOU	Zephyrs (Columbia)	1-23
—	24	I KNOW A PLACE	Petula Clark (Pye)	1-24
—	25	THE MINUTE YOU'RE GONE	Cliff Richard (Columbia)	1-25
21	26	GOLDEN LIGHTS	Twinkle (Decca)	4-21
26	27	THE "IN" CROWD	Dobie Gray (London)	3-26
—	28	DO THE CLAM	Elvis Presley (RCA)	1-28
—	29	I DON'T WANT TO GO ON WITHOUT YOU	Moody Blues (Decca)	1-29
—	30	FOR YOUR LOVE	Yardbirds (Columbia)	1-30

BEST SELLING POP RECORDS IN U.S.

by courtesy of "Billboard"

(Tuesday, March 9, 1965)

Last Week	This Week	Title	Artist
5	1	EIGHT DAYS A WEEK	Beatles
1	2	MY GIRL	Temptations
13	3	STOP! IN THE NAME OF LOVE	Supremes
2	4	THIS DIAMOND RING	Gary Lewis & the Playboys
8	5	THE BIRDS AND THE BEES	

BEST SELLING LPs IN BRITAIN

(Wednesday, March 10, 1965)

Last Week	This Week	Title	Label
1	1	THE ROLLING STONES No. 2	(Decca)
2	2	BEATLES FOR SALE	(Parlophone)
4	3	BEST OF JIM REEVES	(RCA)
3	4	SANDIE Sandie Shaw	(Pye)
—	5	KINDA KINKS	(Pye)
6	6	LUCKY 13 SHADES OF VAL DOONICAN	[illegible]

With the Stones now home from Scandinavia, John Lennon and the Beatles' road manager Neil Aspinall visited Mick and Keith's flat in Holly Hill, Hampstead where, together, they played records long into the night. The *NME* reported Lennon as saying, 'We must have outstayed our welcome, because when it came time to go home, our hosts had gone to bed.'

A week later the Stones were back on *Ready Steady Go!* but not in its central London studio at Kingsway. On this occasion the programme had moved to studios in Wembley. This week's show had a slight name change to *Ready Steady Goes Live!* as it was the first one in which performers could play for real, rather than miming to their records, thanks to the improved facilities at Wembley.

Appearing on the same show were the Animals, Goldie and the Gingerbreads, Dave Berry, American singer Roger Miller and Madeline Bell. The 22-year-old Miss Bell, from Newark, New Jersey, had recently moved to England and signed to Columbia Records.

The Stones did three numbers: the by now almost ubiquitous 'Everybody Needs Somebody To Love/Pain In My Heart', 'I'm Alright' and 'The Last Time', which was completing its third and final week at No.1.

Two days later they were back in Wembley, although this time it was at the Empire Pool and not at the TV studio. They were there to star, along with the Beatles, at the *NME* Poll Winners' Concert in front of 10,000 fans. It was a star-studded affair with, among others, the Moody Blues, Georgie Fame, Twinkle, the Seekers, Wayne Fontana and the Mindbenders, Donovan, Them, the Searchers, Dusty Springfield, the Animals and the Beatles. The Stones closed the first half of the show and Keith Altham writing in the *NME* said of their performance: 'The Stones entered the arena to the biggest ovation, and Mick swung into his mean and moody routine with "Everybody Needs Somebody To Love", which broke straight into the slower "Pain In My Heart". The faster tempo of "Around And Around" provided Mick with the opportunity of going into his more violent movements, and he whirled around at one moment like a berserk windmill. The Stones showed how important it is not only to give the audience something to listen to, but also to watch, and Mick's facial dramatics during "The Last Time" are an education. They rounded off a wild performance with "Everybody Needs Somebody To Love" as an encore. No one was left in any doubt as to who was the most popular group in this fantastic first half.'

The TV show, billed as *Poll Winners' Concert*, aired over two Sunday afternoons with the Beatles appearing on 18 April and the Stones a week later on 25 April. The Stones

Opposite: 'The Last Time' was the band's third UK single to reach No. 1 on the UK chart

Left: Recording an appearance on *Thank Your Lucky Stars* on 21 March

Below: Keith leaving Manchester on 11 March after the band taped ITV's *Scene at 6.30* TV show

NEW

MUSICAL

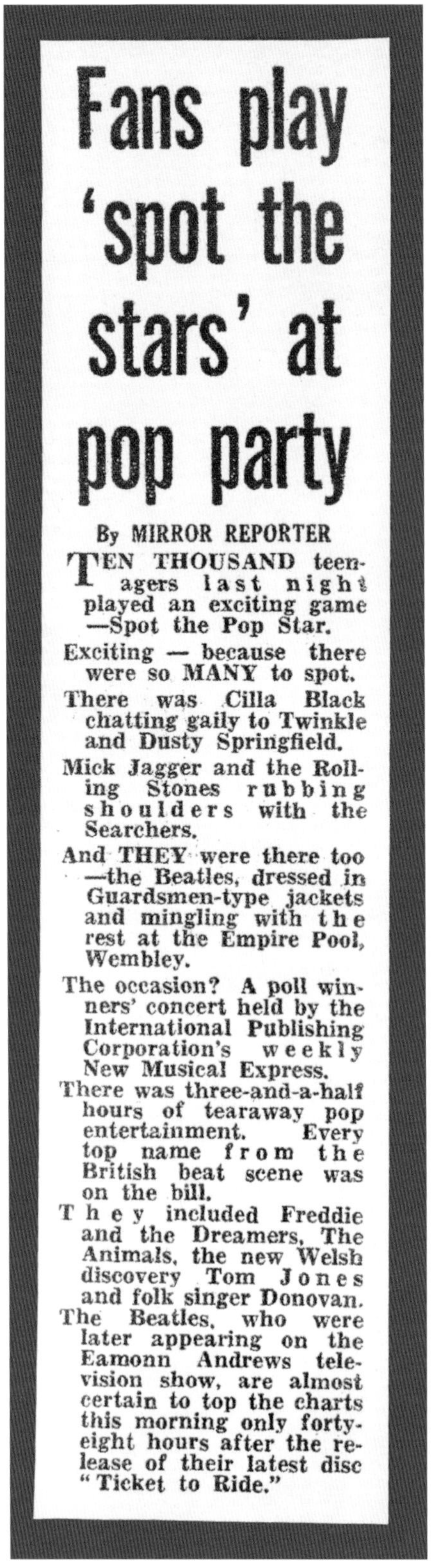

Fans play 'spot the stars' at pop party

By MIRROR REPORTER

TEN THOUSAND teenagers last night played an exciting game—Spot the Pop Star.

Exciting — because there were so MANY to spot.

There was Cilla Black chatting gaily to Twinkle and Dusty Springfield.

Mick Jagger and the Rolling Stones rubbing shoulders with the Searchers.

And THEY were there too—the Beatles, dressed in Guardsmen-type jackets and mingling with the rest at the Empire Pool, Wembley.

The occasion? A poll winners' concert held by the International Publishing Corporation's weekly New Musical Express.

There was three-and-a-half hours of tearaway pop entertainment. Every top name from the British beat scene was on the bill.

They included Freddie and the Dreamers, The Animals, the new Welsh discovery Tom Jones and folk singer Donovan.

The Beatles, who were later appearing on the Eamonn Andrews television show, are almost certain to top the charts this morning only forty-eight hours after the release of their latest disc "Ticket to Ride."

Previous pages: On stage at the *NME* Poll Winner's Concert

Left: The *Daily Mirror* reports on 'three-and-a-half hours of tearaway pop entertainment' at the 1965 Poll Winner's Concert

missed seeing the Beatles on the TV as they were in France for concerts at Paris's Olympia Theatre over three days. The concerts were billed as 'Musicorama' and Europe 1, France's biggest radio station, broadcast one of them live on 18 April. It was a typical set list of the time featuring their three recent UK No. 1s: 'It's All Over Now', 'Little Red Rooster' and 'The Last Time'. At the end of their set they played Bo Diddley's 'Hey Crawdaddy', something they had not done since the heady days at Richmond's Station Hotel.

On their return from Paris the *Daily Mirror* carried a report under the headline, 'Top Beat Boys Snub Palladium'. 'The Beatles and the Rolling Stones are giving a back-stage snubbing to the contract-makers of Britain's number one showbiz spot,' said the article. 'Both "beat" groups have turned down "Top of the Bill" offers on *Sunday Night at the London Palladium*. "It's not our kind of scene," says Mick Jagger. The shaggy-haired Stones, just back from a series of concerts in Paris, said that they had turned down *Palladium* offers five times. They have never appeared on the show. An Associated Television official said, "I understand that negotiations have been going on for some time, but I didn't know they felt this way."' The story featured alongside a photo with the caption 'Reginald Kray Marries'. The photo showed the notorious gangster with his brother and his bride, Frances Shea. Two years later, having left Reggie Kray just weeks after the marriage, and still only twenty-three, she died of a drug overdose.

Two days later the Stones were at Heathrow, once again heading across the Atlantic for what was their third North American tour – missing their own performance on television at *The Poll Winners' Concert*.

'The Beatles and the Rolling Stones were rulers of pop music, Carnaby Street ruled the fashion world ... and me and my brother ruled London.'

Ronnie Kray

DAILY MIRROR, *Tuesday, April 20, 1965* PAGE 5

REGINALD KRAY MARRIES

JUST married . . Reginald Kray, 31 (right) and 21-year-old Frances Shea.

With them, after the ceremony yesterday, is Reginald Kray's twin brother, Ronald.

The couple were married at St. James the Great with St. Jude, Bethnal Green, in London's East End.

Veteran boxer Ted Kid Lewis and former champions Terry Spinks and Terry Allen were among the guests

Good-luck telegrams were received from Judy Garland, Billy Daniels, Lita Roza and Joan Littlewood.

The wedding plans were announced by Reginald Kray two weeks ago, after he and his twin and freelance writer Edward Smith were found not guilty and discharged at the Old Bailey on charges of conspiring to demand money with menaces.

It was their second trial. In the first trial the jury failed to agree.

The twins were in custody for ninety days.

Top beat boys snub Palladium

By DON SHORT

THE Beatles and the Rolling Stones are giving a back-stage snubbing to the contract-makers of Britain's No. 1 showbiz spot.

Both "beat" groups have turned down "top of the bill" offers on "Sunday Night at the London Palladium."

"It's just a drag," says Beatle John Lennon.

"It's not our kind of scene," says Stones' singer Mick Jagger.

'Wrong'

The Beatles have topped the bill twice on the Associated TeleVision show that commands a 17,000,000 audience.

The last time was fifteen months ago. Yesterday John, George, Paul and Ringo said: "Not again!"

Ringo added: "They can't put over our sound. They do it all wrong."

The shaggy-haired Stones, just back from a series of concerts in Paris, said yesterday that they had turned down Palladium offers five times. They have never appeared on the show.

Mick Jagger said: "Some

'JUST NOT OUR SCENE'

of the early-evening beat shows mean more to us, as they go out to our kind of fans."

But an Associated TeleVision official in London said: "The 'bad sound' criticism is really surprising as we have often made live recordings at the Palladium

Opinions

"In recent weeks, Cliff Richard, Cilla Black, Dusty Springfield, Tom Jones, and Frank Ifield have all appeared, and they have not complained.

"About the Rolling Stones, I understand that negotiations have been going on for some time, but I didn't know they felt this way and had definitely turned us down.

"They're all entitled to their opinions, but over the past ten years, pretty well anybody who is anyone in the world of entertainment has appeared on the show."

COLONEL DENIES 'HAIRCUTS' ORDER

American Air Force Colonel Richard Hughes denied yesterday that he ordered a six-member London pop group to get haircuts.

The group, the Ricochets, had claimed that they had to cut their hair before playing at the Colonel's air base near Madrid. Another officer is now said to have given the order

Above: The report on the Stones 'snubbing' *Sunday Night at the London Palladium* shares a page with Britain's most notorious gangsters, the Kray twins

THE WOLF MAN COMETH

Opposite: ***The Ed Sullivan Show*** **on 2 May featured the Stones and Tom Jones**

The Stones left Heathrow to fly to Montreal in Canada on Thursday 22 April. Such was the way of air travel back then that their flight routed via Manchester and Prestwick. There was the usual gaggle of press including TV cameras to record their arrival, along with around 300 fans. This was the band's first visit to Canada and there were concerts over the next four days in Montreal, Ottawa, Toronto and London (Ontario).

The Rolling Stones, Now! was at No.1 on the Canadian album charts as they arrived, so enthusiasm for the band among teenagers was ramped up, even if older people, and especially journalists, seemed a little perplexed. 'Ottawa teenagers scream, shout, faint and fight as shaggy-haired British singing idols belt out the blues,' ran one report. TV appearances seem to have been limited to interviews on programmes including Montreal's *Like Young*, a show for teenagers that ran for over three decades, and *Saturday Date*, a CBC programme filmed in Ottawa.

Whatever acceptance there was among the young for the band, the older generation and particularly hotel managers were not to be counted among their fans. As one hotel manager told the Ottawa newspaper, 'The Stones would never have been booked if we'd known ahead of time who they were. They were booked under individual names, and we didn't know until too late. Unfortunately, these groups encourage an unpleasant element among teenagers.'

Their first concert in America was in Albany, New York on 29 April, and it was here that the first of many local TV appearances was recorded, but again it was an interview rather than a performance. It was not until they were in New York City that they were booked to perform on television, appearing on *The Ed Sullivan Show* on Sunday 2 May, despite the show's host having told the *Toronto Globe and Mail* the previous November that 'he won't have them back' – that's showbiz for you. Rehearsals lasted for much of the day and the Stones hung out with British comedians Morecambe and Wise, who along with Tom Jones were also on the programme.

The Stones opened with 'The Last Time', which had been released in the US in late March. It was currently peaking on the Hot 100 at No.9 where it stayed for two weeks. Later in the show they did 'Little Red Rooster' (despite London Records failing to release it as a single), 'Everybody Needs Somebody To Love' and, as the show faded out, '2120 South Michigan Avenue', the instrumental inspired by recording at Chess Records.

'The Stones are the "Soul" of British beat music. I was driving along in my car. I have a TV installed, and suddenly on the screen came the Stones singing my song "Everybody Needs Somebody To Love". What a knock-out.'

Solomon Burke
August 1965

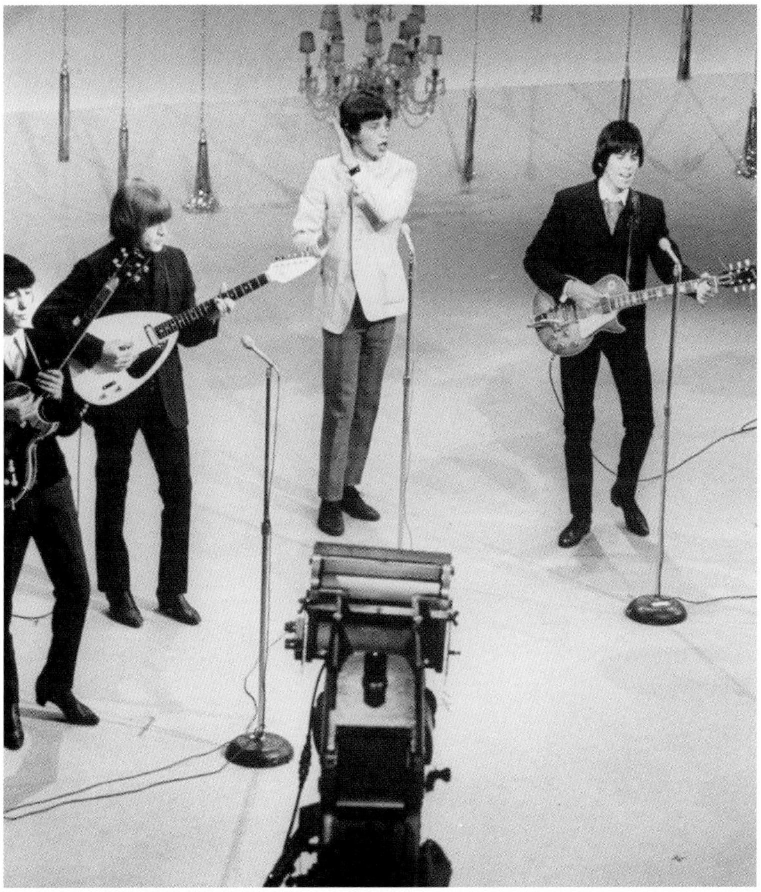

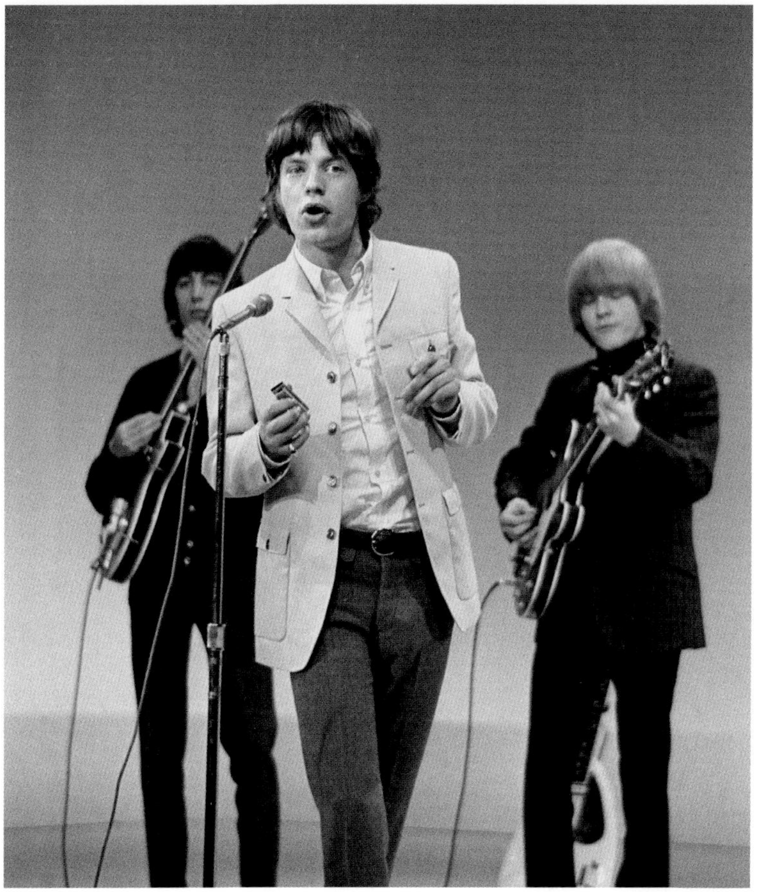

The
Ed Sullivan
Show

The day after *The Ed Sullivan Show* they were back on *The Clay Cole Show* on WPIX Channel 11 for a recording that, when it aired on 29 May, was billed as 'the Beatles vs the Rolling Stones'. There were interviews and once again 'Little Red Rooster', 'The Last Time' and 'Down The Road Apiece'.

On 6 May they played a concert at the Jack Russell Memorial Stadium in Clearwater, Florida and, after the show, Keith woke in the middle of the night at the Fort Harrison Hotel and wrote a riff. The next morning when he played it, Mick came up with the accompanying words: 'I can't get no satisfaction.' Four days later at Chess Studios they recorded Mick and Keith's new song during an afternoon and evening session along with four other numbers.

The following morning they flew to Los Angeles and stayed at the Ambassador Hotel where they did radio interviews with Don Steele for KHJ, whose 'Boss Radio' format was the new big thing in AM radio in California, and also with Rod Barken for KRLA, the other big AM radio station in the city.

The following day they were back in RCA's studio with engineer Dave Hassinger to record seven more songs, including the version of '(I Can't Get No) Satisfaction' that was released as a single.

'Charlie put down a different tempo, and with the addition of a fuzz-box on my guitar, which takes off all the treble, we achieved a very interesting sound.'

Keith Richards
NME
3 September 1965

Opposite: An appearance on *Shindig!*

After playing San Francisco on 14 May, the Stones headed south to San Bernardino and an afternoon radio interview with KMEN. From there it was back to Los Angeles to record an appearance on *Hollywood a Go-Go*, filmed at KHJ Studios on Melrose Avenue. The show was hosted by Sam Riddle, who was a lot more sympathetic to the band than Dean Martin on the similarly named *Hollywood Palace* the previous year, although Riddle may well have become frustrated at the number of retakes that were needed on 'The Last Time' because Brian kept sticking his tongue out at the camera. Aside from their latest single the show also featured 'Play With Fire' and 'Oh Baby (We Got A Good Thing Going)'. During 'Play With Fire', the show's regular Gazzarri Dancers were featured, which added little to the proceedings, but just about every American TV show at the time had its own set of dancers.

The following afternoon the Stones were driven south to the Civic Auditorium in Long Beach where they played an afternoon gig promoted by KRLA Radio that included the Byrds and Paul Revere and the Raiders among the support bands. The show was compered by KRLA DJs Bob Eubanks, Dick Biondi and Dave Hull. With the Stones having played their set and with it time for them to leave, it very nearly went disastrously wrong.

According to *KRLA Beat*, the station's own music magazine, under the banner headline, 'LA Rocks as Stones Roll', 'The Stones rushed off the stage and into a black station wagon parked inside the building directly behind the stage. The get-away plans had been carefully laid, but somebody goofed somewhere. The black wagon was in motion a split second after the Stones had jumped aboard, but it was moving in the wrong direction! After proceeding half way around the arena, the car could not get out, and was spotted by throngs of screaming fans. Once outside, the car was engulfed in a mass of surging bodies.' The Stones had to hold the roof of the car up with their feet to prevent it from caving in from the weight of hundreds of teenagers swarming all over it.

It was all very typical of what the band faced at gigs throughout America, but what is particularly interesting here is the reportage in the Pasadena radio station's magazine. The *KRLA Beat* was first published in October 1964 as a four-page print-sheet of gigs and other news. In February 1965 it became a more professional newspaper headed up by journalist Derek Taylor, who had worked for the Beatles and Brian Epstein before falling out with the latter and moving to California at the start of 1965. The *KRLA Beat* did so much to promote British bands in California and

Opposite: Recording an appearance on *Hollywood a Go-Go* on 15 May

Left: The Byrds in London's Trafalgar Square sporting Brian Jones-inspired haircuts (left to right): Jim (Roger) McGuinn, Chris Hillman, Mike Clarke, Gene Clark and Dave Crosby

Below: Sonny & Cher on *Shindig!*

Following pages: Draped across a Rolls Royce on *Shindig!*

the Stones in particular benefited. It continued to be published until May 1968.

Following the terrifying incident at Long Beach, the band were taken by helicopter back to Los Angeles and then driven straight to KABC-TV's studios to record an appearance on *Shivaree*. The show, which had only gone on air for the first time in April, was hosted by KFWB-AM DJ Gene Weed, LA's top night-time presenter. The Stones taped four numbers that aired during the rest of 1965 on this thirty-minute show.

A concert at San Diego's Convention Hall followed the next day after which they had a couple of days off before they were once again to appear on *Shindig!*, although this time it was at ABC Television Center on Prospect Avenue, Los Angeles. The show went out on a Wednesday and this edition was filmed a week earlier on Thursday 20 May. Initially the show had been a thirty-minute slot but since January 1965 its popularity had seen it expanded to an hour.

Among the many guests on this week's edition were Sonny and Cher, Adam Wade, Bobby Sherman, Jackie DeShannon and Howlin' Wolf. The Stones played a short version of 'Down The Road Apiece' live, featuring on

Right: Mississippi blues musician Son House

Opposite: The Stones watch Howlin' Wolf perform his spot on *Shindig!*

keyboards the 19-year-old Billy Preston, who was also a member of the programme's house band, the Shindogs, as well as the obligatory dancers. Later, and somewhat ironically given Wolf was also on the show, the Stones performed 'Little Red Rooster', with Mick, moodily lit, twirling his harmonica throughout. This was followed by 'The Last Time', 'Play With Fire' – with the Stones draped over a Rolls-Royce and the song incorrectly referred to as 'Playing With Fire' on the accompanying graphic – before they closed the show with 'Satisfaction'.

The band recorded backing tracks for the other numbers and Mick sang live, apart from on 'Satisfaction', which was mimed – not to the version that we've all come to know and love, but the recording they had done at Chess. It featured Brian on acoustic guitar and Keith playing his Gibson Firebird which he had bought a few days earlier in Los Angeles.

It was the Stones who had asked for Wolf to be on the show, and presenter Jack Good insisted on referring to him as Mr Howling in his proper English accent. It was not unknown for black artists to appear on the show, but it was very much against the norm. Wolf performed 'How Many More Years' and was introduced by Mick and Brian who were themselves interviewed by Jack Good. According to Brian Jones, 'He's one of our greatest idols and it's a great pleasure to find him booked on your show. So it's about time you shut up and we had Howlin' Wolf.'

Throughout his performance the Stones sit at Wolf's feet alongside some of the other guests while he sings. The backing band is the Shindogs, which in addition to Preston featured James Burton on guitar, Chuck Blackwell on drums and Delaney Bramlett on bass.

A young white guy from Boston, Dick Waterman, who had found the legendary Delta bluesman, Son House, in New Jersey after searching Mississippi for him, had gone to the studio to reintroduce the 63-year-old to the younger Wolf as they had known each other in the 1930s. Having managed to get into the studio with little problem it was, according to Waterman, quite a meeting: 'Wolf saw Son and recognized him and Wolf came out of his seat like an elephant coming out of a phone booth. He came up in sections and Son looked at him and says, "Man, he has got his growth." Because Wolf was about 260 lbs. One of the Stones was watching me and then came up to me and tapped me on the shoulder. "Excuse me, who is the old man that Wolf thinks is so special? Wolf is in awe of that old man, who is the old man?" I said, "That's Son House." And he turned to me and said, "Ah, the one that taught Robert Johnson." It was Brian Jones and then he went back and told the others.'

After three more Californian dates, the Stones headed east to play New York's Academy of Music on 29 May and they then flew home to the UK, where less than a week later they were back on British television for their first appearance in over a month.

SOMETHING SPECIAL

The Stones were back on *Ready Steady Goes Live!* on 4 June with Burt Bacharach, the Kinks and the Yardbirds, who had taken over the band's residency at Richmond's Crawdaddy Club in 1963. The Yardbirds now had a new guitarist, Jeff Beck, who was making an early TV appearance with the band following the departure of Eric Clapton, who had objected to the group's move away from the blues into more pop-orientated material. Two days later, the Rolling Stones had a trip to Birmingham to record *Thank Your Lucky Stars* and, with no new single to promote, they were instead busy plugging their new EP that was released on 11 June.

Got Live If You Want It is a corruption of Slim Harpo's 'I've Got Love If You Want It', a single released on Excello Records in 1957. The Stones' EP was recorded during their UK tour in March and features Bo Diddley's 'I'm Alright' along with 'Route 66', which both featured on the TV shows, while on *TYLS* they also did Hank Snow's 'I'm Moving On'. *TYLS* aired on 12 June and two weeks later the EP was No.1 on the chart. On *RSG!* the Stones played live but on *TYLS* it was, as usual, mimed. Before *TYLS* aired, they appeared on *Top of the Pops* miming to 'I'm Alright'.

'The EP captures on wax the unadulterated in-person excitement of a Stones stage show. This is the Stones as they sound on stage, and very good it is too.'

Decca Records
press release

Right: The Yardbirds performed on *Ready Steady Go!* in 1965
Opposite: The Stones appearing in June

VOX

This and previous pages: In the studio and backstage at *Thank Your Lucky Stars* on 6 June

Following their *TYLS* appearance, the Stones did a short four-city tour of Scotland, staying at the world-famous Gleneagles Hotel. When they returned to London, Mick was interviewed for the long-running radio programme, *Woman's Hour*, and another called *The Teen Scene*, both for the BBC's Light Programme.

When Mick got back from America he briefly stayed with the photographer David Bailey at his flat in Gloucester Road before moving in, temporarily, with his girlfriend, Chrissy Shrimpton, who lived at 14 Sinclair Road in Kensington. However, even before the programmes aired Mick had moved into his own place in Bryanston Mews East in central London. The BBC contract showed that Mick was paid a little under £7, which equates to around £130 at today's values.

Woman's Hour has been a flagship programme for the BBC since it first broadcast in 1946 and it is still running today, with little change to the overall format. Mick's appearance was none-too-inventively billed as 'A Rolling

Right and below: Recording *Thank Your Lucky Stars*

Stone Gathers No Moss'; views on an old proverb that also featured writer and broadcaster Kevin Fitzgerald. The programme aired on 6 July, by which time the Stones had been on another Scandinavian tour.

In Scandinavia, the usual round of TV newsreels were filmed, showing the band's arrival and even a short clip of them performing 'I'm Alright' at Oslo's Messehallen. It was also after Mick's *Woman's Hour* appearance that '(I Can't Get No) Satisfaction' went to No.1 on the *Billboard* Hot 100, the first Stones' record to top the US charts. It was on 10 July that it made the top spot, which was also the day that Radio Luxembourg featured the Stones and the Beatles in their *Battle of the Giants* programme on which records were played and the audience had to vote on which was the best band.

Five days later it was announced that the Rolling Stones had polled more votes than the Beatles and they were duly awarded the 'Getaway trophy' at a lunch on a boat on the River Thames attended by Brian, Keith and Charlie. The day after the announcement, the Stones played Exeter in Devon on the first date of a six-day mini-tour supported by Steampacket, a group that included Long John Baldry, Brian Auger, Rod Stewart and Julie Driscoll. The penultimate night of the tour was in Leicester on 26 July, Mick's twenty-second birthday, and the tour ended on 1 August at the London Palladium.

Halfway through their mini tour there was TV and radio coverage of a different kind about an incident that has since become part of Stones' folklore. Back in March, following the last night of their UK tour with the Hollies at the ABC Theatre in Romford, Essex, and on their way back into London by limo, Bill Wyman was caught short. Desperate for a pee, he suggested they stop at a petrol station in Stratford, east London.

According to an eyewitness report in a newspaper at the time, 'Mr Eric Lavender, 22-year-old youth club leader, had stopped for petrol. And there was an incident, said Mr Lavender, which led to him and a mechanic reporting two members of the pop group to the police. It was about 11.30 p.m. when the big black car pulled up and a long-haired type wearing dark glasses got out. Mr Lavender told them their "behaviour was disgusting" and they started shouting and screaming.'

Having been refused use of the lavatory, Bill had relieved himself against the garage wall, which is what really caused all the fuss. On 22 July, Mick, Brian and Bill were in the dock at East Ham Magistrates Court, while Charlie and Keith were in court to give their support. Mick, Brian and Bill were charged with using insulting behaviour, while Bill alone was charged with using obscene language. All three pleaded not guilty and all were found guilty of using insulting behaviour whereby a breach of the peace may have occurred. They were fined £5 each, and ordered to pay 15 guineas costs; Bill was found not guilty of using obscene language.

'I kept out of trouble. I was asleep in the back seat of the car, man.'

Charlie Watts

Following pages: Onstage in Copenhagen, Denmark in June

The main BBC and ITN news programmes that evening had a field day covering the incident, reporting Mr A. Morey, the magistrate, as saying, 'Whether it is the Stones, the Beatles or anyone else, we will not tolerate conduct of this character. Because you have reached the exalted heights in your profession, it does not mean you have the right to act like this. On the contrary, you should set a standard of behaviour which should be a moral pattern for your large number of supporters. You have been found guilty of behaviour not becoming of young gentlemen.' The following day even the BBC's World Service featured the incident in a piece called 'Streets of London', on which Mick, Brian and Bill were interviewed. The Stones had become global news.

On Mick's twenty-second birthday, on their way to play Leicester's ABC Cinema, the band stopped off at Alpha Studios in Birmingham to record an appearance on *Thank Your Lucky Stars*. They mimed to 'Satisfaction', which was on its fourth week at No.1 in America, but had still not been released in the UK. Decca finally issued the single on 20 August, probably delayed as they had been keen to let the Stones' EP continue to sell. The day before 'Satisfaction' was released they mimed to their new single at the BBC's Manchester studio in Rusholme for *Top of the Pops*. The footage was shown on five occasions before the year was out; the first was a week later, after the single had entered the charts, following which it topped the charts for two weeks in September. It was also repeated on the Christmas Day *Top of the Pops* special.

On the day that 'Satisfaction' was released, the Stones were back at the BBC recording two radio programmes. The second of the two shows they recorded was *Yeh! Yeh!* hosted by Tony Hall, which aired on 30 August, and was their first appearance playing live on the radio since March. As well as their new single they did 'Mercy Mercy', 'Oh Baby' and 'The Spider And The Fly'.

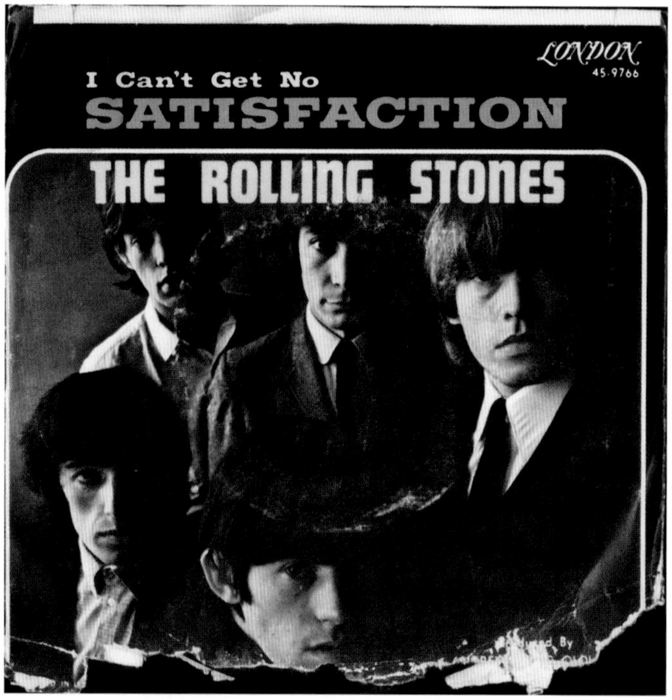

Top: Appearing on *Ready Steady Go!* at the Wembley studios
Right and opposite left: '(I Can't Get No) Satisfaction' was released in the US in early June, two months ahead of the UK; it was the band's first single to top the Hot 100
Opposite right: 'Satisfaction' makes in to No.1

faces of today : sounds of tomorrow
spots, not gauze, and peepers of truth
an audience in a sea of fear
for big daddy doesn't relate any more
this does : so float into tomorrow

Out Now !

(I can't get no)
SATISFACTION
b/w The spider and the fly

THE ROLLING STONES

F 12220

produced by andrew loog oldham

DECCA

The Decca Record Company Limited
Decca House · Albert Embankment · London SE1

Stones' new disc is top of the pops

By MIRROR REPORTER

SATISFACTION . . . That is what the Rolling Stones have got out of their ten-day-old disc, which they aptly call — "Satisfaction."

For yesterday they were told that the record is Number One in the New Musical Express charts. And the Melody Maker puts it in second place.

Pushed

"Satisfaction," written by lead singer Mick Jagger and Keith Richard, another member of the pop group, has already sold 1,250,000 discs in America.

And in Germany, a quarter of a million fans have bought it.

It has pushed Sonny and Cher — singing "I Got You, Babe"—into second place in the New Musical Express charts. The Beatles are third with "Help!"

Pop 30.—See Page 14

Saturday Club was the first show they appeared on and, like *Yeh! Yeh!*, it was recorded in Studio 2 at Broadcasting House in Upper Regent Street in London's West End. Brian Matthew as usual hosted the show and the Stones performed two additional tracks (both shows shared the new single and two of the other songs) – 'Cry To Me' and Buster Brown's 'Fanny Mae'. The latter song featured a distinctive harmonica riff that the Stones also used on their own song, 'Under Assistant West Coast Promotion Man', the B-side of the American release of 'Satisfaction' and a track on both the UK and US versions of *Out Of Our Heads* (their fourth US and third UK album); the Beach Boys copped the same riff on their March 1965 hit, 'Help Me Rhonda'.

Three days later, the Stones were back at Granada TV in Manchester for *Scene at 6.30* to mime to 'Satisfaction'. They were besieged in the building, according to the *Daily Mirror*: 'A fireman turned a hosepipe on 200 screaming girls as they rushed the gates of a TV studio. The hysterical teenagers thought the Stones were being smuggled into the Granada studios in a furniture van. A gate was broken down as the girls swarmed forward. Then the fireman did his bit with the hose. The cold jet stopped the rush, but some of the girls danced in the water and sang "We shall not be moved" and "We shall overcome".'

'The Stones arrived later the back way, in an Austin Princess saloon. The fireman acted on his own initiative. He picked up a piece of plastic piping which was attached to a tap. He squirted it up in the air and on the ground. It was very effective.'

Granada TV spokesman

Left: Fans outside the Granada studios where the Stones were recording an appearance on *Scene at 6.30* in August
Opposite top: Andrew Loog Oldham in discussions with Allen Klein at the London Hilton in August
Opposite bottom: Celebrating their new No.1 in a Manchester hotel

Scene at 6.30 aired on 26 August and the following day it was time for another appearance on *Ready Steady Go!* – the promotion for 'Satisfaction' was in full swing. At Wembley Studios, the Stones played a couple of other songs and over the closing credits Keith, Brian, Charlie and Bill played the Shadows' instrumental hit, 'Apache'. The audience at *RSG!* got a little over-excited and started pulling the band off stage and into the audience.

Two days later they were back in Birmingham to mime to 'Satisfaction' for *Thank Your Lucky Stars* Summer Spin, but not before news of a major change in the Stones' business, and potentially creative, affairs. According to London's *Evening News*, 'The Stones have signed an agreement for their record company Decca to finance fully five films to be made over the next three years. The deal coincided with the news that the Stones' business management had been taken over by an American, former accountant Allen Klein, to further the group's financial success. The Stones' co-manager, Andrew Oldham, will work with Mr Klein as creative manager.' Other papers carried news of the fact that Eric Easton had been eased out of his management role.

'I believe the whole group scene is going to disappear in six months, with the exception of entertainers like the Beatles, the Stones and the Animals.'

Allen Klein
NME
3 September 1965

The Stones really were on a roll at this point. They had secured their first US No.1 single; *Out Of Our Heads* had become their first American No.1 album; 'Satisfaction' was about to top the UK singles chart – their fourth in a row; they had had their third UK No.1 on the EP charts and the UK version of *Out Of Our Heads* was set for release in the third week of September. It was little wonder that *RSG!* decided to record a 'Rolling Stones Special' on 2 September for airing eight days later. According to *Disc*, 'Two years ago, the Stones were viewed by many parents with horror. The cry went up: "Cavemen!" "Disgusting!" "Animals!" A lot of people still wouldn't feel comfortable if the Stones gate-crashed a vicar's garden fete.' Clearly, though, the youth felt differently.

Along with the Stones, the *RSG! Special* featured Manfred Mann, Chris Farlowe, Goldie and the Gingerbreads and a group from south-east London whose new single was produced by Bill Wyman. The Preachers was Bill's group before he joined the Stones and now included drummer Tony Chapman, who briefly played with the Stones in late 1962 prior to Charlie joining. The band, who were introduced on the show by Bill, also included a 15-year-old guitarist by the name of Peter Frampton.

As well as promoting 'Satisfaction' and several other numbers, the Stones, along with Andrew Loog Oldham, participated in a somewhat bizarre sketch with Cathy McGowan during which they mimed to Sonny and Cher's 'I Got You Babe'. It was introduced by Mick.

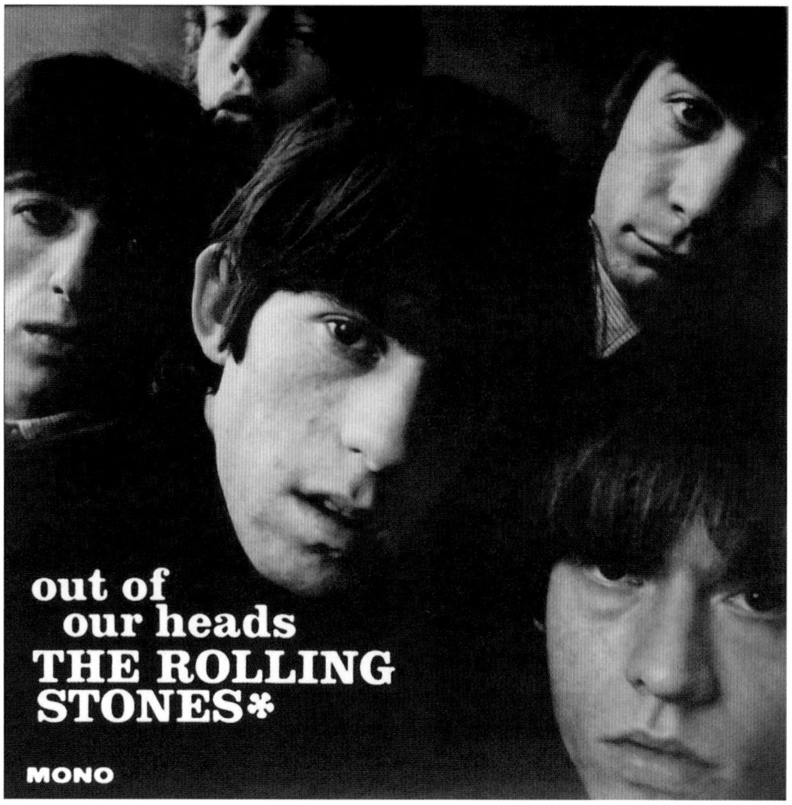

'The one thing I miss on Ready Steady Go! is the miming; we haven't had any for a long time and here's a new lot from Leighton Buzzard who are going to do their best for you.'

Mick Jagger

Above: *Out Of Our Heads* was released in September
Opposite: The Stones appeared on *Thank Your Lucky Stars* five times in 1965

It begins with Cathy and Brian in a duet, with Keith, wearing sunglasses, in the background playing a euphonium. Charlie enters carrying a giant flower before Andrew Loog Oldham, dressed in a huge fur coat, takes over the Cher role and sings to Mick. It's all very camp, and very Sixties.

The show aired on 10 September, by which time 'Satisfaction' had topped the UK charts; the Stones had played concerts in Dublin and Belfast which were turned into the film, *Charlie Is My Darling*; they had flown to Hollywood where they recorded 'Get Off Of My Cloud'; and flown back to London, arriving on the morning of 8 September, before then flying to Douglas in the Isle of Man to play the Palace Ballroom that evening. Just your average eight days in the life of the all-conquering Rolling Stones.

This page and opposite: Between takes on *Thank Your Lucky Stars*, with Brian playing his Gibson Firebird

IN THE CLOUDS

The day after the *RSG! Special* was on television, the Stones flew on Lufthansa to Dusseldorf, West Germany, where there were 5,000 fans at the airport to greet them, as well as police water cannons to quell their enthusiasm. It was the same everywhere they went. At the Grugahalle in Essen, the Stones performed behind steel crash barriers; nevertheless thousands surged towards the stage and mounted police charged the teenagers. In Hamburg, police with hoses and batons fought rioting fans outside a hall and according to the *Daily Mirror*: 'When the Rolling Stones set foot on German soil … they unleashed a typhoon of destruction.' It was all captured by numerous newsreel and TV news crews and plastered across every TV channel in Germany; it was so bad that it even made the BBC television news.

The Stones flew from Vienna to London on 18 September, arriving shortly after *Saturday Club* had broadcast the recordings they had done in August. Three days later they were at *Top of the Pops* to record another appearance playing 'Satisfaction', although this was at the BBC's Television Centre in west London. Three more days after that, *Out Of Our Heads* came out and a week later it made No.3 on the UK album chart. The following week it was at No.2, prevented from reaching the top by the soundtrack album to *Help!*, in November when the Stones returned to No.2 on the charts they were kept from the top by *The Sound of Music* – the Julie Andrews film stayed there until mid-December when the Beatles' *Rubber Soul* finally knocked it off the top, although the film soundtrack returned to No.1 in early 1966.

Any possible respite for the Stones was on hold because on 24 September it was the first date of a twenty-four-night UK tour – it really was relentless. Before the Stones took the stage each night there was an appearance by the Spencer Davis Group who, when the tour began, had three minor hit singles. A month after the tour ended they were on their way to No.1 with a cover of Jamaican singer

Above: Mick interviewed by Radio Free Europe (RFE) the US government-funded station that broadcast to Communist Europe

Opposite: Some typically obtuse, but thought-provoking, Andrew Loog Oldham copy on this advert for their new UK single

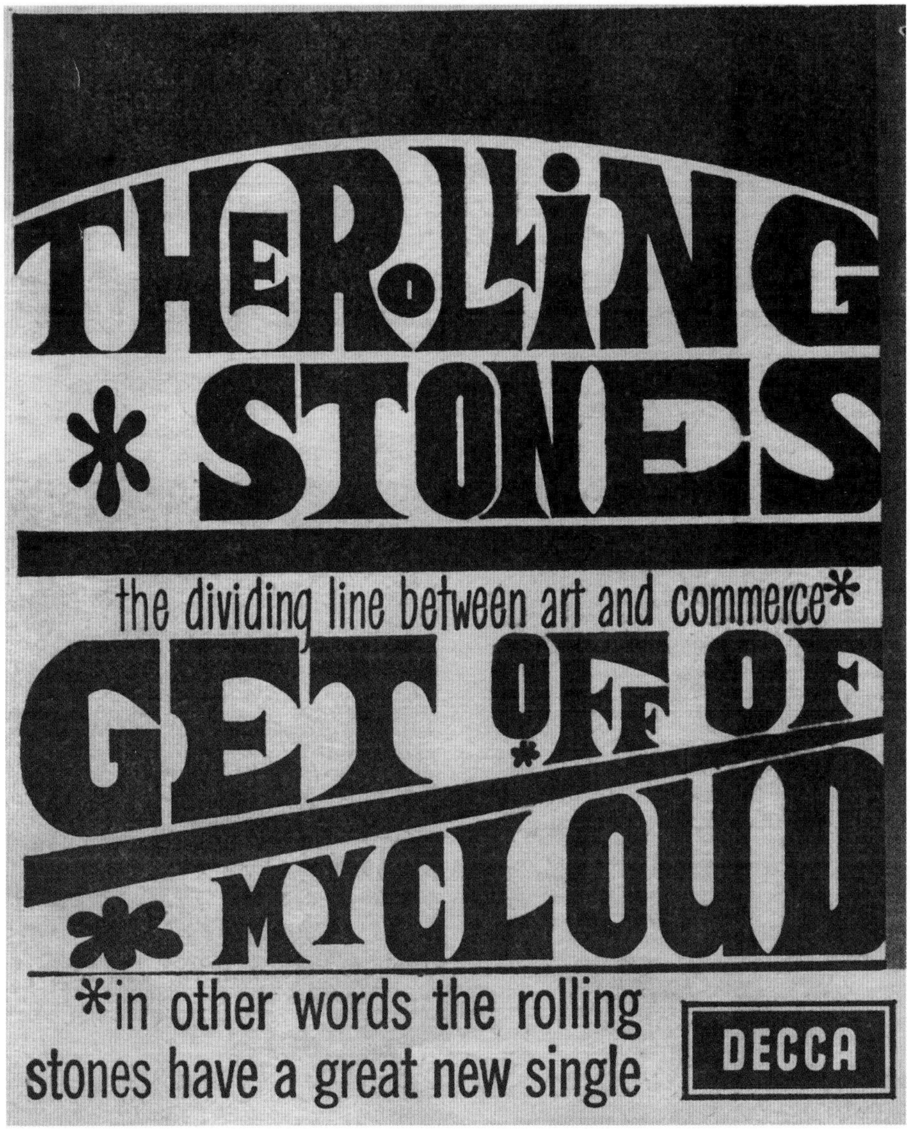

Jackie Edwards' 'Keep On Running', featuring 17-year-old Stevie Winwood on organ and vocals.

Having only been recorded twenty days earlier in Los Angeles, 'Get Off Of My Cloud' was released by London Records in America on the day the Stones played the second night of their UK tour in Southampton. British fans had to wait until 22 October for Decca to release the single in the UK, five days after the tour had been completed.

With the Stones committed to the road, filming a TV or radio appearance was difficult, so *Top of the Pops* used footage filmed by Peter Whitehead for *Charlie Is My Darling* on screen as the single played on the show on 14 October. Meanwhile the Stones themselves were playing the Odeon Cinema in Birmingham. Two days after the tour ended in south London at Tooting's Granada, they were back at the BBC's Television Centre in Shepherd's Bush to mime to 'Get Off Of My Cloud'. The recording was used on *Top of the Pops* on another four occasions, including the Christmas Day special and on a *Man Alive* special, entitled 'Love Me or Leave Me', a film about Brian Jones's wayward – in the extreme – love life. The Stones were paid a basic £183 15 shillings for their appearance on *TOTP*, with an additional £91 17 shillings and sixpence for each additional time it was shown; in today's money that's close to £12,000 for their recording.

On the day 'Get Off Of My Cloud' was released, the Stones were back on *Ready Steady Go!* plugging it, along with 'She Said Yeah' and 'Cry To Me', both of which were included on the UK version of *Out Of Our Heads*. Five days later, the Stones flew from Heathrow to New York's JFK Airport to begin what was to be their fourth tour of America. They were greeted by a 100-foot illuminated billboard in Times Square announcing their next US album, *December's Children (And Everybody's)* – just four months after their last one had been released.

EACH
SWL

Opposite: ***The Ready Steady Go! Rolling Stones Special*** **at Studio One Wembley, London, in October**

Following pages: Recording the ***Ready Steady Go! Rolling Stones Special***

'The sound, face and mind of today is more relative to the hope of tomorrow and the reality of destruction, than the blind who cannot see their children for fear and division. Something that grew and related five reflections of today's children ... The Rolling Stones.'

The Times Square billboard

A few days later the billboard was dark, along with the rest of New York, during a twelve-hour power cut. Brian Jones was in his hotel room jamming with Bob Dylan and Robbie Robertson from the Band ... sadly, no tapes exist.

The tour got underway in Montreal on 29 October and during the next thirty-eight days the band played in twenty different states, along with Washington DC and three cities in Canada. After seven and a half weeks away from home, the tour ended on 5 December in Los Angeles. They had just seven days off.

A few days after the American leg of the tour got underway, the Stones featured on *Shindig!* playing 'Good Times' and 'Mercy Mercy'. These promo films had been recorded at ABC's studios in Twickenham. Another song filmed that day was 'Satisfaction', which aired on the same show in mid-September, although to protect delicate audience sensibilities the 'trying to make some girl' line was taken out. Meanwhile 'Get Off Of My Cloud' was at No.1 in the UK and the US, their fifth single in a row to top the British chart and second in America.

On 11 November, a notional 'day off' between gigs in Raleigh, North Carolina and Washington DC, the Stones flew to New York to appear on one of the few significant American music shows of the era on which they had not so far appeared, *Hullabaloo*. It first broadcast on 12 January 1965 and ran on prime-time NBC-TV as a direct competitor to ABC's *American Bandstand*, a show on which the Stones never appeared.

They filmed their segment at what was then called the RCA Building in Manhattan in Studio 8H, which had been built for the conductor, Arturo Toscanini and the NBC Symphony Orchestra and later still is where *Saturday Night Live* was recorded; the building is now 30 Rockefeller Plaza. *Hullabaloo*'s USP was that it had a different celebrity host each week and on this edition it was Barry McGuire, whose song, 'Eve Of Destruction' had topped the Hot 100 in September; other guests were Brenda Lee, the Kingsmen and Barbara McNair.

EACH

The Stones sang 'She Said Yeah' and 'Get Off Of My Cloud' to pre-recorded backing tracks. Bizarrely, or perhaps not, the *Hullabaloo* studio orchestra played 'Satisfaction' over footage from *Charlie Is My Darling*. It was perhaps not too surprising as it got around the issue of the perceived risqué lyrics that *Shindig!* had struggled with. This was the Stones' one and only appearance on *Hullabaloo*, which only ran until April 1966.

Even with the tour over, they did not fly straight home. As they were in Los Angeles it was convenient for RCA's Hollywood studios and so between 3 and 10 December they recorded some new tracks. Among the songs they did were 'Mother's Little Helper, '19th Nervous Breakdown' and others that appeared on *Aftermath* and *Flowers*.

Their new US album, *December's Children (and Everybody's)*, was released on 4 December and a week later it made the *Billboard* chart, eventually making No.4. It's very much a cobbled-together LP made at various locations, with the earliest song having been recorded in August 1963. The most recent song on the record had been recorded at London's IBC Studios on 26 October 1965, where the Stones had done some of their earliest demos. It features Mick Jagger and a string quartet on 'As Tears Go By'. On Saturday 18 December, Keith's twenty-second birthday, it was released and became the Stones' ninth US single to make the charts, peaking at No.6.

'Marianne Faithfull's version was already a big, proven hit song ... It was one of the first things I ever wrote.'

Mick Jagger
on 'As Tears Go By'

Left: The Hullabaloo dancers
Opposite top: The Stones appear on *Ready Steady Go! – The New Year Starts Here*
Opposite right: The *NME Annual* came out just before Christmas 1965 and features a shot taken by Gered Mankowitz

Instead of flying straight home, some of the band took Caribbean holidays, with Brian the last to arrive in England on 26 December, just in time to appear on *Ready Steady Go! – The New Year Starts Here*, which aired from 10.52 p.m. until after midnight. Aside from the Stones, who did 'Satisfaction' and 'Get Off Of My Cloud', there was the Who, the Animals, Dusty Springfield, the Kinks, Lulu, Tom Jones and a host of others.

It had been the most successful year imaginable for the Rolling Stones, but they had certainly earned that success through a punishing schedule of recording, TV, radio and live shows, all conducted in the intense white light of media scrutiny. They had gone from being the bad boys of pop to fully fledged tabloid fodder, with their every move scrutinized by a media that had come to realize that pop music sold papers and put audience figures on TV and radio shows.

1965 SELECTED TV & RADIO APPEARANCES

6 JANUARY 1965
Six-Five Show, Belfast, Northern Ireland
Little Red Rooster' (Willie Dixon) – at rehearsal, part only

13 JANUARY 1965
(aired 30 January)
Thank Your Lucky Stars, Teddington Studios, Middlesex, UK
Down Home Girl (Jerry Leiber/Arthur Butler), **Under The Boardwalk** (Arthur Resnick/Kenny Young), **Susie Q** (Dale Hawkins/Eleanor Broadwater/Stanley J. Lewis) – playback

15 JANUARY 1965
Ready Steady Go!, TV House, Kingsway, London, UK
What A Shame (MJ/KR), **Time Is On My Side** (Jerry Ragovoy/Jimmy Norman), **Down The Road Apiece** (Don Raye) and **Everybody Needs Somebody to Love** (Bert Russell/Solomon Burke/Jerry Wexler)

21 JANUARY 1965
Interviews with various TV and radio stations at the Chevron-Hilton Hotel, Sydney, Australia

25 JANUARY 1965
Interviews with various TV and radio stations in Brisbane, Australia

28 JANUARY 1965
Interviews with TV stations and radio at Essendon Airport, Melbourne, Australia, including KZ Talk Radio Melbourne. A half-hour programme aired on GMV-6 TV in Melbourne on 17 February

29 JANUARY 1965
(aired 12 February)
Rolling Stones Special Big Beat Show, ATV-O Channel 10 Studios, Melbourne, Australia
Walking The Dog (Rufus Thomas), **Heart Of Stone** (MJ/KR), **Little Red Rooster** (Willie Dixon) and **Around And Around** (Chuck Berry)

17 FEBRUARY 1965
Interviews with various TV and radio stations in Tokyo, Japan

26 FEBRUARY 1965
Ready Steady Go!, TV House, Kingsway, London, UK
Play With Fire (Nanker Phelge), **The Last Time** (MJ/KR) and **Everybody Needs Somebody To Love/Pain In My Heart** (Bert Russell/ Solomon Burke/Jerry Wexler) (Allen Toussaint)

27 FEBRUARY 1965
(aired 28 February)
The Eamonn Andrews Show, Teddington Studios, Middlesex, UK
The Last Time (MJ/KR) – playback

1 MARCH 1965
(aired 6 March)
Top Gear, Studio 2, Broadcasting House, London, UK
Everybody Needs Somebody To Love (Burt Russell/Solomon Burke/Jerry Wexler), **Down The Road Apiece** (Don Raye), **If You Need Me** (Wilson Pickett/Robert Bateman/Sonny Sanders) and **The Last Time** (MJ/KR)

2 MARCH 1965
Pop Inn, The Ideal Homes Exhibition, Olympia, London, UK
Interview with MJ and BJ by Keith Fordyce

4 MARCH 1965
(aired 11 and 18 March, possibly 13 July and 25 December)
Top of the Pops, Studio A, Dickenson Road, Rusholme, Manchester, UK
The Last Time (MJ/KR) – playback

11 MARCH 1965
Scene at 6.30, TV Centre, Manchester, UK
The Last Time (MJ/KR)
Granada in the North, TV Centre, Manchester, UK
Interview with MJ

21 MARCH 1965
(aired 27 March)
Thank Your Lucky Stars, Alpha Studios, Aston, Birmingham, UK
The Last Time (MJ/KR), **Play With Fire** (Nanker Phelge), **Off The Hook** (Nanker Phelge) and **Everybody Needs Somebody to Love** (Burt Russell/Solomon Burke/Jerry Wexler) – playback

1 APRIL 1965
(aired 4 April)
Pop 65, P2 (Swedish radio station), Stockholm, Sweden
Interviews with all five Stones, recorded backstage between gigs
San Francisco Bay Blues (Jesse Fuller) – sung by KR and BW with KR playing guitar

2 APRIL 1965
(aired 8 April)
Popside, Cirkus Building, Stockholm, Sweden (broadcast in Sweden, Denmark, Norway and Finland)
Everybody Needs Somebody To Love (Burt Russell/Solomon Burke/Jerry Wexler), **Tell Me** (MJ/KR), **Around And Around** (Chuck Berry), **Little Red Rooster** (Willie Dixon) and **The Last Time** (MJ/KR)

9 APRIL 1965
Ready Steady Goes Live!, Studio 5, Wembley, London, UK
Everybody Needs Somebody To Love/Pain In My Heart (Bert Russell/Solomon Burke/Jerry Wexler) (Allen Toussaint), **I'm Alright** (Ellas McDaniel) and **The Last Time** (MJ/KR)

11 APRIL 1965
(aired 25 April)
Big Beat '65, NME Poll Winners' Concert, Empire Pool, Wembley, London, UK
Everybody Needs Somebody To Love/Pain In My Heart (Bert Russell/ Solomon Burke/Jerry Wexler) (Allen Toussaint), **Around And Around** (Chuck Berry), **The Last Time** (MJ/KR)

18 APRIL 1965
Musicorama, L'Olympia Theatre, Paris, France.
Europe 1 Radio broadcast the whole concert live, including **Everybody Needs Somebody To Love** (Bert Russell/Solomon Burke/Jerry Wexler), **Around And Around** (Chuck Berry), **Little Red Rooster** (Willie Dixon) and **The Last Time** (MJ/KR)

22 APRIL 1965
(aired 24 April)
Like Young, Hotel Maritime, Montreal, Canada
Interview with all five Stones

24 APRIL 1965
Saturday Date, Ottawa, Canada
Interviews

2 MAY 1965
The Ed Sullivan Show, New York, USA
The Last Time (MJ/KR), **Little Red Rooster** (Willie Dixon), **Everybody Needs Somebody To Love** (Burt Russell/Solomon Burke/Jerry Wexler) and **2120 South Michigan Avenue** (Nanker Phelge)

3 MAY 1965
(aired 29 May)
The Clay Cole Teen Show, WPIX TV, New York, USA
The Last Time (MJ/KR), **Little Red Rooster** (Willie Dixon) and **Down The Road Apiece** (Don Raye) – playback

15 MAY 1965
(aired 22 May)
Hollywood a-Go Go, KHJ Studios, Los Angeles, CA, USA
Oh Baby (Barbara Lynn Ozen), **Play With Fire** (Nanker Phelge) and **The Last Time** (MJ/KR) – playback

16 MAY 1965
Shivaree, KABC-TV Studios, Los Angeles, CA, USA
(aired 5 June and 28 August)
Play With Fire (Nanker Phelge) and **The Last Time** (MJ/KR)
(aired 10 July and 11 December)
Down The Road Apiece (Don Raye) and **Little Red Rooster** (Willie Dixon)

20 MAY 1965
(aired 26 May)

Shindig!, ABC Television Center, Los Angeles, CA, USA

Down The Road Apiece (Don Raye) – live with Billy Preston on keyboards

Little Red Rooster (Willie Dixon), **The Last Time** (MJ/KR) and **Play With Fire** (Nanker Phelge) – live vocals on prepared backing track

(I Can't Get No) Satisfaction (MJ/KR) – mimed to version recorded at Chess Studios on 10 May 1965

4 JUNE 1965

Ready Steady Goes Live!, Studio 5, Wembley, London, UK

Oh Baby (Barbara Lynn Ozen), **Good Times** (Sam Cooke), **I'm Alright** (Ellas McDaniel), **Play With Fire** (Nanker Phelge) and **I'm Moving On** (Hank Snow)

6 JUNE 1965
(aired 12 June)

Thank Your Lucky Stars, Alpha Studios, Aston, Birmingham, UK

I'm Alright (Ellas McDaniel), **I'm Moving On** (Hank Snow) and **Route 66** (Bobby Troup)

21 JUNE 1965

Teen Scene, BBC Broadcasting House, London, UK (aired 6 July)

Woman's Hour, BBC Broadcasting House, London, UK – interview with Mick Jagger

28 JULY 1965

Shindig!, ABC TV Studios, Twickenham, Surrey, UK (aired 16 September)

(I Can't Get No) Satisfaction (MJ/KR) – playback

(aired 6 November)

Mercy, Mercy (Don Covay/Ronald Miller), **Good Times** (MJ/KR) – playback

19 AUGUST 1965
(aired 2, 9, 16 and 30 September and 25 December)

Top of the Pops, Studio 2, BBC TV Centre, Shepherds Bush, London, UK

(I Can't Get No) Satisfaction (MJ/KR) – playback

20 AUGUST 1965

(aired 30 August)

Yeh! Yeh!, Broadcasting House, London, UK

Mercy, Mercy (Don Covay/Ronald Miller), **Oh Baby** (Barbara Lynn Ozen), **(I Can't Get No) Satisfaction** (MJ/KR) and **The Spider And The Fly** (Nanker Phelge)

(aired 18 September)

Saturday Club, Broadcasting House, London, UK

(I Can't Get No) Satisfaction (MJ/KR), **The Spider And The Fly** (Nanker Phelge), **Oh Baby** (Barbara Lynn Ozen), **Cry to Me** (Bert Russell) and **Fannie Mae** (Buster Brown)

23 AUGUST 1965
(aired 26 August)

Scene at 6.30, TV Centre, Manchester, UK

(I Can't Get No) Satisfaction (MJ/KR) – playback

27 AUGUST 1965

Ready Steady Go!, Studio 1, Wembley, London, UK

Mercy, Mercy (Don Covay/Ronald Miller), **The Spider And The Fly** (Nanker Phelge), **(I Can't Get No) Satisfaction** (MJ/KR) and **Apache** (Jerry Lordan) – without MJ

29 AUGUST 1965
(aired 4 September)

Thank Your Lucky Stars Summer Spin, Alpha Studios, Aston, Birmingham, UK

(I Can't Get No) Satisfaction (MJ/KR) – playback

2 SEPTEMBER 1965
(aired 10 September)

Ready Steady Go! The Rolling Stones Special Show, Studio 1, Wembley, London, UK

Oh Baby (Barbara Lynn Ozen), **That's How Strong My Love Is** (Roosevelt Jamison), **(I Can't Get No) Satisfaction** (MJ/KR) and a mimed parody of **I Got You Babe** (Sonny Bono)

14 OCTOBER 1965

Top of the Pops – featured clip from Peter Whitehead's film Charlie Is my Darling overdubbed with **Get Off Of My Cloud** (MJ/KR)

19 OCTOBER 1965
(aired 4, 11, 18 November and 25 December)

Top of the Pops, Studio 2, BBC TV Centre, Shepherds Bush, London, UK

Get Off Of My Cloud (MJ/KR) – playback

22 OCTOBER 1965

Ready Steady Go!, Studio 1, Wembley, London, UK

Cry to Me (Bert Russell), **She Said Yeah** (Sonny Bono/Roddy Jackson) and **Get Off Of My Cloud** (MJ/KR)

11 NOVEMBER 1965
(aired 15 November)

Hullabaloo, RCA Building, New York, USA

She Said Yeah (Sonny Bono/Roddy Jackson) and **Get Off Of My Cloud** (MJ/KR) – playback with live vocals

31 DECEMBER 1965

Ready Steady Go! The New Year Starts Here, Studio 1, Wembley, London, UK

(I Can't Get No) Satisfaction (MJ/KR) and **Get Off Of My Cloud** (MJ/KR) – playback

1963
1964
1965
1966

1967
1968
1969
Gibson

1966

Previous pages: On set at *Ready Steady Go!* at Wembley Studios on 27 May

In the first UK singles chart of the year who was No.1? Yes, it was the Beatles again and despite there being some credible names in the Top 10 there was the usual mix of middle-of-the-road artists, notably two singles by Liverpudlian comedian Ken Dodd. And while long-playing records by 'thinking bands' were beginning to appear – *Rubber Soul* was at No.1 – the chart reflected older, middle-class money buying what it liked and enjoyed. There was the soundtrack to *The Sound of Music* at No.2, another film album at No.3, *Mary Poppins*, and a third occupying the No.5 spot, *My Fair Lady*. Thank God for the Who at No.4.

America was in a similar state. At the top of the singles chart were Simon and Garfunkel with 'The Sound Of Silence', the Beatles were at No.2, then by the following week they were back at the top, and James Brown was No.3. At No.4 in the charts were the Byrds, the Californian band in which every member seemed to have modelled their hairstyle on Brian Jones.

On the US album charts on the first week of 1966, Herb Alpert and the Tijuana Brass held two of the top four places, including the best-seller. *The Sound of Music* was at No.2 and the Stones' *December's Children* was at No.5.

Understandably, given their punishing schedule over the previous three years, the Stones were showing signs of slowing down, just as the Beatles were doing (the Fab Four played their last concert together on 29 August 1966 at San Francisco's Candlestick Park, other than their impromptu performance on the roof of Apple building). TV and radio were becoming increasingly important in getting across the music that artists wanted to sell. In February, the Stones appeared on *The Ed Sullivan Show* where, for the first time, they were seen in colour, rather than black and white.

Not that touring was unimportant to the band. It was also in February that they embarked on another tour of Australia and New Zealand. The following month it was a European tour, taking in Holland, Belgium, France, Sweden and Denmark, albeit a short one. June and it was back to America for their fifth tour, followed by another UK tour in late September and early October.

It was in April that *Aftermath* topped the UK charts, helped in no small way by the band playing tracks from the album on both radio and television. When it finished its eight-week run at No.1, *Aftermath* was replaced by none other than the soundtrack to *The Sound of Music*, which, apart from being replaced by the Beatles' *Revolver* during the late summer, was still there come 31 December.

The UK album chart by the end of the year was a reflection of the taste of the nation ... a broad church. Val Doonican and Jim Reeves represented the old guard, with Cliff Richard, the Seekers and Herb Alpert firmly in the middle of the road. But nothing was more indicative of the power of television than *Here Come the Minstrels*. It was an LP by the George Mitchell Minstrels, a group of black-faced (i.e. white) 'minstrels' that had a weekly television show on the BBC singing about the Swanee River.

As the year came to a close, there was another punctuation mark in the history of British pop; *Ready Steady Go!* broadcast for the final time. Given its popularity it was difficult to see why it was taken off the air, but possibly it reflects what had been happening throughout the year. Bands were maturing and some were even seeing a future beyond just the normal cycle of pop that lasted three years or so, followed by a possible career in the movies if the singer was good-looking enough. Cream, the 'supergroup' made up of Eric Clapton, Ginger Baker and Jack Bruce, released their first album in December 1966 and it made the Top 10 in the UK. The Who were also on the final album chart of the year and, as we now know, they along with Eric Clapton and the Stones have all lasted.

If Britain was changing, then so was America, if at a slightly slower pace. Network TV in the UK made a difference to what was popular, and the pace by which it achieved popularity. In America, when the networks got behind something it really did work. Which is why the final No.1 of 1966 in the US on the album charts were the Monkees, the made-for-TV group, who had their first No.1 single in November 1966. Their second single, 'I'm A Believer', was No.1 on the final Hot 100 of the year. Never underestimate the power of pop ... or television.

CHANGING TIMES

January 1966 was the band's first complete month without a single gig in three years; it was a time for all five Stones to spend time relaxing and pursuing their own personal projects. Keith and Bill recorded a single with Stu, credited to Ian Stewart and the Railroaders. Mick sang some backing vocals on 'Think', a song he and Keith had written that was recorded by Chris Farlowe for Andrew Loog Oldham's Immediate label.

Many sources claim that the Stones appeared on *Top of the Pops* on 20 January, performing 'As Tears Go By', the B-side of the single they were about to release. However, no documentary evidence for this appearance exists – no BBC contract or newspaper listings. In actual fact, there was so little happening that Andrew Loog Oldham, ever the publicist, told the *New Musical Express* that the band's next album, scheduled for release a few months hence, was to be called *Could YOU Walk On The Waters?* The Decca press office went into meltdown, saying, 'We would not issue it with *that* title at any price!'

In fact, the band's first UK TV appearance – though it was indeed on *Top of the Pops* – was not until 3 February. The Stones' next single was released a week earlier and, aside from 'As Tears Go By', which just features Mick and Keith and a string section, it had '19th Nervous Breakdown' on the A-side, a song they had recorded in Los Angeles at the start of December 1965.

Unusually, the Stones recorded two different TV segments for which they were paid £367 5 shillings, double what they would normally receive. They rehearsed their appearances between midday and 6 p.m. at the BBC's Television Centre in west London, as well as taping their second appearance before the show went out live at 7.30 p.m. Of even more interest was DJ David Jacobs, who presented *Top of the Pops* this particular week, interviewing Mick and Keith. This marked a definite shift because previously it had usually been Mick and Brian who took the interviews.

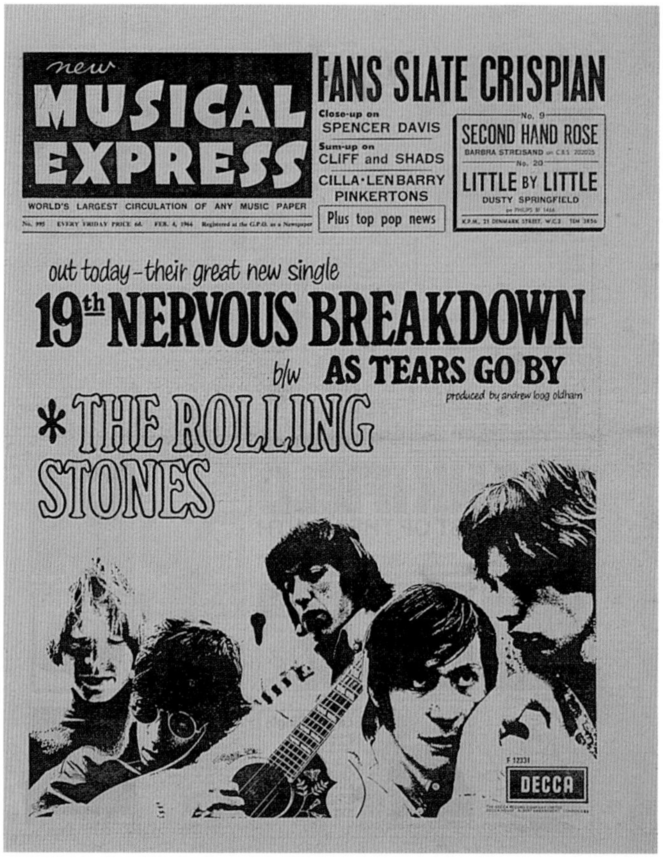

Opposite: A front-page ad for the new single

Below: The band performed '19th Nervous Breakdown' on *The Ed Sullivan Show* in February

'We're not Bob Dylan. "Breakdown" is not supposed to mean anything. It's just about a neurotic bird, that's all.'

Mick Jagger
NME
11 February 1966

Three days later they were on *The Eamonn Andrews Show*, with live vocals against a prepared backing track. Mick was also interviewed and involved in a discussion with the artist, Arthur Dooley, actress Moira Lister and Conservative peer, Quintin Hogg. It prompted a letter to the *NME* from a Scottish reader in Rutherglen, Glasgow, saying, 'At last Mick Jagger has been on *The Eamonn Andrews Show*. Now adults won't be able to say the Stones are dirty and ignorant. I think even Eamonn was impressed. I know my mother was and she is definitely anti-Stones!'

Six days after *The Eamonn Andrews Show*, '19th Nervous Breakdown' entered the UK charts at No.14, the highest new entry of the week, and seven days later it went to No.2. However, it was kept from the top spot for this and the next two weeks by Nancy Sinatra.

On 11 February, the band flew with TWA to New York's Kennedy Airport to film an appearance on *The Ed Sullivan Show* two days later. The day after their arrival, London Records issued '19th Nervous Breakdown' in the States, but coupled with another of Mick and Keith's compositions, 'Sad Day'; the UK B-side had already been an A-side in America, peaking at No.6 on the Hot 100 during the last week of January.

The Stones rehearsed for the *Sullivan Show* on Saturday 12 February and again the following afternoon. They then hung around the studio until the evening when it was time for them to appear live. The show was broadcast from coast to coast, reaching between 15 and 20 million viewers. They played 'Satisfaction', as well as their new single and, with just Keith playing an acoustic guitar and Mick singing, they did 'As Tears Go By' without the rest of the band. This was the first time the Stones had appeared on colour television, despite it having been around for over a decade; it was only in the mid-Sixties that colour TV sets became more widespread. The show also featured Ethel Merman, Hal Holbrook reciting Abraham Lincoln's second inaugural speech, singer Wayne Newton and a Romanian folk ballet ... redefining what it meant to be a 'variety show'.

On Valentine's Day, they flew to Los Angeles where they changed planes to fly to Australia via Hawaii and Fiji on Qantas Airways. Arriving on 16 February, there was the usual round of TV, radio and press interviews at Sydney Airport. The next day they taped an appearance on Channel 9's *Bandstand*, hosted by Brian Henderson. To coincide with their arrival, 'As Tears Go By' and '19th Nervous Breakdown' were released as a double A-side by Decca Australia.

What's interesting about Australian TV is that many of their channels screened American TV shows such as *The Ed Sullivan Show* and *Shindig!* This was often several weeks or months after their US broadcast, but it gave Stones fans the chance to see their idols more often than they would have and helped promote their numerous singles released locally. Whereas in the UK Decca had released nine singles, from 'Come On' to '19th Nervous Breakdown', during the same period Decca Australia released thirteen singles, several of which were what had been released by London Records in the US and been played on Australian TV through US TV shows.

The day after taping their TV appearance, the first concert of their Australian tour, dubbed *Caravan of the Stars '66*, took place at the Commemorative Auditorium at Sydney's Showground in front of 6,000 fans. Throughout the tour, the Searchers were also on the bill, along with local artists that included Max Merritt and the Meteors, Tony Barber, Marty Rhone and the Four Fours.

Sydney's largest radio broadcaster at the time, 2UW FM, carried the first of the Stones' shows, live. This was the first of a number of their shows on this tour that were broadcast by Australian radio stations. On 22 February, Radio 4BH in Brisbane broadcast the second of their two shows, which had taken place at City Hall the previous day. The Stones visited radio station 3UZ in Melbourne on 23 February and the following day the station recorded one of their two concerts (6 p.m. and 8.45 p.m.) at St Kilda's Palais Theatre and broadcast it sometime later. While they were in Melbourne they appeared on GTV-9's Telethon on Friday 25 February, following their two concerts at St Kilda earlier in the evening, in aid of the local children's hospital.

'I hope our filmed insert came over all right. We were all worried that we'd all look a bit skinny. I've lost a bit of weight, but on film it looks as though I've lost loads.'

Mick Jagger
Disc
12 March 1966

Opposite: Mick and Keith performing 'As Tears Go By' on *The Ed Sullivan Show* in February

Opposite: Rehearsing *The Ed Sullivan Show* on 13 February

While the band were in Brisbane they filmed an appearance for *Top of the Pops*. It was at the beach and all the Stones were in swimwear, except Bill, who was not very keen on the water. A waiter arrived carrying a tray and glasses of champagne to serve the band, at which point Bill walked into the sea fully clothed. The segment was shown on 3 March, with '19th Nervous Breakdown' still at No.2 on the UK charts.

After a couple of shows in New Zealand and one in Perth, the Stones flew home via Los Angeles where they once again took the opportunity to record at RCA with Dave Hassinger. Over a four-day period, starting on 6 March, they recorded over twenty songs, including 'Lady Jane', 'Out Of Time', 'Paint It Black' and 'Under My Thumb'. According to Andrew Loog Oldham at the time, 'Brian's contribution can be heard on every track. You can hear his colour all over the records like "Lady Jane" or "Paint It Black". In some instances it was more than a decorative effect. Sometimes Brian pulled the whole record together.'

Arriving back in the UK, Keith finalized the purchase of a house he had viewed prior to their Australian tour. Called Redlands, it was near the coast at West Wittering in Sussex, and it would play its part in the myth and legend surrounding the band. For most of the rest of the month the Stones were free and despite winning the 'Most Outstanding Group of 1965' at the Carl Alan Awards that were televised on the BBC on 21 March, they didn't attend to receive their award personally. It marked the beginning of a subtle change in the band's activities. Prior to this time, they were happy to appear and do just about anything to get media coverage. Now, with five UK No.1s and a No.2 hit under their belt, they could afford to become a little less available.

On 26 March, they began a two-week European tour, taking in Holland, Belgium, France, Sweden and Denmark, appearing in seven separate cities, playing to around 22,000 fans. They played L'Olympia in Paris on 29 February and both shows aired live on Europe 1's radio show, *Musicorama*; Brigitte Bardot turned up at their hotel, the Georges V, after the show to meet the band. The following day they played Marseilles, where, during the second show, someone threw a part of a wooden chair at the stage, hitting Mick over the right eye while they were playing 'Satisfaction' at the end of the show; Mick was taken to hospital for the cut to be treated.

After playing Lyon on 31 March, the band flew home, all except Brian and Bill who returned to the Georges V. Unusually, *Ready Steady Go!* had decided to film an edition of the show at La Locomotive Club in the city, hosted as usual by Cathy McGowan, but with French singer Dick Rivers as her co-host. Both the Who and the Yardbirds appeared on the show, along with several French singers including Mireille Mathieu. Bill and Brian had met Keith Altham, a British PR guy, in Paris and he had persuaded them to go to the club for an unscheduled appearance on *RSG!*

However, the unplanned interview infuriated Andrew Loog Oldham, who wrote to them saying, 'Although I am quite sure your motives were innocent and were done without knowledge of anything I might be doing on your behalf, I would be grateful if in future you could refrain from appearing on television shows such as *Ready, Steady, Go!* without consulting me.' He went on to write: 'I have been negotiating with Rediffusion for us to do our own "special" in place of a *RSG!* which I consider undesirable for you, at the moment. To have you turn up on their TV show rather made a mockery of my plans. The fact is, you are supposed to be the number two group in the world although that status is at times difficult to maintain, and I do not want you just dropping in on TV shows.'

The European tour got back underway on 2 April in Brussels, with newsreel footage of the band's arrival as well as interviews with them. When they returned to London, Mick and Charlie were interviewed at the airport about their forthcoming album release.

TOWARDS THE END OF AN ERA

April was another month of little work for the band. Following their return from Europe it wasn't until mid-month that they were back in the public eye, with an appearance on *Top of the Pops*, but with viewing figures of between 12 and 15 million a week for the show that's a lot of eyeballs. The Stones had no new single to push; instead they played the first track from their new album, *Aftermath*, which was released in the UK the following day. Given their lack of UK shows and their huge popularity at this time, the NME reported that '*Top of the Pops* have taken strong precautions to stop possible gate-crashers on the show.' Johnnie Stewart, the producer of *TOTP*, told the paper: 'We have to take precautions like this when artists like the Stones appear.'

'Mother's Little Helper' was the song they played, another of Mick and Keith's compositions, as were all fourteen tracks on their new LP. Recorded in December in Hollywood, with Brian playing sitar, the song referenced the growing popularity of prescribing drugs to housewives, to 'calm them down', and the potential this created for an overdose. Given the BBC's obsession with drug references that began around this time, it was surprising that it was aired and repeated two weeks later, although the 26 April version was a different staging of the song; they also recorded the band performing 'Paint It Black', which was to be their next single. By 23 April, *Aftermath* was No.1 on the UK album charts where it stayed for eight weeks, helped in no small part by the BBC. The Stones' album finally replaced the soundtrack to *The Sound of Music* at No.1 but was in turn knocked from the top spot by Julie Andrews and co.; in all, *The Sound of Music* spent seventy weeks at the top of the UK album charts.

BEST SELLING LPs IN BRITAIN

(Wednesday, May 25, 1966)

Last Week	This Week	
1	1	AFTERMATH Rolling Stones (Decca)
2	2	SOUND OF MUSIC Soundtrack (RCA)
3	3	SMALL FACES (Decca)
4	4	RUBBER SOUL Beatles (Parlophone)
7	5	MOST OF THE ANIMALS (Columbia)
8	6	SHADOW MUSIC Shadows (Columbia)
5	7	SWEET THINGS Georgie Fame (Columbia)
10	8	TAKE IT EASY WITH THE WALKER BROTHERS (Philips)
—	9	ANIMALISMS Animals (Columbia)
9	10	MANTOVANI MAGIC (Decca)
—	10	SONNY SIDE OF CHER (Atlantic)

On 1 May, the Stones were back at the Empire Pool Wembley to appear at the *NME* Poll Winners' Concert, along with the Beatles; the Spencer Davis Group; Dave Dee, Dozy, Beaky, Mick and Tich; Roy Orbison; Cliff Richard and the Shadows; the Small Faces; the Walker Brothers; the Who and the Yardbirds. The Stones played 'The Last Time', 'Play With Fire' and 'Satisfaction', for which they picked up an award. But none of these three songs, nor the performances of the Beatles, were shown on ABC TV's two seventy-minute programmes that aired on 8 and 15 May. Both bands refused to be filmed performing. According to Don Short, writing in the *Daily Mirror*, 'They said that the sound system was not good enough. ABC TV paid £8,000 to film the concert.'

Two days later, Mick was back on TV to be interviewed for a relatively new BBC TV show, *A Whole Scene Going*, which went on air for the first time on 5 January 1966. The premise of the show, introduced by *Private Eye* magazine's Barry Fantoni, was all things hip and happening in swinging London – over the opening titles, a very BBC announcer said, 'Get down and get with it!' The first show introduced a brand new craze that was sweeping California, skateboarding, featuring a film with the Beach Boys' 'Don't Worry Baby' playing in the background. In reality the craze was not that new; Brian Wilson had written a song for Jan and Dean back in early summer 1964 called 'Sidewalk Surfin', but back then things took a lot longer to cross the Atlantic.

'It's been great working with the Stones, who, contrary to the countless jibes of mediocre comedians all over the world, are real professionals, and a gas to work with.'

Dave Hassinger
Aftermath liner notes

TV ban—by Beatles and Stones

By DON SHORT

FIVE TV cameramen watched the climax of the world's biggest-ever pop concert yesterday . . . because they were unable to film a second of it.

For the Beatles and the Rolling Stones both refused to face the cameras.

Both groups complained that the sound system in the vast Wembley Empire pool—filled with 12,000 fans—was not good enough.

All the other stars on the bill—including Dusty Springfield, Roy Orbison, Herman, Cliff Richard, the Walker Brothers—agreed to the ABC cameras being there.

ABC-TV paid £8,000 to be at the concert—which will be split into two 70-minute programmes to be screened next Sunday and the Sunday after.

Television bosses tried to persuade the Beatles and Stones to change their minds.

But Brian Epstein, the Beatles manager, told me: "This would be very bad, as the sound system is well below standard."

And Andrew Oldham, manager of the Rolling Stones, said, nodding at the rostrum: "No one has a chance out there."

The stars were at Wembley to receive awards from the New Musical Express.

Opposite: *Aftermath* was released on 15 April and was at No.1 a week later
Right: The Beatles' and Stones' refusal to be filmed performing at the *NME* Poll Winners Concert made the national press
Following pages: Mick with Chris Farlowe on *Ready Steady Go!* in June (left); Brian Jones plays sitar for the band's performance of 'Paint It Black' on *Ready Steady Go!* in May (right)

Mick's appearance finally aired on 15 June, on what was the last ever show of the short-lived series, which was not recommissioned despite it attracting over 4 million viewers each week. As well as Mick being interviewed, this edition featured Chris Farlowe and the Thunderbirds performing Mick and Keith's 'Out Of Time', which Mick also produced. The record was released the same week and shortly afterwards it made the charts, climbing to No.1 at the end of July, on the same day as England won the football World Cup – the most-watched programme in British television history with over 32 million people tuning in.

On 8 May, the band were driven to Alpha Studios in Birmingham to rehearse miming to their new single, 'Paint It Black', for an appearance on *Thank Your Lucky Stars*. They also mimed to 'Lady Jane', with Brian on dulcimer and all the band sitting on stools. They closed the show by miming to their new single, with Brian playing sitar. In between the two songs, the show's host, Jim Dale, briefly interviewed Mick, mentioning Ringo Starr's quote that the Beatles just had an hour off and asking whether the Stones had had much free time recently.

The following Thursday there was another appearance on *Top of the Pops*, miming to their new single – their performance had been recorded back in April – and the following day 'Paint It Black' was released. A week later it entered the charts at No.5 before topping the best-seller list the following week. With their single at No.1 they appeared on *Ready Steady Goes Live!* to play their new hit, as well as another couple of numbers. It seems inconceivable now that what was one of the most brilliant and exciting Stones' singles from the 1960s could only manage a week at the top. The reason was simple: 50-year-old Frank Sinatra came along with his new song 'Strangers In The Night' and swept all before it.

'We find it easier now as we don't work as much.'

Mick Jagger
Disc
12 March 1966

In the middle of June, with the release of Chris Farlowe's cover version of 'Out Of Time', Mick appeared on *Ready Steady Go!* talking to Cathy McGowan about his involvement with the record. A week later the band flew to New York for what was to be their fifth American tour. On their arrival, the band held a press conference on the *SS Sea Panther* on the Hudson River. Among the photographers and interviewers was 24-year-old Linda Eastman, who a year later would meet Paul McCartney in London. Shortly after that, they began a relationship that saw them married in 1969.

Since their fourth US tour, six months earlier, the Stones had had three Top-10 American hits and their greatest hits album, *Big Hits (High Tide And Green Grass)*, had got to No.3 on the charts. Four days before the tour opened at the Manning Bowl in Lynn, Massachusetts, the US version of *Aftermath* hit the record stores and by the time the tour was over it was at No.2 on the charts. Their single, 'Paint It Black', was toppled from the top spot on the Hot 100 by the Beatles' 'Paperback Writer', the day after their opening night.

During the tour they visited Canada and twenty US states, as well as playing in Missouri, Oregon, Utah, Virginia and Hawaii for the first time. However, there were no TV

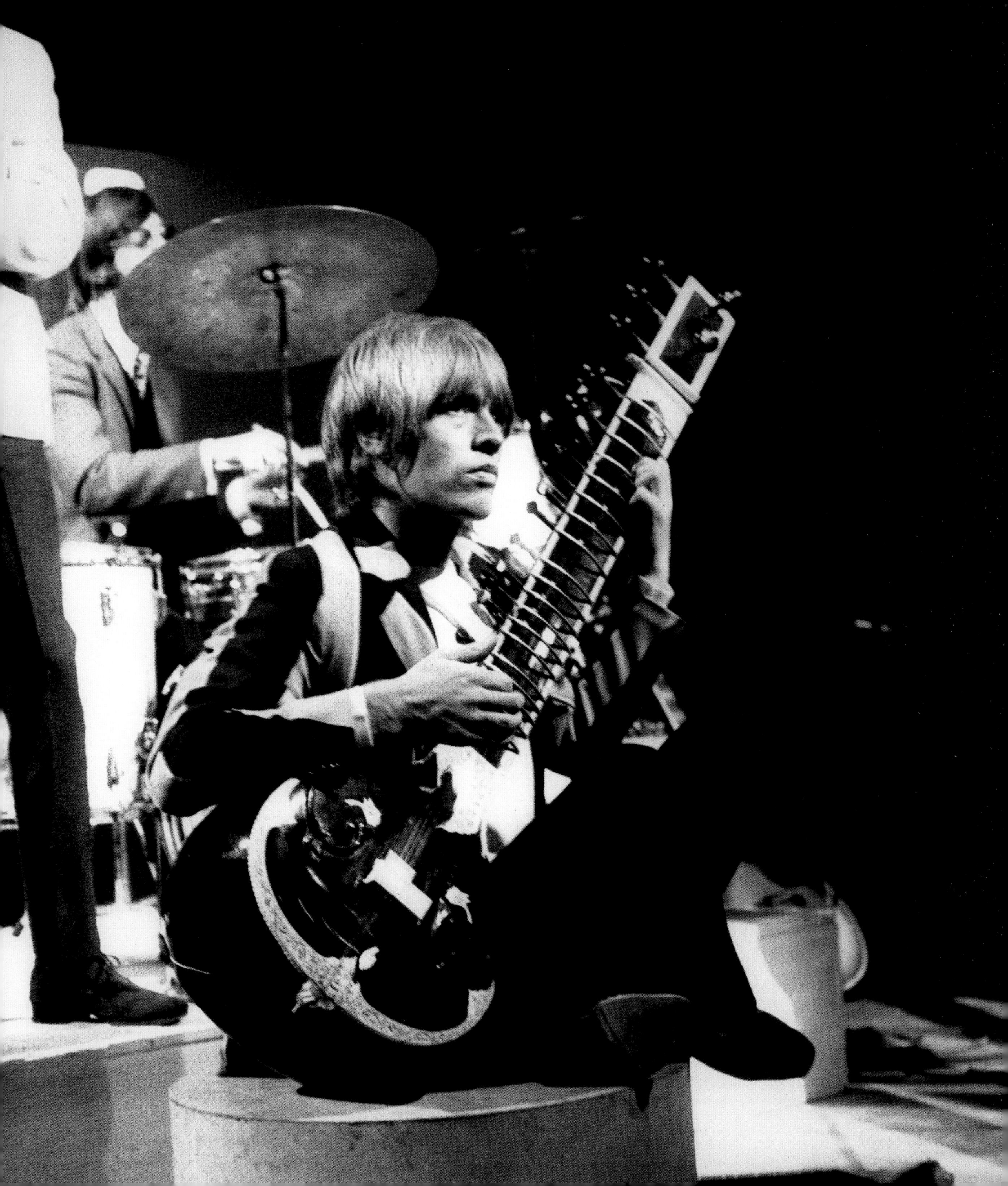

Opposite top: *Ready Steady Go!* 27 May
Opposite bottom: Brian on *Thank Your Lucky Stars* in May
Right: Rehearsing *The Ed Sullivan Show* on 11 September

appearances featuring the band performing. It may have been an accident of timing with their single having been out for a while, and yet they did release 'Mother's Little Helper' backed by 'Lady Jane' on 2 July. The lyrics may have put off TV producers, but it is strange that none of the network shows booked them, nor do there appear to be any regional TV appearances. It possibly affected the chart position of 'Mother's Little Helper', which could only reach No.8 on the Hot 100.

Instead, the TV coverage focused on the riotous behaviour of fans on news bulletins across the nation. At the opening concert in Lynn, some of the 15,000 fans tried to storm the stage; the police ended up using tear gas. It was a familiar scenario that continued throughout the tour and TV (and other media) lapped it up as usual. The other thing that fascinated the media was the news that the Stones were going to get $1 million for their first feature film, which was to be called *Only Lovers Left Alive*, and the fact that Mick and Keith were writing seven new songs for the movie.

Radio remained the most important medium for getting Stones' records heard across America and during their tour it was announced that 'Satisfaction' was the most played song on American radio during the previous twelve months, sharing the top spot with Staff Sgt. Barry Sadler's 'Ballad of the Green Berets' – it's hard to imagine a greater juxtaposition between two No.1 records. Radio stations continued to sponsor concerts in their home cities, as WKNR did in Detroit, KILT in Houston, KAFY in Bakersfield and KHJ in Los Angeles.

In one interesting break from the norm, when the Stones got to Hawaii to play the Honolulu International Convention Center, a deal had been done with local station K-POI to broadcast the concert in its entirety, which ran for a little over half an hour, as it did everywhere on the tour.

Just as the tour was ending, the *Daily Mirror* ran an unusual story concerning Radio Caroline, the pirate station anchored in the North Sea that broadcast to the UK. 'Mr Justice Plowman was told in the High Court about an advertisement, from Radio Caroline, which appeared in *Queen* magazine,' the Mirror reported. 'It showed Mick Jagger with the director of an advertising agency. Mr Colin Duncan QC, for Jagger & Oldham, said the magazine played a dastardly trick on Jagger, by telling him that the photograph was for a future article, and failed to mention it was to be used in an advert. The judge granted a temporary injunction ordering *Queen* not to publish the advertisement.' The injunction was lifted a few days later. Ten days or so later, there were articles in the UK music press about Radio Caroline banning the Stones. However, it was all over very quickly and it was not going to be long before it did not matter much at all what the pirate radio stations did, as the British Government was about to ban them altogether.

With the tour over, WABC in New York conducted interviews over the phone with Keith and Mick, just prior to the band returning to RCA Studios for some recording with Dave. The band drifted home from America at various times in August, as they did not have work commitments to worry about. Brian's relationship with the

Left: Filming *The Ed Sullivan Show*, 11 September

Below: The *Daily Mirror* carried the 'Stones in drag' photo promoting 'Have You Seen Your Mother Baby, Standing in the Shadows'

Opposite: Rolling Stones 66 was the first live tour the Stones had performed in almost a year

Italian actress and model Anita Pallenberg was in full swing, even if his relationship with the rest of the band and Andrew Loog Oldham was not what it had been. With Keith and Mick writing the band's material, Brian's role was as a 'decorator', decorating their records with his innate musical sense, but no longer was he at the heart of the band. Brian was even working on a separate musical project, the soundtrack of the film, *A Degree of Murder,* which also featured Jimmy Page and keyboard player Nicky Hopkins.

One of the tracks that had been started in Los Angeles in early August was 'Have You Seen Your Mother, Baby, Standing In The Shadow?' and there was more recording and overdubs on the song in London at the very start of September. Then, on 8 September, Mick, Keith, Andrew and Stu flew to California and went to RCA Studios to finish the track. The following day, Brian, Charlie and Bill flew to New York to meet up with the others, who had flown in from Los Angeles; they were all there to appear on *The Ed Sullivan Show.*

On 9 September, they performed three songs that Mick sang live over pre-recorded backing tracks. When it aired on Sunday 11 September, 'Lady Jane' and 'Have You Seen Your Mother, Baby, Standing In The Shadow?' were featured at the top of the programme and towards the finale they did 'Paint It Black'; Brian was unable to play guitar because he had injured his hand in an accident in his bathroom two weeks earlier.

Oh! Brian, Keith, Mick, Charlie and Bill.. HOW YOU'VE CHANGED

THIS extraordinary picture was taken last Saturday afternoon in a back street off New York's Third-avenue, and Mr. Andrew Loog Oldham confessed that he was a little worried about it at first.

He manages the Rolling Stones—and the picture is of his charges. The Jean Harlow type on the left is Brian Jones.

In line with him from the left are Keith Richard, Mick Jagger (he is made up to look coloured) and Charlie Watts. Bill Wyman sits this one out—in uniform.

They got all togged up like this in wigs and furs and skirts to illustrate the theme of their new record, which is entitled

by PATRICK DONCASTER

"Have You Seen Your Mother, Baby, Standing In The Shadow?"

"It is about the attitude that exists between parents and their children," explained Mr. Oldham.

The Shadow is the uncertainty of the future. The uncertainty is whether we slide into a vast depression or universal war.

And the Stones, in this picture, set out to give their idea of what some of the mothers of today's generation might have looked like in the Shadow of the warring Forties. "They are parodying the theme," said Mr. Oldham. "New York is quiet on Saturdays. And only three fans were about when the picture was taken."

It will be used as a record sleeve in the United States. And it is likely to cause a storm there when it is issued next month.

Because Americans don't take kindly to such parodies of Motherhood.

The song will be issued in Britain next week. Musically, it's a jolly romp that will have the fans dancing rather than worrying about war or want. Or that picture.

Doncaster's Discs—Page 20.

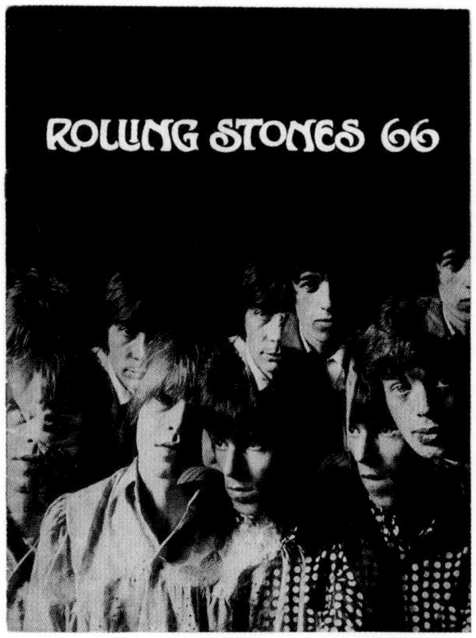

‘The tour has been an enormous success because it’s brought the young people back again. It was getting all “draggy” and quiet. We were in danger of becoming respectable. Now the new wave has arrived, rushing the stage just like old times.’

Keith Richards

On the Saturday, the band filmed two promo videos with Peter Whitehead for ‘Have You Seen Your Mother, Baby, Standing In The Shadow?’ in which they are shown being made up in drag and as the finished articles on the streets of Manhattan. They called themselves Sarah (Mick), Molly (Keith), Flossie (Brian), Millicent (Charlie) and Penelope (Bill). After the video shoot, photographer Jerry Schatzberg took pictures in a street off Third Avenue.

The Stones’ new single was released simultaneously in the UK and America on 23 September and on the day before its release, *Top of the Pops* showed one of the films shot in New York with the band in drag. A week later, with the single the highest new entry on the UK charts, the second video was shown on *TOTP* along with footage of the band receiving gold discs at a party at the Kensington Palace Hotel on 23 September.

Before the party, the band played the first night of a twelve-date UK tour at the Royal Albert Hall, which ran until 9 October. These were the first UK live dates, aside from their brief appearance at the NME Poll Winners’ Concert, in almost a year. Joining them for the tour were Ike and Tina Turner, Peter Jay and the Jaywalkers (featuring the great Terry Reid on vocals), and the Yardbirds, including both Jeff Beck and Jimmy Page.

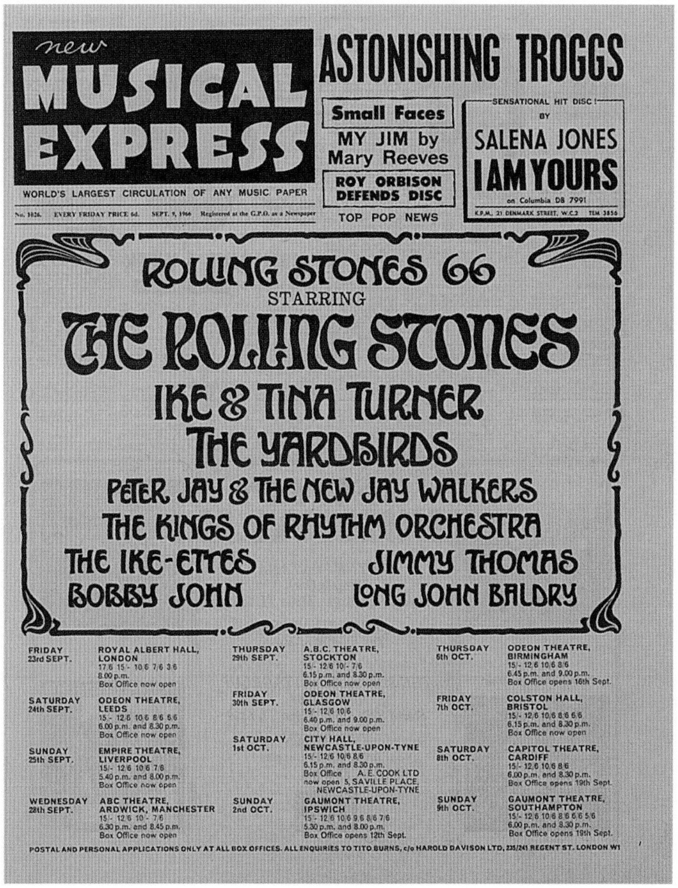

new MUSICAL EXPRESS

WORLD'S LARGEST CIRCULATION OF ANY MUSIC PAPER

No. 1026. EVERY FRIDAY PRICE 6d. SEPT. 9, 1966 Registered at the G.P.O. as a Newspaper

ASTONISHING TROGGS

Small Faces

MY JIM by Mary Reeves

ROY ORBISON DEFENDS DISC

TOP POP NEWS

SENSATIONAL HIT DISC! BY SALENA JONES I AM YOURS on Columbia DB 7991

K.P.M., 21 DENMARK STREET, W.C.2 TEM 3856

ROLLING STONES 66

STARRING

THE ROLLING STONES

IKE & TINA TURNER

THE YARDBIRDS

PETER JAY & THE NEW JAY WALKERS

THE KINGS OF RHYTHM ORCHESTRA

THE IKE-ETTES

JIMMY THOMAS

BOBBY JOHN

LONG JOHN BALDRY

FRIDAY 23rd SEPT. — ROYAL ALBERT HALL, LONDON — 17/6 15/- 10/6 7/6 3/6 — 8.00 p.m. — Box Office now open

SATURDAY 24th SEPT. — ODEON THEATRE, LEEDS — 15/- 12/6 10/6 8/6 6/6 — 6.00 p.m. and 8.30 p.m. — Box Office now open

SUNDAY 25th SEPT. — EMPIRE THEATRE, LIVERPOOL — 15/- 12/6 10/6 7/6 — 5.40 p.m. and 8.00 p.m. — Box Office now open

WEDNESDAY 28th SEPT. — ABC THEATRE, ARDWICK, MANCHESTER — 15/- 12/6 10/- 7/6 — 6.30 p.m. and 8.45 p.m. — Box Office now open

THURSDAY 29th SEPT. — A.B.C. THEATRE, STOCKTON — 15/- 12/6 10/- 7/6 — 6.15 p.m. and 8.30 p.m. — Box Office now open

FRIDAY 30th SEPT. — ODEON THEATRE, GLASGOW — 15/- 12/6 10/6 — 6.40 p.m. and 9.00 p.m. — Box Office now open

SATURDAY 1st OCT. — CITY HALL, NEWCASTLE-UPON-TYNE — 15/- 12/6 10/6 8/6 — 6.15 p.m. and 8.30 p.m. — Box Office now open A. E. COOK LTD 5, SAVILLE PLACE, NEWCASTLE-UPON-TYNE

SUNDAY 2nd OCT. — GAUMONT THEATRE, IPSWICH — 15/- 12/6 10/6 9/6 8/6 7/6 — 5.30 p.m. and 8.00 p.m. — Box Office opens 12th Sept.

THURSDAY 6th OCT. — ODEON THEATRE, BIRMINGHAM — 15/- 12/6 10/6 8/6 — 6.45 p.m. and 9.00 p.m. — Box Office opens 16th Sept.

FRIDAY 7th OCT. — COLSTON HALL, BRISTOL — 15/- 12/6 10/6 8/6 6/6 — 6.15 p.m. and 8.30 p.m. — Box Office now open

SATURDAY 8th OCT. — CAPITOL THEATRE, CARDIFF — 15/- 12/6 10/6 8/6 — 6.00 p.m. and 8.30 p.m. — Box Office opens 19th Sept.

SUNDAY 9th OCT. — GAUMONT THEATRE, SOUTHAMPTON — 15/- 12/6 10/6 8/6 6/6 5/6 — 6.00 p.m. and 8.30 p.m. — Box Office opens 19th Sept.

POSTAL AND PERSONAL APPLICATIONS ONLY AT ALL BOX OFFICES. ALL ENQUIRIES TO TITO BURNS, c/o HAROLD DAVISON LTD, 235/241 REGENT ST. LONDON W1

Right and following pages: Performing 'Paint It Black' on *Ready Steady Go!* on 4 October

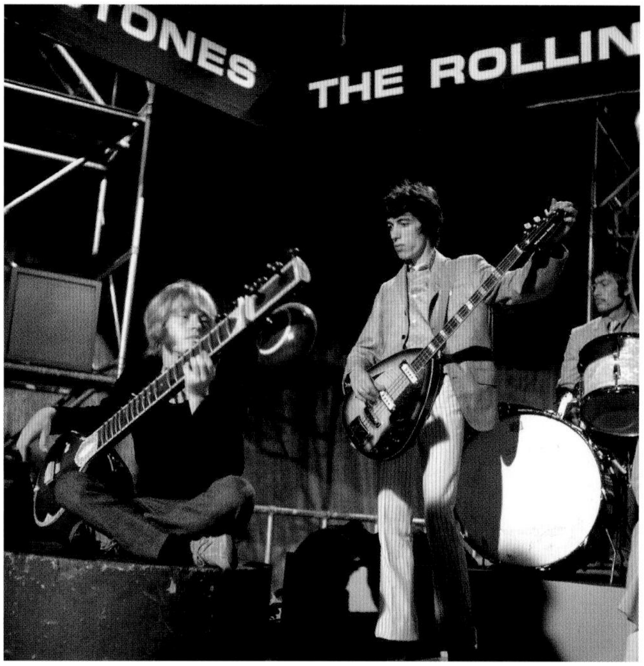

Between dates in Ipswich and Birmingham, the Stones went to the *Ready Steady Go!* studios in Wembley to record an edition of the show that was arguably closer to their collective heart than any other contemporary British TV pop programme. They mimed to their new single, as well as 'Paint It Black' and 'Lady Jane'; it was the band's last-ever appearance on the show before it was decommissioned. Two days later, 'Have You Seen Your Mother, Baby' was again on *Top of the Pops* and a week later it peaked on the UK charts at No.5. Jim Reeves' 'Distant Drum' was at No.1; Dave Dee, Dozy, Beaky, Mick and Tich's 'Bend It' was at No.2; The Who's 'I'm A Boy' was at No.3; and the New Vaudeville Band's 'Winchester Cathedral' was at No.4. Despite all the promotion and the tour, the Stones had failed to score a Top 3 hit for the first time in nine single releases.

There was much talk in the press of the Stones not being quite the force they had been. On 4 November, *Big Hits (High Tide And Green Grass)* came out in the UK with a slightly different track listing from the American release. It was almost as though this was some kind of punctuation mark in the band's career and it reached only No.4 on the album charts. The day after the album's release, Bobby Elliott of the Hollies, when asked what he thought of the Stones' latest single, said, 'The record was just basically above the fans' heads. It was too hippy and those photos showing the Stones in drag put the youngsters off a bit.' He may well have been right. The Stones were moving away from being a pop group and in the cycle of pop, three and a half years is a lifetime.

A few days later, the band recorded at Olympic Studios in Barnes, west London, for the first time; it became their studio of choice over much of the following five years. Among the songs they recorded before the month was over were 'Back Street Girl', 'Let's Spend The Night Together' and 'Ruby Tuesday'. After one all-night session the band went to Primrose Hill, in north London, where photographer Gered Mankowitz took shots for what would become the cover of their next album.

As the year came to an end, the Stones appeared on *Top of the Pops* on 22 December, miming to 'Have You Seen Your Mother, Baby', and the following day just Mick was on the final ever edition of *Ready Steady Go!* At this farewell party show Mick sang both 'Out Of Time 'and 'Satisfaction' with Chris Farlowe. On 26 December, the Christmas edition of *Top of the Pops* used recordings '19th Nervous Breakdown' and 'Mother's Little Helper' from earlier in the year.

1966 SELECTED TV & RADIO APPEARANCES

20 JANUARY 1966
Top of the Pops, Studio 2, BBC TV Centre, Shepherds Bush, London, UK
As Tears Go By (MJ/KR/Andrew Oldham)

3 FEBRUARY 1966
Top of the Pops, Studio 2, BBC TV Centre, Shepherds Bush, London, UK
(aired 3, 10, 17 February and 25 December)
19th Nervous Breakdown (MJ/KR) – version 1 (aired 24 February)
19th Nervous Breakdown (MJ/KR) – version 2

6 FEBRUARY 1966
The Eamonn Andrews TV Show, Teddington Studios, Middlesex, UK
19th Nervous Breakdown (MJ/KR) – live vocals to backing track and interview with MJ

13 FEBRUARY 1966
The Ed Sullivan Show, New York, USA
(I Can't Get No) Satisfaction (MJ/KR), **19th Nervous Breakdown** (MJ/KR) and **As Tears Go By** (MJ/KR/Andrew Oldham) – MJ and KR only

17 FEBRUARY 1966
(aired 20 February)
Bandstand Special, Channel 9, Sydney, Australia
Get Off Of My Cloud (MJ/KR), **Play With Fire** (Nanker Phelge), **19th Nervous Breakdown** (MJ/KR), **(I Can't Get No) Satisfaction** (MJ/KR) and **As Tears Go By** (MJ/KR/Andrew Oldham) – MJ and KR only – playback

18 FEBRUARY 1966
2UW FM broadcast the Stones' first show from Commemorative Auditorium Showgrounds, Sydney, Australia
Mercy, Mercy (Don Covay/Ronald Miller), **She Said Yeah** (Sonny Bono/Roddy Jackson), **Play With Fire** (Nanker Phelge), **The Last Time** (MJ/KR), **The Spider And The Fly** (Nanker Phelge), **That's How Strong My Love Is** (Roosevelt Jamison), **Get Off Of My Cloud** (MJ/KR), **19th Nervous Breakdown** (MJ/KR) and **(I Can't Get No) Satisfaction** (MJ/KR)

21 FEBRUARY 1966
(aired 22 February)
4BH broadcast the Stones' second show from City Hall, Brisbane, Australia

22 FEBRUARY 1966
(aired 3 March)
Top of the Pops, Brisbane Beach, Australia
Possibly using **19th Nervous Breakdown** (MJ/KR)

24 FEBRUARY 1966
Channel 9 **Telethon Appeal Show,** Melbourne, Australia (aired unknown)
3UZ Radio Show, 3UZ Radio Station, Palais Theatre, St Kilda, Melbourne, Australia

29 MARCH 1966
Musicorama, L'Olympia Theatre, Paris, France. Europe 1 Radio broadcast the whole concert live, maybe both the matinee and evening concerts, including:
Mercy, Mercy (Don Covay/Ronald Miller), **She Said Yeah** (Sonny Bono/Roddy Jackson), **Play With Fire** (Nanker Phelge), **The Last Time** (MJ/KR), **I'm Moving On** (Hank Snow), **The Spider And The Fly** (Nanker Phelge), **That's How Strong My Love Is** (Roosevelt Jamison), **Get Off Of My Cloud** (MJ/KR), **19th Nervous Breakdown** (MJ/KR) and **(I Can't Get No) Satisfaction** (MJ/KR)

14 APRIL 1966
(aired 14 April)
Top of the Pops, Studio 2, BBC TV Centre, Shepherds Bush, London, UK
Mother's Little Helper (MJ/KR) (aired 12 and 26 May)
Paint It Black (MJ/KR)

1 MAY 1966 (aired 15 May)
Big Beat '66, NME Poll Winners' Concert, Empire Pool, Wembley, London, UK (matinee) The Stones refused to be filmed performing but they were shown receiving their award

3 MAY 1966
(aired 15 June)
A Whole Scene Going, BBC TV Centre, Shepherds Bush, London, UK
Interview with MJ

8 MAY 1966
(aired 15 May)
Thank Your Lucky Stars, Alpha Studios, Aston, Birmingham, UK
Lady Jane (MJ/KR) and **Paint It Black** (MJ/KR) – playback

27 MAY 1966
Ready Steady Go!, Studio 5, Wembley, London, UK
I Am Waiting (MJ/KR), **Under My Thumb** (MJ/KR) and **Paint It Black** (MJ/KR)

28 JULY 1966
K-POI broadcast the Stones' concert from Honolulu International Center, Honolulu, Hawaii
Not Fade Away (Norman Petty/Charles Hardin Holly), **The Last Time** (MJ/KR), **Paint It Black** (MJ/KR), **Lady Jane** (MJ/KR), **Mother's Little Helper** (MJ/KR), **Get Off Of My Cloud** (MJ/KR), **19th Nervous Breakdown** (MJ/KR) and **(I Can't Get No) Satisfaction** (MJ/KR)

9 SEPTEMBER 1966
(aired 11 September)
The Ed Sullivan Show, CBS Studios, New York, USA
Paint It Black (MJ/KR), **Lady Jane** (MJ/KR) and **Have You Seen Your Mother, Baby, Standing In The Shadow?** (MJ/KR) – live vocals on a prepared backing track

10 SEPTEMBER 1966
(aired 22 and 29 September)
Top of the Pops, promo film shot in New York
Have You Seen Your Mother, Baby, Standing In The Shadow? (MJ/KR)

27 SEPTEMBER 1966
Pop Inn, BBC Broadcasting House, London, UK
Interview with MJ

4 OCTOBER 1966
(aired 7 October)
Ready Steady Go!, Studio 5, Wembley, London, UK
Paint It Black (MJ/KR), **Lady Jane** (MJ/KR) and **Have You Seen Your Mother, Baby, Standing In The Shadow?** (MJ/KR) – playback

5 OCTOBER 1966
(aired 6 October)
Top of the Pops, Studio 2, BBC TV Centre, Shepherds Bush, London, UK
Have You Seen Your Mother, Baby, Standing In The Shadow? (MJ/KR)

14 OCTOBER 1966
The David Frost Show, ABC Film Studios, Wembley Park, London, UK
Interview with MJ

17 DECEMBER 1966
(aired 22 October)
Top of the Pops, Studio 2, BBC TV Centre, Shepherds Bush, London, UK
Have You Seen Your Mother, Baby, Standing In The Shadow? (MJ/KR)

20 DECEMBER 1966
(aired 23 December)
Ready Steady Go! (final show), Studio 5, Wembley, London, UK
Out Of Time (MJ/KR) and **(I Can't Get No) Satisfaction** (MJ/KR) – duet with MJ and Chris Farlowe – just some of both songs were shown. Interview with MJ

1963 1964 1965 1966

1967
1968
1969

1967

1968

1969

Previous pages:
Filming *The Rock and Roll Circus* TV special, December 1968

We've all come to think of 1967 as the year that the 'Summer of Love' occurred – hippies, kaftans and beads were de rigueur and everyone was at peace. Musically, along came *Sgt. Pepper's Lonely Hearts Club Band*, the album that became the soundtrack to the summer, but it was also a year of much change and even more diversity.

Sgt. Pepper topped the album chart for twenty-three straight weeks and only two other LPs made the No.1 spot all year: *The Sound of Music* and *The Monkees*, the latter's show having begun broadcasting on British television.

Amidst the kaftans and droopy moustaches, Engelbert Humperdinck topped the UK charts with 'Release Me', which prevented the Beatles' 'Penny Lane/Strawberry Fields Forever' from reaching No.1. Before the year was out, the man born Arnold Dorsey went on to have another No.1 with 'The Last Waltz', which became the biggest-selling single of 1967. It really was a funny old year.

For the Stones, the infamous Redlands drug bust cast a shadow over everything, including their recordings. To begin with all was well when 'Let's Spend The Night Together' was released in January, making No.3 in the UK. In America, 'Ruby Tuesday'– the single was a double A-side – made No.1, thanks in part to Ed Sullivan making the Stones change the lyric to 'Let's spend some time together'. It did well despite the fact that many radio stations banned it altogether on account of its 'disgusting lyrics'– the same stations that were quite happy to play countless records with 'rock and roll' in the title, which is far more suggestive.

The Stones tried to capture the mood of the moment with *Their Satanic Majesties Request*, an album that was redolent of the times, but lacking in the kind of cohesion normally associated with the band; Mick and Keith, as well as Brian, were all having issues with the authorities. Mick, especially, went from being seen on TV singing to more frequently being touted as the 'voice of a generation'.

Brian's drug busts lead to him being virtually certain of being barred from entering America by US immigration, which meant that 1968 became a year of staying put. In an effort to right their recording ship, the Stones brought in Jimmy Miller as producer, Andrew Loog Oldham having broken all ties with the band in the summer of 1967. The first thing they did together was to record 'Jumpin' Jack Flash', which took them back to the top of the UK chart and to No.3 in America. In another subtle shift, the Stones made a video to promote the record for showing on television around the world when visiting in person was not an option.

Beggars Banquet came out in December and reaffirmed the band's status as the best rock band in the world. Close on its heels, the band filmed their own TV spectacular, *The Rock and Roll Circus*. It was a bit of a shambles, for many reasons, but it was also a pointer as to where things were going. Throughout *The Rock and Roll Circus*, Brian looks dreadful and they decided to shelve it at the time, not releasing it for close on thirty years.

As 1969 came around, the band's lawyers confirmed that there was no way that Brian would be allowed to enter America to tour, effectively ending the band's career. The inevitable happened. Brian was ousted from the band and Mick Taylor brought in as his replacement.

For their first gig with the new line-up – their first proper concert since 1967– the Stones played a free concert in London's Hyde Park in July, a few days after Brian Jones died at home in his swimming pool. The concert in the park was an audacious affair and a TV documentary was made of the event that was shown on UK television a month before the Stones started a mammoth US tour in October 1969.

It was at Hyde Park that the band were announced to the crowd, for the first time, as 'the greatest rock and roll band in the world'. At this point they may not quite have been that, but by the end of the US tour they most certainly were. It was a tour that ended in the tragedy of Altamont.

All this added to the myth of the band. And yet, consider one thing. Following the reminder of their own mortality at Altamont, just three days later, they were back at the BBC's TV studios in London recording appearances on *Top of the Pops*. With the benefit of hindsight it barely seems possible that this could happen. Yet for the Rolling Stones it did, as it continues to do.

They are still the greatest rock and roll band in the world ...

CONTROVERSY

Below: Performing 'Ruby Tuesday' on *The Ed Sullivan Show*, 15 January 1967

Opposite top: Jimi Hendrix backstage at the Saville Theatre, London, 4 June 1967

Opposite bottom: Leaving the Palladium Theatre in London after appearing on *Sunday Night at the London Palladium*

It was a busy, and controversial, start to 1967 for the Stones. On 13 January Decca released 'Let's Spend The Night Together', coupled with 'Ruby Tuesday'; the following day it was released by London Records in America. Their record companies were becoming increasingly aligned.

Mick, in an upbeat interview, told *Disc* in the first week of January, 'It's true we didn't sell so many discs in England during 1966 as in the previous year, but neither did the other groups. As far as abroad goes, America is OK and we broke the Italian and German markets in 1966. We haven't quietened down. It's madder now than ever before. We couldn't possibly go on doing ballrooms and cinema appearances all the time. All the groups seem to be cooling off in this respect.'

'If anyone is going to match our success and that of the Beatles ... it'll be someone completely new that we've never heard about.'

Mick Jagger
Melody Maker
7 January 1967

A week earlier, Jimi Hendrix's 'Hey Joe' featured for the first time on the UK charts; times were definitely-achanging. The day before the Stones' single's release, all the band, except Mick, flew to New York, with Mick following on Friday 13th. Fortunately, Mick's flight was not late as the band had a rehearsal for *The Ed Sullivan Show* that evening.

On Sunday, they were back at the studio for a final rehearsal and an argument with Mr Sullivan, who was shocked and appalled by the lyrics of 'Let's Spend The Night Together'. At first the band and Andrew Loog Oldham refused to change the words, before eventually acquiescing: it was clear that there was no way the broadcast could go ahead with the risk of shocking the delicate sensibilities of 15 million Americans.

Nor did Sullivan mention the offending song in his introduction. Instead, he dodged the issue by simply saying, 'Here are the Rolling Stones.' With Keith at the piano, Brian playing a recorder and Bill bowing a double bass they performed 'Ruby Tuesday'; Charlie looked mildly disgusted throughout. For the potentially offending song, Brian switched to piano and Keith to guitar; Mick duly obliged by changing the lyric ... 'the night', became 'some time'.

In the weeks that followed, some radio stations were equally outraged, bleeping out the word 'night', while some stations went as far as banning it altogether, all of which meant 'Ruby Tuesday' got a lot more airplay. As a result, 'Ruby Tuesday' topped the charts, while 'Let's Spend The Night Together' could only make a lowly No.55. This was in part because the *Billboard* chart in America was compiled from a combination of radio plays as well as the records that were sold.

Home from America, the band's sixth UK album, *Between The Buttons*, was released on 20 January and it was the last of the band's official albums to feature a different track listing to the American version. Ten of the twelve tracks on the UK version featured on the US album that came out on 11 February; the two that were different on the American version were both sides of the latest single, replacing 'Back Street Girl' and 'Please Go Home'.

Two days after the release of their new album, on Sunday 22 January, the Stones were again the centre of a controversy. They had at last relented and agreed to appear on *Sunday Night at the London Palladium*, the ultimate in British light entertainment programmes in the 1960s, but true to form they were going to do it their way. Quite why they had relented, none of the band remembered afterwards.

VOX

'Personally I didn't want to do it, and I'm not sure why we did. I suppose it was a challenge. It's always done more harm than good to anybody I've ever seen on it.'

Charlie Watts
Melody Maker
4 February 1967

Previous pages: Appearing on *Sunday Night at the London Palladium* on 22 January 1967
Above: Rehearsing *Sunday Night at the London Palladium*, watched by Andrew Loog Oldham and the show's producer, Alfred Locke
Opposite: The controversy over the Stones' non-appearance on the 'roundabout' got every national newspaper's attention

On the show, the Stones mimed playing their instruments, while Mick sang live to 'Ruby Tuesday', 'Let's Spend The Night Together', and 'Connection', the latter being a track from *Between The Buttons*. The most likely reason for their appearance was that opportunities to appear on TV were much more limited following the demise of *Ready Steady Go!* and other pop programmes. It was also true that *Sunday Night at the London Palladium* had a huge audience, close to 10 million.

According to the show's producer: 'They arrived with all their music on a tape. Their manager Andrew Oldham sat alongside me checking the sound level. I was so disappointed in my dealings with them. Not only were they late for rehearsal but I feel I was confronted with ill-mannered, studied rudeness.' But then again, according to Keith, speaking in *Disc*: 'The show's so bad we couldn't rely on them to get the sound we wanted. It's not as if we can't play live.'

It was not the use of a backing track that was controversial; it was the Stones' refusal to appear on the closing sequence of the TV show. They declined to stand on the revolving stage, where all the performers and the show's guest compere, Dave Allen, were expected to smile and wave to the audience. Andrew Loog Oldham had a row with Mick about it, and in the following days angry viewers took to writing letters to the press.

One lady from Oxford in a letter to the *Daily Mirror* suggested, 'They should take a lesson from the real stars like Gracie Fields, Margot Fonteyn, Frankie Vaughan, etc., none of whom would dream of being so rude to either their fellow artists or the public.' While another disgruntled Home Counties viewer wrote to the same paper, suggesting: 'It is too late to prevent this record going on the market, but for goodness sake let us ban any sequels before the entire business has a harmful effect on our nation as a whole.' Good to know the Stones remained as polarizing and controversial as ever.

The row seemed to go on for weeks. Those of a certain age couldn't comprehend why the Stones had been invited to appear, younger people couldn't care less about the fuss, and some others probably felt just like the Stones themselves – why had they bothered going on it? But as Mick told the *NME*, 'The only reason we did the show was because it was a

Mick Jagger argues his case with manager Andrew Oldham and Stones' recording engineer Glyn Johns.

STONES IN A PALLADIUM ROW

Story by KENELM JENOUR

Picture by TOM KING

We won't join roundabout, says Mick

A BITTER row flared at the London Palladium last night when the Rolling Stones broke a show business tradition by refusing to "revolve" at the end of the Sunday night TV show.

The rumpus began at rehearsals, two hours before the show was due to go out to millions of viewers.

And it lasted until the show began.

"They are insulting me, and everyone else," shouted the show's director, Mr. Albert Locke, when the Stones refused to join the other artists for the "roundabout" finale.

Singer Mick Jagger, Stones manager Andrew Oldham and Mr. Locke became involved in a heated argument.

Andrew Oldham held a hurried conference with Mick, but the singer refused to give in. Then Mr. Locke called on compere Dave Allen to rehearse an ending without the Stones.

Mick Jagger told me: "Anyone would think that this show is sacred or something. That revolving stage isn't an altar. It's a drag."

Mr. Locke commented: "Who do the Stones think they are?

"Every artist that's ever played the Palladium has done it."

But the Stones didn't. At the end of their act, they walked off as the "roundabout" began.

Leader Mick Jagger

THE STONES SIGN UP FOR PALLADIUM

By CLIFFORD DAVIES

THE Rolling Stones, who have always turned down bookings for ATV's Palladium Show have now agreed to top the bill.

Their decision endorses the opinion that pop groups can no longer rely on teenage viewers alone to get TV bookings, but must appeal to a wide audience.

Mick Jagger, the group's lead singer, said yesterday: "Times are changing. Today the Palladium show is diversified.

"And with the changing times comes a different market—one market. We think the Palladium is ready for the Stones, and the Stones are ready for the Palladium."

The group, which will top the bill on the Palladium show on January 22, hopes to present a new number—"Let's Spend the Night Together."

The disc will be released early next month,

good national plug. Anyone who thought we were changing our image to suit a family audience was mistaken.' Brian Jones was also quoted as saying, 'Our generation is growing up with us and they believe in the same things we do – when our fans get older I hope they won't require a show like the *Palladium*.' Sadly, if anything, it's got even worse.

On the following week's *Sunday Night at the London Palladium*, comedians Peter Cook and Dudley Moore were the stars of the show. Pete and Dud had become friendly with the Stones and to show their solidarity with the band they went on the revolving stage with life-size cardboard cut-outs, created by Gerald Scarfe, of all five Stones.

Amidst all the controversy, 'Let's Spend The Night Together'/'Ruby Tuesday' reached No.3 on the UK charts, helped also by an appearance on *Top of the Pops* on 26 January, as well as 2 and 9 February. And then there was yet more of a storm, this time over the band's appearance on *The Eamonn Andrews Show* on 5 February. The day had started badly for Mick, because the *News of the World* had begun an exposé of drugs and pop. The newspaper said that Mick had taken LSD at the Roehampton home of the Moody Blues; as was so often the case, they had it all wrong, misquoting a conversation a journalist had had with Brian Jones in May 1966. *The News of the World* story claimed Mick said, 'I don't go much on it [LSD], now the cats have taken it up. It'll just get a dirty name. I remember the first time I took it. It was on our tour with Bo Diddley and Little Richard [this was in the autumn of 1963, well before practically anyone in Britain had even heard of the drug].' Nothing could have been further from the truth and Mick asked his lawyer to issue an injunction.

It undoubtedly had a negative effect on Mick's mindset when it came to the band's appearance later on *The Eamonn Andrews Show*. The band had intended to mime, as was the norm, but the Musicians' Union decided to challenge the fact that they were not going to play live; the Stones had a long-running feud with the MU in their early days. The show's producer caved in and insisted that the Stones play a live song and, with no time to rehearse and perform their new single to the standard they felt was necessary – it did after all have a lot of overdubs and complexity to it – they decided to do 'She Smiled Sweetly' from *Between The Buttons* instead.

Eamonn Andrews also had Mick involved in a discussion with the other guests on the show, comedian Terry Scott and singer Susan Maughan. Andrews asked Mick if he felt responsible for fans following the things he did in his private life.

'Everyone is fallible, but the teenager of sixteen to eighteen really more or less knows his or her own mind. But I don't believe I have any real moral responsibility to them at all. They will work out their own moral values for themselves.'

Mick Jagger
The Eamonn Andrews Show
5 February 1967

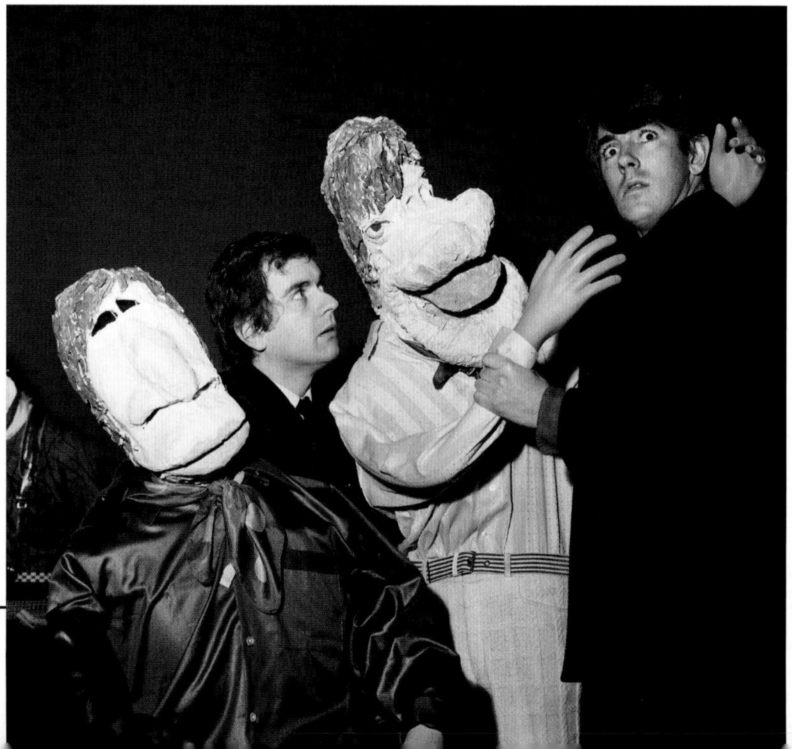

Right: Comedians Dudley Moore and Peter Cook with dummies of Mick Jagger and Charlie Watts before their appearance on *Sunday Night at the London Palladium* on 29 January 1967

Opposite: Recording *Top of the Pops*, 25 January 1967

Mick, who was twenty-three years old, was increasingly becoming the spokesman for his generation, but he was not alone. Brian too was upset with the way he was treated and told the *NME*, 'Our real followers have moved on with us – some of those we like most are the hippies in New York, but nearly all of them think like us and are questioning some of the basic immoralities which are tolerated in present-day society – the war in Vietnam, persecution of homosexuals, illegality of abortion, drug-taking. All these things are immoral. We are making our own statement – others are making more intellectual ones.'

Five days after the TV appearance, Mick and Keith joined the Beatles at Abbey Road where they were doing a promo film for 'A Day In The Life' featuring a forty-piece orchestra. And the following day, when *Between The Buttons* went on sale in America, things really bottomed out for the band, and Mick and Keith especially. During the late afternoon, the band recorded at Olympic, after which Mick and Keith, Mick's new girlfriend, Marianne Faithfull, and some friends drove down to Sussex to spend the rest of the evening at Keith's house, Redlands.

What happened has become the very stuff of rock 'n' roll legend, the beginning of a period that nearly broke Mick and Keith, as well as the band. When the story of a drugs bust broke in the *News of the World* on 19 February it did not mention Mick and Keith by name, instead saying: 'Several stars, at least three of them nationally known names, were present at the party.' It was not until 18 March that Mick and Keith were summoned to appear in court on 10 May at Chichester in Sussex. Then and in May, the TV and radio news was full of stories and the background to what has become known as the Redlands Bust.

Opposite: ***Top of the Pops*, 25 January 1967**
This page: Rehearsing for *The Eamonn Andrews Show* in February 1967
Following pages: Rehearsals at Teddington for *The Eamonn Andrews Show*, 5 February 1967

TV

THE VOICE OF A GENERATION

Less than a week after the story of Mick and Keith being summoned to appear in court broke in the press, the band were back on the road to begin a European tour that included their first shows in Italy, Greece and Poland (their first trip behind what was then the Iron Curtain). These were also their first concerts in nearly six months and nearly everywhere they played, the fans rioted, and nowhere more so than in Germany.

The band's appearances on television were mainly restricted to news programmes showing footage of their concerts and the rioting fans. Other than that, it was Mick, as the spokesman, who was interviewed on various TV stations. The *Daily Mirror* reported, 'Police detained 154 Austrian beat fans after a riot. Smoke bombs were thrown in the 14,000 capacity Stadthalle in Vienna.' With news of the drugs bust common knowledge throughout Europe, local customs officers and police took the opportunity to become somewhat more vigilant than they had been in the past. Right from their arrival in Sweden, customs regularly detained them for in-depth searches of their luggage. Nothing was ever found.

The only musical recording of note on this tour was Europe 1 in France broadcasting their Olympia show on 11 April on its *Musicorama* programme. It featured all their recent hits as well as 'Yesterday's Papers', which was included on both the British and American versions of *Between The Buttons*, and 'Goin' Home' from *Aftermath*.

The tour ended in Greece, after which Mick told the *Melody Maker*, 'We've virtually given up one-night stands. The one-night scene is dead, terrible – there's just not enough entertainment value in tour shows now. The people need something much more interesting to watch. I have got some ideas on how to change things – to do something different, but I don't want to say what they are.'

'We shall never tour America again. It is very hard work and one bring-down after another. You have no idea of how terrible it is unless you've been through it.'

Mick Jagger
Melody Maker
22 April 1967

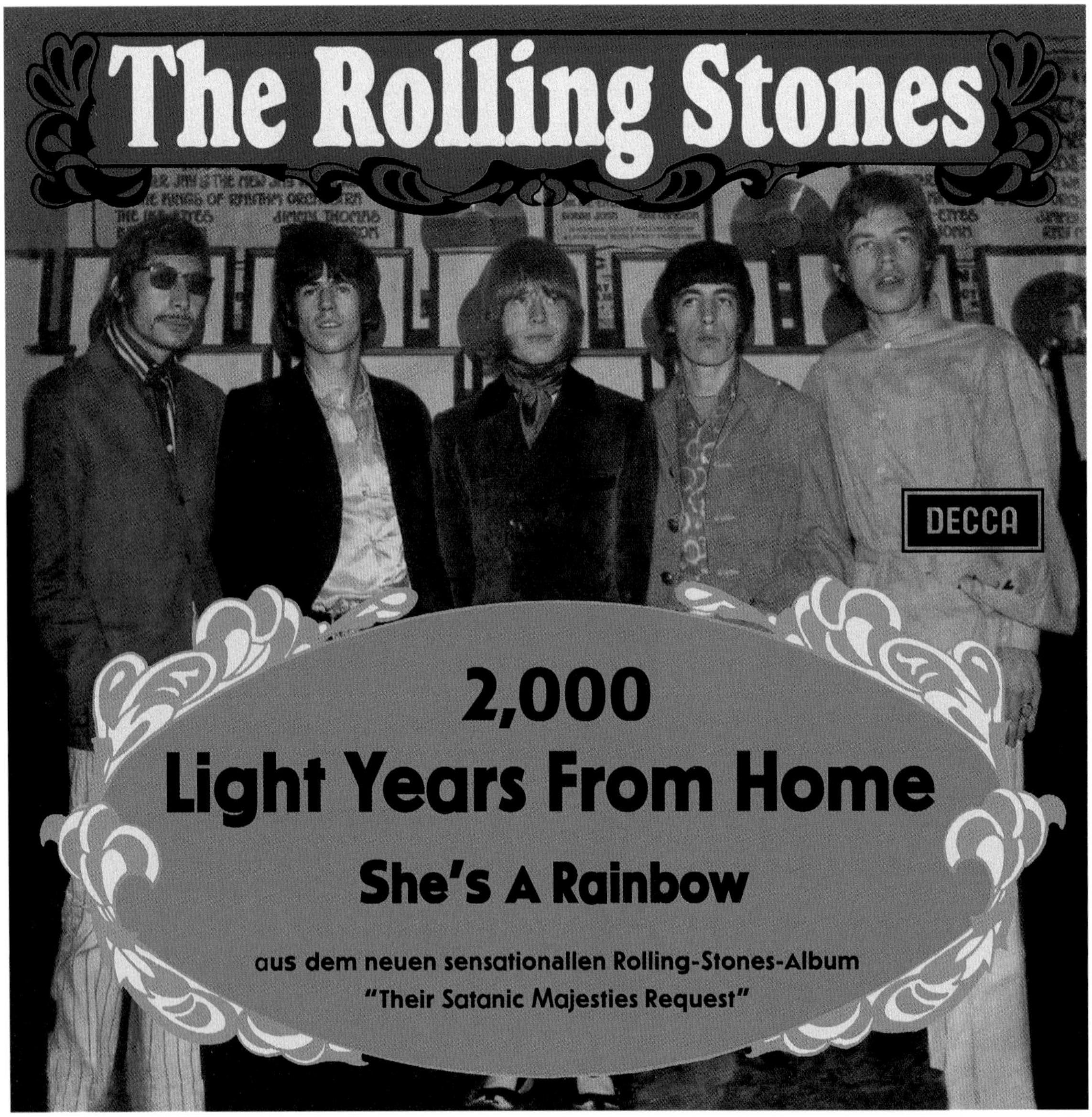
The Rolling Stones
DECCA
2,000
Light Years From Home
She's A Rainbow
aus dem neuen sensationallen Rolling-Stones-Album
"Their Satanic Majesties Request"

Opposite and right: Appearing at L'Olympia, Paris, France, on 11 April 1967; the gig was broadcast live by Europe 1

Above: Decca Germany's release of the Stones' single from *Their Satanic Majesties Request*

Mick, as they all were, was aware that the pending court case could well put a stop to future American tours. The hearing that took place in Chichester on 10 May was all over the evening television news, which showed the heavily guarded court. Mick was seen wearing a green jacket, white shirt and dark grey floral tie and Keith a navy-blue jacket and pink tie, while their co-defendant, the art dealer Robert Fraser, wore a light grey suit. Though no one watching knew this, of course, as the news was still shown in black and white.

At the hearing, all three elected to go to trial, with the date set as 22 June. Following the hearing, the band got down to recording a new album, if not too enthusiastically. Sessions at Olympic in May were sporadically attended, but there were some songs recorded, including 'She's A Rainbow' and an early version of 'We Love You'. And then on Friday 2 June, Charlie's twenty-sixth birthday, Brian was at West London Magistrates Court following the discovery of marijuana, methedrine and cocaine at his apartment; he too elected for trial by jury, a fact covered on both BBC radio and TV news.

Two weeks later Brian went to the Monterey Pop Festival in California and nearly two weeks after that Mick and Keith were found guilty and sentenced to short jail sentences. Both elected to appeal and after spending the night in jail (Mick had already spent the previous night in prison) they were granted bail. Among some sections of the media there was a sense of outrage at their treatment, not least William Rees-Mogg, the editor of *The Times*, who wrote his famous piece under the headline 'Who Breaks the Butterfly on a Wheel?'.

'The Rolling Stones are one of Britain's major cultural assets, who should be honoured by the kingdom instead of gaoled.'

Allen Ginsberg
letter to *The Times*
12 July 1967

While all this had been going on, the 'Summer of Love' was in full swing and the Beatles had released *Sgt. Pepper's Lonely Hearts Club Band*. Meanwhile the Stones were struggling to record a new album. Two days before their court appearance, however, Mick, Keith and Brian were on the television with the Beatles.

The Beatles had agreed to appear in *Our World*, the first multi-country satellite TV link-up that would bring together twenty-five networks from around the world in front of an estimated audience of 400 million. John Lennon's 'All You Need Is Love' was the perfect evocation of the Summer of Love and the Beatles were filmed performing the track in Studio One at Abbey Road. On Sunday evening, 25 June, at 9.36 p.m., the pre-recorded backing track was used for the actual broadcast, while the vocals, bass, guitar solo, drums and orchestra were performed live. The broadcast ran for a little over six minutes and Mick, Brian and Keith as well as Eric Clapton, Keith Moon from the Who, Gary Leeds from the Walker Brothers and Graham Nash from the Hollies were all seen during the broadcast.

With Mick and Keith's court appeal put back to the end of July, life continued. The BBC demonstrated their total grasp of the concept of the Summer of Love by threatening to edit Mick and Keith out of the 'All You Need Is Love' promo film to be shown on *Top of the Pops*; Brian Epstein was incensed. 'I would object most strongly if cuts were made from the film. The Beatles want Mick and Keith in,' he declared.

On 26 July, Robert Fraser's conviction was upheld and on 31 July, with Mick in court and Keith in a side room because he had chicken pox, Keith's conviction was quashed. Mick's was upheld but his sentence was quashed. They were free and every TV and radio news report was full of the Stones. Following his release, Mick was driven to Spain's Hall, Ongar, Essex, to take part in a televised debate with establishment figures Lord Stow Hill, William Rees-Mogg, John Robinson (the Bishop of Woolwich) and Jesuit priest Father Thomas Curbishley. This was filmed for ITV's flagship current affairs programme, *World in Action*, and billed as 'a dialogue between the generations'; Mick gave a spirited defence of the rights of the individual in society. The idea for the programme came from a 22-year-old researcher named John Birt, who would later become Director General of the BBC.

Brian spent some time in the Priory Clinic, not far from Eel Pie Island and Richmond's Crawdaddy Club where the band had established their reputation in 1963. He was trying to sort out his drug problems; he was also rumoured to be leaving the band. The insecurity surrounding the band was worsened by poor relations between Andrew Loog Oldham and Allen Klein, which were getting more difficult by the week. Not long after this, Loog Oldham relinquished his position.

In mid-August, the band's new single, 'We Love You'/'Dandelion', was released in the UK and managed a disappointing No.8 on the charts. It had limited exposure on the TV with just one showing of Peter Whitehead's promo film – which included a parody scene of the trial of Oscar Wilde, with Mick playing the part of Oscar, Marianne as Bosie, and Keith as the Marquess of Queensberry – on the BBC's *Late Night Line-Up* on 24 August, two days before it made the charts.

Top of the Pops refused to show it, saying, '[The producer] considered the film was unsuitable in the context of the programme, which is about pop music.' Instead they played the song and featured stills of the band and the studio audience dancing along.

'Pop music today is a socially committed form and the BBC are being irresponsible to ignore what is happening in the whole of the pop business today.'

Peter Whitehead
Melody Maker
26 August 1967

Opposite top: Mick and Keith following their release from prison on 30 June 1967

Opposite bottom: Mick with John Lennon at Abbey Road Studios, London, for The Beatles' *Our World* live television broadcast

Above and right: Mick with William Rees-Mogg (left), John Robinson (the Bishop of Woolwich, centre) and Lord Stow Hill (right) recording World in Action in the gardens of Spain's Hall in Ongar, Essex

In mid-September, the band flew to New York to shoot the cover for their new album, *Their Satanic Majesties Request*. At JFK Airport, US immigration officials initially refused Keith entry, then relented and allowed him 'deferred entry'. Mick, having been in Paris, flew in on a later flight, and met the same fate. The following day, they were given permission to stay for three days; they were also told that US immigration would decide whether they would be allowed in again, after they studied the reports of their cases.

A month later, Brian appeared in court, where he pleaded guilty to possessing cannabis and was sentenced to a year in prison; following an appeal Brian was given three years' probation. As with Mick and Keith, the TV and radio news covered the whole thing extensively.

On 30 November, Mick, Brian and Charlie were at the BBC in central London to record a by now rare appearance on radio, on Radio 1's *Top Gear*. The show, presented this time by Tommy Vance, who had been a DJ on Los Angeles KHJ, played the album in its entirety with the three members of the band providing a commentary. Three weeks later, the band appeared on *Top of the Pops* with two promo films of '2000 Light Years From Home' and 'She's A Rainbow' from their new album. Two days later it made the UK album chart at No.10. *The Sound of Music* was still at No.1, having replaced *Sgt. Pepper* at the top of the charts in October.

As the year drew to a close, the Christmas edition of *Top of the Pops* featured a rerun of 'Let's Spend The Night Together', taped in January. Meanwhile, two days later, the BBC's flagship current affairs programme in its review of 1967 showed footage of Mick at his post-acquittal interview in July. It neatly summed up the ying and yang of what pop had become.

Right top: Released in August 1967, 'We Love You' features uncredited backing vocals by John Lennon and Paul McCartney

Right centre: Mick and Keith with filmmaker Peter Whitehead during the filming of the 'We Love You' promotional film in Essex on 30 July 1967

Right bottom: Brian, Mick and Charlie with DJ Tommy Vance, seated, and Bernie Andrews, the producer at BBC's *Top Gear* on 30 November, when *Their Satanic Majesties Request* was played in its entirety

THE END OF AN ERA

In February 1968, John Landau of *Rolling Stone* magazine wrote, '*Their Satanic Majesties Request*, despite moments of unquestionable brilliance, puts the status of the Stones in jeopardy.' It was not the only warning sign. In the NME's poll at the end of the previous year, the Stones, who had been running the Beatles a close second, were now in fourth place in the world vocal group section, behind the Beach Boys and the Monkees, and only just ahead of the Bee Gees.

Their Satanic Majesties Request was about as successful as the band's previous album, *Between The Buttons* – they both reached No.3 on the UK album charts – and yet they hadn't managed a Top 20 record on the *Billboard* chart since 'Ruby Tuesday' at the start of 1967. *Their Satanic Majesties Request* made No.2 in America, but it was a success based on past glories, rather than hope for the future.

Brian's drug problems were getting no better, but the band needed to get back on track. A few days before Brian's twenty-sixth birthday (28 February), the Stones were in a rehearsal studio in south London working on some of Mick and Keith's songs. They had also begun working with Jimmy Miller, a 26-year-old American producer who had come to Britain at the invitation of Chris Blackwell of Island Records. Among the songs they worked on was 'Jumpin' Jack Flash' and another that was called 'Primo Grande', but would become 'Street Fighting Man'. Work continued throughout March and April; sometimes Brian was there, but as often as not he wasn't.

Opposite: The Stones performing and backstage for their final appearance at the *NME* Poll Winners Concert on 12 May 1968

'Oh yes. We are hoping to make several live appearances shortly from our wheelchairs. In fact, I think you can safely say that live appearances are a thing of the future.'

Mick Jagger
NME
16 March 1968

On Saturday 20 April, Michael Lindsay-Hogg, with four camera crews, filmed the band at Olympic Studios for a promo for 'Jumpin' Jack Flash'. The following weekend at an unknown location in the countryside the band were filmed miming to 'Child Of The Moon', and later at Olympic Studios, they were again filmed playing 'Jumpin' Jack Flash'.

'Jumpin' Jack Flash', set for release at the end of May, was arguably the most important single of the Stones' career; they needed to prove they were not a spent force. Anything less than a big-selling record would have been a severe blow. The Stones decided to play at the *NME* Poll Winners' Concert on 12 May, at which they performed their forthcoming single, as well as 'Satisfaction'. Mick recorded an interview backstage with Tony Blackburn for ITV's *Time for Blackburn*, which aired six days later.

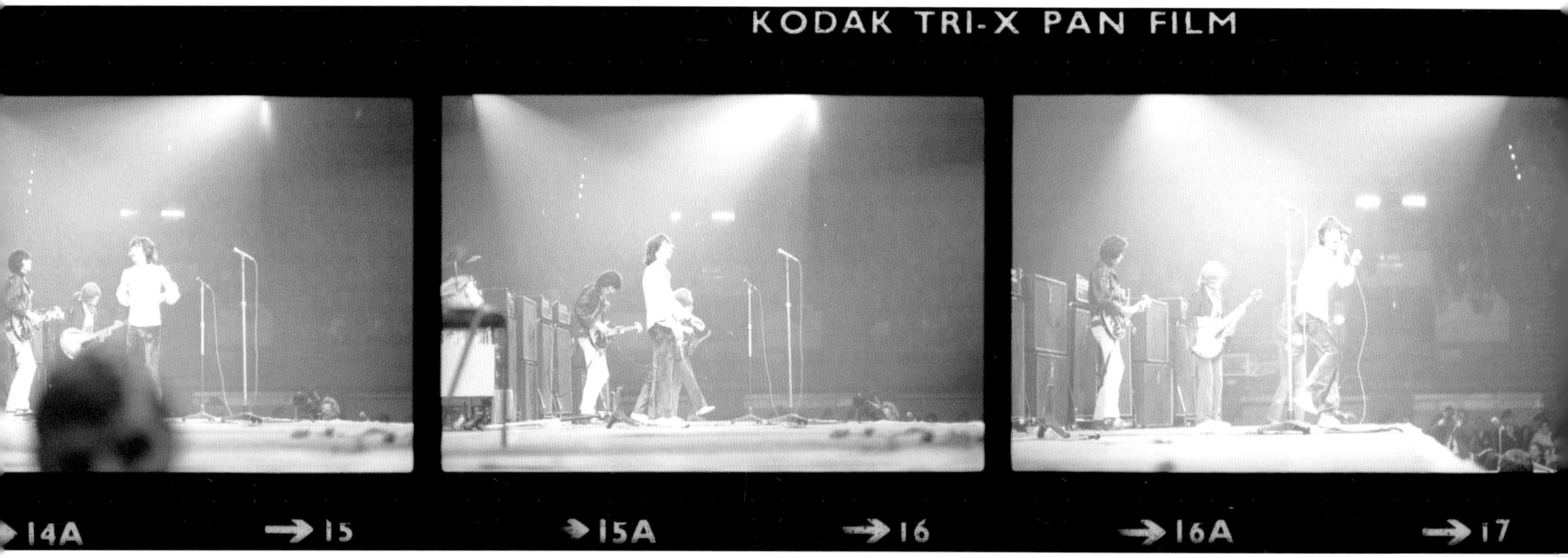

Above: Filming the 'Jumpin' Jack Flash' promo film
Opposite top: The infamous launch of the *Beggars Banquet* album took place in the Elizabethan Room of the Gore Hotel at 190 Queensgate in London on 5 December 1968
Opposite centre: Performing 'Sympathy For The Devil' on *Frost on Saturday* with Rocky Dijon on congas, Brian's last TV appearance with the band
Opposite bottom: Mick and social campaigner Mary Whitehouse being interviewed by David Frost

While Brian was struggling with his own demons, he was still popular with fans and he appeared along with Mick on several BBC Radio 1 shows, including *Top Gear*, to support the release of the new single. Mick told the *Melody Maker* that he hoped their new album would be out at the end of July and told *Disc* that the Stones would like to play live again but not by travelling around doing endless one-nighters. Because they were not about to, and arguably not able to, visit America, the band between them did over thirty interview tapes for US radio stations.

When *Top of the Pops* showed the 'Jumpin' Jack Flash' promo film – including the band with painted faces – on 23 May, Mick and Brian were there to be interviewed; two weeks later *Top of the Pops* repeated the film.

If it was not quite a media onslaught it was helpful in promoting their new single, which of course received extensive airplay simply because it is so good. On 22 June, 'Jumpin' Jack Flash' went to No.1 on the UK charts, where it stayed for two weeks. Pop was morphing into rock and the Stones were one of the principal architects of the transition.

Despite all this success, things were going from bad to worse for Brian. Not long after 7 a.m. on the morning of 21 May, he was woken up by policemen knocking at the door of his Chelsea home; they had a warrant. Brian didn't open the door immediately and when they eventually gained entrance they found him sitting on the floor calling his solicitor on the telephone. After finding things at the flat that could be related to drug-taking, Brian was taken to Chelsea Police Station where he was charged with possessing a quantity of cannabis. Granted bail later that day, Brian went to stay with Keith at Redlands; Mick was there too, and they better than almost anyone understood Brian's predicament.

Beggars Banquet was the title of the Stones' new album, named by the Stones' old friend Christopher Gibbs, who came up with the idea while decorating Mick's new Chelsea home. The name inspired the band to rent a house in Hampstead in which they staged the banquet, to be photographed for the inner sleeve of the album. A couple of weeks later the Stones agreed to appear in Jean-Luc Goddard's film *One Plus One*; they were featured working on 'The Devil Is My Name', later renamed 'Sympathy For The Devil'.

Brian had elected for trial by jury and it took place in September. Much against the odds, he was released with just a small fine. They all must surely have expected he would be sent to prison given the fact that he was on probation for his earlier offence. Over the summer, Brian had visited Morocco and recorded the Master Musicians of Jajouka in the Atlas

Mountains. He also bought Cotchford Farm, in Hartfield, Sussex (fifty miles south-east of London), the former home of *Winnie the Pooh* author A. A. Milne.

On 9 October, the day that Che Guevara died in Bolivia, the Stones were rehearsing to get the band fit to go back on the road. For the launch of their new album they unsuccessfully tried to hire the Tower of London, but instead settled on the Elizabethan Rooms at the Gore Hotel in Kensington.

The Stones' own 'Beggars Banquet', for seventy invited guests from the media, took place at lunchtime: the event was as over the top as the inside cover of their album, with serving wenches and food and drink in abundance. Near the end of the lunch an all-out food fight ensued, led by the Stones, but including the principal guest, Lord Harlech, Chairman of the British Board of Film Classification. It was covered extensively by ITV news, but it appears there was no coverage on the BBC.

A week before the album launch, the Stones appeared on television performing 'Sympathy For The Devil' on *Frost on Saturday*, filmed at ABC Film Studios, Wembley Park; it was to be the last time that they appeared on TV with Brian.

'Not quite the sort of party I'm accustomed to, but thoroughly enjoyable.'

Lord Harlech

Beggars Banquet was released exactly a year after *Their Satanic Majesties Request*, though that's where the similarity ends. Their earlier album was indulgent, lacked clarity and was in no way a reflection of their roots; *Beggars Banquet* is a focused, blues-based tour de force, one of their finest LPs. Making the charts on both sides of the Atlantic on 21 December, it went on to go to No.3 in Britain and No.5 in America.

Jann Wenner in *Rolling Stone* magazine said, 'The Stones have returned, and they are bringing back rock and roll with them.' The *International Times*, an underground paper in the UK, was moved to write: 'This album is to "Beatles" as Courbet [is] to Manet, Michelangelo to Tintoretto, Realism to Expressionism.' Take your pick …

To cap it all, the band decided to create their own TV spectacular, *The Rock and Roll Circus*. All too soon the budget rapidly escalated to £32,000 (£550,000/$700,000 today), but it promised to be spectacular. On 10 December, rehearsals began for the band's TV project, directed by Michael Lindsay-Hogg, but the whole thing proved to be just a step too far for everyone. Besides the Stones, there were John Lennon and Yoko Ono, the Who, Jethro Tull, American bluesman Taj Mahal, Eric Clapton, Mitch Mitchell from the Jimi Hendrix Experience, clowns, a tiger in a cage, classical pianist Julius Katchen, Israeli violinist Ivry Gitlis, and members of Robert Fossett's Circus, including a fire-eater. It was all filmed at Intertel Studio A in Wembley. When the band saw the sections of the show in which they performed they decided to reshoot them, but with events unfolding over the following months, nothing ever happened and it was finally released in 1996. In so many ways the ill-fated film was a fitting end to what had been a tough year.

Left and opposite: Keith and Mick on the set of *The Rock and Roll Circus*, with Nicky Hopkins on piano

Bottom: On set for *The Rock and Roll Circus*: Yoko Ono, Julian and John Lennon and Eric Clapton, seated, Bill, Charlie and Brian standing with Keith Moon, drummer with The Who

Following pages: *The Rock and Roll Circus*, from left: John Entwistle, Keith Moon, Pete Townshend, John Lennon, Yoko Ono, Keith, Mick, Brian, Charlie, Bill, Eric Clapton and Marianne Faithfull

'The Stones are to produce their own TV spectacular – for sale all over the world. They will star in an hour-long show, which will cost £20,000 to make. Worldwide sales are likely to earn them about £250,000.'

Daily Mirror
13 November 1968

THE ROLLING STONES
ROCK AND ROLL CIRCUS

STONES FREE

As 1969 began, *Beggars Banquet* peaked at No.3 on the UK album charts, the same position as their previous three albums. In the US, it could only manage No.5, not even as good as *Their Satanic Majesties Request*. There was much speculation about the band's US tour scheduled from late March to early May – would it even go ahead? Naturally it was the uncertainty around Brian's position that concerned the rest of the Stones. Their lawyers were consulted about the need to inform the American Embassy that they were applying for a visa for Brian. The overriding problem was that Brian's appeal against his latest drugs conviction was thrown out in late January. This all but ruled him out of a US tour.

For the Stones to continue as a cohesive group they needed to be able to tour America; without their being there, record sales would begin to dry up, a fact underlined by the relatively poor performance of *Beggars Banquet*. While relationships with Allen Klein had become increasingly strained, they were strained still further when he took over the running of the Beatles' Apple Company.

By February, they were back at Olympic Studios to start recording once again, tour plans on hold. In interviews, mainly for the music press, it was now being suggested that the end of the year was the likely timeframe for a tour. While they were working on 'Let It Bleed' and 'Midnight Rambler', as well as adding a choir to 'You Can't Always Get What You Want', trouble with Brian once again reared its ugly head. He looked far from well during the filming of *Rock and Roll Circus* and was soon back in the Priory Clinic in Richmond.

In late May, the NME announced that Mick was to star in a film about the nineteenth-century Australian folk hero

'Right now I feel I'm old enough to get out of the group scene and go into something completely different.'

Mick Jagger
in *The Teenbeat Annual*
released Christmas 1968

Opposite: Brian with the Stones in 1968

and bandit, Ned Kelly. At the same time, Brian's position with the band had become untenable. It was Ian Stewart who came up with the suggestion of a replacement, a young guitarist by the name of Mick Taylor. At twenty years old he was a good bit younger than the rest of the Stones, but he had been with John Mayall's Bluesbreakers since May 1967, having replaced Peter Green. In March 1969, Mick Taylor left Mayall to do his own thing – his timing was perfect.

Mick J. phoned Mick T. and told him that Brian was thinking of leaving the band and asked him along to a Stones session at Olympic on Saturday 31 May. On the second evening they worked on 'Honky Tonk Women', a song they had been trying to nail for some time. The session initially didn't go well, but by 3 a.m. the next morning they had got a great take; it was Charlie's twenty-eighth birthday, and the Stones had their new single and a new guitarist.

Over the next few days, work continued on 'Honky Tonk Women' and by the weekend rumours began to spread about Brian leaving the Stones; this was not the first time such rumours had arisen so no one got very excited. On Sunday 8 June, Mick, Charlie and Keith spent the afternoon at Olympic and – almost on the spur of the moment, because they knew something had to be done – they drove to Sussex to see Brian. They arrived at Cotchford Farm in a little over an hour and had a thirty-minute talk with him.

The facts made it inevitable. Brian was not going to get a work permit allowing him to perform in America yet the Stones had to tour. There was also Brian's health; his visits to the Priory Clinic were becoming more frequent. It was agreed that Brian should make a statement and later that evening it was officially announced that he had left the Stones, and Mick Taylor was taking his place.

On Wednesday 16 June, the Stones went to the Mayfair Theatre to record a segment for David Frost's American TV show. The band mimed to backing tracks for both sides of their new single – 'Honky Tonk Women' and 'You Can't Always Get What You Want' – while Mick sang live. The latter song was aired on 7 July; it was the first time America saw a Brian Jones-less Stones.

Eleven days later, a press release went out from the Stones saying, 'Rolling Stones' Free Concert in Hyde Park on July 5th. Announcing the concert this week the Stones' office said, "No final arrangements for the rest of the bill have been made but those who attend the concert will have a total of five hours non-stop entertainment completely free of charge." The concert will start at 1 p.m. and will be held in the "Cockpit" area of the Royal Park.'

Brian had begun living at Cotchford Farm at the time of the *Rock and Roll Circus* and following his departure from the band he began talking to people about his future plans. On the evening of 2 July, however, following dinner with friends, Brian tragically died while swimming in the pool at Cotchford. The following day the tragedy received fulsome coverage on every media outlet in the UK and across the world.

'You become some kind of spokesman for your generation. You're expected to be some kind of philosopher and you're not.'

DJ John Peel

This page and opposite: Just a couple of days after returning to the UK, on 12 December 1969, the Stones recorded an appearance on *Top of the Pops* performing 'Honky Tonk Women', which aired on the Christmas Day edition of the show

For the Stones that day, there was an appearance already booked on *Top of the Pops* at the BBC's Lime Grove Studio and it went ahead. While this may seem slightly shocking it has to be placed in the context of Brian having been increasingly difficult to work with and he and the band had become largely estranged from one another. The Stones recorded two separate versions of 'Honky Tonk Women' with Mick singing live to a prepared backing track. The first version aired on 10 July, the single entered the UK charts two days later, and over the coming weeks both versions were used by *Top of the Pops* after it topped the charts for five weeks from the end of July.

The Stones decided to go ahead with their free concert in Hyde Park and to dedicate it to Brian. In so doing, it marked a major turning point for the band. If the concert had not taken place there would be so much about their history that would have been so very different. And while Brian's death cast a shadow over the day, in truth he had left the band to all intents and purposes a long time before.

Open-air concerts on a large scale were not particularly new, but the sheer size of the Hyde Park concert set it apart from others. Did Brian's death make any difference to what happened? In points of detail, yes, but overall no, although perhaps his passing helped to make it the very-laid back affair that people remember with such fondness, even if some people struggle to remember the minutiae. Fortunately, the whole thing was filmed for a Granada TV documentary, which did so much to portray the quintessential Englishness of the whole affair.

A month after the Stones played Hyde Park, 'Woodstock: the Aquarian Music and Art Fair – Three Days of Peace and Music' took place, casting a mythological shadow across every future festival, one that was brought into focus by the film of the American festival. While America talks of the 'Woodstock Generation', in Britain it ought to be the 'Hyde Park Generation', and television helped here too.

'We will do the concert – for Brian. We have thought about it an awful lot and feel that Brian would have wanted it to go on. He was music. I understand how many people will feel – but now we are doing it because of him.'

Mick Jagger
4 July 1969

Right and opposite: The band play Hyde Park, Mick Taylor's first gig with the band. Keith plays his Gibson ES-330

ENTERPRIS

In a unique, yet prescient move, fifty Hells Angels were drafted in by concert organizers, Blackhill, as security; in truth they were just a bunch of posing bikers. There's a certain irony here, given what would happen almost five months to the day at the Stones' free concert at the Altamont Raceway in California.

The crowd grew steadily and by 11 a.m. the police estimated there were 25,000 people in the area immediately around the stage. The Hells Angels in their ridiculous swastika-adorned clothes, seemingly impervious to the heat, strutted around the VIP enclosure in front of the stage demanding to see the special blue access passes.

Since first light, camera crews had been setting up their gear and capturing the scene in the park, and every aspect of the build-up, for the TV documentary that was made by Jo Durden-Smith. There was plenty for them to film, long before any of the bands took to the stage, as by lunchtime the crowd had swelled to around 200,000 people.

The Third Ear Band took to the stage shortly after 1 p.m. Next on were a new band, King Crimson, followed by a south London band named Screw, who no one seems to remember now. The Stones' old friend, Alexis Korner, showcased his new drummerless band, New Church, as a late addition to the bill, before Family played a rousing set and then the Battered Ornaments. Every band on the bill was on a hiding to nothing, though; everyone just wanted to see the Stones.

When the Stones arrived, aboard a former army ambulance, they were anxious to establish exactly what was going to happen when they went on stage. Enter 26-year-old Sam Cutler, who was working for Blackhill and running the onstage announcements and introductions. Mick explained that he was going to read a piece of Shelley's poetry before the band played, but he needed some quiet. As Mick finished talking, Cutler dropped a bombshell. 'I reckon there's 650,000 people out there,' he said. 'No!' was all that Mick could reply.

The crowd was not 650,000. There has always been doubt about the real figure, which was probably closer to 250,000, but as it was free nobody counted, nor cared. It was certainly the largest crowd ever to assemble in Britain for a concert; the myth of half a million fans was perpetuated by a TV programme that suggested this figure.

At 5.25 p.m., Sam Cutler took to the stage and said into the microphone, 'The greatest rock and roll band in the world. They're incredible ... let's hear it for the Stones!' It was the first time the band had ever been called that, a far cry from Mick telling *Jazz News* in 1962 prior to playing their

Previous pages: Immediately in front of the stage an area was cordoned off with crash barriers to house the Stones' special friends, families and anyone else who knew someone well enough to blag their way in

This page and opposite: Previous concerts in Hyde Park had a four-foot high stage, for the Stones it was ten-feet high and there was a huge photo of Brian at the back of the stage.Thousands of butterflies were released in his memory

first gig at the Marquee, 'I hope they don't think we're a rock and roll band.' Cutler's introduction was spontaneous and has become entirely appropriate and synonymous ever since. Cutler used the same words to introduce them throughout their US tour later in the year and it can be heard on *Get Yer Ya-Yas Out!*, their live album recorded on the tour.

Following Mick reciting Shelley's poem, 'Adonais', the band began their set, not with one of their own hits or even a song that most of the audience knew. Instead they played 'I'm Yours And I'm Hers', written by Texan albino blues guitarist Johnny Winter, from his debut album. It had only been out for a month and Keith had suggested they play it. It was the one and only time the band has ever performed it on stage.

Their set was longer than they had ever played before, and very different from what their audiences of old would have been expecting. But with over two years' absence from touring, and several new releases behind them, it was bound to be much altered from the days of the package tours or the thirty-minute sets that they were playing on their 1967 tour.

Engineer Ray Pickett did a great job in supplying the soundtrack for the TV film capturing the band's performance on the eight-track Pye Mobile Studio. It was one of their first concerts to be recorded warts 'n' all; previous Stones' live performances had been heavily overdubbed in the studio and in some cases had not even been recorded live – screams were simply added to studio recordings to give the effect of an in-concert recording.

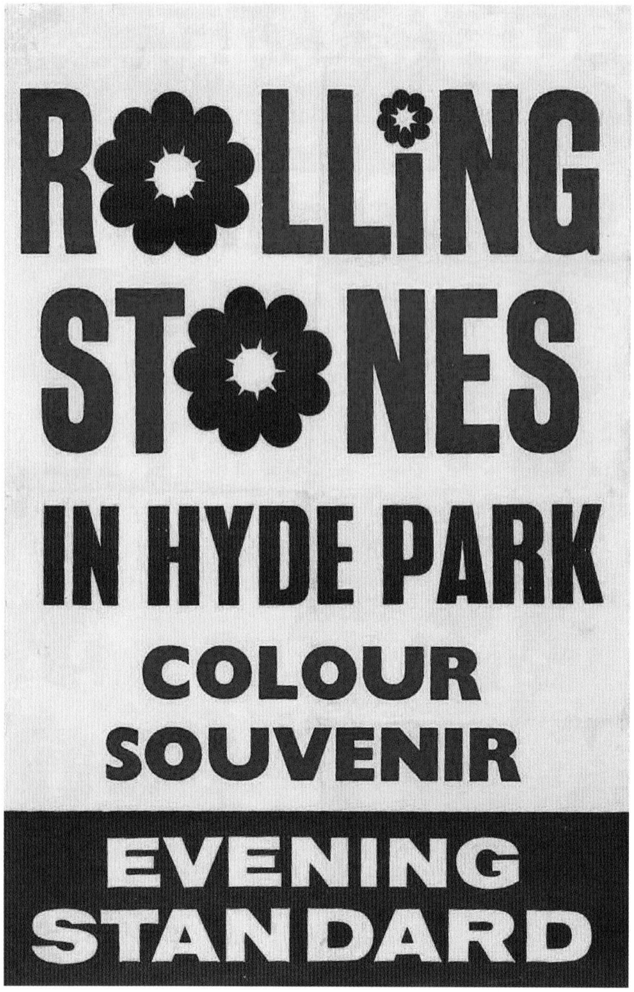

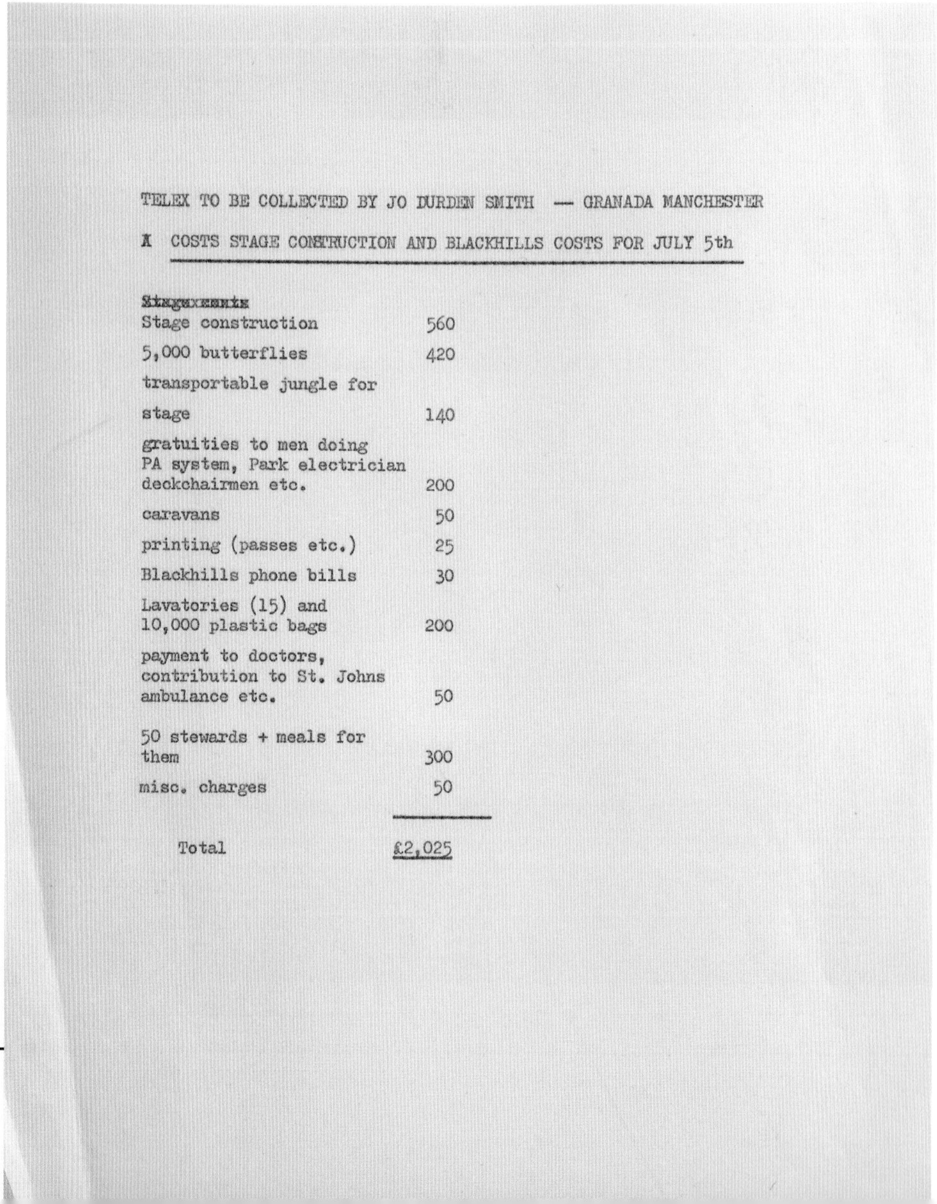
TELEX TO BE COLLECTED BY JO DURDEN SMITH — GRANADA MANCHESTER

X COSTS STAGE CONSTRUCTION AND BLACKHILLS COSTS FOR JULY 5th

Stage construction	560
5,000 butterflies	420
transportable jungle for stage	140
gratuities to men doing PA system, Park electrician deckchairmen etc.	200
caravans	50
printing (passes etc.)	25
Blackhills phone bills	30
Lavatories (15) and 10,000 plastic bags	200
payment to doctors, contribution to St. Johns ambulance etc.	50
50 stewards + meals for them	300
misc. charges	50
Total	£2,025

B.P. 123 Ref. No. BRP/ 534

ROYAL PARKS

PERMIT FOR SOUND RECORDING EQUIPMENT OR CAMERA CAR, ETC.

The Minister of Works hereby permits Representatives

of Granada T.V.

to take photographs/recordings in Hyde Park

using Tripod camera + portable sound.

on/~~until/between~~ Sat 5th July 1969

no vehicles to park in other than in authorised areas

and no vehicles to drive off the carriage Rds.

D. Daly
for Minister of Works

SUBJECT TO THE CONDITIONS PRINTED OVERLEAF

This and following pages: The Hyde Park gig was organised by Blackhill Enterprises, whose costs increased from the original budget submitted to Joe Durdon Smith at Granada Television. Jo Bergman was the Stones' PA

The Rolling Stones

Telephone 01-629 5856
Telex 266934

46a Maddox Street
London W1

Joe Durdon Smith,
Granada Television,
36 Golden Square,
Wl.

8th July, 1969.

Dear Joe,

Letters are sometimes superfluous, but maybe you can stick this one up in a well lit corner.

We have never ever worked with television people who were so organised, professional, incons= picuous, intelligent, aware, (roll on the adjectives) and just plain lovely.

Please pass on our thanks to everyone who had anything to do with the whole operation, it was indeed a triumph, and we love you all.

Regards,

Jo

Jo Bergman.

BLACKHILL ENTERPRISES LIMITED
32 ALEXANDER STREET, LONDON W2. TEL 01-229 5714/8

21st July, 1969

J. Durdon Smith, Esq.
Granada Television Limited
P. O. Box 494
36, Golden Square
LONDON, W1R 4AH

Dear Jo,

Thank you for your letter....we think that you too are easily the nicest people we have ever worked with intelevision. I hope we will be able to carry on scratching each other's backs ~~next~~ this week as per our recent telephone conversation. AK

In the meantime, here is the nitty gritty...

S.G.B. Stage (with damage to canvas and four boards)....	£ 700
Caravans (plus damage).	62
Van Hire (plus damage to roof of van)	22
Equipment insurance (Marshall amps and speakers).	25
Trees and plants hire for stage	120
Butterflies (3,500)	100
Location food van (meals for 80).	100
Passes, press release paper, etc.	35
Gratuities:	
WEMS personnel.	40
Parks' Electricians	10
Stewards (25 Angels & 55 others at £5 each)	400
Tom Keyloch's ten pro heavies	80
John's van for transporting Stones.	10
Drinks (AEK for Parks people, Forte's, etc.).	20
Dr. Sam Hutt, on duty	10
Hi-Watt personnel on duty	20
Gratuities - Road Managers:	
Family. (two)	10

DIRECTORS: PETER JENNER, ANDREW KING

Jo Durdon Smith, Esq.

Balance Forward:	£1,764
Gratuities: Road Managers (cont'd)	
Screw.	£ 5
Third Ear Band	5
King Crimson (two)	10
Alexis Korner.	5
Battered Ornaments	5
Stage Hands: Alan, Peter and Charlie.	30
Gibson Maestro (lost).	160
Screw's mikes and Battered Ornaments stand (lost). . . .	80
400 Stones' single	100
Ginger's drummers	80
Misc. expenses: Food for Stones, flowers, taxis, etc). .	60
Ministry of Public Buildings & Works	400
Sam Cutler (one month's hard work)	200
Blackhill concert management fee	500
Total:	£3,404

You will observe with your customary acumen that Blackhill have awarded themselves a concert management fee of £500. Obviously, this is a rough estimate, basically of the cost to us in terms of the time devoted to that concert over a long period. I think you will agree that it is a very reasonable figure, and I hope that you will use your best interests to secure the balance of money owing to us as soon as possible.

I realise that the total is over £3,000; this is mainly due to stolen equipment and damage for which we inadequately estimated. I always maintained that £3,000 was cutting it very fine.

Jo, you are BIGGER than S.P. Eagle...with humblest regards,

Yours sincerely,

Andrew

Andrew E. King

The day after the concert, Mick was interviewed on BBC Radio 1's *Scene and Heard* programme and five days later, on the day 'Honky Tonk Women' was shown for the first time on *Top of the Pops*, Brian Jones was buried in his home town of Cheltenham. Mick had already left the country as he had flown to Australia to begin filming *Ned Kelly*. In the Sunday papers, more than anything the Stones sang or did, the focus was on what Mick had worn in Hyde Park, a Greek-inspired voile dress that he borrowed from designer Michael Fish's shop on Clifford Street, just off Piccadilly.

An exercise in contrasts

By L. MARSLAND GANDER

"IT'S extremely loud," warned a glamorous organiser at a preview of the "Stones in the Park" programme seen on the I T V network last night.

Watching it without the privilege of access to the volume control was an experience I have had only on three or four occasions.

It compared in deafening degree with the open cockpit of a Handley Page bomber, the flight deck of the Ark Royal and the preliminary bombardment at the final offensive on Cassino.

A Granada team of 55 people in six film units tackled the formidable task of portraying what happened in Hyde Park on July 5 when a vast crowd, guessed at 500,000, assembled to be hypnotised by Mick Jagger.

As a technical exercise in TV production the resultant film was a remarkable, balanced achievement contrasting the juvenile feverishly abnormal with the humdrum.

We saw horses trotting along Rotten Row unperturbed by the uproar, a solitary fisherman oblivious. But as a programme it emphasised the yawning gap between the generations.

Why should the leather-jacketed rockers suddenly become the custodians of order, crowned with German helmets and splashed with swastikas? Why should we all be terribly surprised when a vast uncomfortable crowd of young people gather together and don't start punching one another or throwing petrol bombs?

Was it entertainment? I dare not pronounce except to say that Ginger Johnson's African drums won the rhythm contest. The joint producers were Jo Durden-Smith and Leslie Woodhead.

'STONES' FAIL IN FESTIVAL

By PETER KNIGHT in Monte Carlo

THE Rolling Stones were given the thumbs down by the jury at the International Television Festival in Monte Carlo yesterday after the showing of their programme, "The Stones in the Park."

Granada had entered the programme in the hope of repeating its success last year, when Freddie Jones won the actor of the year award for his performance in the series, "The Caesars."

But the Stones' programme, recorded at an open-air concert in Hyde Park and shown in England last year, was greeted with almost open hostility and no praise. A typical comment was: "It was so ugly and so noisy. In a festival with international peace as its theme it seems to have no place at all."

WIDELY PRAISED

Now Independent Television's hopes of a prize rest on a documentary from Westward Television, made on a shoestring budget. This is "The Loss of the S.S. Schiller," which was widely praised when shown in England last year and has since been warmly received at other international festivals.

The B.B.C.'s chances at the festival have also received a setback. Its entry "A Hot Day," from its 30-Minute Theatre series, was submitted in colour but will have to be shown in monochrome because there are no facilities for showing colour programmes on videotape at the festival.

Its main hope, however, rests on an episode from its Civilisation series. The one entered is "The Pursuit of Happiness", presenting the music of the 18th century,

'It's very masculine and we've sold several. They cost 85 guineas each.'

Michael Fish's business partner at Mr Fish

Only 12 years divide '6.5 Special' from **Stones in the Park** (Granada), but how we've changed. Actually it wasn't all that good as a film, largely because of over-editing. There were far too many tricks (if I were a television dictator I'd ban the use of the zoom lens for at least a year), but the main fault was that in its determination to achieve the jagged *cinéma verité* look it messed about with the continuity and lost any sense of climax.

I wish, too, there'd been more interviews with the audience. Jagger is a very glamorous figure. He has a Byronic aura and he dances beautifully, but as a talker he's no great shakes you know, like it's not his buzz, you know, like you know.

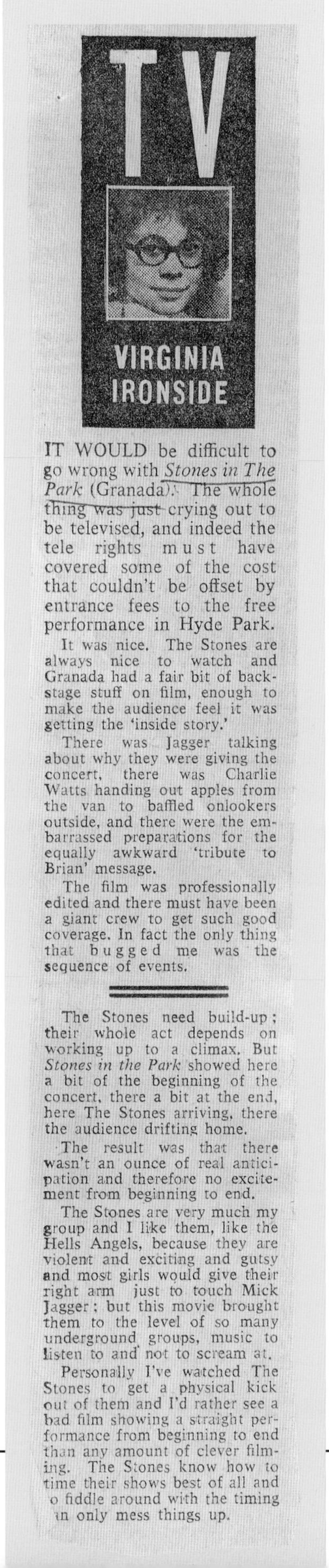
TV

VIRGINIA IRONSIDE

IT WOULD be difficult to go wrong with *Stones in The Park* (Granada). The whole thing was just crying out to be televised, and indeed the tele rights must have covered some of the cost that couldn't be offset by entrance fees to the free performance in Hyde Park.

It was nice. The Stones are always nice to watch and Granada had a fair bit of back-stage stuff on film, enough to make the audience feel it was getting the 'inside story.'

There was Jagger talking about why they were giving the concert, there was Charlie Watts handing out apples from the van to baffled onlookers outside, and there were the embarrassed preparations for the equally awkward 'tribute to Brian' message.

The film was professionally edited and there must have been a giant crew to get such good coverage. In fact the only thing that bugged me was the sequence of events.

The Stones need build-up; their whole act depends on working up to a climax. But *Stones in the Park* showed here a bit of the beginning of the concert, there a bit at the end, here The Stones arriving, there the audience drifting home.

The result was that there wasn't an ounce of real anticipation and therefore no excitement from beginning to end.

The Stones are very much my group and I like them, like the Hells Angels, because they are violent and exciting and gutsy and most girls would give their right arm just to touch Mick Jagger; but this movie brought them to the level of so many underground groups, music to listen to and not to scream at.

Personally I've watched The Stones to get a physical kick out of them and I'd rather see a bad film showing a straight performance from beginning to end than any amount of clever filming. The Stones know how to time their shows best of all and to fiddle around with the timing can only mess things up.

Left and opposite: Lukewarm reviews of the Hyde Park film

Following pages: Appearing on *The Ed Sullivan Show* on 18 November 1969

Mick's Australian filming was over by the first week of September and he flew home to where work had been continuing on the Stones' new album. Ten days before Mick arrived home, Granada aired their fifty-three-minute film, *The Stones in the Park,* at 10.30 p.m. on Tuesday 2 September. With an edit that jumped around, failing to show the whole set or the songs in the order in which they were played, it failed to meet with universal approval – but can anything filmed in such a way ever live up to the expectations or capture the enormity of such an event? Despite the criticism, *The Stones in the Park* was nominated to represent ITV at the Monte Carlo Television Film Festival in February 1970. Watched today on reissued DVDs it gives a real sense of what the day was all about.

Even before it aired in the UK, German TV's *Beat Club* showed footage of the concert in early August – whether this was from the Granada documentary or shot by one of their crews is unclear. The Dutch pirate station, Radio Veronica, broadcast most of the concert from a recording made on a portable Sony tape recorder.

Two days after Mick flew home from Australia, it was announced that the band would begin their sixth US tour on 26 October, giving them a little over six weeks to get everything together. Work was largely completed on the new album that Keith had decided should be called *Let It Bleed,* and with another greatest hits album just released in both America and Britain, everything was ready for the Stones to go back on the road.

On Friday 17 October, the band flew to Los Angeles to prepare for the tour. Joining them were B. B. King, Ike and Tina Turner, Chuck Berry and Terry Reid, but not all of them at every show. Before the tour began, Mick and Keith finished *Let It Bleed,* including Merry Clayton's great vocals on 'Gimme Shelter'; this was barely a month before the album's release. *Through The Past Darkly,* their greatest hits album, was sitting at No.2 on the US charts, on its way to selling a million copies.

On Friday 7 November, the tour's opening night was at the State University in Fort Collins, Colorado. Tickets for this seventeen-date, twenty-three-show tour sold out in a matter of a few hours and extra shows in New York and Los Angeles were added. Basing themselves in either New York or Los Angeles, the Stones flew to their gigs, but the logistics caused major difficulties, with the band often appearing late, at 4 a.m. on at least one occasion. Midway through the tour, their gig at the Forum in Los Angeles grossed $260,000, beating the record set by the Beatles at Shea Stadium in 1966 by $20,000.

Nine dates into the tour, on 18 November, the Stones were filmed at CBS in Los Angeles for an appearance on *The Ed Sullivan Show*. It was very different music from any they had played before on American TV. They sang live to backing tracks of 'Gimme Shelter' (with Merry Clayton on the backing track), Robert Johnson's 'Love In Vain' and 'Honky Tonk Women'. The performance aired five days later in the show's regular Sunday evening slot.

Another five days and they finished the tour in West Palm Beach, Florida, at the International Raceway, before flying to Alabama to record at Muscle Shoals Sound Studio in Sheffield. They cut tracks that would eventually appear on *Sticky Fingers*, released 504 days later.

On the evening of Friday 5 December, the band arrived in San Francisco and a little over twenty-four hours later, the Stones and more than a dozen others were crammed on board a helicopter struggling to get airborne to escape the nightmare of the Altamont free concert, which they had added midway through the tour. This was a concert at which the Hells Angels, hired as security guards, killed a member of the audience.

What almost defies belief is the fact that after a full-on US tour, three days of recording and the horror of Altamont, just six days later the Stones were back in the more genteel surroundings of the BBC's TV studios being filmed for three separate shows, including *Top of the Pops*, which was to air on Christmas Day.

The Stones were also about to play two London dates, the first at the Saville Theatre, on 14 December, which was filmed by Pathé News (one song, 'Satisfaction', was also used on American television). A week later, a second concert took place at the Lyceum. In between their London shows, on 18 December, Keith celebrated his twenty-sixth birthday. It had been a year when everything had changed.

One of the BBC shows for which they recorded a track on 12 December in Studio E of Television Centre was *Ten Years of What*, which aired on 28 December. The Bonzo Dog Band appeared on the programme as well as the music of the Beatles, Bob Dylan, and an extract from Vaughan Williams' *A Sea Symphony*. John Peel spoke about 'the youth revolution' and others on the show included MP Enoch Powell and fashion designer Mary Quant. It was very much 'of its time'.

For their final appearance on television in the Sixties, the Stones appeared on a seventy-five-minute colour programme celebrating a decade of popular music, made in conjunction with West German TV's ZDF network. *Pop Go the Sixties* also included footage of the Beatles who, like the Stones, were not in the studio; their clip was from the Shea Stadium concert. The majority of the rest of the performers – which included the Who, the Kinks, the Hollies, Cliff Richard and the Shadows, Dusty Springfield and Sandie Shaw – were live in the studio. The Johnny Harris Orchestra did a version of '(I Can't Get No) Satisfaction' while the Ascot Dancers did their thing. The whole thing was compered by German TV's Elfi Von Kalckreuth and British DJ Jimmy Savile. Savile, exposed as a sexual predator after his death in 2011, has been cut out of frequent re-screenings of this programme and numerous others he made for the BBC.

The Stones were filmed playing 'Gimme Shelter' for their Sixties swan song. Its lyrics addressed so much about what had been happening over the previous few years around the world – violence on the streets, the Vietnam War, and other atrocities. Mick sings, 'Gimme, gimme shelter, or I'm gonna fade away.'

For the Rolling Stones, nothing could have been further from the truth.

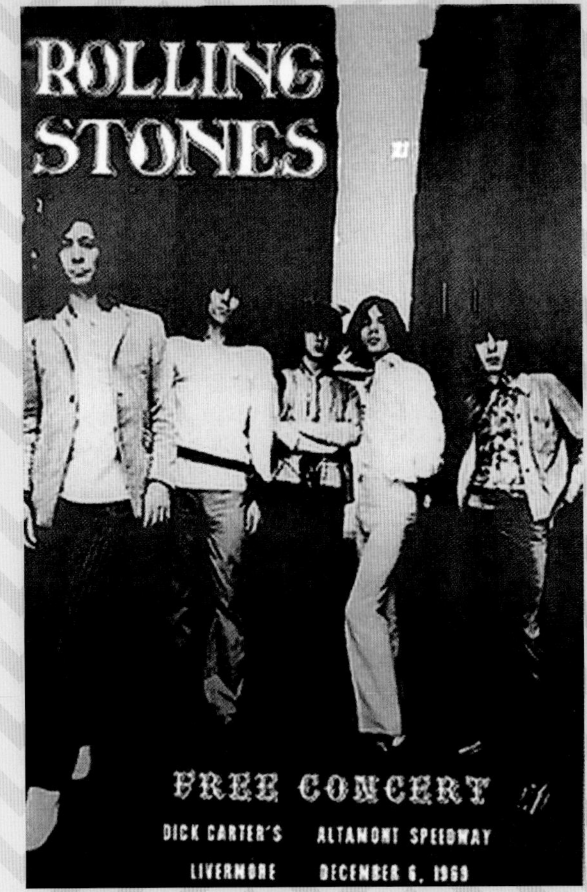

Right: A poster advertising the free concert at Altamont

Below: Recorded on 12 December 1969, the same day as their *Top of the Pops* recording, the Stones performed 'Let it Bleed' for *Ten Years of What*, a show that was a nostalgic look back at the decade

CONFIDENTIAL
TO: TELEVISION ACCOUNTANT
LONDON

TELEVISION SERVICE PROGRAMME ALLOWANCE
PROGRAMME ESTIMATE

PAGE No. 1 OF

PROGRAMME TITLE: TEN YEARS OF WHAT?
BBC 2
PROJECT No. 053595461
REC. DATE 20th Dec. 1969

PRODUCER: JEREMY MURRAY-BROWN
OB POINT OR STUDIO: T.C.1
TX DATE 28.12.69

FIN. DIV. USE — TELEVISION SERVICE USE — FIN. DIV. USE

CARD 1: P | CODE 2: 6 | SOURCE 3: E | MAIN PROJECT No. 4-12: 053595461 | INSERT PROJ. No. | PERF. DATE 64-68 (DD MM Y): 28 12 9

NOM. ACC. 13-15	£	s	d	DESCRIPTION 32-55
101				ARTISTS
	157	10	0	Enoch Powell
	52	10	0	Steven Rose
	15	15	0	Alasdair MacIntyre
	31	10	0	John Peel
	75	0	0	Sir Francis Chichester
	52	10	0	Yehudi Menuhin
	52	10	0	Thomas Berman - fee
	139	0	0	- expenses
	157	10	0	Malcolm Muggeridge
	300	0	0	Bonzo Dog Band
	100	0	0	Arthur Schlesinger jun. - fee
	450	0	0	-Air fare and expenses (est.)
	332	0	0	Jeremy Murray-Brown's visit to the USA
	100	0	0	James Mossman (est.)
	210	0	0	Jimmy Savile
	52	10	0	C. Day-Lewis
	31	10	0	Archbishop of Canterbury
	31	10	0	David Sheppard
	31	10	0	Cardinal Heenan
	36	15	0	Susan Hampshire
	31	10	0	Canon Collins (est.)
102	183	15	0	The Rolling Stones
	12	12	0	Winnie Taylor
	115	10	0	10 girl extras from Denton de Gray Agency.
	2752	17	0	
103	78	15	0	STAFF FEE - Robert Dougall
104				REPEAT FEES -
	5	5	0	Al Mancini - extract from TW3
	5	5	0	Lance Percival "
	5	5	0	David Kernan "
	5	5	0	Wendy Berry "
	5	5	0	David Frost "
	5	5	0	William Rushton "
TOTAL ESTIMATED COST C/F	2863	2	0	

VTR Nos.
ADDITIONAL DISTRIBUTION COPIES:-
STANDARD DISTRIBUTION COPIES:- PROGRAMME ORGANISER
SENIOR COST ACCOUNTANT
PROGRAMME FILE, REGISTRY
SIGNED

PRODUCER DAYS	80
PRODUCERS ASSISTANT	155
P.A.	150
S.M. XX studio director	15
R.A.	NIL

SHOT LIST

Page 1

PRODUCTION: THE SIXTIES
EDITOR:
PRODUCER: Jeremy Murray-Brown
TRANSMISSION DATE:

SHOT NO:	DESCRIPTION	SOURCE	FOOTAGE
		Pennant	PBU's
	XXXXXXX	* 1.	De Gaulle
	35mm BP	* 2.	Kennedy
1	Reprise of 16mm Montage 35mm BP	3.	Wilson
2	3¼" BP - TITLE (4 copies)	4	Macmillan
3	3¼" BP - MACMILLAN	* 5.	Monroe
4	3¼" BP - KENNEDY	* 6.	Biafran Boy
5	3¼" BP - JAGGER	* 7.	Vietnam
6	35mm BP - GAGARIN	8.	Ian Smith
7	3¼" BP - POPE PAUL	* 9.	Pope Paul
8	35mm BP - WILSON COMMERCIAL	* 10	Mini / Maxi
9	3¼" BP - LUTHER KING	11	Rocket
10	35mm BP - KENNEDY FUNERAL	12	Footballer
11	XXXXXXXXX 3¼" BP - KENNEDY FUNERAL	* 13.	Riot
12	3¼" BP - MENUHIN	* 14.	Adv.
13	3¼" BP - AIR HOSTESS	15.	Adv.
14	3¼" BP - ARCHBISHOP OF CANTERBURY	16.	Adv.
15	3¼" BP - WORLD CUP	17.	Adv.
16	3¼" BP - CHICHESTER YACHT	18.	
17	3¼" BP - CONCORDE	19	
18	3¼" BP - DE GAULLE	20.	
19	3¼" BP - ADEN - CRATER	21.	
20	3¼" BP - CAERNARVON		
21	MOON LANDING 1) View of Earth 3¼" BP		
	2) Down steps on to Moon 3¼" BP		
	3) Reflection in Aldrin's Visor 3¼" BP		

SIXTIES NEWSPAPER HEADLINES

1960

mirror	17th May	✓	Breakdown of summit conference
mirror	23rd May	✓	Eichmann captured.
Times	16th July		Picasso exhibition opens to public
mirror	6th July		Mutiny in Congo
Times	9th August (Sep 22.)		Laos Civil war starts
Times	18th Oct.		End of news chronicle

1961

mirror	22nd April	✓	Algiers Revolt
Times	31st May	✓	S. Africa leaves Commonwealth
mirror	2nd July	✓	British Forces land in Kuwait
mirror	31st July	✓	British Application to join Common Market
? mirror	21st August	✓	Goya's 'Duke of Wellington' stolen
Mirror	31st August	✓	Russia resumes Nuclear Tests
Mirror	18th Sept.	✓	Death of Dag Hammarskgold
Mirror.	20th Dec:	✓	Selwyn Lloyd announces government decision to opt for decimal courage.
Sunday Times	Dec 3.	✓	Thalidomide

1962 17th Repeat.

Times	Dec 31st Jan 1st ?	✓	22 missionaires murdered in Congo
mirror	March 19th	✓	Ceasefire in ~~Nigeria~~ Algeria
Mirror?	July 1st	✓	Referendum in Algeria
mirror	July 10th	✓	Telstar launched
Times	Oct. 20th	✓	China + India offensive
mirror	Dec:	✓	US offer to supply Polaris missiles to British nuclear submarines following decision not to proceed with Skybolt

1963

mirror.	14th Jan	✓	De Gaulle vetoes British entry into Common Market
Mirror	27th March	✓	Beeching report on Railways
Mirror	6th April	✓	Anglo - US Polaris Agreement
mirror	4th June	✓	Profume scandal breaks
Mirror	5th Aug:	✓	Partial testban treaty signed (not France)
Mirror	8th August	✓	Great Train Robbery
Sketch Sep 21st.	26th Sept. ? 20.	✓	J.F.K. at UN 'Man on Moon this decade'.
Times	31st Dec. Jan 1 '64		Dissolution of Central Africa Federation

THE SIXTIES CONT:

1964

mirror (binding) Sketch	21st Aug:	?	3 topless dresses in Street - guilty of indecendy.

1965

mirror	7th Feb:	✓	U.S. commences bombing in N. Vietnam
Mirror	6th April	✓	Early Bird launched May 1st - first broadcast.
Mirror	6th Sept.	✓	India attacks Parkistan
mirror	11th Nov.	✓	U.D.I.
Times 65. Mirror	15th Nov.	✓	Ken Tynans Four letter word.

1966

(mirror)	10th Jan	✓	Tashkent Agreement ?
(mirror)	14th Feb	✓	Russian Sinyarsky + Daniel Sentenced
?? Times [illegible]	31st March	✓	General Election
Mirror	19th April	✓	Moors Murder Trail opens.
Times (Times)	18th July	✓	France withdraws from NATO
mirror	10th Nov	✓	Wilson applies to join Common Market.

1967

Mirror	13th March	✓	L.S.E. Boycott
(Mirror)	16th March	✓	De Gaulle Vetoes British entry into Common Market
(Mirror)	29th May	✓	Biafra declares itself a republic
Mirror	5th June	✓	6 day war starts
	~~July 1st~~		~~Non-Proliferation Treaty~~
	~~July 29th~~		~~Pope on Pill~~
(times) try Guardian.	2nd Oct	✓	1st Polaris Sub. commissioned
	~~9th Oct.~~		~~Smith talks on HMS. Fearless~~

SIXTIES & NEWSPAPER HEALINES CONT.

1968

(Express) July 1st   Non-Proliferation Treaty signed.

Mirror July 29th ✓   The Pope on the Pill

(Mirror) Oct, 9th ✓   Smith talks on HMS Fearless

1969

(Mirror) 17th Jan ✓   Jan Paloch sets fire to himself

Times 17th Jan ✓   NATO defence ministers set up joint naval force in
                                    Mediterranean

Mirror 24th Jan ✓   L.S.E. Students smash down gates

(Times) 25th Jan   1st session of full scale peace talks on Vietnam
(Guardian)   open in Paris

(Guardian) Feb 6th   Reagan declares state of extreme emergency at University
                          of California - Berkely.

Times March 2nd   Russia/China clash on Ussuri River

Guardian March 12th   Foreign office under secretary William Whitlock
                          driven out of Anguila by Mafia type organisation

(Mirror) April 18th ?   Dr. Husak replaces Mr. Dubcek

Mirror April 20th ✓   Government of N. Ireland request assistance of troops
                          to guard   key installations

            April 27th   French Referendum

            June 8th   Nixon withdraws 25,000 troops from Vietnam

            June 30th   Lagos bans the Red Cross from co-ordinating relief
                                    supplies for Biafra

            July 8th   80 marines flown out to Bermuda at request of
                                    Bermuda's government

            July 21st   Edward Kennedy charged in connection with accident
                                    involving death of Mary Jo Kopechne.

**This page and opposite:
The events of the
1960s to be included
in *Ten Years of What***
**Following pages:
The band rehearsing
before their gig at
the Saville Theatre,
14 December 1969**

SIXTIES - NEWSPAPER HEADLINES CONT.

1969 Cont.

August 15th   Government of N. Ireland request assistance of
                          troops to restore law and order

Sept. 17th   Nixon announces 35,000 more U.S. troops to be
                          withdrawn by Dec. 15th.

GRETSCH

HIWATT
HIWATT

1967–1969 SELECTED TV & RADIO APPEARANCES

15 JANUARY 1967
(aired 13 July)
The Ed Sullivan Show, CBS Studios, New York, USA
Ruby Tuesday (MJ/KR) and **Let's Spend The Night Together** (MJ/KR)

22 JANUARY 1967
Sunday Night at the London Palladium, London, UK
Connection (MJ/KR), **Ruby Tuesday** (MJ/KR), **It's All Over Now** (Bobby and Shirley Womack) and **Let's Spend The Night Together** (MJ/KR) – live vocals on prepared backing track

25 JANUARY 1967
Top of the Pops, Studio 2, BBC TV Centre, Shepherds Bush, London, UK
(aired 26 January and 26 December)
Let's Spend The Night Together (MJ/KR) – playback (aired 2 and 9 February), **Ruby Tuesday** (MJ/KR) – playback

5 FEBRUARY 1967
The Eamonn Andrews Show, Teddington Studios, Middlesex, UK
Interview with MJ
She Smiled Sweetly (MJ/KR)

11 APRIL 1967
Musicorama, L'Olympia, Paris, France – Europe 1 Radio broadcast the whole concert live
Paint It Black (MJ/KR), **19th Nervous Breakdown** (MJ/KR), **Lady Jane** (MJ/KR), **Get Off Of My Cloud** (MJ/KR), **Yesterday's Papers** (MJ/KR), **Under My Thumb** (MJ/KR), **Ruby Tuesday** (MJ/KR), **Let's Spend The Night Together** (MJ/KR), **Goin' Home** (MJ/KR), and **(I Can't Get No) Satisfaction** (MJ/KR)

31 JULY 1967
(aired 1 or 7 August)
World in Action, Spain's Hall, Ongar, Essex, UK
MJ in discussion with Lord Stow Hill, William Rees-Mogg, the Bishop of Woolwich and Father Thomas Curbishley

30 NOVEMBER 1967
(aired 3 December)
Top Gear, BBC Broadcasting House, London, UK
Interview with MJ, BJ and CW by DJ Tommy Vance, as he played tracks from **Their Satanic Majesties Request**

21 DECEMBER 1967
(aired 28 December)
Top of the Pops, Studio 2, BBC TV Centre, Shepherds Bush, London, UK
2000 Light Years From Home (MJ/KR) and **She's a Rainbow** (MJ/KR) – promofilms
Interview with MJ

11 MAY 1968
(aired 23 May, 6 June and 25 December)
Top of the Pops, Studio 2, BBC TV Centre, Shepherds Bush, London, UK
Jumpin' Jack Flash (MJ/KR) – promo film
Interview with MJ and BJ live on 11 May

12 MAY 1968
(aired 18 May)
Time for Blackburn, Teddington Studios, Middlesex, UK
Interview with MJ

3 SEPTEMBER 1968
(aired 6 September)
Frost on Friday, ABC Film Studios, Wembley Park, London, UK
Interview with MJ

12 OCTOBER 1968
Frost on Saturday, ABC Film Studios, Wembley Park, London, UK
Interview with MJ and discussion with Mary Whitehouse

29 NOVEMBER 1968
(aired 30 November)
Frost on Saturday, ABC Film Studios, Wembley Park, London, UK
Sympathy For The Devil (MJ/KR) – live vocals on prepared backing track

24 FEBRUARY 1969
Scene and Heard, BBC Broadcasting House, London, UK
Interview with MJ by Chris Denning

16 JUNE 1969
The David Frost Show for broadcast in the USA, Mayfair Theatre, London, UK
Interview with MJ
(aired 7 July)
You Can't Always Get What You Want (MJ/KR) – live vocals on prepared backing track
(aired 21 August)
Honky Tonk Women (MJ/KR) – live vocals on prepared backing track

3 JULY 1969
Top of the Pops, BBC Lime Grove Studios, London, UK
(aired 10, 17 and 31 July)
Honky Tonk Women (MJ/KR) version 1 – live vocals on a prepared backing track
(aired 7, 14 and 21 August)
Honky Tonk Women (MJ/KR) version 2 – live vocals on a prepared backing track

5 JULY 1969
(aired 2 September)
The Stones in the Park, Granada TV documentary, Hyde Park, London, UK

18 NOVEMBER 1969
(aired 23 November)
The Ed Sullivan Show, CBS Studios, New York, USA
Gimme Shelter (MJ/KR), **Love In Vain** (Robert Johnson), **Honky Tonk Women** (MJ/KR) – playback with live vocals

12 DECEMBER 1969
(aired 28 December)
Ten Years of What?, Studio E, BBC Television Centre, London, UK
Let It Bleed (MJ/KR) – live vocals with backing track (aired 19 December)
Pop Go the Sixties, BBC Television Centre, London, UK
Gimme Shelter (MJ/KR) – live vocals with backing track (aired 25 December)
Top of the Pops Christmas Special, BBC Television Centre, London, UK
Honky Tonk Women (MJ/KR) – live vocals with backing track

INDEX

PICTURE CREDITS

ABKCO RECORDS:
73 The Rolling Stones EP UK
74 The Rolling Stones
224 Out of Our Heads

ALAMY:
85l, 182, 286t Everett Collection Inc.;
118l INTERFOTO;
57b, 69, 145cl, 283t Trinity Mirror/Mirrorpix;
44, 45, 51, 62/63, 88, 111, 134r, 147l, 147r, 208, 210, 250, 265t, 281b Pictorial Press Ltd;
43, 46b, 50l Tony Gale/Pictorial Press Ltd;
120 Tracksimages.com
130b ZUMA Press, Inc.;

BBC WRITTEN ARCHIVES:
24, 26, 27, 30, 55, 56, 57t, 76, 112, 113, 140, 162, 163, 164, 165, 166, 167, 168, 169, 170/171, 172, 173, 174, 191b

CAMERA PRESS LONDON:
284 Photograph by Peter Shillingford

FREMANTLEMEDIA:
103, 212/213, 214, 226

GETTY IMAGES:
32t, 32b, 190 Keystone Features/Hulton Archive;
86/87 Frank Martin/Hulton Archive;
104/105 Michael Ward/Hulton Archive;
107t Albert McCabe/Hulton Archive;
116b Express/Hulton Archive;
122 Central Press/Hulton Archive;
132/133 Hulton Archive;
136, 137 Stanley Bielecki/ASP/Hulton Archive;
205t Victor Blackman/Hulton Archive;
220b Blank Archives/Hulton Archive;
256, 257, 258 Photoshot/Hulton Archive;
274/275 Larry Ellis/Hulton Archive;
277b RDA/Hulton Archive;
7, 13b, 25r, 89, 91t, 91c, 96/97, 120c, 121c, 128, 157, 202, 204, 206/207, 209, 234, 244 Michael Ochs Archives;
8, 41, 281c, 283c, 291 Mark and Colleen Hayward/Redferns;
17l Echoes/Redferns;
17r Gilles Petard/Redferns;
252t & c Ivan Keeman/Redferns;
50r, 58, 309t GAB Archive/Redferns; 135t Jeremy Fletcher/Redferns;
82l Redferns;
90, 189, 192r Val Wilmer/Redferns;
102t, 195t, 195c, 216b, 225, 227, 252b, 271, 272 David Redfern/Redferns;
102b, 215, 216t David Farrell/Redferns;
134 bl K & K Ulf Kruger OHG/Redferns;
143 Peter Francis/Redferns;
220t CA/Redferns;
238/239, 251 Jan Olofsson/Redferns;
13t Charles Trainor/The LIFE Picture Collection;
146b Grey Villet/The LIFE Picture Collection;
201tl John Loengard/The LIFE Picture Collection;
205b Bill Ray/The LIFE Picture Collection;
67b, 68, 70/71, 116t, 285t, 299t Popperfoto;
99, 100/101, 108/109, Terry O'Neill;
127b, 153bl, Roger Viollet;
130t Bettmann;
146t, 201tr, 201bl, 201br, 243, 247, 253, 254t, 264, 306/307 CBS Photo Archive;
150/151 INA;
153tl, 153c, 153br Giancarlo Botti/Gamma-Rapho;
178/179, 191t Bob Thomas Sports Photography;
186, 187b The Sydney Morning Herald;
218/219 Jan Persson;
228 ullstein bild;
230 Philippe Le Tellier/Paris Match Archive;

GRANADA TELEVISION LIMITED:
300r, 301, 302, 303, 304, 305, 309bl & br, 310, 311

RICHARD HAVERS:
25l, 29t, 29l, 31, 39, 40, 42, 49, 53l, 75, 77, 80, 81, 123, 124, 135b, 138, 149, 154, 155, 159, 161tl, 194, 229, 235b, 242, 248, 255, 277t, 281t, 300l

MIRRORPIX:
34, 60, 66, 67t, 72, 78/79, 84, 85r, 91b, 92, 93, 95, 106, 107br, 119b, 121tl, 121bl, 121tr & br,125, 126, 127t, 139, 141, 144, 145br, 145t, 145bl, 152, 183, 192l, 193, 195b, 196/197, 198, 199, 221, 222, 223, 249, 254b, 260/261, 265b, 269, 270, 273, 278t, 282/283, 286b, 288/289, 294b, 296/297

REX/SHUTTERSTOCK:
276 Andre Csillag;
312/313 Daily Mail;
28, 29r, 48, 115, 185t, 187t; 211, 232/233, 235t Dezo Hoffmann;
107bl Tony Gibson/Associated Newspapers;
287 Globe Photos;
266/267, 268, 280, 285c, 285b, ITV;
114 George Konig;
46t, 278b David Magnus;
294c, 295, 298 Alan Messer;
59 Chris Morris;
294t, 299b, Peter Sanders;
185b Trevor Watson

TOPFOTO.CO.UK:
117

PHILIP TOWNSEND:
2/3; 7; 18/19; 20/21; 36; 38; 52

©CHRIS WALTER/WWW.PHOTOFEATURES.COM:
292, 293

NO SOURCE:
37, 82r, 118r, 119t, 161b

COVER PHOTOGRAPHS:
Getty Images/Hulton Archive; Mirrorpix

PHILIP TOWNSEND 1940–2016

The publishers would like to pay tribute to Philip Townsend, who offered invaluable help with the book and kindly gave permission for the use of his images.

'In those early days of '63 and '64 the Stones gave many photographers a few minutes, a couple of rolls of film. Their snaps surface occasionally and have their value as ephemera, but the time Philip spent shooting the Stones meant something more. They were sensitive enough to know that there was a fine line between notoriety and buffoonery. They trusted Philip and knew that he wouldn't make them ridiculous, though some of his suggestions elicited a bratty smirk. As I myself was trying to do in the studio and in the press, Philip gave them room to become themselves. The Stones, of course, were always much photographed and many of the early images are timeless. But Philip's work with them in particular, like that of Richard Lester in *A Hard Day's Night*, captures a very specific time and feel, when the mere idea that someone would want to take a photo of them was still a novelty.'

Andrew Loog Oldham

'Philip's best-known images were of the Rolling Stones, and he was able to gain access to the group because of a friendship dating back to his teenage years with Andrew Loog Oldham, their first producer... Philip photographed the band around Chelsea, London, in 1962, keeping their spirits up with chicken and beer. On subsequent occasions, he shot the Stones wearing check jackets – the opposite of their bad-boy image.

Philip's work is held in the V&A and the National Portrait Gallery. An exhibition of his images, 'Mister Sixties', was held at the Lowry Gallery, Salford, in 2010. His work was prominent in the exhibition 'Rolling Stones: 50' at Somerset House, London, in 2012, and is included in 'Exhibitionism', the Stones exhibition now touring the world.'

Julian Wilkins – the *Guardian*

10 9 8 7 6 5 4 3 2

Virgin Books, an imprint of Ebury Publishing,
20 Vauxhall Bridge Road,
London SW1V 2SA

Virgin Books is part of the Penguin Random House group of companies whose addresses can be found at global.penguinrandomhouse.com

Penguin Random House UK

First published in the United Kingdom by Virgin Books in 2017

www.penguin.co.uk

A CIP catalogue record for this book is available from the British Library

ISBN 9780753557556

Text: Richard Havers
Project manager: Caroline McArthur
Editorial director: Lorna Russell
Assistant editor: Lucy Oates
Production manager: Phil Spencer
Picture research: Claire Gouldstone
Design: StudioFury

Printed and bound in Italy by L.E.G.O. SpA

Penguin Random House is committed to a sustainable future for our business, our readers and our planet. This book is made from Forest Stewardship Council® certified paper.

FSC www.fsc.org MIX Paper from responsible sources FSC® C018179